34

Social History of Canada

H.V. Nelles, general editor

K.P. STICH is a member of the Department of English and the School of Graduate Studies at the University of Ottawa.

Laura Goodman Salverson's sensitive and finely wrought autobiography describes the struggles of a young immigrant woman to rise above an early life of poverty, isolation, and upheaval. A rare, first-person account of growing up different in Canada, *Confessions of an Immigrant's Daughter* also depicts, sympathetically and graphically, the agonizing process of an immigrant community adjusting itself to life in the New World.

The Icelanders left their homeland to escape economic pressures and the threat of erupting volcanoes. Salverson was born into the uprooted and transplanted community in Winnipeg in 1890. Following her father's *wanderlust*, the family travelled, in search of stability, to Minnesota, to the Dakota country, to Selkirk, Duluth, and ultimately to the Mississippi Valley in the deep south. His schemes unrealized, Lars Gudman brought his family back, time and again, to the security of the Winnipeg sweat shops. In recalling these wanderings, Salverson documents a wide swath of western history.

Against this nomadic background, Salverson tells of the trials of growing up, of the ostracism and condescension, of being 'hopelessly Icelandic.' But the story reflects also her indomitable inner spirit, which led to the discovery of libraries and the world of books and to the eventual fulfilment of her dream to be a writer with the publication in 1924 of her first novel *The Viking Heart*.

Confessions of an Immigrant's Daughter, which won the Governor-General's Award in 1939 but has been long out of print, is an important book for the light it sheds on the social history of Canadian women and immigrants; it is also a Canadian classic, a major achievement in Canadian literature.

In his introduction, Professor Stich reviews the significance of Salverson's recollections as a vigorous defence of women as well as of non-British immigrants in the Canadian west and their part in shaping its complex cultural heritage.

LAURA GOODMAN SALVERSON

Confessions of an Immigrant's Daughter

WITH AN INTRODUCTION BY K.P. STICH

UNIVERSITY OF TORONTO PRESS
Toronto Buffalo London

Confessions of an Immigrant's Daughter
FIRST PUBLISHED IN 1939. ALL RIGHTS RESERVED
COPYRIGHT HELD BY GEORGE SALVERSON

Introduction by K.P. Stich
© University of Toronto Press 1981
Printed in Canada

Reprinted 1996

ISBN 0-8020-2424-6 bd. ISBN 0-8020-6434-5 pa.

Canadian Cataloguing in Publication Data

Salverson, Laura Goodman, 1890-1970.
   Confessions of an immigrant's daughter

   (Social history of Canada)
   First published: London: Faber and Faber, 1939.
   ISBN 0-8020-2424-6 (bound). – ISBN 0-8020-6434-5 (pbk.)
   1. Salverson, Laura Goodman, 1890-1970 – Biography.
   2. Authors, Canadian – 20th century – Biography.
   I. Title. II. Series.
   PS8537.A48Z53 1981   C813'.52   C81-094104-X
   PR9199.3.S24Z464 1981

Cover illustration by Chris Palmer

Social History of Canada 34

This book has been published with the help of the block grant programs
of the Canada Council and the Ontario Arts Council.

Confessions of an Immigrant's Daughter was first published in October
1939 by Faber and Faber Limited, London, England, and distributed in
Canada under the Ryerson Press imprint; this edition was reissued,
with the author's foreword, in 1949 by the Reprint Society of Canada
Limited, Montreal, by arrangement with the Ryerson Press, Toronto.

K.P. STICH

Introduction

North American autobiographers have been fond of fusing their self-portraits with images of America. Their views of America – be it the United States or Canada, be it William Bradford's Plymouth Plantation or Frederick Philip Grove's Manitoba – usually present an idealized New World in conflict with seemingly crude environmental and cultural realities. The resulting polarities provide functional foregrounding for the authors to dramatize their public and private lives, the ostensible topic of their narratives. While in general the reader may expect historical reliability from sincere autobiographers, it is essential to remember that their accounts are *processed* by memory. The probability of vague, purposively selective, and perhaps even transformed memories in close alliance with the double theme of New Man in the New World calls for guarded responses to the objectivity and subjectivity of autobiographies. At any time, however, the inevitable amalgamation of recollection, imagination, events, ideologies, ideals, and aesthetics remains impressive in the service of such books to the fields of literature, psychology, history, and sociology. Operating on personal and social levels alike and with explicit or implicit emphasis on historicity, good autobiographies are complex cultural documents of life in a specific society. This is the case with Laura Goodman Salverson's *Confessions of an Immigrant's Daughter*. It is a rare first-person account of growing up Icelandic in the New World, of the agonies and joys which shape the process of discovering one's identity as a woman and as a Canadian.

Confessions concerns the years between 1890, when Salverson was born in Winnipeg, and 1923, when her first novel, *The Viking Heart*, appeared in New York, London, and Toronto. It was the period of unprecedented mass immigration to the west and of the celebration of the prairie frontier as the source of Canada's imperialist visions of economic greatness.[1] Above all, it was a time of far-reaching cultural changes as a result of the growing political and social power of womanhood and feminism in 'the fields of temperance, child welfare, urban reform, city government, public health, child and female labour, and suffrage.'[2]

The non-British immigrant woman, of course, easily became the symbol of the extent to which, aided by the women's movement, the ethnic frontier of the newly settled west would threaten to transform the prevalent nineteenth-century Britishness of the Canadian social order. While the title 'confessions of an immigrant's daughter' spells out Salverson's subject, it also implicitly mocks popular fears of the ethnic inferiority and moral looseness allegedly accompanying the 'strangers within our gates' against whom Rudyard Kipling, among others, warned Canadians in 1908 and again in 1910:

> The Stranger within my gates,
>   He may be evil or good,
> I cannot tell what powers control –
>   What reasons sway his mood;
> Nor when the Gods of his native land
>   May repossess his blood.
>
> The men of my own stock,
>   Bitter bad they may be,
> But, at least, they hear the things I hear,
>   And see the things I see;
> And whatever I think of them and their likes
>   They think of the likes of me.[3]

The 'things' Salverson recollects for us mainly from her life in Duluth, Minnesota, and Winnipeg, Manitoba, deal with social exploitation, moral injustice, and North American materialism in a male-oriented society. In response to such iniquities her recollections become a vigorous defence of women as well as immigrants in the new Canada of the west. Being of Icelandic descent and, appropriately of course, a former member of the Leif Ericson Society of America, she easily attracts our attention to her book as an historical narrative of immigrants' struggles. The book's fascination, however, comes with its power as a personal narrative of a girl's self-formative journeys out of a transplanted Icelandic world towards emergence into womanhood and selfhood in the New World.

When in 1887 Salverson's parents, Lars and Ingiborg Goodman,[4] arrived in Manitoba from Iceland, two of their children had died en route. 'It was a prophetic beginning –' comments Salverson in *Confessions* (p. 79), 'a foretaste of the high cost my parents were to pay for the rights of citizenship in the new country.' They were able to pay the cost because as Icelanders, Salverson maintains, they had learned to value mind and spirit over matter. Stressing the significance of heredity and philosophies of life rather than environment, history and culture rather than place, she examines her own Icelandicness through portraits of her parents, her relatives, and other fellow Icelanders who had arrived in the west before, all bringing their Norse heritage with them. Such cultural reflections occur intermittently whenever the crudeness, particularly of the urban west, threatens to foreclose the Goodman family's quasi-mortage on their transplanted lives.

On the one hand, Salverson admires her father for his love of literature and the imagination, his individualism tempered by gregariousness, his social compassion, and his intellectual inquisitiveness; in short, his romanticism that manifested itself so patently in his *wanderlust*. It was his restlessness together with his hardships as an impoverished gentleman farmer in Iceland that had made him an easy believer in Canada's immigration salesmen with their 'marvellous reports ... of the immigrants in that matchless country. Already most of them were on the high road to fortune' (71). On the other hand, she admires her mother for her classical rather than romantic temperament, for 'her life-long battle for respectability' (93) softened by humour and warmth: 'Mamma was my unquestioned voice of authority, my inspiration and source of wisdom' (211).

Initially, her father's *wanderlust* took his family to Winnipeg, the gateway to the Icelandic settlements first established on Lake Winnipeg in 1875. By 1912, however, the Goodmans had moved to Minnesota, North Dakota, back to Winnipeg, to Selkirk, back to Winnipeg, to Duluth in Minnesota, Mississippi, Duluth again, and finally back to Winnipeg.[5] Then Salverson's independent wandering began with her temporary return to Duluth, her marriage in 1913 to George Salverson, a Norwegian-American, and their numerous Canadian places of residence. This is why her autobiography, she says half in jest, 'might well be the chronicle of the child of Vikings. On the move so constantly she can never tell with assurance where home is; she conceived this book by the waters of Lake Superior, planned it in Edmonton, wrote it in Calgary, Alberta, Vancouver Island, and on various trains and vessels in between, and read the proofs in Winnipeg, Manitoba. Written over one quarter of the continent, the book itself covers her wanderings in still another quarter. This constant travelling is thanks to her husband ... whose position with the Canadian National Railways takes him spasmodically from one to another of Canada's cities.'[6]

The Salversons' moves, however, lack the psychological urgency of Lars Goodman's repeated starts to keep his 'soul alive in this harsh country' (49) of the west on both sides of the 49th parallel, where neither the urban nor the rural realities would come close to the capitalist, pastoral idylls promised by immigration propaganda.[7] Although he always found work in Winnipeg for his skills as a saddler, the sweatshop working conditions meant near-poverty as well as physical and spiritual exhaustion.[8] Added to this, the demands of his growing family and the little time left for his literary contributions to Icelandic periodicals quickly turned expectations of the fabled 'last best West' into bitter disappointment. Lacking capital, the Goodmans' alternative attempts at farming in Manitoba and ranching in North Dakota proved to be similarly disheartening, though at least not as humiliating as work in a sweatshop. The next alternative was to move to an American city, namely Duluth, from where Lars Goodman's sister had written her brother that 'Canada wasn't much of a country anyhow. So far as she had been able to make out, not even the English thought of it in favourable light' (172). The Goodmans' move to Duluth in 1890 was typical of the times. About half a million people left Canada for the United States between 1882 and 1891 alone,[9] thinking similarly to Salverson's aunt that 'the United States was a self-respecting country – not just the tail-hair of the British Bulldog! ... The United States offered you a chance to prove *yourself*' (172).

From Salverson's recollection, Duluth appears as not much of an improvement over Winnipeg: 'Squalid in every respect was this American counterpart of the frontier town we had just quitted. There wasn't a splinter to choose between them! The same ugly, hastily erected houses offended the eye; the same unkempt streets and dirty alleys despoiled an otherwise decent plain. We still fetched water from a pump that rose like an iron-wraith from an oozy grave. The same sort of rigs rattled over the ruts and the same sort of humdrum humanity hurried by' (180). Yet it was to be Duluth where Salverson spent most of her adolescence and youth; there she learned English at the age of ten, received her elementary and secondary school education, signed her first library card as 'Laura Goodman,' and felt the urge to write books in English.

Literature and nature offered her sanctuary from the dilemmas of being the child of immigrants who were so un-American in appearance and customs, and from the concomitant 'tangle of social commandments' (245) that stood between her and Middle America's ideals of puritanical daughters of the Republic. Her strong sense of actuality and her moral integrity, however, soon put an end to such school-induced social aspirations. Alert to the exploitation of women, witnessing her mother's unwanted pregnancies, working as a domestic for the money-rich, and experiencing the exploitation of workers in general at the end of America's so-called Gilded Age, Salverson turned inward and to her Icelandic heritage. Sound practical scepticism protected her from languishing in moods stirred by William Cullen Bryant's *Thanatopsis* and similar poems. It protected her even when thanatopsis became acute with the Goodmans' brief move to a Mississippi hamlet with its quasi-Faulknerian world of poor-whites and blacks: 'Built in an hour, destined for a day, the village had something primeval about it. Something old as time, and imperturbable as the trees whose death song hummed all day long from the greedy mills' (298).

In the South, death from malaria threatened Salverson in a way reminiscent of her near-death from diphtheria during her Winnipeg childhood. This north-south polarity dramatizes the futility of any geographic quest for the promised land in North America. From disillusionment with the pastoral capitalism in the 'last best West' in the north to the unlikely kinship with the remains of colonial plantation America in the south, the Goodmans' expectations tended to conflict with social reality. Salverson's first romance, which significantly occurred in Mississippi, clarifies her strong sense of irony about the family's American journeys; instead of the proverbial Southern gentleman the immigrant's daughter would marry an immigrant's son.

With the Goodmans' return to Winnipeg in 1912 eventually came material comfort. To the autobiographer's discerning eyes, however, 'Life was so barren now. So safe! Sold to prosperity and commercialism' (360). She noticed this change above all in the Icelandic society of which her family had been part in Winnipeg, just as in Duluth earlier:

Having suffered ostracism and condescension because of their foreignness; it seemed as though all the national energy of the people had been expanded to acquire a blameless Canadian skin, Canadian habits, and Canadian houses.

This struck me as a little ironic, considering how contemptuous the general run of Canadian was of his own country. The deprecating manner towards everything Canadian was something else that struck me very forcibly, coming, as I had, from a country that believed in its own destiny, and took pride in American endeavour (357).

Acceptance of anglo-conformity, of assimilation into the dominant society, had begun to replace the Icelandic minority's Norse culture that Salverson has recorded so well in the portraits of her parents. Assimilation, of course, has always tended to belie ethnic pride in the Canadian west. Ethnocentrism, 'the firm conviction that one's culture is superior to that of any other ethnic group,'[10] has been easier to maintain in Canada than in the United States because of our long-standing support of multiculturalism. The cultural voice of some large non-British minorities in the west was being heeded in school districts as early as the 1890s when 'the three language groups of Manitoba were English, French and German; a fourth, the Icelandic, accepted public education in English while maintaining the mother tongue in the home and Icelandic press. By 1911, many other groups had been added, of which two, the Polish and the Ukrainian, were devoted to the maintainance of their native languages.'[11] Even though Manitoba enforced a unilingually English school system in 1916, multi-culturalism was to remain characteristic of the west; so much so, in fact, that it attracted Stephen Leacock's humorous attention in 1937: 'The publication of foreign language newspapers in the Prairie Provinces of Canada has, so far as I know, no parallel in the world. The only thing one could compare it to would be a cocktail party of the League of Nations at Geneva.'[12]

The general public's attitudes towards immigrants like the Goodmans tended to lack humour, tolerance, and understanding. Partly in response to ethnic tensions in the urban centres, mainly Winnipeg, and partly out of concern that the west not become 'the Old World's dumping ground,'[13] J.S. Woodsworth compiled his pioneering study, *Strangers within Our Gates* (1909). Always a fighter for human dignity and social justice, Woodsworth set out to refute some common prejudices of the inferiority of immigrants, particularly non-English-speaking Europeans. He pleaded somewhat cautiously for their acceptance as new Canadians in assimilable numbers but he also called for responsible immigration policies. Federal and local administrators clearly needed to go beyond concerns with work force statistics, economic bigness, CPR profits, and romantic visions of Winnipeg's rivalling London, Berlin, or Paris in civic greatness.[14] There was little grandeur in the *de facto* segregation of foreigners into Winnipeg's North End. This so-called foreign quarter was on the proverbial wrong side of the tracks, CPR tracks and yards, which cut across the city. 'By 1913 only two overhead bridges and two subways provided access to the North End,' thus facilitating the segregation of immigrants that 'was encouraged by Winnipeg's developers and real estate agents.' Residential mobility, of course, was not uncommon, particularly among Scandinavians and Germans with their cultural closeness to Anglo-Canadians.[15]

Woodsworth, like many Anglo-Canadians, welcomed such integration for the purpose of assimilation. His book thus gives the Icelanders a 'leading part in the development of the West' and, in keeping with traditional European stereotyping, considers Scandinavians as 'accustomed to the rigors of a northern climate, clean-blooded, thrifty, ambitious, and hard-working.'[16] This well-worn emphasis on sobriety, industry, and assimilation envisions a new Canadian society in the old spirit of Benjamin Franklin's tract, 'Information to Those Who Would Remove to America,' and of the third of St Jean de Crèvecoeur's *Letters from an American Farmer*, entitled 'What Is an American.' The compromiser Franklin praised the 'general happy mediocrity' of society in the New World, and the Tory continentalist de Crèvecoeur saw 'a pleasing uniformity of decent competence' emerging out of an initially multi-ethnic North America. Such seemingly pleasant mediocrity and uniformity by way of ready assimilation and material comforts also characterizes Woodsworth's vision. It would lead to a cultural ebb, to that 'blameless Canadian skin' referred to by Salverson above.

Salverson rejects the melting pot principle in her neo-romantic, twentieth-century perspective. Inasmuch as her autobiography is a reply to the traditional Anglo-North American preference for ethnic assimilation, its intention is for *new* and *old* Canadians alike to adopt a less American attitude towards ethnic accommodation. 'It may be,' she says, 'that, like myself, some child of immigrants longs to justify her race as something more than a hewer of wood; dreams in the starlight of the lonely prairie of some fair burnt offering to lay upon the altar of her New Country, out of the love of a small, passionate heart' (414). Salverson's own geographic, national, and cultural quests become sufficiently representative of the sociology and psychology of immigration for her autobiography to serve as a psycho-history of nation-building in the multi-ethnic west.

Next to immigration, women's rights are Salverson's second sustained social theme, frequently intertwined with the former. Her record of her mother's leaving Iceland against her better judgement, her accounts of the exploitation of neighbours' wives and friends, her own experiences as a domestic and unskilled worker, all contribute pragmatically to her rebellion against 'the cruel subjection of women' (378), against essentially the same forces responsible for the subjection of immigrants, namely, prejudice and materialism. What distinguishes Salverson's approach is her unprogrammatic, *gentlewomanly* point of view. She sympathizes with the contemporary rise in prairie socialism and the popular causes of the women's reform movements without becoming partisan or doctrinal; even Christian social work becomes 'just another garden plot of fancy' (377), a sort of questionable homesteading; and the temperance movement registers neither a dry nor an ironic response. Salverson is extremely sceptical of organized reform and organized religion in whatever traditional or fashionable form they manifest themselves.[17]

In this respect she is the opposite of her close friend Nellie McClung, who represented organized social and political reform. Like Salverson, McClung reacted against the 'false flattery which has been given [Canada] by immigration agencies in Europe,'[18] and like Salverson she also believed that immigrants needed to shape the west rather than a myth of the west shape them. McClung popularized these ideas in *Painted Fires* (1925), a somewhat melodramatic novel about a Finnish girl on the urban prairie frontier. Above all, however, McClung's is a didactic voice in the service of temperance and women's rights, whereas Salverson's is a more circumspect, more authentic voice in the Emersonian-Thoreauvian tradition of achievement through simplicity, self-reliance, and action: 'I have seen the fulfilment of a dream. That is something, in a world that prides itself on materiality. A small triumph, for so many years; but a small thing can demonstrate a great truth. That I accomplished so little is beside the point' (413).

Much of her authenticity comes from the confessional nature of her autobiography. The title 'confessions' implies emphasis on inner truth rather than the outer truth of historicity that one associates with memoirs, a different autobiographical form of writing. In other words, the author tells the reader to expect relatively little concern with the documentation of facts: 'It was not my purpose or desire to write factual history of this or that village or event ... I have been concerned only with the human element; with those joys and sorrows and rare moments of spiritual grace which seem to me to encompass all that any of us ever knows of lasting reality.'[19] Such careful abstention from mere historicity in favour of self-revelation was also her advice to McClung: '"Be more personal in your new [autobiography] ... Break down and tell all! We want to see you and know how your mind was working."'[20]

Admirable advice, but Salverson herself rarely breaks down and tells all. Her 'confessions' are neither Proustian recollections nor psychological self-portraits in the manner of a D.H. Lawrence or a Frederick Philip Grove. *Confessions* is rather like a portrait of the author as a young woman against a domineering foreground of the prairie frontier and immigration and against an imposing background of romantic idealism. Warmth, humour, irony, occasional satire, humility, sincerity, courage, and, at times, a consciously child-like perspective shape the personal and social dimensions of Salverson's autobiography. Naturally, she refers to it as a *personal* chronicle' and a *rambling* narrative' (5, 413, emphasis added) of 'those happenings that stirred my imagination' (131), be they Winnipeg sweat shops, unwed mothers, poverty, immigrants, prairie sunsets, spiritualism, Norse lore, or school-days. Between wolves' 'savage tongues' which so ominously introduce the New World in chapter one and Salverson's adoption of a new native tongue in her literary apprenticeship, *Confessions* helps to illuminate the so-called structure of feeling on the last traditional frontier in the New World.

How does one re-evaluate the dynamics of immigration to the west when the notion of 'Canada's Century' was at its height? How does one begin to re-evaluate the complex cultural heritage which has shaped the mindscape of the west? In light of G.F.G. Stanley's belief in serious historical study of 'the literature of Western Canada as a reflection of our Western Canadian mind,'[21] such re-evaluations need to give self-evident attention to remembered lives, memoirs, confessions, as well as autobiographical novels. *Confessions of an Immigrant's Daughter* is an obliging text by itself and stands well in the company of related books such as *Wheat and Women* (1914) by the Englishwoman Georgina Binnie-Clark; *A Search for America* (1927) and *In Search of Myself* (1946) by the German immigrant Frederick Philip Grove; *Taking Root in Canada* (1954) by the Ukrainian-Canadian Gus Romaniuk; *Wolf Willow* (1955) by the Norwegian-American Wallace Stegner; *Under the Ribs of Death* (1957) by the Hungarian-Canadian John Marlyn; and Salverson's own *The Viking Heart* (1923), all of which are available in recent editions.

NOTES

I am grateful to Mr George Salverson, son of Laura Goodman Salverson, for his gracious support of this edition and to the National Library of Canada for permission to quote from the Salverson Papers.

1 Robert Craig Brown and Ramsay Cook, *Canada 1896-1921: A Nation Transformed* (Toronto: McClelland and Stewart 1974), 4, 83

2 Linda Kealey, ed., *A Not Unreasonable Claim* (Toronto: Women's Educational Press 1979), 2

3 Kipling, *Letters to the Family: Notes on a Recent Trip to Canada*, 2nd ed. (Toronto: Macmillan 1910), 39-40

4 Salverson normally uses the Anglicized 'Goodman' as the family name in the book, but occasionally she gives variations on the original Icelandic 'Guðmunð.' Etymologically, 'Goodman' is of course not directly related to 'Guðmunð,' which means 'God's gift to the bride.'

5 Icelandic migration between Manitoba and the Dakota territory was common towards the end of the nineteenth century. See Thorstina Walters, *Modern Sagas: The Story of the Icelanders in North America*, with an introduction by Allan Nevins (Fargo: North Dakota Institute for Regional Studies 1953), 62-3

6 Laura Goodman Salverson, 'Biographical Note,' typescript, National Library of Canada, Salverson Papers, envelope no 3, p. 3

7 See K.P. Stich, '"Canada's Century": The Rhetoric of Propaganda,' *Prairie Forum*, I, 1 (1976), 19-30; and Doug Owram, *Promise of Eden: The Canadian Expansionist Movement and the Idea of the West, 1856-1900* (Toronto: University of Toronto Press 1980).

8 For a documentation of social conditions in the Winnipeg of Salverson's *Confessions*, see Alan F.J. Artibise, *Winnipeg: A Social History of Urban Growth, 1874-1914* (Montreal and London: McGill-Queen's University Press 1975).

9 James B. Hedges, *Building the Canadian West* (New York: Macmillan 1939), 91

10 Jean Leonard Elliott, ed., *Immigrant Groups* (Scarborough: Prentice-Hall of Canada 1971), 8

11 W.L. Morton, 'Manitoba Schools and Canadian Nationality, 1890-1923,' *Canadian Historical Association, Annual Report* (1951), 54

12 Leacock, *My Discovery of the West* (Toronto: Allen 1937), 157-8

13 J.S. Woodsworth, *Strangers within Our Gates* (Toronto: Stephenson 1909), 201. This book was reprinted in the Social History of Canada series in 1972.

14 See, for example, C.F. Roland, 'The City of Winnipeg,' in *A Handbook to Winnipeg and the Province of Manitoba* (Winnipeg: British Association for the Advancement of Science 1909), 46

15 Alan F.J. Artibise, *Winnipeg: An Illustrated History* (Toronto: Lorimer and National Museum of Man 1977), 66, 68

16 Woodsworth, *Strangers*, 93, 92

17 Walters, in *Modern Sagas*, 82 ff., documents liberal protestantism among the great majority of Icelanders in North America.

18 McClung, *Painted Fires* (Toronto: Allen 1925), 241

19 Salverson, unpublished 'Author's Preface' to *Confessions*, Salverson Papers, envelope no 10, pp. 1-2

20 McClung, *The Stream Runs Fast* (Toronto: Allen 1945), 145

21 Stanley, 'The Western Mystique,' in *Prairie Perspectives*, ed. David P.

Contents

4 Contents

Author's foreword

When the publishers very kindly suggested that I should write a foreword to the new edition of *Confessions of an Immigrant's Daughter* I had not the wit to foresee the inhibiting difficulties ahead. For after all what can one say of a self-portrait, and more especially a portrait of a young self one knows to have existed, as have seasons past whose gay and gloomy aspects are now no more than a faded dream.

But dreams have a vitality which outride time and to that incontestable fact I must pin my hope that the substance of this book has merit pertinent to the future. In this hope I am further encouraged by the many United Kingdom reviews which, almost without exception, found the book a singular departure from the usual autobiography. This I take to mean that I may have succeeded in what I tried to accomplish: namely to make of a personal chronicle a more subjective and therefore more sensitive record of an age now happily past. For that past was difficult indeed for the immigrant who had the temerity to value his own traditions and dared to dream of justifying those traditions to the enrichment of his adopted country.

Today our attitude is less insular, and I cannot help but feel that any newcomer to our Dominion has only himself to blame if he fails to find some measure of human satisfaction. How many opportunities he will find which did not exist in the days of which I write in this book! Opportunities to make the most of himself whatever his talent or bent. Books on every conceivable subject; extension courses within the range of the most meagre purse; all sorts of study groups where the give and take of considered opinion is freely encouraged. Priceless things unknown in the recent past which I for one rejoice to bury without a single tear.

Then why write a book about it? Why not let it lie in dusty peace with all the other debris of disenchantment and frustration? For the same seemingly obscure reason which prompts an old Salt, cheerfully contemplating a calm sea, suddenly to launch into a tale of stress and storms and black tribulation. The means may be devious, but is not his inference well founded? Is he not saying, through the medium of hardships overcome: How little there is to fear for the voyager of tomorrow!

So there it is. To the best of my ability I have tried to show that a little courage and a lot of humour go a long way towards the fulfilment of even the most impossible. Lastly be it confessed that it was of the dreamer I was principally thinking. The lonely underprivileged dreamer, so seldom understood, and even more seldom successful in the things of this world. But should he therefore despair and doom to failure the timeless things of the heart? Should he not rather ask himself of what substance are those treasures of human culture which alone of man's creation time cannot destroy? The answers will be comforting. For when all is said and done it is by reason of its dream that nations live and mankind advances from the brute to human structure.

Finally, as it has been my own comfort, let me pass on to other obscure dreamers the sturdy motto of my ancient house: To the strong in heart there is no defeat!

Winnipeg, October 1948
L.G.S.

1939 edition	1949 edition
Respectfully dedicated to	Respectfully dedicated to
DR HENRY CHOWN	DOROTHY BRADSHAW
for his devotion to the poor	good companion and devoted friend

PART I

1

The first horizon

The Dakota prairie was an infinity of darkness through which the
buckboard rolled over the rutted trail with an eternal motion. To
the small girl-child crouched on the floor boards beside her
father's legs, the darkness and the rolling motion seemed of
infinite duration. It had started in a confusion of strange activities that shattered her familiar world, back in a blue dusk that
lay in the back of her mind, weighted with perplexing mysteries.
It had gone on and on and on in ever deepening mystery and
darkening shadows to which there seemed no end. Except for the
rumps of the horses, with their whisking tails that brushed the
dashboard with a reedy sound, there was nothing to see and
nothing to hear but the steady clop-clop of their pounding feet
and the creaking noise of the wheels. Everything else was a
wilderness dark, wrapped in a silence so heavy she was afraid to
sleep.

It was all very queer. That morning, which now seemed such
ages ago, she had wakened in a madhouse. The bed opposite her
little cot where her parents slept was in pieces, the feather ticks
and pillows lying in bundles on the floor. The kitchen was full of
boxes. The big stove where she usually struggled into her little
clothes to the comforting crackle of fire and the humming of the
copper kettle, was cold and desolate. The baby, tied in the old
black rocker, squirmed and whimpered unheeded, for mamma
had eyes for nothing but the dishes she was hastily packing in

the wash tub. And papa, equally preoccupied, was unscrewing the legs of the table. Even her brother, who might have been expected to find a teasing word of greeting, was out in the lean-to busily stuffing sheep's wool into a canvas sack. No one had paid her the slightest attention until, the dishes packed, her mother called out sharply:

'Dress yourself, child! Don't stand there like a stick!'

When mamma spoke in that tone of voice, you did as you were told and asked no questions. She had dressed, and a little later had eaten a cold egg, which she hated, and had obediently drunk a cup of milk, which was almost as bad. Eggs and milk and the long prayers she was obliged to say each night were a trinity of unavoidable trials. The eggs always made a sour taste in her mouth, and the prayers frightened her with their vague suggestions of yawning eternities. The milk had at least one element of comfort. If mamma was not looking, the cat could always be prevailed upon to finish the cup.

Oh, but that was the worst of all! The dear grey cat was gone, along with everything else stable and familiar. If only Tabby were here, purring on her breast, the darkness and the endless silence would not matter. Always, when something had gone sadly awry in her small world, it was to Tabby she carried her woe, and, in its inimitable way, the soft little creature had eased away the misery and filled her heart with comfort.

Blinking back tears, the child edged a little closer to her father's legs. By some unerring instinct of intuition, she knew that her mother, sitting stiffly erect with the sleeping baby in her lap, was miles removed in consciousness, shut away from them all in a bitter world of her own. But her father, in whom a poetic temperament made the transition from gloom to gaiety an easy process, might perchance by a little nudge be made aware of her loneliness. If only papa would say something, in his warm, pleasant voice, everything might right itself, and even this sudden endless journey through the prairie might take on reasonable meaning. Papa could always make sense out of non-sense – even mamma admitted that.

But it was her mother's voice, thin and strained, that cut the silence like a silver whip.

'Can't we go faster, Lars? It will soon be black as pitch.'

'We're getting there,' her father replied amiably, flicking the reins. 'A slow gait is a sure one, my dear.'

'I should not think you'd want to keep the Ericsons waiting up half the night for us,' her mother retorted, and caught her breath sharply. For suddenly the night was full of weird sounds, high, shrill, intolerable yapping sounds that raced along the dark horizon as though the air itself had found a thousand tongues with which to lash the silence. The horses jumped in their traces, tossed up their drooping heads, and, snorting with fear, started off at a gallop. The wild lurch pitched the child against the dashboard, but her father's hand shot out of the dark and drew her back to his knees. Shivering, she clung to those knees, too frightened for tears. Besides, now she understood why mamma had sat so straight and still. These awful noises were the terrors that haunted her nights and days. They were the wolves!

She had heard them before, though never so monstrously magnified, so terrifyingly close, and she remembered her mother's blanching face and the bitter words she had flung at papa.

'Now this I will not endure,' she had said, with hard, quiet finality. Other things, too, she had said, which the child could not understand, but now she realized that this race through the night was an effort to get away from the things her mother would not endure. And somehow she knew it was not just the wolves her mother heard in this awful clamour, but the savage tongues of this dark land, itself the voice of the wilderness for which her mother had no heart and against which she fought with cold determined resolution.

'There you are!' her mother cried bitterly. 'We shall be eaten alive! A fine finish to a brave venture.'

Her father laughed, not very brightly. 'That would be history,' he said. 'A pack of coyotes attacking a team at full gallop. Use your sense, my dear – you are so proud of it. I have told you often enough there are no wolves left in this part of the country.'

'You told me the lambs were safe last week. You know what happened.'

'It's a long time since you and I were lambs, my dear. There is a comforting thought,' he rejoined, with a chuckle, that eased the strain in the little girl's body. But her mother refused to be comforted.

'If you had as much wisdom as wit, we should not be here,' she said.

To which her father replied, 'Well, we won't be here long, Borga. And wit has a way of dying in the sweat shops of the city.'

A cry from the back of the buckboard, where her brother sat perched on top of bundles and boxes, put an end to the argument. 'Look! Look! There's a light!' he shouted. 'We're all right now, mamma. That's the house!'

So it was. Far ahead, in the midst of an ocean of darkness, two small jets of light stood out like candle flames braving the night. Why it should be so, I cannot say, but those wavering jets of yellow light marked a division of time for the little girl at her father's feet. From that moment her little thoughts and starry impressions were distinctly individual, and she herself no longer just the little girl who existed as a small, obedient extension of her mother. Struggling to her numbed feet and leaning against her father's knee, she stared in silent fascination at the nearing points of lights, and suddenly, for no apparent reason, a delightfully wicked thought popped into her head.

'Even if it's a troll's house, I WON'T eat an EGG!' she resolved.

In which fine frenzy a predestined rebel was born – the rebel who is myself.

The Ericsons, I was to learn much later, were considered a queer pair. In those good old Victorian days, the slightest departure from the accepted conventions was sufficient to earn one a suspect reputation. To question the Trinity, fail to hang your clothes out on Monday morning, or give houseroom to a book of Thomas Ingersoll, any of these was enough to arouse the criticism of the righteous. So far as I ever knew, the Ericsons were innocent of such monstrous errors, but they kept a 'heathen beast' (of which more later) and they had no children. That, in itself, was a suspicious circumstance in an age of step-ladder families, and argued either the wrath of God or a wilful obstruction of His blessed favour.

Beyond that, it seems the queer pair behaved normally. They had come to Dakota with that fugitive band of Icelanders who, despite the remonstrances of the Canadian Government, had quit the fly-ridden marshlands of Manitoba, to which they were consigned, and, the men on foot, their women in ox-carts, trekked to the fertile plains across the border. They were industrious; the furrows lengthened year by year, and neither the grasshopper plague, the furious winds, nor the thieving wolves, had dampened their faith in the country. Indeed, it was this glowing faith, communicated over a mild glass of toddy, which had persuaded my impressionable father that the nearest approach to heaven-upon-earth was a sheep ranch in Dakota. To obtain this leasehold on bliss, a neat little cottage with a white picket fence around its patch of green garden was sacrificed, much against my mother's will and better judgement. As for the ranch, it consisted of a log house for which my mother had an unreasoning hatred as the lowest habitation possible to men; I don't know how many acres of unbroken scrub prairie; a dozen sheep; a cow.

But now the venture was over. Once again, penniless, and with nothing but the bedding, our clothes, and a few pieces of furniture, we were on the move, our immediate destination the sod-roofed cabin of the hospitable though queer Ericsons.

That visit stamps the beginning of memory – the first of a chain of unrelated events, insignificant in themselves, and yet each one having its ineradicable, subtle effect upon my future reaction to life. That I should remember so much of that visit after almost forty-four years is not particularly remarkable. Extremes of emotion leave indelible marks. And certainly that was a night of tragi-comic extremes.

The Ericsons, two bent gnomes peering anxiously into the darkness, were waiting in the open doorway. They had almost despaired of our coming that night, and were about to go to bed, when they heard the horses. They were pleased as children to be cheated of their rest, and bustled us into the house with embarrassing effusion. They were short and dark and leathery, and, to my childish eyes, differed in nothing, except that Mr Anderson had a tuft of hair on his chin and was dressed in baggy brown homespun trousers, whereas Mrs Anderson's tuft was under her nose, and she wore a wide skirt, of the same material.

Their voices were high-pitched and thin – as though they had worn them threadbare calling to each other across the windswept fields. And when either one made a statement, it was referred back to the other, prefixed by a question:

'Ha? Kvad heldur pú, Runa? Eh? What do you think, Runa?'

'Ha? Pú sejir satt, Noni! Eh? You are right, Noni!'

The house was very hot and smelled of boiled mutton, for we had been expected for hours, and the stewpot still simmered at the back of the stove. There was a wall lamp with a tin shield behind it that dazzled my eyes and made me think of the fierce-looking angel in the story-book who stood at the gates of Eden brandishing a crooked sword.

A table was spread with plates of doughnuts, liver sausage, pickled sheep's head, bread and butter, and the omnipresent, ever-heated eggs. A bureau with a marble top and a cracked mirror occupied a place of honour between the two small windows, and flaunted for all to see a fat, poison-green plush album with real brass clasps!

There my discoveries ended. Something agile and swift leaped from under the table where the cloth had kept it hidden, and, with the ease of a bird, settled on the back of the kitchen chair not a dozen steps from me.

My heart went out to the marvellous creature at once. He had eyes, black and bright as new shoe buttons, that stared at me out of a tiny yellow face no bigger than an apple, yet absurdly human. He capered about on the back of the chair, making the funniest chattering noises that made me think of hail on a window-pane, and a little of mamma when she was very cross.

I was rooted to the spot with mounting admiration. When Mrs Ericson, having settled my mother and the baby in comfort before the fire, came to help me, I suffered myself to be peeled out of my little tight coat without hearing a word she said, nor remembering to hold my hand out politely. Even mamma's voice, gentle now, and full of concern, calling me to the fire, had no effect. I could not leave off watching the intriguing yellow creature.

Still in a daze, I found myself whisked to a milking stool, given a piece of sugar, and told to sit still like a good child and wait for my supper. The sugar slipped into the little pocket of my dress, for, though I detested everything sweet, all through childhood I had a squirrel's instinct to hide such stuff away. But neither sugar nor supper occupied my puzzled thoughts. With what wit I had, I was trying to penetrate the mystery before me. How could anything so much like a baby be covered with fur? And, if it wasn't a queer sort of baby, what was it scolding about? What sort of creature pulled faces like a boy, wagged its head like an old woman, and scratched its yellow stomach with tiny, pink-palmed paws?

He was not a cat, nor was he a dog. And, of course, no ordinary baby was smart enough to perch on the back of a chair, to say nothing of bobbing about, flailing its arms. I could not think what he was, but when he suddenly hooked a long tail round a rung, and popped to the floor, and, quick as a cat's wink, popped up again, an enchanting solution broke on my mind. Completely forgetting that nice little girls were seen and not heard, I shrieked out ecstatically:

'Papa! Papa! It's a king's son in a cat's skin! And I'm going to love him for ever and ever!'

Alas for budding genius! Gales of heartless laughter greeted my heroic invention. It was a bitter blow. Big people were little better than trolls, I thought. Indeed, they were very like them. In the stories that mamma read to me, Tröll-karls and Troll-skessur were always roaring with laughter at the wrong moment. Papa, at least, might have remembered that it was he himself had told me the sad tale of the golden-haired princeling who was changed into a bear, and had to go roaring through the black pine forest for ever and ever – which, of course, meant until the woodcutter's little daughter loved him in spite of the roaring and stole away his hide.

I subsided into humiliating silence, confused, but now convinced. The mystery still remained. The little yellow beast was in a fury because no one understood him, no matter how hard he talked. He jittered and stared accusingly, and sometimes, covered his tiny face in his funny wee paws, and shook pitiably. He could not be happy inside himself!

All through supper the alarming fancy grew on me that here was no mortal household; that Mrs Ericson, with her blue moustache and nimble chatter, was a witch, and no woman at all. It really didn't take much reasoning. You found her house, as you found all witches' houses, after a terrifying gallop through the dark. On the doorstep she waited for you, with a crooked little man at her side, and a bright, blinding light at her back. It was so hot in her house you might fall asleep unawares, and be turned into goodness knows what sort of creature. And, most convincing of all, there was a huge black pot brewing and stewing on her huge black range!

More and more confused, more and more weary, it was perhaps not extraordinary that my behaviour should vex my mother. I not only refused to eat an egg when it was sprinkled with sugar, but I rudely pushed away the stew. No. No. I would not have it, I glowered. No. No. No. I could not and dared not explain that spells were brewed in black pots. I could only shove the dish away with disgraceful impoliteness. My father saved the situation by taking me on his knee and letting me dunk a doughnut in his coffee. The doughnut appeased the disagreeable gnawing under my breast bone, and the warm curve of my father's arm comforted the crink in my back. If only I might have slept there, the scandalous business to follow might have been averted.

But I was snatched from this pleasant shelter. It was time to go to bed. To-morrow we were driving to Crystal, where a train would take us on to Winnipeg. None of which meant anything to me, except that I guessed it was a place mamma preferred to the sheep ranch, and papa, on the other hand, somehow dreaded. For, vaguely, I had become conscious of the conflict of ideas between my parents – a conflict which was never to end, and precluded any solid, satisfying home life, in the conventional sense.

I have no recollection of the bedroom as a bedroom into which my mother led me. But for years I relived in nightmares the terror of that room. There was a big bed in it piled with the usual feather tick and patchwork quilts, but, when my mother threw back the covers, I caught sight of something under the hay mattress that turned my skin to ice. It was a red, hairy hide! In fact, a cow-hide, spread over the home-made rope spring – to me, a *hammur*, the bewitched hide, waiting to swallow my little self. And, to further confuse my infant reasoning, I now remembered with horror an episode which had taken place a few days ago.

I had formed the odious habit of eating paper. No amount of scolding had cured me of the crime. But one morning, on following my mother into the lean-to, I saw stretched upon the wall the gory hide of the little calf which only the day before had been gambolling in the back yard.

'Mamma!' I had shrieked, pointing to the hide, 'that's the little calf, rolled out –!'

'Oh, I know,' replied mamma, seriously, shaking her head. 'You see, the poor thing ate paper.'

Well, I had not eaten paper since, but now it seemed my sins were finding me out. The cow-hide was a menace. The calf who ate paper, the little animal that resembled a baby but wasn't a baby, the old woman with a moustache, and the bubbling black kettle, all combined to make a nightmare of fear in my tired child's mind. When my poor distraught mother reached out to take me on her knee and undress me, I screamed and hit out like a little fiend. She was unaccustomed to such behaviour in her children. I was soundly smacked and severely shaken, all to no effect. Hysteria gave me the strength and viciousness of a wild cat. I fought and scratched and wriggled and squirmed, quite as determined to stay out of that bed as my mother was determined to put me into it.

In the end, after repeatedly flinging me into the feather tick, only to see me roll to the floor, it was she who gave up the battle. Worn out and unhappy, completely mystified by this sudden transformation of a peaceable, pudgy infant into a raging limb of Satan, she left me to sob out my meanness on the floor. All night I lay there, abandoned to wickedness, and only fell asleep when the grey morning light, stealing in through a small, barred window, fell on my cold little face like gentle, forgiving fingers.

2

I discover my birthplace

I have no further recollection of that journey to Winnipeg, nor any clear memory of our arrival in that muddy village. I do remember, however, that we went to live in a row of houses, all built alike, all having bay windows; floors where the frost gathered around the doors and baseboards; and facing upon a street where two planks represented the last word in a civic improvement.

In wet weather, the road, like an angry sea-serpent looping along, dripped a red, gummy spume, through which horses and men slithered and slipped, and often enough, to my vast amusement, sank half-way to their knees. Rubbers were sucked off with a hungry, smacking sound, and the feet of the horses glug-glug-glugged endlessly. In winter patches of ice formed in the low spots, and the little ridges of dirty snow made the sleighs jolt and screech as they flew by to the sound of singing bells.

Winter, I discovered, had compensations. It was bad to have your feet always cold, and disagreeable to run into the kitchen only to find every chair spread with frozen clothes off the line, but it was pleasant to make a clear spot on the snowy window-pane and watch the hurrying world go by. No one ever got stuck in the winter time. Horses were never beaten to make them strain and struggle in a sickening manner. No angry shouts and rumble of ugly words rent the air. In the winter, all sorts of queer contraptions and funny people came to see papa. There was a sleigh, with a top like a house, where a stove-pipe gave off feathers of smoke, and out of which men and women tumbled like the animals out of the Ark. They came from Icelandic River, and sometimes they brought a gift of fish, deer meat, or mutton, and now and then a bag of wool. Most of the men had whiskers and smoked short pipes, which made me think they were all grandfathers. For papa neither smoked nor wore a beard, but only now and then dipped snuff from a pretty silver box; and his moustache was short and carefully trimmed. His hair, too, was sleek and black as the fur on my new tomcat, whereas these visiting grandfathers, for the most part, were thatched with sandy-coloured straw.

The women either brought babies, or, when they left after a stay in Winnipeg, took babies back with them. It was a little tiresome, to be sure, and yet there was a certain thrill in seeing the door fly open, and bundles of people rolling in, with whiffs of frosty air circling them in clouds. There was always a lot of laughter, mysterious headshakes, and once the visit got under way, pots and pots of coffee, with plates of mamma's famous pancakes. Sometimes, too, there was singing, and a queer kind of chanting, which papa called *Kveda*, and told me I should listen, for the verses were full of ancient wisdom. It was a dignified sort of noise, so I usually listened willingly enough, especially if papa let me sip from his saucer when mamma was not looking.

There came a time, however, when papa failed to come home. He had been taken sick, and carried to the hospital. It was a little colder in the house thereafter and the pancakes had a flat taste, and mamma drank her coffee black.

Not long after that, mother dressed me in my little coat, and said we must make a visit to Great-Uncle Jonathan. She had work to do, she said, and I must be a good child and stay with uncle until she fetched me. It was fun following the crack in the plank sidewalk, and speculating upon where we were going. When we got there I saw before us a small white house, with two trees in front of the low veranda. There was a little hall, where mother took off my coat and hung it on a nail. It was queer, I thought, that no one met us. But a moment later, when we

stepped into the room giving off the hall, I understood, and was
struck dumb.

In the middle of the room was a strange sort of chair, with big
yellow wheels and a high yellow back. In the chair sat a man
dressed in a purple gown, his legs covered with a plaid shawl.
His eyes, deep, brown, and luminous, turned on us out of a serious face that looked parchment pale in contrast with the long,
flowing, curly brown beard that rippled down his bosom.

It was an awesome moment! Made doubly so when I heard my
mother say, quite calmly: 'Kondu saell godi min.'

I clutched her skirt. Surely even a mother ought not to say to
the Lord, careless-like, 'How do you do, my dear!' But no thun-
derclap followed. Just a very human rumble, replying, 'So-so-so-
so – what have you got there behind your skirts!'

I decided to risk a peep. The bearded monarch was smiling –
actually smiling. Oh, thought I, with boundless relief. It was not
the Lord God Almighty after all. God was not the smiling sort. It
must be Moses ...

Even that was not quite accurate, I learned to my astonishment. The venerable gentleman was very like a patriarch, and, as
I was many years later to see, actually resembled Michelangelo's
Moses, but he was just my Great-Uncle Jonathan, an old, old sea
captain, many years home from the sea.

That was the beginning of the happiest months of my entire
childhood. Great-uncle was confined to an invalid's chair, having suffered a stoke which left his legs paralysed. It was a secret
between us that I took care of uncle, and not uncle of me. He was
a beautiful old man of impressive dignity, and full of quiet
humour. His little, plainly furnished room, which we very
shortly turned into a lively universe, round which we shipped
from port to port, lives unspoiled in my memory.

There were shelves with books, and shells and stones, and dried
sea-urchins, Sometimes uncle secreted raisins on these shelves,
for which we cruised under full sail. The raisins I disliked, as all
sweets, but I ate them in the same reckless spirit in which Mother
Eve ate of the forbidden fruit. Raisins came from Spain, great-
uncle said, and in Spain the señoritas were a joy to behold.

'Ah, there were pretty girls for you!' said my uncle, stroking his beard, and twinkling at me with his warm brown eyes. 'Little devils, too. They danced the heart from your breast, wore it for a posy a day or two, and tossed it away with a laugh.'

In Barcelona there was a girl he still remembered. A slip of a black-eyed thing with a rose in her midnight hair, and laughter on her scarlet lips. Ah, she made a merry fool of more than one poor sailor, said my uncle, sighing. But it was all so long ago, he remembered nothing very clearly, except the sound of her twinkling feet – he sometimes heard them now, on the windowpane, when the hard, bright prairie rain was falling.

I, too, heard her after that. When the dusk came down on a wet and windy day I loved to sit at my uncle's feet, listening for the tiny castanets, and the swish of invisible, silken garments. For her sake I would have eaten a pound of raisins and never turned a hair!

There were other reminiscences, less appealing, but full of thrilling marvels. Great-uncle had been a deep-sea sailor, and visited many 'foreign parts.' For instance, he had been to Scotland, where the gentlemen wore petticoats; to England, too, in the days when the good queen, now so pious and severe, was a little young thing with lively grace in her eye.

Grace of heart, too, she had, said my uncle, 'God save her Majesty!' Why, when the Queen learned that little boys no bigger than myself were poked up the chimneys of rich people's houses – and, possibly, the palace – to clean away the soot, she put her foot down instantly. It had to stop, she said – or the chimneys widened to admit bigger boys.

What was more, the little queen put an end to gibbets, said my uncle. Gibbets were something bad people dangled from, and blew about in the wind like socks on a line. It spoiled the landscape, and hurt the feelings of any nice young lady who came upon such a sight at the cross-roads. So all the gibbets were instantly chopped down. There were other things which the young queen did not like: women crawling about in mines, when they ought to be home raising babies for the nation; riots in Ireland, where the people were always short of potatoes, and just as short of temper, so uncle said. And much more of which I have no recollection, because it was entirely outside my infant ken.

When he spoke of the sea, and the flying ships, with the winds of the world at their backs, I did not have to understand. I could feel the wet spray in my face, and see the dolphin dancing in the sun. I shivered when the storms blew up, and knew beyond doubt what trials lay ahead for crew and cargo when a red ring lay around the moon. It did not frighten me when 'another poor devil went overboard,' nor seem at all strange that his poor, grey ghost should be seen aimlessly flitting up and down the rigging. Ghosts held no more terror for me than the make-believe spirit inside myself, the irrepressible creature that played in the puddles by the corner pump, thought nothing at all of climbing the roof to touch the stars, and even said, in its heart, a hundred times: I won't be a girl to sew a fine seam and rock a little cradle!

Sometimes we kept off the sea, and pillaged about on the land. 'Now, let me think,' great-uncle would begin, as soon as the door closed behind mamma. 'Where should we go faring to-day, little one?'

'Not on the seas, uncle dear, the good ship needs repairing after the gale yesterday.'

'True, true, so she does,' he replies. 'Well then, we shut our eyes and fly to Iceland, where the Hidden People found a lasting refuge when the Lord God cast them off.'

How was that, I wanted to know, suspecting that the Lord God had started another flood, or burned another Tyre for the fun of it.

'It was like this,' my uncle began. 'Mother Eve had spent a busy day setting her new house to rights. A very tiresome business for a body straight from Eden, where work was quite unknown. It was coming on evening, with a nice wind blowing from the coco-nut groves. Adam was daudling down by the well, most likely admiring his beard. There was no help to be had from him, and the children were all unwashed and dirty. All but Cain and Abel, that is. They, to be sure, had their faces scrubbed, and sat on a bright new stool, swinging their legs. At that moment, poor Eve looks towards the palms, and sees where the Lord is walking, taking the air, communing with himself. What's to be done, thinks Eve, terrified to be found as bad a mother as she was once found a mischievous maid. The Lord God was coming to call. Oh, she knew that in her bones. And here were all the little wretches, except Cain and Abel, covered with bramble scratches, berry stains, and plain dirt to boot.

'"Quick, my little ones!" Mother Eve spoke sharply and waved her broom. "Run and hide, and for goodness' sake keep quiet!"

'So the Lord God finds a tidy house, a tidy woman, and, very politely, Cain and Abel leap down to let Him have the stool.

'"How goes the struggle, Mother Eve?" the Lord asks, very kindly.

'"Not too badly," says Eve, "not badly at all, except that Adam leans too long on his hoe, to my thinking."

'"Hmm," says the Lord, a bit of a twinkle in his eye. "And how are the children?"

'"They could be worse," says Eve, making a sign to Cain to stop digging up the dust with his toe. "They do very well on the earth, if I may say so."

'"Hmm," says the Lord, surprised-like, but still very gentle. "And are these all the children, Mother Eve?"

'Eve hung her head. How could she bring those little wretches into the presence of the Lord God, who was dressed in purple and gold with the power of life and death in His hands?

'"Lord, these are all," she said.

'"Yea, only these," poor Eve forswore.

'Then the Lord rose, and His robes made a sweeping sound, as of many winds, and His voice was terrible as thunder.

'"Hear me, then, Eve. What thou hast hidden, let be for ever hidden!"

'That my little lamb, is how the Hidden People came to be,' uncle finished. 'And I'm not sure they got the worst of the bargain.'

Nor was I, when he had told me a tale or two. They had no souls of course – neither heaven nor hell was open to them. But it was very jolly to flit about, lightly as shadows, to live in little knolls, and build homesteads and churches in the heart of a mountain. It was worth doing without a soul, when you could disappear through walls, walk on water as easily as on dry land, and enter a rock as readily as a mortal entered a doorway! What was more, the Hidden People had magic powers against which mere mortals were helpless. If they chose to build a house in a nice green knoll in the bishop's field, his lordship knew better than to have the grass cut. Once, a foolish fellow attempted such a trick, and all his hay flew away in a wind that swooped out of a calm sky, like a hawk a-hunting. Oh, it wasn't safe at all to disturb the peace of fairy dwellings! Indeed, if you were wise, you kept the larder unlocked, just in case it was a hard year below, and the hidden tenants needed a bit of meal or slice of smoked mutton. When they were treated with kindness, the Hidden People watched your cattle, and saw to it that no evil befell them.

They were kindly baggages, on the whole, said my uncle – a little too given to vain attire, perhaps, and to the light fantastic, but for that he could not seriously blame them. A wench in homespun, with lead in her feet, was a sad sight anywhere. No, if they had any real fault, it was the passion for stealing human babies. Poor things, they could not forswear the hope of somehow obtaining an immortal soul.

These tales were a perpetual joy. They absorbed me so completely that sometimes I wondered if I were not a changeling myself. It might very well be, for my thoughts were very foolish, I knew, and, moreover, I had overheard mamma telling a visitor I had been the smallest baby. In fact, a funny little thing, only four pounds, and with black hair to my shoulders! That was odd, when you came to think of it. The last two babies – whom God had given and taken away, as seemed to be His habit – were much bigger than that, and with very little hair on their little round heads.

But, if uncle's stories absorbed me, the day arrived when another obsession obscured every common fact. That was when I mounted an empty apple box, and started telling tales myself. Time flew, thereafter, and if mamma was late in coming for me, I scarcely noticed. Indeed, I sometimes forgot I was her little girl at all, and bound to go home to a chilly house and a dish of porridge. And not until the day when mamma was much later than usual, had it ever occurred to me that uncle might have a family. He had always been alone in his quiet kingdom of dreams when we arrived in mid morning, and we had left him in similar, cheerful peace, at five in the afternoon. On this occasion, however, a tall, angular lady, in a long black dress that poked out at the back, like the hump on the kitty when something scared him, swept in on a gust of cold wind.

'Skotan's vedur!' cried she, kicking the door shut with her heel, for there was a big bag in one hand and an umbrella in the other. The autumn wind was cold, but she was colder, I thought, watching her put away the umbrella, the bag, and the stiff black hat from the top of her head, and hang up her jacket, that had a thousand buttons from chin to stomach. The wind was dreadful, the streets were dreadful, the dressmaking shop where she worked was dreadful – in fact, everything in this dreadful place worse than dreadful, she said, in a running-river voice that raised the goose-flesh on my skin.

Striding to my dignified uncle, she kissed the top of his head, yanked the pillow he liked under the small of his back up under his shoulder-blades, and, with a crack of a smile in her thin, sallow face, said smartly:

'That's better! How are the feet? Were you cold? Did you eat the sole I fixed for your lunch?'

Then, as if seeing me for the first time, she exclaimed, eyeing me severely: 'So that is Lala! Goodness, child, what makes your face so red? I hope you aren't getting a nasty fever!'

'The little thing is shy, Bella,' uncle defended me.

'Nonsense! Don't put ideas in her head,' Bella retorted. 'Here, child, you need not be shy with me. Come, I'll fix you a nice drink to cool your blood.'

I did not want anything to drink, but when she reached out a strong, lean hand for me, I went along to the pantry. I remember the rites of that drink to the last detail. She took a glass, into which she poured a little vinegar, added a spoonful of sugar, some water, and a pinch of soda to make it fizz.

It had a dreadful taste, but I knew better than not to drink it, and said, besides, 'Thank you,' as bravely as I could.

On the way home, that evening, I plucked up courage to question mamma. 'Who is Bella?' I wanted to know.

'Bella is your uncle's wife,' mamma astonished me by saying. And then I saw that she was laughing in a silent way, that she always had when greatly amused. So I dared to add:

'But, mamma – uncle is awfully old!'

'That was the trouble,' she said. 'Yes – that was the trouble.'

There the matter rested. Years later, I was to hear a common version of that belated marriage. Uncle Jonathan had been caught in a weak moment, while he was ill! Too old for adventure, and retired from the sea, Bella's practical ministrations were doubtless a welcome panacea for his loneliness. A good wife she proved, at that! So my mother always declaimed, a bit militantly. A good, sensible wife, who cared for him in sickness and health. But I, who remembered the twinkling castanets, that danced for him in the prairie rain, sometimes wondered – for what had a bed, and a fire, and a piece of fried sole, to do with happiness?

3

Introducing Job's cycle

These happy days came to an end. My father was home from the hospital, and, although far from well, was soon at work again. There was no one now to whom I could tell my thoughts. Mamma was for ever busy. She had a passion for keeping things scoured and scrubbed. Even the stove had its face rubbed until it shone like a mirror. When you carried water from a pump half a block away, or melted snow after the winter had set in, all this washing and cleaning consumed a lot of time. Moreover, these household activities were only the beginning of mamma's labours. There were endless socks and stockings and mitts to knit, besides clothes to be mended and made for others.

The knitting had compensations. It was generally dusk before she got round to it, and then she would pull up the high-backed rocking-chair to the side of the shiny black stove, where the kettle hummed its own little tune and the cat purred under the fire-box. It was fun to draw up my little chair, too, and watch the glinting needles fly in mamma's small, pretty hands. She was proud of those hands, and proud of her beautiful, chestnut hair, coiled in heavy braids at the back of her head. She had other pride, as well, which I could not then understand. And yet, when she sat there, small, and straight, and still, in her high-backed chair, I always half expected she might wave her hand, like the good queen who put down gibbets, and, in a trice, transform the sad old house. And quite often something not unlike that did happen.

For mamma would tell me a story. Not the saucy sort of yarn that great-uncle loved to unfold with lavish detail, and laughter in his eye. There were no twinkling toes and fleeting gallantries in mamma's sagas. While the cat purred and the kettle sang, I was made to feel how seldom the high-hearted pursued the pleasant paths of common happiness. Heroes fell upon their swords, forsworn to honour, and their ladies, equally stern, shunned such ignoble weaknesses as tears and lamentation.

There was Brynhild, the gleaming warrior maid; Isolde the Unlucky; and Gudrid the Fair – though what was fair about a maid so full of vengeance, I never could see. Her wilful story cast a chill on my child heart, and yet, when mamma recited the famous confession Gudrid made to her son, when she was old, and become a holy recluse, tears choked me: 'Now will I tell thee this: to him was I worst whom best I loved!'

There was something grandly tragic beyond my ken in those sagas. I heard them with interest, not unmixed with awesome fear. What I liked much better were the times when mamma brought out the spinning-wheel, and I sat at her feet, carding tufts of wool, listening to the fascinating histories of Snow White and Rose Red and the Seven Dwarfs, Kitty, the King's Daughter, and the pretty tale of Laufey and Lineik.

There came a morning, however, that put an end to these lovely pleasures for quite some time. I awakened with a horrible, choking sensation, that rapidly increased. My body was on fire, my head spun with queer noises, and nothing that any one could do eased the growing misery. The old doctor who had dosed us for simple ailments wrung his hands in despair. He had thought this a case of aggravated croup, he said, but now he surmised that the 'infant-killer' had picked me for its victim. It was diphtheria!

My poor parents looked at each other in fear. If he had said it was the bubonic plague their hearts would have suffered no greater chill. For, in those not so distant days, diphtheria was almost as fatal a scourge. If only we were nearer the centres of civilization, the old doctor moaned. He had read of an anti-toxin just discovered, that was being used with miraculous effects. But we were not on the highroads of civilization. We were in an isolated frontier town, far from all such blessings.

That I am still alive to tell the tale is certainly due to a singular circumstance. A friend of my mother who lived at a considerable distance, was suddenly obsessed by the feeling that she should visit us. It was very cold, and, so far as she knew, there was no particular reason for the nagging urgency that oppressed her. By all the rules of common sense, she should have waited for decent weather. But neither common sense, nor the prospect of a long, tiresome walk in sub-zero weather, was strong enough to obliterate that odd feeling of urgent need calling her. At twilight, she could resist the pull no longer, and started out, feeling a little foolish but determined to act on the driving impulse.

Once inside our stricken house, this wonderful woman took matters into her own hands. She sent for her own physician, Dr Chown, at that time one of Winnipeg's outstanding medical men. Neither prestige nor poverty affected his zeal. He fought for life as grimly and tirelessly as a soldier fights for the shining thing he calls honour, on whatever battle-front. Dr Chown literally leaped at the case, because the odds were all against him – if there were even one chance in a thousand, he meant to fight for that chance. And so the long struggle began.

What frantic measures were attempted are of no particular consequence now. But I remember, with ineradicable vividness, the first of many evils. I remember the insufferable tent, made of heavy blankets, where my father was to hold me over a tub of boiling water, kept at white steam heat with hot stones. I remember it so well because, in my choking agony, I clutched at papa and moaned: 'Take me out, papa – I'm gone any way!' Yes, I remember it, for suddenly my father's tears were a cooling rain on my burning face, and the smothering walls fell away ...

Dr Chown eventually called in a young surgeon whose reputation was already enviable. What his exact theory was, in regard to this particular case, only heaven knows. But he decided that the most feasible way of saving me was by the insertion of some sort of tube into my throat – presumably to act as a repository for the phlegm and poisonous secretions. It was to remain not more than twelve hours. Thereafter, the pressure would be too great.

The brilliant surgeon may have been overly busy – those were days of an under-staffed hospital – or he may simply have forgotten that an immigrant's child was battling for life in an obscure corner of the town. At any rate, he failed to return in the twelve hours. But when Dr Chown made his call, that awful morning, he took just one glimpse of the purple, squirming bundle that fought for breath, bleeding at the nostrils, mouth, and even the finger nails, and out he flew to his rig, and across town, in a mad chase that was to become history in our slice of the world.

A chastened surgeon returned with him. Somehow, that frightfully entangled device was literally torn up from my tortured throat. How, I mercifully never knew, for nature had done what medicine dared not do – I was unconscious.

The point of all this came much later. One morning, awakening from a foggy sleep, I overheard voices: 'She will live,' some one said, 'but I'm afraid her voice may be lost – that she may not speak —'

Terror, such as only a helpless child can know, almost stopped my heart. Oh, I knew the meaning of those whispered words. Never to sing at the top of my voice when I was alone in the house and mamma busy elsewhere. Never to speak, even to myself, the crowding thoughts that flocked to my head. I opened my mouth to scream, only to find how right the whisperers were. No sound came out! Frozen with fear, I lay there, my little body too weak to move, and the voices going on and on just beyond the doorway. It was then, all at once, that something fierce, something stronger than fear, rushed to my aid. I remembered those stories told on an empty apple box. I would not lose my voice. No, no, I would not! I had to have a voice to go on telling Uncle Jonathan my little stories ...

When my mother came in, I was crying soundlessly. That was another thing I must not do, I was told. It would hinder my getting strong again. I must be quiet, and very, very still. I must go on patiently taking the endless broths, fed with a spoon, and swallow without complaint the syrupy stuff, bitter sweet, from the big brown bottle the doctor had left.

Days and nights dragged out their endless length. Except for the visits of the doctor who each morning left something in my numb little hands: a yellow orange; a bright red apple; and sometimes a silver shiny coin; nothing relieved the pain-filled monotony. The nights were the worst, however, for then, so often, I broke into a sweat, reliving the choking horror, and all that went with it. Those nights would have been an unrelieved nightmare, but for my faithful, black cat, who so often crept into my bed, and, quite as though he understood my misery, snuggled, warm and loving, close to my troubled heart.

My father had lost many days' work while I was so desperately ill, and now was compelled to work overtime, late into the night, in the futile hope that somehow or other he could thereby meet the cost of this protracted illness. His worry must have communicated itself to Dr Chown, who, perhaps, understood that one may be poor with honour, and that the handicap of language does not necessarily condemn one to insensitive ignorance. At any rate, one Sunday Dr Chown simulated the greatest interest in a chest of drawers papa had made from an old oak bed. It was marvellously done, he said. Papa's bookshelves were another wonder – although made from nothing better than cheap pine boards. Now, if only he could get flower-boxes made as well as that, said the doctor, sighing. But, of course, skilled craftsmen in any line were not to be picked up for odd jobs like that. Naturally, my father understood what genuine human goodness prompted these reflections. Very gladly he made the doctor's flower-boxes, and what else the generous physician invented as his need. But papa was not prepared to receive, for these inadequate tasks, a cancelled bill! Such kindness had not been our experience in Canada. It was a miracle that melted some of mamma's bitterness against what had always been little better than humiliating exile. There were tears in papa's eyes when he told her of it, and I remember the white look of her face when she answered:

'So then – there are gentlefolk in this country!'

No doubt, she was thinking back to her old home at Reygholt, in the famous deanery, where life moved with dignity, and charity was something more than a pious word. To that ancient, historic estate, where a noble Norse chieftain had raised his booths and written his famous laws, and where, in later times, dignitaries of the Church pursued their homely ways, cherishing many admirable customs. Kindly customs, such as the house-readings, of which mamma so often spoke, when all the household assembled in the *badstofa*, and the old dean read from the ancient sagas, from poetry, or holy writ. And, always, at the close, in that quaint household, the mistress and her daughters waited on the servants, for this was their hour of respite, and the little courtesy an unspoken reminder of the Greatest Servant, who came, not to be served, but to serve others.

That way of life, almost feudal in its dignity, and fixed, substantial habits, my mother never forgot – and, perhaps, never forgave herself for leaving, as she had done on a romantic impulse, and against her people's wishes. But of that, I as yet knew nothing, nor could then have understood. I only knew that Dr Chown softened her attitude toward the new country, and perhaps raised a hope that one day her children might redeem themselves from the bitter bondage of straitened circumstances. For never, like my incurably idealistic father, could she console herself with poetic fancies – believe any but concrete deeds were of any particular value. One kindly, quiet deed eclipsed a million easy sympathies, in her estimation. And good impulses froze in the human heart when one's circumstances prevented their natural expression. So she believed, and, neither then nor at any future time, was she ever to modify that opinion.

The doctor's generosity had relieved my parents of a financial burden, but the anxiety over my voice still remained. Six weeks had passed, and not a sound came from my stricken throat. I was able to be up a few hours daily, and in all other respects was well on the way to recovery, although the doctor predicted bronchial difficulties, and urged the most stringent care. Kind friends came and patted me on the head, and said what a good child I was. Certainly, I was passive enough, and quiet enough, for there was nothing left of the lively spirit that had spun such enchanting vagaries in uncle's fairy kingdom. I was no longer so frightened at being mute, for I had acquired a sort of infant stoicism, and by some instinctive reasoning accepted the futility of expecting any one to understand what really troubled me. But I so often wept furtively, when left to myself, thinking of those happy days in the little house that held an entire world.

There came a day, however, which has a place by itself in memory. Mamma had dressed me in the red cashmere frock she had made to celebrate my recovery. Round my neck was a string of white beads from papa, and on my feet little patent-leather slippers he had made after working hours. My long, yellow hair was tied back from my forehead with a fine new ribbon, and once again the time had come to take a special medicine and try my voice. Mamma drew up my little chair to her knees, and, when I was seated, poured out the sticky substance for me to swallow.

'Now try to say something, child,' she urged, as she had gently urged a hundred times before. Suddenly, I was afraid – terribly afraid. I had tried so often. Without much hope, my lips parted. I don't know what I meant to say. I only remember the shock of amazed delight, when a thin, wavering squeak sounded in my ears. And then, all at once, I was in mamma's lap, crying and crying, her arms tight, tight about me.

In a really smart chronicle, any struggle ends at a prescribed climax, preferably with a happy recompense for all concerned, save the wilful sinner. But, unfortunately for the artistry of this tale, life is not smart. Life is a colossus too great for smart declensions, and as indifferent to human vanities as to individual destiny. It cares nothing for the canons of art, and pursues its ironic rhythm, piling up anticlimaxes as a tidal wave piles up the wreckage it has made of some once seaworthy ship.

It would certainly be more agreeable, and, in the happy convention, to end the vicissitudes of my childhood with the recovery of my voice, and some divinely ordered recompense. But, as a matter of fact, that unforgettable illness was only the beginning of a prolonged Job's cycle – a sort of melodramatic introduction to years of intermittent suffering. And the only compensation, truth compels me to acknowledge, was a gradual deadening of the acute sensitivity which had registered so many earlier impressions. Each illness seemed to thrust me deeper and deeper into a kind of mental stupor, which rendered the greater part of those years a blank.

4

Humours of the last frontier

The poor attract malicious fate. A few weeks after my recovery a neighbour suggested to my mother that she should rent an upstairs room to a widow who was seeking a modest shelter. When she arrived to inspect the room she brought a child whose pasty complexion struck my mother as unhealthy.

'I hope your little girl isn't unwell,' she said to the woman. 'I have a child who is just recovering from a serious illness, and have to be careful.'

'Oh, there is nothing wrong with Lena but a touch of cold,' the other said.

The cold was whooping-cough! Mother never forgave that lie, and promptly evicted the woman when the ugly truth came out. But the damage was done. I had contracted the worst of all ailments, under the circumstances – one which left me with a permanent bronchial weakness.

Thereafter I was the prey of every raging epidemic. Those who remember the institution of the Little White Hearse, which was a commonplace on the streets of old Winnipeg, know the frequency of those epidemics and their fatal virulence. Those were the good old days when every mother was warned against 'the second summer' for her baby. When old wives stood ready with such simple remedies as lime-water, flour steamed in cotton sacks, the powdered inside of the caked ball to be administered for dysentery. When camphor bags about the throat were believed to lessen the chances of contagion, and paregoric was thought to have beneficiently soothing effects. When onion poultices, mustard baths, linseed packs, and various homeopathic remedies were the order of the hour, and most doctors were still very dubious about the possible effects of night air.

In these partially enlightened times the 'second summer' myth connotes sheer superstition, but there was ample justification for the belief in the days when milk was peddled in cans from door to door, and dished out in quart measures by indifferent delivery boys; when the water-supply came from wells in a low, flat plain, where sewers were undreamed of, and the height of sanitary arrangement was the swill wagon that nosed up and down the back street, like some prehistoric monster, intent upon slaking its thirst from innumerable barrels round which bluebottles sang an eternal dirge.

That wagon ought to have been preserved for posterity. It was a huge affair, with a long, canvas-covered rubber hose that swayed to and fro, like the trunk of an elephant, as it lurched up and down the rutted back lanes, drawn by a team of heavy *percherons*. You could hear its thunderous approach, punctuated by regular gurgles as it pursued its civic passage from barrel to barrel.

The actual process was a perpetual interest. The horses came to a stop, dropped their heads for a wink in the sun, and the driver leaped nimbly down from the wagon seat. Whistling cheerily, he removed the burlap cover from the reeking barrel, and, unhooking the trunk, inserted it into the boiling sour contents – and kept on whistling, while the monster glug-glugged contentedly.

There were other back-yard conveyances, that moved in the night, to save the sensibilities of the citizen, which are better left to the imagination. But some idea may be gathered of the plague of flies that swarmed over lane and alley of whatsoever section of the town. On the outskirts, small dairies, and the thrifty individual of whom sentimentalists sing such praises to-day, added their unpleasant quota by way of chicken-runs, pig-sties, and the family cow. In town, it was little better. Almost every block had a livery barn, with its malodorous accumulation uncontested by civic authorities. It was indeed a fragrant time! Even the rich had no defence, other than stands of Manitoba elms or maples, that screened the rear of their Victorian houses from similar, unsightly manifestations of wealth outside the barn and coach-house door.

In those good old days, which the reactionary likes to believe were an idyllic interlude of healthful, simple living, scarcely a day passed without the appearance of the Little White Hearse, with its smart span of grey horses, before some doorway flying a long white *crêpe*. And, if the peril of 'second summer' was successfully averted, the ever recurring epidemics of measles, chicken-pox, scarlet fever, and bronchial pneumonia waited, unseen and unpredictable enemies, to pounce upon the growing child.

Fortunately for most of us, the subconscious mind has its own beneficent defence mechanism, which enables us to inhibit and forget what would be intolerable to remember. In any case, those dreary years are a vague interval, where only an occasional event stands out from the grey panorama of seemingly unrelated happenings, and even these memorable bits are unrelated and refuse to appear in any sort of chronological order.

Sometimes these incidents had to do with little trips I made with my father to the Hudson Bay Company, where a chilling sort of dignity seemed to hover over the jumbled merchandise, and greasy squaws and incredibly wrinkled old men sat smoking on the curb before the door. On one such occasion, in early spring, when the Red River was dangerously high and the citizens were marking its angry progress with anxious eyes, father pointed out for me a tall, sardonic Indian who was strutting up and down the river bank.

'That's Laughing Joe,' papa said. 'No doubt he is waiting for a larger audience. When there are enough to make it worth while, you'll hear the Red Man's version of Paleface mirth.'

As papa said, when enough idlers had gathered to justify the performance, Old Joe threw down his hat, with a horrible leer which was doubtless intended as polite persuasion, and certainly brought results. 'The old wretch looks capable of murder,' said a man, as he tossed a coin into the tattered hat. Other coins followed in a fleet silver shower. When satisfied his talent was sufficiently rewarded, Old Joe threw back his unkempt head, opened his mouth in a hippopotamus yawn, and was off on a round of laughter that rocked his whole body and made his listeners instinctively draw closer to one another, however broadly they grinned.

As for me, I clung to my father's coat tails, waiting for the thunder to cease. A little later, when papa and I sat under a red willow bush, watching the muddy waters coiling by, I said:

'That wasn't happy laughter, was it, papa?'

'No, child,' papa smiled, patting my hand. 'Old Joe hasn't much to be happy about – least of all, when he imitates the white man's cruel laughter.'

'Why is it cruel, papa?' I wanted to know.

'Because it is always cruel to laugh in the face of misery,' said papa. 'But that is something conquerors never trouble to know.'

Another time, we went to the immigrant sheds to meet some Icelanders who were arriving from 'home,' and had neither relatives nor friends in this country. It was not unusual for such people to write to my father, for he was known through his writings in the Icelandic periodicals, and he seemed to take it for granted that he should help these strangers through the ordeal of endless questionings, medical inspection, customs ritual, and, finally, steer them to some sort of temporary quarters.

It was Sunday, on this occasion. In one respect, this was a happy circumstance, for it meant no loss of time from his work at the saddlery, where he eked out a meagre living under the time-honoured piecework system beloved of all sweatshop autocrats. On the other hand, it meant precious hours away from his hobby, from the one thing that kept him alive – his cherished writing.

'Six days, I may be a slave,' papa used to say. 'On Sunday, I am my own man, and live to please myself.'

It was quite a ritual. Breakfast coffee over, he shined his shoes, washed, put on his white shirt, dark trousers, and a rusty old

Prince Albert, and when he was sure not a hair was out of place, his moustache neatly trimmed and his tie perfectly straight, he pocketed his silver snuff-box, and, cane in hand, set out for a little walk. Sometimes he went to church – preferably to the Unitarian Meeting House, where ideas, not emotions, were exploited. Sometimes he called on a sick friend. But, invariably, when he came back, and dinner was over and done, he retired to his barren room to write for the rest of the day, perfectly contented, and unconscious of what went on in the rest of the house.

Now, however, he had to visit the immigrant sheds. It was a warm summer's day, with not a cloud in the sky, or a murmur of wind. The air would do me good, he told mamma, a little defiantly. That was another bone of contention between them. Papa maintained I should run about more freely, but my poor mother, always terrified that I might go the way of her other babies, would have wrapped me in mothballs and locked me in a glass case if she could. This time, the perfect weather and a patchwork quilt she was eager to finish spoke in our favour. So there I was, dressed in a clean pinafore, with ruffles on the shoulders that stood out like wings, and my pigtails neat, yellow ropes bobbing from under a little straw hat, walking sedately beside papa, who had faithfully promised to keep a slow pace, so that I should not get a fit of coughing from breathlessness.

There was really no danger of excessive haste. Papa knew his own weakness, and had set off in ample time. A few houses down the street a stout woman was picking marigolds in her patch of garden. She was puffing and blowing, and red as a beet, and her mouse-coloured hair straggled down from a hard knot at the back of her neck. Papa stopped, leaning on his cane.

'How fine you look, Marta,' said he, with a hint of flattering surprise. 'My, my, what flowers! It is easy to see you have the touch a lovely garden needs.'

Marta stifled a gasp, as she straightened her cricked back, mopping a wet brow, and smiled at papa.

'I'm not so bad, thank God,' said she. 'But those devils of cutworms come up in droves after the rain – and that was quite a shower we had last night. Three or four o'clock it was, I know, for I hadn't shut an eye, what with my bad leg, and Benjamin a snorer.'

'Those are beautiful flowers,' papa interrupted an impending deluge, pointing to a bed of sweet-william and verbena.

'Brightish, kind of,' Marta agreed. 'If I didn't see you are visiting-bent, I'd give you some, and welcome – maybe the little one would like a posy any way.'

'Your heart is as good as your garden, Marta,' papa rejoined. 'I'd be glad of a few flowers, if you can spare them. We are off to the immigrant sheds – you know how it is for the stranger.'

'What a thoughtful soul you are!' exclaimed Marta, and set to work selecting her choicest flowers for a fragrant offering. With these in my arms, we continued our leisurely way.

Safely out of earshot, I said: 'Papa, did you really want these – for the strangers?'

'Perhaps not, Lala,' papa smiled at me. 'Perhaps I wanted the old woman to be happy. It makes people happy, to share beautiful things.'

Our next stop was a corner store, where papa bought a little round carton of snuff, and a red apple for me. The storekeeper limped with sciatica, and papa recommended 'cupping,' and a bitter. In Dakota, papa had had a pain in the back, and a cupping had drawn off the fever. 'Sure, I believe you,' said the storekeeper, but where in Winnipeg was a good 'cupper' to be found? No one cultivated the old healing arts in this country. Why, you couldn't even get your ears pierced to draw off the soreness from watery eyes!

A street or two farther on, a big man with a ruddy complexion and Dundreary whiskers met us at an intersection. 'Ha! Ha! Lars Gudman! Why aren't you at the meeting-house?' he demanded truculently, and glowering.

'I wanted to keep the peace,' said papa. 'It's a pleasant pastime. I'd recommend it even to a man of God.'

'You're a saucy fellow,' the big man retorted. Then, a grin spreading over his face, he added: 'None the less, I wish you'd recommend it to my daughters – the baggages are quite out of hand. Inga won't get married like a sensible girl, and Sofie wants to start a bake-shop!'

'My, my! Little Inga is in a bad way,' papa twinkled. 'But the shop seems a womanly venture.'

'Baggages! Baggages!' roared the big man. 'If they were boys, I'd birch them. But you can't beat a woman, and they know it! Where are you going, may I ask?'

'To the immigrant sheds. Perhaps you'd like to come?'

'Not I! I've no heart to greet a parcel of fools. Why don't they stay home? They'll end up in the harvest fields and the ditches! Well, if you can't find a roof for all of them, there is a bed in my attic,' the big man concluded, tweeked my ear gently, and trod away, frowning.

At last we neared the confluence of the Red and Assiniboine Rivers, and saw, down on the bank, the long, low structure that was the immigrant shed. I don't remember much about it, except that it was a grimy, forbidding place, with dirty windows and battered doors. We stepped out of the brilliant prairie sunshine into a grey gloom, and exchanged the sweet summer air for a stale, indescribable smell, which haunts me to this day. It was a sickening compound of rancid oils and animal odours that seemed to be carried on every faintest current of breeze from the room which gave off the small information office wherein we stood.

Papa coughed, took out his snuff-box, hastily inhaled a pinch of the pungent powder, coughed again, and hurried to the information desk. Yes, the Icelanders had arrived, the clerk informed him. They were waiting in the second room to the right. Papa glanced dubiously towards the doorway whence the evil smells drifted.

'Go ahead,' the man told him. 'Just a bunch of Doukabors in there. There's nothing to stop you.'

No, there was nothing to stop us, except a hundred human forms stretched out upon the dirty floor, close-packed as locusts in a year of plague. Strange, human bundles, which, to my terrified glance, seemed more like animals, than men, for they were all wrapped in greyish, woolly, skin garments, that reeked with horrible odour. That they were human beings I realized, however, as we picked our way, stepping over a sprawling leg or outflung arm or an entire inert form. Sometimes, a heavy head would lift from its sheepskin collar, and eyes like coals stare at us out of a thicket of matted hair and beard. Sometimes, a beardless face turned on us, vacantly, blinked empty eyes, and dropped back to the comfort of a sheepskin sleeve, or the hill of a smaller bundle, which may have been a child, or a tightly rolled feather tick.

To my excited fancy, they seemed a race of hairy monsters, stewing in their own reek, like the animals in a circus. I could not skip through them fast enough. That is how I came to trip, sprawling on a huge fellow who lay spilled out in peace just inside the door I was so eager to reach. Of course, I lost my Marta's gift of flowers, and if I didn't scream, it was because the fright was shocked out of me when the huge bolster jacked-up like a spring, and the big, bearded face stared at me, crinkled with smiles. What was more, the surprising creature retrieved the bouquet of flowers, which had fallen behind him. Before he could hand them back, however, as was his evident intention, a woman beside him snatched them from his hand, and buried her hot, grimy face in their sweet petals.

'Come child,' papa's voice called me.

'But, papa, my flowers —'

Then I saw that papa was smiling in a queer way at the woman, who seemed to be seeing nothing but the little bunch of flowers from a prairie garden.

'Come, my dear,' he repeated, softly.

5

Treasured portrait

The arrival of the peddler was always a pleasant break in the daily monotony. For many seasons our part of town was covered by a little Italian woman, whom I called 'Mrs Yes-mam,' because 'yes ma'm',' 'no ma'm',' punctuated every other phrase that rippled from her agile tongue, and it struck me as highly amusing, for I had no knowledge of English, and thought it a form of expletive, like *Herra Gud*. She was always welcome, even if our purchase was nothing more than a spool of thread or a paper of safety-pins for the latest baby. She was small, and extremely dark, with alert, black eyes that must once have been extremely fine, and heavy, raven hair that was as neatly arranged as wind and weather permitted. She wore bright cotton clothes in summer, green and red usually, the blouse set off with strings of coloured beads that dangled down her bosom, and there was always a little gold cross at her withered throat. The skirt was full, gathered into the waistband all around, and sometimes an apron of black sateen, with bias bands of red and green tape at the bottom, completed the garb. But what fascinated me were the big brass ear-rings that swung against her sallow cheeks as she bobbed up and down, displaying her wares.

Yes-mam carried an ingenious pack. It was made of oilcloth, and opened and shut like a tobacco pouch, by means of innumerable curtain rings and a stout linen cord. When she threw the pack to the floor, all the rings jangled gaily, and put one in an expectant mood. Yes-mam never made the mistake of opening the pack at once. She hovered above it like a protective Byzantine angel in a plate-glass window, waving her nubbed arms up and down like attenuated wings, and declaimed upon the weather, the gumbo, the latest plague, and hoped that the Holy Mother of God had kept all evil from our house.

When she opened the tantalizing pack it was done with a smart flourish: a quick pull on a string, and lo! the mysterious contents lay before you, and a delectable perfume assailed your nostrils. That perfume of the pack was something to remember. It was the democratic incense of coloured soaps, sachet bags, bottles of toilet water, hair tonic, and those now forgotten scented hearts, which the knowing maidens of the day wore in their bosoms. I remember them well, for mamma bought me one to wear round my neck at a church concert. It was made of some shiny, filigree stuff, and enclosed a purple waxy substance that smelled very pleasantly of English lavender. I wore it on a string of purple baby ribbon, and thought myself very fine indeed.

There were other luxuries in Yes-mam's pack. Silk handkerchiefs, embroidered with butterflies and birds and exotic flowers of every hue. They were fine silk, and the workmanship such as one rarely sees to-day on a similar type of handkerchief. There were cheap ones, to be sure. Five- and ten-cent scraps of silk with gaudy cabbage roses in the corner. But sometimes Yes-mam displayed a square of ivory-coloured silk, beautiful as the petals of a rose, sewn with hair-like silks in the most delicate shades, which some skilled Chinese lady must have worked long hours to execute. There were shawls, too, in that mysterious pack, of soft wool and cashmere, and Bulgarian silk; cards of lace, both fine and coarse; crochet cottons; mending wool; aprons; and, of course, stockings of black lisle for women, and of stoutest cotton for children; mitts with rainbow tops: comforters for baby; spools of thread; and an assortment of tape, rick-rack braid, and kneedles and pins; with sometimes strings of rosaries at the bottom of the notions tray, completing the store.

We seldom had money to buy any of these alluring treasures, but Yes-mam never passed our house, for she was always sure of a cup of hot coffee and a welcome rest. If she happened to come on a day when papa was home, either too sick to work or on a half-day taken to make something for the house – a cupboard or chest, or simply to sole our shoes, the visit stretched to several cups, and all manner of confidences. Papa had a friendly interest in everybody. He could ask more questions, without offence, than any one I have ever known. In no time at all perfect strangers confessed their secret sorrows and dearest ambitions. Mamma always deplored this habit. If it were not downright impertinent, it was certainly insincere, she contended. Papa could not possibly be interested in the private lives of individuals he might never even see again, she thought. He could not possibly mean the flattering comforts he invented on the spur of the moment! But, to papa, wiser than she knew, the moment was supremely important, and the measure of sincerity and truth and good it brought about.

Yes-mam found papa home with lumbago one chilly autumn day. She was full of concern, and called upon the saints to exorcize the misery from papa's back. Ah, she knew what a bad back was! Years with the pack, bowing and scraping at inhospitable doors, put a crink in the spine and aches like dagger-thrusts in the old bones. 'Poor woman! Poor woman!' papa sympathized. It was curious how fate tricked one, he said. Very curious! For, of course, it was easy to see that Yes-mam had not always been a slave of the pack – a handsome woman like she.

Yes-mam lifted her hands heavenwards. The signor said the truth. There had been better days in the vineyards of Italy. Sunny skies, sunny dreams – but always there was some one to care for. First, the little brothers and sisters. Then, the old parents. And a girl's heart gets her into trouble. Her particular trouble was a good-for-nothing husband. But that was past and done. The signor must understand she was not complaining. Life was hard, for a peddler, to be sure, but she had her little shack down where the river sang to the willows all night through. No, no, she was not complaining. There was nothing much troubling her now, except the wretched behaviour of her sewing-machine. The devil had it in a spell, to be sure, and not a stitch would it sew!

Now, that was too much! said papa. The devil must be taken down a peg. If the weather was clear to-morrow he would like to take a look at the bewitched piece of machinery.

Yes-mam called upon the saints to witness her gratitude to the signor for the generous thought. He with a bad back! Yes, if she ever forgot, she implored the holy ones to smite her on the spot. And in this exalted mood she whipped out a yellow silk handkerchief, which she hoped the *bambino* would accept without price – though it cost twenty cents.

That is how I came to visit Yes-mam's shack, which perched like a lone, grey cormorant on the river bank at Point Douglas. While papa tinkered with the machine I had a lovely time playing with an enormous cat, and wondering what ailed the saints, whose painted faces gazed at me mournfully from a dozen faded prints on the walls. But there was one thing of beauty in that cluttered house: a little image of a woman, whose delicately sculptured face was as serene as a midsummer night. Who, of the heavenly company old Yes-mam implored, she represented, I never knew. I only know the impression she made upon my youthful imagination has remained through the years, lovely as a cameo cut from alabaster.

6

I meet the august ancestors

A child's mental life is essentially egotistical. It revolves around its own emotions and sense impressions, untouched by the wider awareness which distinguishes the adult from the infant. A child is in the world, yet not of it, for his sense extensions are limited and weak. He swims about in the waters of his own emotions as unconscious of the outer world as a goldfish in its little glass bowl.

A series of sad jolts might, conceivably, increase the sensitivity of a goldfish – a cat clawing the water would no doubt inspire a spurt of exceptional energy. There was always something stirring the quiet of my private world. This something had, generally, a sting that whipped my small mental processes to the point where I found myself dimly aware that strange, alien powers existed beyond my little bowl.

There was the place where papa worked, for instance. It exercised a definite spell, which cast an uneasy shadow on the whole house. Before six in the morning papa set out with his lunch-box and bottle of coffee, and whenever he was well enough, he remained in this mysterious place until nine or ten o'clock at night. That his many illnesses were somehow connected with these strange visits I began to suspect, for he was always so tired when he came home. And sometimes there was a grey look in his face that made him seem a stranger. I was usually awake, for my cough tormented me, and often, too, I had bilious attacks that prevented sleep, and so nothing would do but I must sit on papa's knee for a minute.

I remember those ghostly nights, when the kitchen lamp, turned low to save coal oil, struggled against the dark, and the stove made equally inadequate headway against the cold. Papa was often too tired to eat anything, though mamma always had a kettle of soup or porridge waiting for him. He ought to eat, she said; there was no nourishment in bread and coffee. And soup was the mainstay. Boiling beef or brisket with potatoes made a fine dish, the broth thickened with flour or a dash of oatmeal, and sometimes stepped up with an onion or a turnip when the budget permitted such luxuries.

Yes, he ought to eat. Papa knew that, but how could a man eat when his whole body ached and his lungs felt clogged with dust and his senses reeled with weariness? How could you sit for almost fourteen hours at a bench, stitching by hand the heaviest traces, fighting time for a few cents because it meant life for your family – stitching, stitching, stitching, with the devil at your heels, a sort of frozen despair in your heart, and come away with enough life even to feel hunger?

Yes, mamma knew that it was hard to keep one's soul alive in this harsh country. She was sympathetic and cheerful, though at times a note of bitterness, not unmixed with accusation, coloured her sentiment. In a vague way, I understood that this feeling had its source in something far beyond my tiny goldfish bowl. It had to do with the incomprehensible world in which mamma lived before I was born, which was harder for me to visualize as tangible and real, for mamma referred to it seldom, than the glamorous reign of the Ancestors, on whose achievements she liked to dwell. They too were outside my small, immediate world, but represented a ghostly court of equity, to whom it was my duty to refer the record of my deeds and misdeeds.

The old-fashioned Icelander, like the ancient Chinese, does not cherish his ancestors idly. It is not with him a question of recounting with pride achievements once illustrious and long forgotten, for nothing better than pleasurable vanity. One walked warily before this ghostly assembly, and shuddered to be found wanting in commendable behaviour. Consciously and unconsciously, my mother's judgements were invariably coloured by this final court of appeal.

Hardships she endured with exemplary courage, but no flight of sentimental eloquence ever swayed her the slightest from what she believed as right and becoming in the sight of that formidable company. Where my father would have cheerfully opened his house to any one with no better hospitality than a cup of coffee and some easy conversation, mother thought it beneath the dignity of respectable behaviour thus to inflict one's poverty on others. She had no gift for light friendship, and preferred an old book to the companionship of indifferent people.

She was a woman descended from an ancient family, stiff-necked, righteous, and unbending in their unconscious pride. The sagas record their knightly deeds – bold, fearless, not always wise, yet never, I think, inconsistent with the cold pride that impelled them. Gunnar Hamundson, the hereditary chieftain, to whom the numerous branches of the family look back with justifiable veneration, was the last of the great Vikings. By which I mean last of the Norse nobles to acquit himself in the Viking manner, serving at court, sailing his own dragon ship on seaways of adventure, presiding at parliament, keeping open house in the regal style, paternal towards his dependents, keeping himself responsible for their justice at Thingvellir, and, as a matter of course, the champion of his less fortunate kinsman in all their quarrels. Immortalized in the sagas by reason of his own attainments, his family was already old and established long before they came to Iceland. Gunnar's great-grandfather, Baugur Raudson, was one of the Landnamsmonnum – the first band of nobles who took possession of the country and established the old Norse Republic. His great-grandfather was Kjarvalur (Ceabhall), a colourful chieftain, who, in the good old Irish fashion, dubbed himself king of Ossory in Munster. He died there in 888.

True to the sentiments of his race, Gunnar preferred to die at the hands of his enemies rather than submit to a three-years' banishment, although, for so renowned a knight, the sentence would have resolved itself into nothing more drastic than an extended visit at the court of the Norwegian king. But he loved his Icelandic dales; and the green slopes of the little hills, where lacy waterfalls came sweetly down from the crags above, were more precious in his sight than the pageantries of any court. Against the counsel of his wisest friends, he refused to fly. These heaths were his homeland. Why desert them because a feud of which he was spiritually guiltless might lead to death?

'Death is not so great a matter,' he contended. But the manner of one's dying – ah, that was something else. A man's departure from the vanities of existence ought to be consistent with the code he practices. 'Aldrei ad guggna!'

They knew no compromise, those headstrong clansmen, and that unyielding quality has characterized their descendants, often with ill effects and unhappy consequences. But if they were often short on mercy, they seldom failed in justice, and rarely broke the bonds of loyalty.

After the fall of the Norse Republic and the rise of the medieval church, which, in Iceland as elsewhere in those god-bitten days, arrogated unto itself powers and principalities that formerly rested with the nobles, many an ancient house was brought to ruin, and only those individuals who, in the course of time, managed to slide into the pontifical service rose once more to public place. That, I suppose, rather than piety or special virtue, accounts for the priests and prelates that distinguished my mother's family. However dire the economic fortunes of the country, some one of the line always managed to pop up in ministerial robes, and their daughters, as a matter of course, were predestined to the high service of husbands similarly placed. But the same quality which on the one hand upheld the old traditions without flinching might, on the other, pursue a tangent, and meet with grief.

My poor great-great-grandmother was a case in point. She was a pretty woman, the youngest of several sisters, all of whom, in due course, snared her minister, and, according to the tale, were a credit to the family. They were forceful, vigorous, wilful women, who knew, without a shadow of doubt what was right, not only for themselves, but for their youngest sister, whom they dearly loved, but secretly suspected of a doubtful gentleness. They had seen her, on several occasions, listening with too wrapt attention to the silly verses of a handsome young nobody from a neighbouring farm. Being their sister, they could not of course, accuse her of indiscretion, even in thought. The most they could do was set her at weaving whenever the young man came to discuss the law and the prophets with papa. And, to prevent her mind from wandering, one or another dear sister would read her something really inspiring from the Latin-threaded tomes of the bishops' archives.

Yet, the unthinkable befell. One morning the sisters gathered in the *badstoffa*, their faces drawn and white, their glances veiled under shamed lashes. Their breakfast coffee drunk, the eldest, lifting her burning eyes, broke the dreadful silence, voicing what must be said.

'Margot has gone,' she said. 'Gone – you understand? There are to be no inquiries. No explanations. When affliction strikes a house, it must be borne in silence. The Lord gives and the Lord taketh away ...'

That was the end of the matter. So they thought. But they had reckoned without that other nagging virtue, loyalty. Margot was officially dead, but her memory burned in their hearts. They never spoke of her, yet each knew when, by some roundabout means, word reached one or another, and a sort of gloom would hang over the house for days. It did not surprise them that poor Margot's happiness was short-lived, or that the shock of disillusionment and the break with her family was undermining her health. That was the natural consequence of an unnatural act. Margot had wilfully betrayed the laws of common sense. She had thought that romantic love could cancel the incompatibilities inherent in such a misalliance as hers. She had thought that her husband's flare for poesy would stand between her and the harsh realities of a poverty-stricken life.

No, the sisters were not the least surprised that Margot went about her humble duties like a wistful ghost, seldom speaking, and never heard to laugh. But that was a year of bad harvests and fearful weather, and often, after the winter had closed in upon them, the sisters would stop in the midst of their labours, and their thoughts, though unspoken, were plain to all. How was Margot faring in that wretched place? Had she even the common necessities of life ...

It was spring when the news reached them. Margot was dying of consumption. She had borne a child, and the doctor suspected she had had such a bad time of it because she was undernourished. The dreadful tidings were brought by Jon himself. To his personal misery the sisters were blind and deaf. That the poor young man was half dead with grief, and was come to beg their help humbly for Margot, apparently touched them not at all. Margot had no hand in his coming, he said – but she was dying.

The sisters held a council. Margot must come home – they must send for her at once – but she must come as she had left, unencumbered, alone. One look at their cold, hard faces, and whatever plea the poor husband may have had in mind for his helpless infant died unspoken. Perhaps he understood them better than they knew. They were just without mercy, utterly incapable of comprehending the graces of a truly charitable mind. They would be good to Margot. They would welcome her without recrimination, since that was the only procedure that could wipe from their minds the ghastly nightmare of her wilful behaviour.

So the prodigal came home to die in the bosom of a solicitous family, to whom, however, she dared say nothing of the little one left in the desolate crofter's hut. But, when she was dead, the sisters had the child put to foster with a highly respectable family. They would have none of it themselves, for that would remind them of too many bitter memories. Still, the child had its rights – it must not grow up in ignorance, condemned to the stupid existence of an utterly commonplace person.

That disowned, not quite commonplace person, was my great-grandmother, and, from all accounts, her plebeian contribution had little effect on the sterner qualities peculiar to the family on which she was so haplessly grafted. But in that I may be wrong. Certainly, in the eyes of her people, mother repeated that wretched mistake when she married my father.

It was a wild, windy day that blew an arctic chill from the mountains when father first rode into the wide courtyard before the ancient deanery, seeking shelter. Mother was a little girl of ten, with a small delicate face and great ropes of bronze-coloured hair dangling down her back. She had been sent to the church, which stood at a little distance from the house, to fetch a hymnal for the dean, who was preparing the house-service for his people. It was she who first sighted the young men riding down from the hills, singing at the tops of their lungs, and making a gay spectacle in their riding-clothes and finely appointed accoutrements. The little horses stepped to the wind and sailed, heads high, tails streaming behind them, into the ancient court-yard.

Their coming must have created an uncomfortable stir, and, no doubt, a consequent pleasurable excitement. For the dean was famous for his zeal in the church, whereas, at least one of the young gallants, my future father, was infamous for his heretical intellectualism, and was a divorced man besides!

From all reports of father at that time, he was a dashing young man, too handsome for his own good, and possessed of a pleasant, persuasive voice. He was gay and witty, a radical in thought, and, like so many young men of his generation, given to pleasure and the glass that cheers. He was the son of a landed farmer, whose patch of precious earth, nestling under the dark shadow of mountains, was a source of deep affection. It was historic ground. Scarcely a foot of it but was consecrated by some event in ancient story. It was truly the land of their fathers, romantically loved and dearly treasured. How deeply loved can be judged by the fact that, a generation after it had passed from the family, my aunt in Winnipeg commissioned an artist to paint the homestead that so much of it at least might be preserved to its spiritual children.

They called it Ferry-Cot, and even in its painted semblance it looks a jolly place, as though something of its former rash hospitality lingered through the years. The beautiful White River winds lazily by, skirting the haylands, and the vagrant roads drop down from the mountain flanks – river and roads that brought so many ever-welcome visitors to the friendly old house. It is a sturdy house, as befits a dwelling where turbulent spirits worked out their turbulent destiny. It has the look of having weathered many storms, and settled at long last to sadly sweet dreams.

Those who are kindly inclined say that grandfather's mismanagement of Ferry-Cot dated from the death of his first wife, Fru Anna, a woman of refinement and charm, and a singer of considerable merit. She had a way with her, say the old folk, a gentle persuasion that kept her impetuous husband from many a folly. She smiled upon his blustering, smoothing away irritation, and, without seeming so to do, really steered the domestic craft. When she died grandfather thought the world had come to an end. His grief was genuine and tragic – his choice of solace, no doubt, inexcusably weak and unwise. He was seldom sober, though never drunk, and took to riding about the country with his cronies, leaving the management of his land to servants. He could not bear the chill loneliness of that motherless house, and the sight of his bereaved children only increased his misery. He was sorry for them, but sorrier for himself. 'I had the fairest woman to wife,' he is quoted as saying, 'and I had not the sense to appreciate her.'

It is difficult in this day and age, to give any adequate picture of what an old-fashioned Iceland farm was like, or to define the peculiar position of servants in such a patriarchal institution. But nothing is further from my mind than to create an impression of wealth in regard to grandfather's humble, though comfortable, estate. That there were many working folk (*vinnu folk*) on the place was so from necessity, not because of affluence or vanity. In those days a farm was a miniature manufacturing plant, a self-contained institution. Almost everything needed and used in the home was made there. It was not merely a question of raising sheep and cattle and laying in the supplies of fodder necessary to their keep. Hides were tanned for shoes, the wool transformed into yarn for spinning and weaving, and this in turn meant that men and women proficient in such crafts must be employed, either by the season or permanently, as was more often the case on a large estate.

Horses were the only means of transportation, and there was always a large number trained, either for riding, which meant breaking them to pacing, since no Icelander would ride a horse that trotted, or for work as pack ponies. Every farm had, therefore, its smithy and in the smith a man who understood and loved horses. The cattle and sheep required herdsman and shepherd, and since sheep are milked in Iceland, a number of milkmaids, who had charge of the buttery and cheese-making. Meats were cured, fish dried and salted, huge kegs of skir prepared for the winter. An Icelandic *bur* was something to delight a woman's heart, its shelves lined with cheeses, piles of flaky flatbread, firkins of butter, the rafters hung with sweet-smelling smoked mutton, and on the floor huge tubs and barrels of pickled meats, pressed sheep's heads, spiced rolls of flank lamb, and bales of dried fish. The making of these edibles was entirely in the hands of women, as was the yearly supply of soap, and the thousands of candles required through the long winter.

Tailoring of both men's and women's wear was carried on in the home, and, of course, in that pre-machine age it was done by hand. Yet I have never seen a more neatly turned lapel than one shown me by an old woman trained in those ancient days, and the work of her patient fingers.

All manner of handicrafts were expertly done on such farms; needlework of various sorts, the most beautiful of which was the *baldering* – gold and silver embroidery used on festal garments – an art perfected by Viking women; delicate crochet, weaving, knitting, the making of dyes, and, on the men's part, carving in wood and bone, cabinet-making, bookbinding, leather work of many kinds, and, most respected of useful arts, the copying of ancient manuscripts. Indeed, many a rough-looking chap, who spent his days pitching hay and tending cattle, might of an evening, and by no better light than a tallow candle, turn out an illuminated page in script as fine as copper type, his capitals a work of sheer art, delicately shaded in blues and gold and scarlet.

It is perhaps not so difficult to imagine that so many people, living under one roof-tree, each contributing something toward the general welfare, should retain a self-respect and an independence not to be found among our servants of modern employers. There was never any stigma attached to labour in Iceland, and yet no people were ever more conscious of race. Individual integrity and attainments – which were expected of well-born people – these were the criteria, and no amount of money could supply the deficiency.

Grandfather may well have been as unwise in his selection of workers as he was in his choice of companions. At any rate he awoke, one day, to the disagreeable fact that his affairs were badly handled. When Fru Anna was at the helm everything had run smoothly enough. The solution, therefore, was another wife. He found her in a widow with a son about the same age as my father. From all reports, she was a sensible, amiable woman, who accepted the proposal in good grace. Amiable she proved, indeed, but anything but a manager. As the hasty wooer soon discovered, the new Frua was indolent and much too fond of physical comfort to inaugurate any vigorous improvements. She was a stout, cheery soul, who firmly believed in the road of least resistance. She was careless and untidy, and often drove grandfather into tantrums by leaving her personal ornaments strewn about the buttery.

'Well, well, who is to steal them, my dear?' she would laugh. 'If they aren't safe in the buttery, they won't be safe in the bedroom.'

Some of these heirlooms, which once graced a butter tub, are now in the national museum. Quaint old pieces of silver filigree, fine as lace, and dating back no one knows how many generations.

But Frua had her loving attributes. She was a kind stepmother. She was as kind to my father as to her own son and the little daughter she bore to grandfather. Father's eldest sisters seldom spoke of her. Perhaps they resented that a woman so different from their beloved mother had taken her place. Being women, they doubtless were more critical of niceties and more apt to be antagonistic. Father always thought of her with sincere affection, and loved to recount how mischievously he and her own son behaved toward the poor lady.

She grew heavy with the years, and consequently, more devoted to comfort. She was, too, I gathered, not above believing in the Hidden People. When she was busy in the *bur* the boys thought it rare sport to terrify the good soul with moans and groans and mysterious noises. Then the fun began: having drawn a shriek, the young imps pounced out, hooting their glee, and Frua, flying into a temper, would seize a ladle or a whisk, and chase her tormentors, crying: 'Impish little worms! Wait till I lay hold of you!' The chase generally extended round the house, till, breath and bulk exhausted, Frua gave up and laughingly told the little worms to behave themselves.

'You should have a hiding, so you should, *skratans ormarnir*! But look, now – if you behave, you can have a cookie!'

A kind, generous-hearted woman, her indifferent management was not, as grandfather discovered, likely to save the household from disaster. Year followed year, and, instead of improvement, it now became apparent that something drastic must be done if the farm was not to pass from their hands. The solution grandfather hit upon this time may sound like a fantastic invention, but it must be remembered that over sixty years ago a father was something more than an apology for being.

At any rate, grandfather needed money, and suddenly he remembered that a friend of his, though blessed with means, was burdened with a plain daughter. A colourless, insignificant miss, who could never make a likely match, except at some sacrifice to her papa. Well then, let the wench pay off the debts on Ferry-Cot with her dowry! She must marry his son.

This heaven-sent inspiration in mind, grandfather straightway rode off to share the happy thought with his crony. The scheme had much to commend it, thought his friend, but what of the prospective bridal pair? Were they not too young to know their own minds, he wondered.

'Ha! I could wish them younger still,' said grandfather. 'Something tells me they will be hard enough to manage as it is.'

Which certainly proved true. The girl wept and pleaded. My father argued and stormed. They did not want to be married. They had no interest in each other, nor anything in common. They fought a good fight to no purpose. Grandfather meant to save the farm, and the bride's papa to see that no daughter of his passed up an opportunity to better herself. What either of them thought now, in their foolish immaturity, did not matter, said the fathers. They had their duty to face – their Christian, filial duty to perform.

In desperation the two young things met at a secret rendez-vous. They were pale as death, outraged in their innermost feel-ings, and miserably conscious of their utter helplessness. The unhappy youth apologized for the bitter things he had said of his proposed bride. He had not been thinking of the tearful girl before him.

'Oh, I know, I know,' the poor girl sobbed. 'You can't like people just because you are told to – I guess I'm kind of plain, and – and papa thinks nobody will have me, except – well, like this. But he's wrong! I – I don't know how to tell you, without seeming to be foolish –'

'Don't tell me!' the young man cried. 'It's bad enough as it is. What a country! What a blind, belly-ridden country! If those old men thought of anything except their damned sheep and cattle – but they don't. They think of everything in terms of chattel, even their flesh and blood, and that's what we are until we come of age.'

'Yes, that's what we are,' the girl echoed, brightening a little, because she sensed a touch of sympathy in the firebrand before her, although his eyes flashed and his coal-black hair, gleaming in the moonlight, gave him a cold, tragic air. 'I thought of run-ning away, but where could I go? Wherever I went, I'd be returned to my father's house. I guess there is nothing we can do except – except try not to hate each other too much.'

'Oh, but you are wrong,' he told her, with bitter intensity. 'That is exactly what we must do. Hate each other. Hate each other so effectively that this sort of thing will end. What if they brand us with that Christian ceremony, like they brand their sheep? Does that mean we have to live together? Look here, don't worry about me. I'll find a way to keep out of the way. And when I'm of age —' He drew a deep breath, and the look on his face brought a lump to her throat.

Oh, poor boy, she thought, he is just as badly hurt as I.

'When that time comes, and it is not so long,' he concluded vehemently, 'you shall see how well I'll carry out the good work our dear fathers began. But I'll go to the devil in my own sweet way!'

Father was not the kind of man who details, out of vanity, or for idle pleasure, his amatory history. This tragic episode, which undoubtedly coloured his whole existence and bore much bitter fruit, was told me by an older member of the family when I myself was a woman grown, and all the painful memories were gentled over by the years.

It is said that those two young people faced the churchly prelate, who pronounced upon them an eternal obligation, with frozen, ghostly calm, tears in their desperate eyes, and who can say what hate in their hearts? The subsequent fate of the little bride has no part in this story, but much that was reckless and paradoxical in my father's conduct thereafter may be attributed to this unfortunate circumstance.

In accordance with the times, and the means of a small landowner, father acquired considerable learning at home. He was a scholar at heart, passionately devoted to the sagas, and well grounded in the antiquities. He was always a romanticist, demanding something more than dull, realistic details of obvious faults and incidents in poetry or prose. He loved Robert Burns because of his tenderness and pity, and understood that except for his weaknesses he could not have reacted so surely to the sufferings of men. He used to say that there was no uniform perfection in anything but mediocrity – 'and from that may the good gods save us!' He was devoted to letters and the language, and whatever he wrote was carefully and conscientiously composed. Not that he had any desire to pose as a stylist, but because he held that a thing worth saying at all was worth saying well.

He was, moreover, an original, fearless thinker, not the least affected by conventional thunders or pious bigotry. Curiously enough, he was abetted in his heretical rationalism by a young cleric, the Reverend Oddur, who was his tutor for a season, and a lifelong friend thereafter. This young man had been educated in Copenhagen, and while there had hobnobbed with the rising intellectuals, who, in due course, were to cause such scandals in their respective countries, denouncing tyrants and disputing the Trinity. Perverse individualists, who refused to believe that man is a miserable worm, conceived in sin and shapen in iniquity. Mad hatters, who even went so far as to contend that women might be trusted not to wreck the earth if, now and again, they were permitted to toy with a vision that transcended the cradle and the kitchen.

There is no doubt but that, had grandfather not followed his heavenly inspiration with regard to his son, my father would have settled down to the pleasant life of an Icelandic farmer, spending his time in debating the pros and cons of advancing thought and current poetry, and of the hated Danish suppression. The monotonous details of farming would have fallen to others, while he himself tinkered about as fancy dictated, devoting what time he pleased to his own chosen craft or chosen hobby. In my father's case it was saddlery. He was an expert craftsman, and derived as much satisfaction from a meticulously executed pattern, the leather handsomely tooled and the cloth fittingly embroidered, as from a pointed discussion on the latest theological schism.

In old Iceland the hand and the head were never at enmity, nor was any man condemned to ignorance and the company of clods because he earned his bread by some humble employment. Some of our greatest poets were poverty-stricken farmers, and even a bishop might on occasion join in the haymaking in the short summer season. It is not surprising, therefore, that when my father decided to come to Canada he should think of his skill as something on which he might rely to provide a decent living for himself and his children. It would have been surprising had he even dreamed that a good craftsman, despite a very decent education, could so effectively be reduced to the status and the misery of a slave in the glorious country that ballyhooed its magnificent opportunities by way of press and prophet.

But that was yet to come. Father had no thought of America in his youth, and, from all reports, led a hectic, erratic career after that hapless marriage ceremony. It was dreadful, said the grundys, how he neglected his poor young wife and flashed about the country with his godless companions. It really seemed as though any pretty baggage with inviting eyes was more interesting to the wayward husband than his lawful spouse. Which was doubtless quite true. But all these excursions abroad were not quite so iniquitous as the good folk honestly believed. There were times when father went to some isolated mountain farmstead and behaved himself with decided decorum.

In fact, he spent happy months teaching the children the time-honoured reading, writing, arithmetic, and what he pleased of history and literature. How agreeably he lent himself to the task may be gathered from the fact that more than fifty years later father received a touching letter from an obscure old woman who had been his pupil. Style and handwriting were so ridiculously imitative of father's that our first impulse was to laugh – but we did not laugh. She was a widow now, she wrote, and life had never been easy on the farm. But her children had all bettered themselves, had pursued 'the happy path of knowledge.' That was what she wanted papa to know, for it would please him. Herself, she had not been able to make much of his instruction, but she had not forgotten him, nor the hope he had set before her. And she signed the letter: 'Your loving little Stina.'

There was a film of tears in father's eyes as he gazed at that signature a moment, trying to recall what those devoted lines wished him to remember: a little girl with flying yellow hair and eager, inquisitive glances. Yet, when he spoke, the familiar satiric humour sang in his voice.

'Oh, yes, my little Stina was a winsome lass, with no head for figures, God bless her – but what a gaunt old warhorse she had for a mother!'

These tutoring days were a pleasant interlude that left its homely memories, but the restlessness and inner revolt tormenting him seem to have rendered every place quickly distasteful, and all quiet occupation intolerable. He must turn to something else, go on and on, seeking he knew not what, but fully determined to repudiate the ties and obligations imposed upon him by paternal authority.

There are varying and contradictory tales of those aimless years, the common denominator of which seems to be that some overpowering impulse of curiosity drove him from one extreme to another. His most industrious moments were tormented by doubts of futility, his wildest excesses overcast by vague regrets. It might be that in his wandering, in his eager yearning, he had somewhere glimpsed those fateful fairy lights that the Norsemen called *Vafurlogar*. Strange, unpredictable hungers seized the spirit that looked upon this light; and none could tell to what quest it bound one, whether after riches, or beauty, or some dimly guessed knowledge beyond the stars. There was only one thing certain: once those silver torches had fired the fringe of consciousness, only death ended the searching wanderlust of the soul.

It is true, at all events, that nothing so plagued my father as the smug monotony most people mistake for spiritual grace and happiness. In common with his godless companions, he subscribed to the tolerant doctrines of liberalism, and doubtless drained too many tankards to the glory of the newly liberated spirit of man. Also, like those other hotheads who punned against a graft-ridden government and thumbed noses at its pious beneficiaries, he is said to have serenaded too many susceptible damsels by the melting light of the midnight sun.

There were other deeds of which less was said – impulse, kindly deeds. There was the time a poor, filthy beggar died in his hut on the outskirts of a hamlet where father happened to be. The sheriff could find no one willing to prepare the wretched creature for decent burial. Alive, he had been a disgrace, scarcely tolerated in the cowsheds. Let him lie to the last judgement in the state he had chosen!

'But he must once have thought like a man – dreamed like a man,' cried my father. 'Who can say where the blame rests? In him, or another, that he lost that dream.'

'Fine words, fine words!' muttered the sheriff, glowering at the fastidious romanticist. 'You wouldn't mind the dirty task yourself, I suppose – you'd fair jump at it, now wouldn't you!'

'I will do it very gladly,' said my father.

7

Introduction to exile

Other similarly distasteful things father performed when he thought they should be done to justify man's existence and set him on a plain above the beast. Trivial gestures, no doubt, born of a vagrant idealistic moment, yet as irrepressible and impellent as the adventurous streak that nothing ever quite destroyed. The new, the strange, the unknown, these never lost their fascination for my father, however cramping his circumstances might be.

It was adventure more than anything that sent him, as a young man, to the north of Iceland to serve as a coast-guard. Patrolling those wild, hazardous waters was always an unpredictable venture. The rockbound coast with its whipping gales and gloomy fogs and churning sea wore a perpetual air of evil doom, as though some god of the deep, resenting the greedy persistence of the warring fishing fleets, had vowed everlasting destruction. Of all the famous northern preserves none was more feared than this, and never a season passed without its bitter toll of human lives, and sturdy schooners ground to matchwood. It was the duty of the coast patrol to salvage such wreckage, and whatever else tragic or treasurable the sea might yield.

It was here after a storm of unusual fury that father had a curious experience which, since he was neither superstitious nor religious in the narrow, conventional sense, may bear retelling. The storm had lasted for days, beating up from intermittent squalls to a raging tempest. A Brittany fishing schooner had fought the waters within sight of shore, and, despite every effort of the patrol to come to her assistance, was crushed like an eggshell by the savage waters. The first lull in the storm came at dawn and all that day the exhausted patrol searched for the dead among the numerous skerries and jagged rocks that characterized the treacherous coastline. By the time the early dusk terminated the dreary task, many poor, broken bodies had been brought to the little chapel, which, chained to the rocks, sounded a note of sublime challenge to the angry sea. Their immediate duty done, father and his two companions, almost dropping in their tracks, stumbled on to their quarters in the barren house of an old woman, long since widowed by these same waters.

They wanted nothing but sleep, uninterrupted, healing sleep. Yet, in less than three hours, father was rudely jolted back to consciousness. His first reaction was sheer rage. Who the devil had dared wake him? Raising himself on an elbow, he peered through the gloom, and thought he saw a figure in the doorway. But, though he called out in vitriolic tones, no one answered, and, as his heavy eyes cleared, he perceived that, except for his sleeping companions, the room was empty and still. He must have been dreaming, he thought, and, grumbling at his own foolishness, he drove back into the pillows and was instantly fast asleep. Not for long, however. This time it was not a sound that broke his rest, but the weird sensation of being shaken. Nor was there any mistaking what he saw. Three figures, clearly distinguished, yet oddly wavering, as though he were seeing them through swirls of fog, stood at his bedside. They stood there in the grey gloom, transfixing him with sombre eyes, their lips moving soundlessly. 'By heaven, now I am dreaming!' father exclaimed, and jumped to hear his own voice ringing through the quiet room.

'Kver fjandin!' His bedfellow started up crossly. 'Why the shouting – have you gone crazy?'

'Perhaps I have, Nonni,' father answered sheepishly. 'Something like it. Thought I was seeing things.'

'Hell!' Nonni yanked the blankets over his head. 'See away, but for the Lord's sake shut up!'

That ended the queer disturbance, and the young men slept until late in the morning, when their kind old housekeeper brought a tray with steaming coffee and flat bread.

'Praise God you've had your rest, I see,' she greeted them mournfully. 'Not but what you needed it, poor lads.'

'Now, don't tell us you had the toothache again,' Nonni sympathized, but father seemed to know what she wanted to say, and frowned at the thought.

'No, not the toothache – a body could stand that better. Nightmare, that's what it was. Me that's used to the sea all my life dreaming three foreigners dripping brine and looking sad as the last judgement. Queer, I call it, and no good omen.'

'Poor old girl,' Nonni muttered, when she had shuffled out. 'Those beastly sights are getting too much for her.'

'Suppose it wasn't a nightmare!' father said. 'Suppose I should tell you I saw the three myself?'

'Bosh! Imagination. That's your ailment, Lars.'

Perhaps. But father decided to comb the beach once more. Dream or a dead man's desire to communicate by some power of the mind not yet understood – whichever it was, there might be some reason for it. And reason there seemed to be, for that morning father found the three bodies almost buried in a sandbar a mile or so up the shore. The outgoing tide would have swept them down to an unmarked grave. That, mayhap, was what they feared. There was nothing by way of identification on the bodies, but all three wore scapularies eloquent of their religious faith. There was no Catholic priest in the vicinity, but father had them buried in the tiny churchyard, a white cross marking the lonely resting-place.

It was after a sojourn in the north that father once again broke a long, wearisome ride at the Deanery. He had no memory of the little girl who, seven years before, announced his first visit and listened to his gay narratives in shy fascination. But I think she did, and that flattering hint of memory must have added to her charm. She was a dainty little person, barely five feet tall, with marvellous hair, a flawless complexion, and humorous eyes. And she had the fascinating manner of a very young girl playing at decorum while her thoughts danced in a saraband of secret fun.

They seem to have been fated to meet at a most impressionable moment. To the man who had followed a dozen whims in the effort to forget a disagreeable interlude, she was a delightful, irresistible discovery. To her, he was the reincarnation of a dream – the poor young man with whom she had sympathized so deeply on that former visit. Persecution had crowned him with peculiar charm. And here he was, whimsical as ever, and with the added attraction of a reputation that set people bickering for and against him. He was charming, yes, but irresponsible. His beguiling manner was apt to make one forget that he had abjured the staid conventions and even repudiated sacred dogma! He was a pleasant companion, but not the sort of man an innocent girl should marry!

Sensible argument, however, as usual, was quite unavailing. That fateful streak of stubbornness, characteristic of the breed, sharpened under pressure into an unshakable devotion. Every one was against him, so, of course, she loved him. In less than a year, they were married – if you could call it marriage when a man had another wife living, and only the law to sanction his behaviour!

Her people were never reconciled to the match. They could foresee only misery and unhappiness in the mating of individuals so utterly different in taste and training. Nevertheless, being what they were, she received a generous dowry. Father had rented a small farm, but the stock, sheep, household linen, and even mother's riding horse, were the gifts of the dean.

They should have prospered. But ten years of haphazard living dedicated to the quest of some rare adventure had unfitted father for a sudden plunge into fleckless domesticity. Moreover, it was soon apparent that those two, who had chosen each other for better or worse, despite bitter opposition, were emotionally unsuited, and apt to clash on any number of inconsequential, yet provocative opinions. Temperamentally, they were poles apart. He was impetuous, warm-hearted, and, like every romanticist, superficial in his emotions: quick to forget both pleasure and pain. On the other hand, she was deeply reserved, somewhat cold in deportment, and, although far too sensible for neurotic brooding, seldom forgot either an injury or a kindness. Father, whose feelings were coloured by the passing moment, found it easy to express himself; whereas mother, whose sentiments were fixed, was always helplessly inarticulate where her innermost sensibilities were concerned. She had the keenest wit, in latter years often devastatingly caustic, but in those early years of growing disillusionment I think she must have suffered mental agonies for which she found no words, and pride drove deeper and deeper into her heart.

From the very beginning everything went amiss. It seems that father either could not, or would not, shake off his former companions. They descended in droves upon the little household, and, however ably they may have settled the seething political questions of the hour, they contributed nothing towards the stability of the farm. The hay might be blowing away in a windstorm, and a dozen sheep need shearing, but a girl-wife could hardly interpolate such commonplaces into floods of glowing eloquence, both patriotic and transcendental! Nor was there any use attempting to stay the crusading company when the spirit moved them to spread their liberal gospel far and wide. Like grandfather before him, father evidently expected the farm to prosper without much help from himself.

That he should have expected an inexperienced girl of eighteen to shoulder all responsibility is scarcely flattering to his judgement, and yet it seems that she might have managed rather well if she had not faced more trying obstacles. To begin with, those trips about the country were costly in more ways than one – and, of course, debts incurred by gentlemen were 'debts of honour,' which must be paid, whatever the state of the family budget. Many a fat ewe was laid on the altar of this delicate honour. And, finally, in addition to financial problems and the hundred and one mishaps incidental to farming, the young wife had her own predestined handicap to contend with. Before her nineteenth year she had nearly lost her life in one of those brutal struggles which even yet are calmly accepted as the divinely ordained lot of women. After three days of unspeakable agonies the blessed reward was twins – still-born – and a fuller realization of the handicap of her sex.

Few sentimentalists measure up to their fine phrases in a distressing crisis. Father seems to have evaded the disagreeable by protracted jaunts over the country. I have a suspicion that he received sympathy with fine grace on these occasions, and responded with charming delicacy. None of which was much comfort for his wife, left alone to face disillusionment and increasing financial worries.

The next few years were anything but enheartening. If father had any talent for farming, he failed to show it. Any bargain he drove was sure to prove disastrous, and one time, in a fit of jollity, he gambled away the better part of the flock of sheep which was their mainstay. Well, one had to lose sometime, he reasoned cheerfully. To-morrow would be different. But to-morrow was never different. For some reason he simply could not settle down to the sober monotony of serious existence. That so many people had hungrily fixed on every caprice from the beginning, and predicted inevitable failure, may have had much to do with it. And I sometimes think that a weaker woman might have managed better than my mother. Like many another strong character, she made the mistake of assuming with embittered patience more and more responsibility. A little guileful flattery and coy appeal to the ever-susceptible gallant in father might have brought astonishing results. If she only could have understood that the poetic temperament requires the camouflage of romanticism to render even the most obvious duties palatable, life might have been less barren for both of them. But that was too much to expect of a young woman, forthright rather than analytical by nature, who, nurtured as she was in the sterner principles, now found herself plunged into an existence that taxed all her strength and ability. Theories and speculations were all very fine – she had listened to them spellbound those first few months of married life – but they did not pay land dues, or add one krona to the budget.

With determination and tireless energy she kept the little establishment off the rocks, working from dawn till dark, whatever the state of her health, her only vacations those enforced rest periods when another blessed event called a halt to the never-ending work at hand. Father, meanwhile, continued flirting with fate.

It was on one of those wasteful trips through the country that he met an immigration agent who was enthusiastically selling Canada to the Icelanders. Marvellous reports were detailed of the immigrants in that matchless country. Already most of them were on the high road to fortune.

'Think of it!' said the gentleman. 'Over there, any able-bodied man can instantly find lucrative employment in the city, or, better still, take advantage of the generous homesteading grant, which makes him the owner of a tract of land of such fertility as is undreamed of in barren Iceland. As to the other avenues of wealth – well!' Here the agent laughed significantly. He really didn't dare enlarge upon the possibilities open to trappers, hunters, fishermen, and freighters, for no one would believe him.

Unfortunately for many, they did believe him. They believed him with eagerness born of long suffering. The country was entering upon a slow period of arduous adjustment, which, to be thoroughly understood, requires more explanation that seems pertinent to introduce here. However, passing mention must be made of the iniquitous trade monopolies, which, operating as they did over a period of three hundred and eighty years, had almost reduced the country to economic slavery. It began with the Hanseatic League, to which company of German merchant princes the Danish crown sold the Icelandic fishing trade for two hundred and forty years. Their policy of absolute control and unabating greed rapidly reduced the native fisherman to abject poverty. He could neither buy nor sell through any other agency, and the slightest deflection brought swift and instant punishment. Once in the bad books of a tyrannical factor, and a man never knew what the day had in store. He might be black-listed in the fishing fleet, or his catch discounted as unfit for foreign shipment. Yet he dared not dispose of it on home soil, nor steal a bite for himself or his children.

The Hanseatic League, aided and abetted by miserable agents, left a bitter memory behind it, yet its policies were angelic as compared with those of the Harkraemer Syndicate, which fol-lowed and bled the country for one hundred and forty years.

This infamous house added secret settlement and intimidation of the vilest sort to the sufficiently unsavoury practices of its predecessor. As before, the prices were fixed for the Icelanders, but, whereas the Hanseatics had at least maintained a pirate's rough justice, the Harkraemer agents were adepts in dishonesty. Not content to estimate every catch at the lowest possible value, they resorted to crooked balances, and each succeeding season they raised the costs of outfitting the fleets and the prices of commodities required by the people. For instance, in 1702 a bar-rel of flour sold at two rigsdaler – by 1800 it had risen to ten. Yet a *skipspund* of fish (160 kilograms), for which the Icelander might have received from thirty to forty dollars in other markets, had to be sold to the Danish syndicate for seven dollars. But even this did not satisfy the greed of these 'princes.' They began importing rotten food and wormy flour!

It is a moot question whether the Icelanders, who, first of northern races, instituted a republic and a democratic parlia-ment, could have been reduced to such servile straits if nature had not aligned herself with their aggressors.

Ravages from volcanic disturbances defy adequate description. To begin with, there are 107 volcanoes in a country which is only one-fifth larger than Ireland. Since historic times twenty-five vents have caused almost inestimable damage, while count-less others, still extant, have been fitfully active. Lava streams from these various sources cover an area of 4,650 square miles.

Odadahraun (Lava of Evil Deeds) on the tableland of Skapta Jökull, two to four thousand feet above sea-level, covers thir-teen hundred square miles, and represents the accretion of countless eruptions from twenty vents whose activity antedates historic record. As an indication of the fearful effect of such eruptions over a period of centuries I shall mention three recorded instances.

On the 5th of April 1766 the southern countryside was plunged into terror. From the summit of Mount Hekla a huge pillar of black sand was seen slowly ascending the heavens, to the hideous accompaniment of subterranean thunders. Then a coronet of flame encircled the crater, giving the mountain an unholy air of satanic grandeur. The next instant, masses of red rock, pumice, and magnetic stones were hurled up from the inferno in such continuous showers as to resemble a swarm of bees clustering over the crater. The stones were flung to incredible distances; one boulder, six feet in circumference, was pitched twenty miles, another, of magnetic stone, for fifteen miles. The air was so darkened that one hundred and fifty miles away it was impossible to distinguish white from black at a little distance. On the 9th of April the lava began to flow, and ran for five miles in a southwesterly direction, bringing death and destruction to all before it.

Yet this was as nothing compared with what the country had suffered from former eruptions of the historic mountain, or to that which was in store for the people from an unsuspected quarter. From the confines of Skapta Jökull, solitary monarch of an impenetrable desert comprising four hundred square miles, cradled among icefields, descended the most spectacular visitation ever known to that ill-fated land. Toward the end of May 1783, following a winter and spring of exceptionally fine weather, a light bluish fog began to float along the wastes of Skapta, and was followed early in June by great tremors of the earth. On the eighth of the month immense pillars of smoke gathered over the hill country to the north, and, coming down against the wind in a southerly direction, enveloped the whole district of Sida in darkness.

A whirlwind of ashes swept over the country, and on the tenth innumerable fire-spouts were seen leaping and flaring amid the icy hollows of the mountain, while the River Skapta, one of the largest of the island, having rolled down to the plain in a vast volume of fetid waters mixed with sand, suddenly disappeared. Two days later a stream of lava, issuing from sources no one has been able to penetrate, came sliding down the bed of the dried-up river, and, though the channel was six hundred feet deep and two hundred feet wide, the glowing deluge quickly overflowed its banks, crossed the fertile low country of Medalland, ripping the turf up before it like a tablecloth, and poured into a great lake, whose waters rose, hissing and steaming, into the air. Within a few days the basin of the lake itself was filled, and the unexhausted torrent again commenced its march, in one direction overflowing some ancient lava beds, and in the other re-entering the channel of Skapta, and leaping down the lofty cataracts of Stapafosse. Nor was this all. Another lava flood was working similar havoc on the plains of Hvervis Fljot, rushing through the country with even greater velocity. The historian to whom I am indebted for the above colourful, yet authentic, record, goes on to estimate the losses in livestock in this one eruption. They are as follows: 11,500 cattle, 2,800 horses, 190,000 sheep, which in itself represents almost an Inquisitorian death sentence to a people whose economic resources were so wickedly exploited. In actual figures, the ensuing famine carried off 9,500 human lives, and left thousands more with permanently impaired health.

In this day and age we are accustomed to relief agencies that rush in with help of every kind to any people similarly afflicted. It is, therefore, difficult to visualize a state of conscience which left the so-called protectors of the Icelanders not only indifferent to their frightful misery, but which actually spurred them to further aggrandizement. Yet such is the truth. With all the unction of medieval Christianitiy, the Harkraemer Company increased its trade demands under the cloak of beneficent helpfulness. The destitute had only to sell themselves, body and soul, for the privilege of keeping alive!

Another vital factor enters into the sinister picture. Such violent eruptions are not only destructive on land, but, through furious subterranean action, affect the tides, thereby killing the spawn and driving off the shoals of fish. Consequently, the one remaining livelihood of the helpless people was seriously disrupted, and their unscrupulous masters given a plausible excuse for further extortion.

There were other sources of misery. Church and State, scarcely less avaricious than the traders, had long since cunningly usurped most of the productive lands. To be exact, the elected saviours of the poor now claimed over two thousand tax-free estates, while the total of private holdings was no more than that number, many of which were little more than strips of herbage in the midst of lava wastes. But let no one imagine that mercy was shown the deluded mortal who presumed to set the needs of his stomach above the royal tax, or the tithes to the diocese! Such worldly consideration died with the poor laws of the ancient heathen republic.

The seventeenth century was by all accounts the darkest in Iceland's tragic history. It is neither strange nor remarkable, therefore, that the Harkraemer Syndicate should have looked upon this fresh catastrophe as a divine act predicated to their favour – that now, at last, the rebellious Norse spirit must subside for ever. They were mistaken. They had forgotten, or perhaps had never known, that long before a paradoxical code of ethics had been forced upon the Icelanders they had been effectively converted to an imperishable belief in the dignity of the human spirit. As Norsemen, they had so loved liberty that rather than accede to the demands of a king whose policy of beneficent dictatorship offended their ancient rights, they chose exile on a barren island at the world's end. Centuries of mishap and the corrosive sentimentality of a negative faith had starved the ancient fires, but now, out of the ashes of deepest despair, a thousand tongues leaped to life once more. Wherever two or three gathered together, the gospel of liberty sounded. Desperate young men, defying all sorts of degrading punishments – public whippings, imprisonment, exile – flashed up and down the country, stirring the hearts of the people.

Yet these political firebrands might have failed in their monumental task if their message had not been caught up and impregnated by the immortal ideology of the national poets. Without the magic of impassioned poetry to fix and hold the public mind to the vision of a liberated Iceland, the inertia of woeful poverty would certainly have defeated those rebel hopes.

But, thanks to those inspired singers, the quickened spirit of liberty was never again to be quelled, howsoever the heroic agitators might suffer. Penalties and punishments were so much added fuel to the fire. Individuals might be silenced and destroyed, a dozen others leaped into the breach. The fierce old Viking soul had found a tongue once more to raise such a storm that, at long last, even the Royal Ear was disturbed, the August Conscience troubled. As a result, the Crown abolished the Harkraemer charter in 1850, thereby ending all trade monopoly. That memorable date marks the beginning of an amazing struggle for rehabilitation by the Icelandic people – a struggle fraught with every imaginable handicap, to the complete vindication of the tenacious Viking spirit. In 1904 Home Rule was established, and in 1918, Iceland became an independent nation.

This sketchy reference to the historic past is not so extraneous to my story as it appears. Economic pressure, and nothing else, was responsible for the only group emigration of Icelanders to Canada. In 1875 occurred the last of those major eruptions which I have chosen out of many to illustrate the unpredictable disasters that hounded the little nation. On this occasion it was Askja, a relatively insignificant volcano, that erupted, and yet such was its violence that a rain of ashes fell for eleven hours and forty minutes on the west coast of Norway. Fifteen hours later the city of Stockholm, Sweden, was plunged into semi-darkness by the onrushing clouds.

It was this fresh catastrophe that, in aftermath, so weakened the resources of the people that word of their suffering reached Lord Dufferin, one-time Governor-General of Canada. It was he, who, with the best of intentions, first drew attention to the Icelanders as possible settlers for Canada. Lord Dufferin had visited Iceland, and, as his *Letters From High Latitudes* tend to show, had found the people interesting and admirable. It was his hope that in Canada the qualities he had marked and admired might take root and contribute to the cultural life of the dominion.

8

Exile

Unfortunately for us, the zeal of the immigrant agents somewhat outstripped their veracity. The tales they told had less point in truth than fiction. But, to my adventure-thirsting father, the glowing recital was a potent inspiration and the answer to all his boredom and perplexity. Why, if even one-tenth of the report were true, a man should prosper in that far dominion! And how good it would be to be done with carping criticism.

Mother seems to have agreed willingly enough. What had she to lose? As it was, she was effectively cut off from her own people. Only once, and that when the old dean lay dying, had she set foot in her home. A tragic occasion, rendered the more bitter because of her obvious poverty. Even her beloved riding-horse had gone the way of other possessions, and she was forced to borrow a shaggy mount, as well as her habit.

What little remained of household effects and farm animals was sold at auction – a dreary transaction which she watched from a green knoll, three small children at her knees and a new-born infant in her arms.

The ship that was to have borne them to Scotland did not put in at Isafjordur as had been promised. Those were days of uncertain sailings between Iceland and the British Isles. No one seems to have had any definite information to offer as to why the vessel had not arrived, or when another might be expected. Their home disposed of, father decided that his best course was to move to

Bolungavik, where he could enter the fishing fleet while they waited for transportation. Poor mother could only pray that the miracle might happen before their little money had vanished.

The heavenly ear may have been dulled by too many needy pleas. At any rate, when, on the 9th of June 1887 they eventually sailed for Scotland, *en route* to Canada, their sole resources were bedding, personal effects, and four small children.

The ship that had been chartered to take the immigrants across the stormiest of northern seas was a disreputable tub, called the *Kamoens*, that creaked in every timber, and was otherwise remarkable for its distinctive trade odours. It had been used to transport horses! In Glasgow they were transferred to slightly better quarters aboard a so-called transatlantic Allen liner. In actual fact, however, there was little to commend the latter ship, except that it was larger, less dirty, and quite seaworthy.

Four families, irrespective of size, were allotted to a cabin, each of which was furnished with four empty bunks and a bare board table. Food for children and adults alike consisted of meagre rations of beef and badly baked bread. The unfamiliar, tasteless diet might have been endured without disastrous effects if the cabins had not been so unconscionably overcrowded that all attempts at cleanliness were defeated, and even the comfort of sleep became impossible. As if to make sure that these miseries worked their utmost havoc the ship ran into heavy weather, through which it battled for days, only to find when the storm lifted a little, that it was far off its course and, apparently, heading into a freshly rising gale. Incredible though it may seem in this day and age of scientific seamanship, air patrol, and radio, the hapless ship remained lost for six ill-fated weeks!

The inevitable result was a violent outbreak of ship's fever, a pestilence feared and familiar in those times of wretched travel. Few, indeed, on that miserable ship, escaped the disease. It was a harrowing experience for all concerned, and even those who feared the best shuddered in retrospect.

Mothers, too ill themselves to move from their improvised beds upon the floor, saw their little ones die, and, too weak for tears, watched dry-eyed as their tiny forms were shrouded in canvas for the saddest of all burials.

Out of the unhappy beings that crowded their particular cabin only mother kept on her feet, comforting as best she could the delirious, starving children. But neither prayer nor selfless ministry were availing. As the dreadful days dragged on she realized that her two youngest babies could not survive. So short a while ago sweetly plump and rosy, they were pitiful skeletons, whose trusting infant glances and futile pleading gestures turned her soul to ice. There was only one cry left in her heart. If only God would spare her that melancholy ritual at sea – somehow, the thought was intolerable.

The ship had found its course, and, striking utmost speed, was hurrying westward with its load of human misery. In mute despair, mother watched the little ones, her faith fiercely fixed upon that one forlorn hope. But even that was not to be. Three days before the ship reached land the elder child was consigned to the sea, and, as they docked at Quebec, the infant died.

It was a prophetic beginning – a foretaste of the high cost my parents were to pay for the rights of citizenship in the new country. Indeed a cruel introduction to a chosen homeland. And yet, what little kindness my mother was to receive by way of comfort or welcome in this new country was experienced here, in the old French port, where she was never to be known, and which she was never again to see.

She used to speak of it sometimes, with gentle wonder. Sitting there, alone with her dead, unheeding the life around her, she had suddenly heard a kind voice, and felt a gentle touch upon her shoulder. It was an old priest in rusty habit who stood beside her, a little stooped and worn. Although she could not understand his speech, her frozen heart melted under the kindness of his face. How good it seemed, in that foreign place, to behold once more a minister of comfort, whose sympathy was not a forced gesture, but the expression of natural sympathy. How healing to her wound was that moment of pity. For here was a man who looked upon her as a sorrowing fellow being, not as an immigrant to be stared at with ill-concealed curiosity. Wakened to this kindness, she became aware that other kindly folk drew near, and that their eyes were full of honest commiseration. It was then that the hard ring of misery compressing her heart loosened. It was then that she wept.

That other dear one had been given to the sea with no better shroud than a shawl and a piece of dingy canvas. But now, through the efforts of the immigrant agent and the sympathetic port officials, this second child was given a decent burial.

'They understood, those good people,' she used to say. 'The little coffin was the finest – white and lovely as the little boy it received.'

Nearly forty years later I stood amidst a gossiping crowd on the terrace of the Hotel Frontenac overlooking the beautiful harbour, but my thoughts were not on what was said. I was trying to see the city through my mother's eyes, trying to relive her gratitude for that understanding generosity. I wanted to forget the palatial hotel behind me, and all those other modern improvements that had altered, but not quite obliterated, old Quebec. I wanted to envision and recapture for my own inner-most memory the ancient city fronting the grey river; to feel, as she had felt, the healing inspiration of the faintly mauve Lauren-tian hills in the background – gentle hills against the gentle blue under whose shadows life had moved in softer tempo, and where God had spoken through a shabby priest for the healing of an overburdened heart.

There is no point in labouring the long journey from Quebec to Winnipeg. The Canadian Pacific Railway had by now spanned the Ontario wilderness, and, compared to the route former immi-grants had been obliged to follow, the new mode of travel was considered in the light of a miracle. The railway carriages were, however, not much improvement upon the prairie schooner and Red River carts. Wooden benches lined the box-like coaches, which were open to wind and weather, to showers of wood ash and flying sparks. As the decimal miles dragged on, their jolting discomfort was in some respects harder to endure than the lum-bering progress of the outmoded schooners had been for former settlers. They had at least enjoyed a more companionable adventure. At night there were welcome bivouacs beside cheery fires, where the tired traveller might stretch his aching muscles and renew his spirit in hopeful conversation and aspiring dreams. But here, in the close confinement of carriages that ground on and on, even the friendliest soul grew taciturn, and the hardiest of mortals succumbed to a listless fatigue that almost amounted to stupor.

One of my father's sisters, a graduate midwife, had come to the country previously, and was now living on Younge Street, in Winnipeg. The family joined her, and set up joint housekeeping as best they could. The prospects were far from bright. Father was still suffering from the effects of ship's fever. Even in normal health, he was not fitted for, nor accustomed to, hard manual labour, which was the only work freely available for the immigrants. It was thought, however, that outdoor activity might be of real benefit, and so it was with hopeful eagerness that he joined a threshing gang bound for Dakota when the harvest season opened. The hope was not justified. He fell seriously ill, and, after six weeks in bed, tormented by anxiety for his family, he returned to Winnipeg, where he worked at odd jobs throughout the winter.

My aunt was a practical, highly ambitious woman, and, although happily married had no intention of confining her life to domestic drudgery. She was a born nurse, if there ever was one, and she had determined to resume that profession so soon as she had acquired the language and could pass the required examinations. She heartily disliked every form of housework, and yet, because she wanted to learn the ways of this country, as well as its speech, she went out cleaning by the day.

Knowing my aunt as I do, I can imagine how the women who attempted to patronize the 'queer foreigner' must have fared. Elizabeth of England was not more certain of her divine birthright than Haldora Gudmunsdottir! Without a particle of vanity, she permitted no infringement upon her self-respect, which epitomized a lively individualism and an unassailable belief in her own judgement. Whatever clashed with her own opinions she dismissed with cheerful urbanity, not to say contempt. 'Ridiculous person!' she once exclaimed at a fault-finding employer. 'Fussing and fuming over a bit of dust on some worthless bric-à-brac, but no thought for the pantry! For what do you think I found there? Sour beans! Let me tell you, I thrust them under her stupid nose.'

Mother was taking care of the house, and contributing towards the budget by what she earned at knitting. She would have preferred to have followed her sister-in-law's example, but some one had to assume responsibility for the children – her own two little ones and aunt's two small boys. What worried her more than anything else at the time was the lack of fresh milk. To her way of thinking, a child was starved without it. When she heard that a certain farmer who was said to be too mean to hire needed help was throwing gallons to his pigs, she offered to do the milking. It meant a daily walk of nearly three miles over a gumbo trail, which, in wet weather, became a river of slippery glue. The farmer was loud in verbal gratitude for her service, but when it came to concrete recompense he thought that two quarts of milk was quite sufficient. After all, he had the pigs to consider.

It must have been galling to think of her old home in the deanery, where the meanest beggar found a welcome hospitality, as she trudged that wilderness trail of an evening, with her little pail of begrudged milk. I know that this, and many similar incidents, embittered her outlook and hardened her into the unswerving Icelander that she remained to the day of her death. A woman who rejected assimilation in any degree with a people whose sensibilities she doubted, and whose culture she therefore refused to admit.

At this time, however, she thought little of the incident. She was young, and magnificently healthy, and with a spirit not easily depressed. The milk would benefit the children, and if only the colour returned to their cheeks the task was worth it. Indeed, as the weeks passed they took heart. The crisp autumn weather, with its brilliant sunshine, inspired cheerfulness, and the pastel beauty of the turning leaves made the landscape a vibrant poem.

The people might not be friendly, nor the tale of ready opportunity more than a myth, but the land itself was cast in a titantic mould, and one day must surely inspire greatness in its children. When the sun flamed red along the limitless horizon, and the winds swept down from untrammelled wastes, it was impossible not to believe that unseen forces brooded over its destiny. Avarice and ignorance, and all the vicious snobberies transplanted from slave-bred civilizations might endure for a day, but in the end they must give way before a wider conception of existence.

These comforting dreams, and the high expectation of peaceful days ahead, were rudely shaken one wintry morning, when father was brought home unconscious from the harness shop where he had found employment. The doctor's verdict was not encouraging. Father was rushed to the hospital: he should have had medical attention long ago. That was the trouble with people, said the doctor crossly. They let things go, and then expected miracles.

It was true that father had been sick. He had been subject to attacks of severe pains in the head, maddening jabs of burning intensity, that left him faint and dizzy, and increasingly fearful lest he be found lagging at his bench. A friend explained these things, and added, indignantly, that if his condition was serious, the sweatshop system under which men laboured in this land of publicized liberty was certainly not blameless.

'Perhaps not – perhaps not,' the doctor muttered, and amended hastily: 'None the less, it would have happened eventually, my good woman.'

His reaction and reasoning were sound enough. His attitude, if not his words, belied what he honestly believed, and for the best of reasons refrained from saying. There was nothing to be gained by putting rebellious ideas into the heads of immigrants, who must, as a matter of course, sweat for their daily bread. No sense in setting the slave against his master, when every good Christian knew, on biblical authority, that obedience was the prescribed duty of the one, and the power of life and death the prerogative of the other. Furthermore, any reasonable person understood what sacrifices an employer made when he invested capital in an enterprise that afforded a livelihood for others.

How true! Something certainly must be said of the over-whelming sacrifices involved in this particular instance. And yet, since truth is generally such an affront to the best people – and, of course, in the very worst taste – I must refrain from men-tioning actual names. I shall call the gentleman Mr Brant, and his philanthropic institution 'The Saddlery.' To further ease the strain on tender sensibilities, be it marked that the good man has long since departed this life for fields of wider, if vaguer, possi-bilities.

Mr Brant was a native of Ontario, and admirably fitted the picture of most so-called supermen of industry. He was shrewd, intelligent, though uneducated, ruthless in principle, and utterly indifferent to criticism. He was a harness-maker by trade, though not a very good one – a detail that in no way affected his career, for his first stroke of genius was the selection of a partner who fur-nished both skill and capital for their initial undertaking. His own contribution was superb executive ability and the iron heel of the born aggressor.

Shortly after his arrival in Winnipeg he set up a small shop, which, due to the nature of the times as much as to business ability, grew with amazing rapidity. It must be remembered that transport was still largely dependent on ox, mule, and horse power. Freighting into the territories and up the lakes, to men-tion nothing else, was a highly profitable occupation that com-manded hundreds of teams, with all that that implies. In other words, harness shops and harness-makers were as essential to that mode of life as the petrol vendor to-day, and required no more genius to exploit their wares.

Every hamlet and town had its harness-maker, who, before the ultimate rise of Mr Brant, derived a steady though modest living from his trade. These brother craftsmen of the future leather luminary differed from him in little, save their point of view. Which is to say, they were simple souls who valued exis-tence apart from business, whereas to Mr Brant anything with-out a dollar mark, plus one hundred per cent profit, was as worthless as a prairie sunset.

When my father entered his employ the business had been moved to an old shop on the market street. It was an abandoned skating-rink, long, low, and gloomy, with small-paned windows that admitted inadequate light and no ventilation. In summer the rain leaked down through the rotting roof, and in winter the frost coated the walls. Mr Brant, with his eye on a fortune, found better uses for his profits than to squander them on emasculating comforts. If some weakling was always keeling over, that was his own misfortune, and no concern of the Winnipeg Saddlery. All that was made very clear to each applicant. Mr Brant assumed no obligations whatsoever, aside from the payment of wages agreed upon. This varied from seventy-five cents to a dollar for a ten-hour day. Piece-work, which was naturally urged upon the uninitiated, was priced so low that, however proficient a man might be, it was impossible to earn more than sixty or seventy cents a day. A six-foot trace of heaviest leather, which had to be doubled stitched by hand, brought thirty cents. No holiday was paid for, nor the slightest favour granted to any one. The oldest, most faithful employee was fined if a moment late, whatever his justification. As might be expected, Mr Brant instantly and effectively killed every effort to unionize the shop. He had no intention of permitting anarchy to take root in his establishment, nor had any need of advice on matters of organization and management. He had perfected a highly satisfactory, not to say ingenious, system whereby his power and profits increased from year to year. It was really a beautiful arrangement, for it cost him nothing financially, and the burden of its operations rested upon his luckless employees.

It was not a new, but a trusty sweat-shop manoeuvre ever dear to the autocrat, whose opportunity is the extremity of others. He kept a sharp watch for arriving immigrants, and hired as many as possible. These unskilled surplus hands were utilized in odd jobs, for which they received a pittance, and free instruction in a lucrative trade. The instructors were, of course, chosen from the best, and, so far as it applies, highest-paid men, who thus dug their own economic graves. For so soon as the new-comers qualified for the jobs, they got them, at a lower wage. And out went the old-timers, unless they accepted a similar reduction.

Because of his skill as a saddle-maker father had not experienced any difficulty in getting his job. The difficulty then and for years to come, was to keep the family alive on the wages. To those who benefited by the times, this may sound like an over-statement, born of malice and resentment. For it is seldom that the fortunate are willing to conceded that a combination of circumstances that favoured them might have ruined others. Yet the truth is that even in those days of supposedly easy opportunity it required some capital to take advantage of them – or, if not capital, its equivalent in unhampered and unencumbered energy. But, without money, the man who had dependents, stood no better chance of attaining to financial security in old Winnipeg than did his fellow workers in other cities of the world.

A little plain arithmetic may absolve me from wilful heresy. Mr Brant's wage scale, it has been seen, made it almost impossible for a piece-worker to earn more than five or six dollars a week. Which, at the most, adds up to twenty-four dollars a month. From that, at least five dollars must be deducted for house rent; another three or four for firewood and kerosene during moderately cold weather, and usually twice that amount in the bitter winter months. At best, then, that leaves only fifteen dollars to spread over the needs of an entire family – that is to say, for food, and clothing, and medical services, and such incidentals as even the poor cannot evade.

But food, we sometimes hear it said, was so plentiful and cheap that no one need have suffered any actual lack. The inference being, that none save the thriftless sinner could have escaped luxury. So far as I remember, however, the Icelandic immigrant was neither given to idleness nor excess, yet his table was restricted to the plainest, most meagre fare. What meat he had was usually pickled sheep's head – for these could be bought at five cents each at the slaughter house (it was not called abattoir then!) – or shank bone for the soup kettle, or now and then a bit of liver, when onions were on hand to dress the dish. As for other commodities: flour sold at $2.50 the hundredweight; sugar at fourteen pounds for the dollar; butter from fifteen to twenty-five cents a pound; lard, five cents; and green coffee, which every housewife roasted in her own bake oven, sold at six pounds for the dollar.

A little quiet speculation on these seemingly low prices, as seen in ratio to the wages paid, will prove, I think, that the average immigrant family that strove to maintain some sort of respectability under these conditions might just as well have dreamed of a mansion on the moon as of sharing in the many profitable opportunities which were open to men of a little means.

I remember that one of the few grievances that my amiable father nursed against fate was that when lots were selling at five dollars on Nina Street (now Sherbrooke) he could never manage to scrape up the money. In a few years those lots were selling for hundreds of dollars, and by the time I had reached my teens many a tidy fortune had been made from those city blocks. But to me, the wonder was, not that the family fell short of financial grace, but that it should have survived those awful early years, unaided and intact.

9

First taste of the New World

It is not my intention to recount all the melancholy privations through which the family struggled, always, by some miracle of inward solace, maintaining a fairly cheerful atmosphere. For nothing ever dampened my father's belief in the essential business of life, which he held to be the evolution of character. Nor was my mother long cast down by tribulation. Her courage and humour was equal to almost any trial. But this first winter brought her to the point of despair.

Father, it was discovered at the hospital, had an abscess in the lower brain, caused by an injury received years before in a shipwreck. It was decided that an operation, though delicate in the extreme, might save him, but the hope held out was slight indeed. Fortunately for us, the Winnipeg Hospital, though small and under-staffed, was none the less fairly well equipped, and the tiny operating-room under a most able surgeon. In view of the difficulties under which the new hospital had had its rise, it seems fitting to mention its early beginning, and those 'old-timers' who bore the brunt of its inauguration.

It was after the first Riel Rebellion that the need for hospital accommodation was first felt. Many of the volunteers had remained in Winnipeg, and new settlers kept pouring in over the newly opened Dawson trail, and by way of St Paul. The houses of the town were soon overcrowded, and consequently when sickness broke out the necessity for some place where patients could be properly cared for became apparent.

Accordingly, in 1871 a meeting was called by Governor Archibald to deal with the problem, and among those present were Robert Cunningham, James Ross, Hon. A.G.B. Bannantyne, Hon. Alfred Boyd, and Dr J.H. O'Donnell. At the meeting, a Board of Health was formed, and steps were taken to begin hospital work. On the 13th of December of the following year the hospital was organized, but it was not until the 14th of May 1875 that Provincial letters of incorporation were taken out – a step rendered necessary by an appeal to the Provincial Government for assistance.

At that time the board of directors consisted of Messrs George Young, Gilbert McMicken, W. Kennedy, W.C. Clark, Thomas Lusted, G.B. Spence, George Bryce, A.G.B. Bannantyne, J.H. Ashdown, Stewart Mulvy, A.G. Jackson, J.H. O'Donnell, Joseph Royal, J.H. McTavish, and W.G. Fonseca.

The first building occupied by the hospital was owned by Mr William Harvey, and was situated on the north-west corner of McDermot and Albert Streets, where the once-famed Marriaggi Hotel afterwards stood. This became the Winnipeg General Hospital. The accommodation here was, however, quickly exhausted, and the hospital was moved to other quarters, somewhere in the rear of the present Bank of Montreal, and shortly thereafter to yet another house on Notre Dame Avenue, owned by Dr Shultz. From there the hospital was transferred to premises owned by Mr John McTavish, situated on the Red River, south of Broadway Bridge. In 1875 another move was found imperative, and the choice fell on property owned by the late Hon. John Norquay, somewhere on Main Street North. And the sixth move was to a house owned by the hospital, between Bannantyne and McDermot, close to the present location, on land donated by the late A.G.B. Bannantyne. This location was selected with a view to placing the hospital in a section of the city which in time would be most central to the needs of the future. The wisdom of the choice continues unquestioned.

The building here erected accommodated sixteen public-ward patients and four private patients, and had a small operating-room. But the hospital had yet another move to make before its final installation in the buildings which formed the nucleus of the present imposing structure. This new 'flitting' was altogether unavoidable. With the beginning of the CPR construction the sudden influx of settlers rendered the little hospital inadequate. While arrangements were being made to collect funds for the necessary extensions, the hospital was moved to the Dominion Immigration Hall on Point Douglas Common, which was purchased from the Government for five thousand dollars. In this building what was then considered a complete operating equipment was provided at a cost of seven hundred and sixty-two dollars, and private wards were improvised by screening off portions of the public wards.

The erection of the new hospital, the central portion of the present buildings, was a long and tedious undertaking. It was decided that the lot donated to the institution by the late A.G.B. Bannantyne and A. McDermot was not large enough, and this was exchanged for a block of ground west of Olivia Street, and the adjoining block was purchased from the executors of the McDermot Estate for five thousand dollars. Penelope Street, between these two blocks, was closed, and here the first buildings of the present group was erected. This decision was made in 1882, and the official opening of the Winnipeg General Hospital took place in 1884.

It was to this arduously acquired little hospital, which the old-timers saw as a symbol of the height of humanitarian progress in the west, that my poor father was taken that bitter day. His case created something of a sensation. Up to that time no such operation had been attempted in the modest surgery. What was lacking in equipment was earnestly supplied by sheer ability and conscientious goodwill. Certainly no surgeon ever accomplished a more skilful operation, despite his own doubts of the experiment, and the complete scepticism of his assistants. No one, it seems, expected the patient to live. It was in the interest of science, rather than of the fever-wracked form on the operating-table, that the brilliant attempt was made. But there was incredible vitality in that pale, slight frame. He not only survived the experiment, but made such a rapid recovery that, ironically enough, it inspired an almost criminal optimism which nearly cost his life. There was certainly no intentional negligence, no one in particular to blame for what happened. Father was cared for as well as the public-ward facilities permitted. But the hospital was crowded. When, therefore, in four weeks' time, he appeared sufficiently recovered, he was discharged. It was February, and bitterly cold. With his head still swathed in bandages, and no better covering than a threadbare tweed lightcoat, he had to walk over a mile through a gathering storm. As might be expected, what should have been a joyous return, and for which my mother had celebrated with pathetic pride – setting the table with coffee and real cream and rolled Icelandic pancakes – resolved itself into overwhelming tragedy. The severe chill brought on brain fever, and for seven weeks he alternated between wild delirium and terrifying coma.

Mother could never speak of those weeks without a shudder. There was no one to whom she could turn. My aunt, who would have been a tower of strength, had moved away, having fixed upon the United States as a much more progressive country. How, then, was the little family to live? Father had to be nursed night and day, a task almost beyond the strength of one woman during those delirious hours. The landlord was willing enough to wait for his rent, but there was fuel and food and medicine to be bought. She tried to knit, which meant that, in the rare intervals when the patient was quiet and she should have slept, she forced her tired eyes to remain open by dashing cold water on them, kept herself from collapsing by drinking black coffee. As a consequence of these pathetic labours her sight was impaired to such an extent that she eventually lost the use of one eye.

Yet, however hard she drove herself, these efforts would not have kept him alive if the best of men had not come to her assistance and lent her a supply of groceries. This benefactor was a Mr Fredrickson, an Icelandic small merchant, whom many a family remembers for similar kindness. Another Icelander, a man who worked with father in 'The Saddlery,' took up a subscription of fifteen dollars from those poor wage-slaves to defer medical expenses and buy a cord of wood. For these things, mother was deeply grateful, yet I think nothing ever hurt her more. She was the kind of woman who found it easy to give but extremely difficult to receive.

Father's recovery was, of course, extremely slow. After weeks at home, the doctor decided that he must have better care, and consequently, as soon as he could be moved with safety, father went back to the hospital, this time to remain for three weary months. So soon as these arrangements had been completed mother gave up the house and took three tiny upstairs rooms for herself and the children. Now, at last, she felt free to go to work, in order to pay off those frightening, pyramiding debts. She had the will and the courage, yet how, she asked herself, could it be done, when the younger child was scarcely more than a baby? In this dilemma she was forced to accept a solution that violated her deeply maternal instincts. A dearly beloved cousin of father's, Malfridur Borgford, offered to adopt the child. It was a cruel decision for mother to make, yet better, perhaps, than shunting the little girl back and forth among strangers who would not consider her best interests. It was a bitter concession to her own helplessness. But then, had not everything been cruelly bitter in this new country? In her despair she tried to reason that, whatever might be her innermost feelings, little Anna would fare better for the sacrifice. She would be loved and conscientiously cared for at the Borgford's. Indeed, she would be spared the wounding privations which, instinct told her, the small son she was keeping would, perforce, have to bear.

Yes, it was highly sensible to let the child go. So she told herself again and again. It was cold comfort, however, when on the appointed day, from her bleak window she watched the little creature trot gaily away, all unsuspectingly, with her Auntie Malfridur. It was a beautiful spring morning, one of those bright prairie days when the eyes are pained by the reflected brilliance of a whitely golden sun. For the watcher at the window, whose tearful eyes were fixed upon a sturdy little figure marching bravely out into the unequivocal distance, there was no beauty in the dazzling white landscape, no light in the sky.

But grief, like everything else, was a luxury, mother told herself harshly. There was no time for tears. She had work to find – any kind of work. And how gladly she toiled! How proudly and gratefully she counted each dollar that, bit by bit, would cancel those intolerable obligations. Yet what must her feelings have been each morning, when she left to his own devices a little boy of six? A merry little fellow, whose youth was already doomed to premature age and responsibility? Poor little lad, how fortunate that, of all her children, he had the sweetest disposition and the most pliable mind. Gravely, the little boy promised to be good, oh, very, very good. Not to forget to feed the cat, nor to let it annoy the neighbours. In the evening his reward would be a story, a very thrilling story of brave men and maids. Perhaps a fairy tale or two if mamma had much mending to do.

So the months passed. When father came home at last the three rooms were very festive. There were curtains at the windows, and two brand-new chairs! The stove shone like the face of a saint, and fumes of freshly roasted coffee made a joyous incense. And, can you believe it, there were five silver spoons and three china cups on the table!

And so this chapter, which I report from hearsay (though, truth to tell, it seems odd I wasn't there to glory in the spoons) comes to an end. For the summer was an uneventful interlude in which the invalid kept house with the little son, and gathered strength for renewed battle. In the autumn father was back at the saddlery, and mother, once more confined to the house, was finally launched upon her life-long battle for respectability.

The next year the family moved to a fairly decent brick house on Bushnell Street. And here, at midday, on the 9th of December 1890, I had the bad manners to interrupt my mother in the midst of making headcheese – and for no better reason than to be born.

10

Subjective interlude

'The thoughts of youth are long, long thoughts.' So says the poet. To which sentiment most people agree, although, too often, without much understanding. The cheerful agreement applies to far, faint, mythical individuals, to people beyond the common ken. For how often, on recalling something that deeply impressed me, I have been told, 'You could not remember that. Of course you could not – you were such a child!' As though there were a point, or divisional place fixed by years, where consciousness begins and a purely vegetable existence ends. As a matter of fact, the thoughts of early childhood are the longest thoughts of all. They persist through life, not, perhaps, as distinct images or ideas, but as sharp, unalterable reactions, such as sympathies and phobias. Vague, unrelated, often distorted and but dimly understood, these child thoughts are, none the less, full of exquisite wonder, wing-swift surprise, and indelible pain. They are indeed the stuff from which the world evolves, the mysterious matrix of which the emotional life is made.

In my own case scarcely any situation in human relationships has escaped a tempering shadow from some such long-gone experience. Not that I reasoned about it, weighed and measured, and drew conclusions. It was all quite unconscious as are all our so-called spontaneous reactions. That there is no such thing as an unconditioned response to the calls of life I sincerely believe. I think that, just as the tonal quality of a violin depends upon the delicate process of weathering, so the sensitivity of the human mind depends, to a remarkable degree, upon the stress and strain of childhood thoughts and emotions.

It follows that events, in themselves, are of no importance except as they incite and react upon consciousness. In its final analysis, life, for each of us, is nothing more than a series of sense impressions. And these impressions, depending as they do upon the normal or abnormal functioning of the physical organs of sense and the sympathetic nervous system, necessarily reveal unto each of us a world thus limited to our individual comprehension and mental reserves. Consequently, none of us can ever actually see 'eye to eye,' as the foolish saying goes, nor sense the same shade of beauty and blemish in any given experience. And yet, because we live for no better reason than to reveal our particular slant on the riddle of existence, we must proclaim truth as we see it. But not, I think, without a qualifying humility which readily admits that, so far as one's individual conception goes, truth is a purely relative term. The same applies to all human judgements. To argue that anything in human experience is of itself, aside from its reactions upon the individual, either great or small, is a confession of insensitive stupidity.

For example, to the man of action physical hardships hold little terror, yet a contest of words with a narrow bigot may put him to rout – which proves nothing, except that each is adept in his own obsession. Furthermore, bound as we are within the individual consciousness, it is ridiculous to expect more than comparative understanding from even our dearest associates. For instance, a practical soul, however generous, would never instinctively understand why any one should weep over the simple act of tossing away a sheaf of withered flowers. Practical natures are not prone to vagrant dreams, nor even dimly aware of the bright immortality of illusive ideas. It is not in such a one to understand how the dreaming heart cries out against the swift eclipse of beauty, and mourns with a mist of tears the golden leaves of a thousand yesterdays. Such facile, foolish pain is very real to me – real as the purple shadows that veil in mystery the sailing horn of the young moon, and the little winds that run before the night on softly whispering feet. Real as are all the innermost senses which life has stirred to passion by its flaming sword.

11

God's fields

I don't know how old I was that early morning when I awakened with a start, and knew at once that something was wrong in the house. It was so unearthly quiet. Ordinarily, at this hour, mamma would be banging about in the kitchen, scraping the breakfast pots, or rubbing away on the washboard. Then, too, little brother, who of late had cried so much in a thin wailing voice, wasn't in his cradle, nor making the least sound, wherever he was. That was queer, I thought, staring at the empty cradle, and straining my ears for the familiar sound. Sitting there on the edge of the bed, it seemed to me that the silence thickened about me, pressed in on me like a September fog swirling in from damp brown marshes, and the chill of it raised sharp pinpricks on my bare arms and legs. I was being foolish, I knew. The make-believe side of my mind was playing tricks on me. It was what I had been told would happen unless I mended my wool-gathering ways. With an effort of will I wriggled forward on the bed, reaching out for my clothes on a near-by chair. And then, more frightening than the silence, came a sound that almost stopped my heart.

It was a strangled cry, that hurt to hear because it was so quickly suppressed, smothered in painful, muffled weeping. Petrified, I sat there clutching my clothes, waiting the world's end. For that was mamma weeping. My cheerful, energetic mamma, whose eyes had a way of twinkling at you even through the misty vapours of the washtub, and who always found a laugh to heal my childish tears. Then, in further confirmation that my small world was sorely amiss, I heard papa's voice, low and indistinct, but with some quality so pitiful vibrating through it that my breath caught in my throat. Gathered in a lump that threatened to choke me. Oh, something was very, very wrong, since papa was home on this shiny summer morning, for I knew he was not sick. But now I must find out for myself, take my share in the terrifying mystery. Oh, hurry, hurry, I said to my fingers, which were suddenly all thumbs as they worked at buttonholes now too small for the buttons. I wanted to rush out to that grief-stricken room, to throw myself on mamma's breast, to comfort and be comforted. That was what I wanted. Yet, when I had dressed at last, I dared not open the excluding door. No, I dared not. With my hand on the knob, and my heart beating in my throat, I somehow understood that those tears and hesitant commiserations were not for me to look upon. I would go, instead, to the front room, and wait for the melancholy sounds to subside.

When I slipped into the small parlour (which was, of course, no real parlour such as the minister had, but just the room where mamma's chest of drawers, her black rocker, a braided mat, and a table with flowering plants gave an air of mild formality) and had shut the door behind me, I beheld a thing that made me rub my eyes. In the middle of the room, supported by two chairs, was the loveliest white bed. I assumed that it was a bed, although so tiny and narrow, for little brother was sleeping in it. He was sleeping so sweetly that I almost feared to breathe as I stole forward on tiptoe for a better look at this strange white resting-place.

Who shall say how knowledge comes to a child? There was nothing but innocent curiosity in my mind as I drew nearer on silent, cautious feet, and yet, all at once, I was filled with the startling consciousness that here was no ordinary sleep. Never before had little brother slept in such waxen quietude, his tiny hands utterly at rest on his small bosom. Strange, inviolate sleep!

Strange, silent little face, that not even the weaving light from the window stirred from its graven peace. What was here I could not understand. I none the less comprehended it was not for me to spy upon. Little brother had acquired some special significance as remote as the stars and too deep for curiosity. He was so beautiful, lying there in his snowy bed, that my whole breast ached, and I envied him a little.

Quietly I crept to the window, and noted with astonishment that, just as on other days, the local boys were playing in the muddy pool by the corner pump. Nothing was changed in the street. There, every familiar activity proceeded as was usual. Like puppies at play, the boys pushed and pummelled each other, their bare feet splashing through the saffron water. A woman in a trailing black skirt hurried by, a wicker market basket on her stout red arm. The baker in his red cart rumbled through the ruts, and the postman, cheerily whistling, plodded on. Nothing at all in this outer shell of the world was the least affected, although the inner citadel trembled around me.

I don't know how long I had hovered there, mutely miserable, when papa came in. 'Come, child,' he said, 'you must dress.' An odd command, surely, for had I not already accomplished that vexatious feat? Could he not see that even my dress was neatly buttoned, and my shoe-laces tied? The look on his face, grave and weary, held me silent. Meekly, I followed into the kitchen, where the smell of coffee enheartened me a little. Then, too, I saw that mamma was not crying now. She sat by the stove, her fine, restless hands for once idle in her lap. She did not look at me, however. Dressed in her dark green alpaca Sunday gown, she sat, straightly and still, with eyes fixed on some inner mystery that left me worlds apart.

We were going somewhere, it seemed. I dared not ask where. I dared not so much as wriggle when papa, unaccustomed to such a task, tried his best to comb my hair, and cruelly pulled the snarls. When he fetched the red cashmire dress from the closet I put it on without a murmur. I even ate a dish of hated porridge because he said I must. It was just as I finished that a knock on the door came as a welcome deliverance, and a big man in a frock coat entered with his hat in his hand. He nodded at papa, and, bowing a little, addressed mamma in a kind, solemn voice.

'I wish I were here on a brighter errand,' he said, 'that there was something I could say – but what are words? It is hard – hard.'

'Thank you, Mr Bardal,' mother answered, in a cold small voice. 'We are ready, as you see.'

We went out and there at the door stood a hack with two black horses switching their gleaming tails. 'Papa – papa,' I whispered in rising elation that instantly died when he touched his lips for silence. It was all beyond comprehension. Here were we, who never went abroad in style, about to ride forth in a fine carriage such as the rich folk used for pleasure, and not one word of joy to be said. One by one, we climbed in and took our places, and then – astonishingly true – the tall stranger brought out little brother's bed, now completely covered with a crinkly velvet lid, and set it between us. Then the horses were off, stepping daintily as ladies over the rutted road.

There was so much I wanted to ask, so many confusing thoughts crowding my troubled mind, but as neither parent seemed even remotely aware of my presence I fell to watching the streets. Strange streets, full of sound and movement, interesting enough in their fashion, for even then the panorama of human beings pouring from an unknown past to an unguessed future intrigued me. Yet all this was quickly forgotten when the noisy streets gave way to an open road. No more ugly houses; no more cluttered shops; no more hasting, harried people. As far as the eye could travel, green fields flowed on and on under a cloudless sky toward a far, blue horizon.

It was the prairie in its sweetest dress, the tall grasses stirring in a little wind, with yellow daisies and shy blue flowers nodding as we passed. It was the prairie as I was always to love it, breathing something fine and free that stole into my heart. It lay there under the amber summer sun, so big and so beautiful that I thought God must have made it in some gentle moment for His own White Company – for the angels that walked the earth by night.

The fancy so pleased me that I could hardly believe my eyes when this broidered carpet of green was rudely broken by a high iron fence. An ugly, chilling enclosure, wherein lay rows and rows of wooden crosses and cold white stones. And here the horses stopped. The tall man, more grave than ever, lifted out the little bed, and mamma and papa stepped down from the carriage. For the first time that morning mamma took note of me.

'Stay where you are, child,' she said. 'Your shoes are thin, and the ground is damp.'

I did not want to enter that place of stones, yet the tears leaped to my eyes. I wanted to run into those wide, green fields, where the variegated flowers waved in the sunlight. I wanted so passionately to set my feet on that soft, sun-drenched carpet rolling away to the blue, that, when I was left, I buried my face in my hands to shut out the beauty I might not share.

I think the tall, grave stranger must have dearly loved children, and read their hearts aright. I think he understood my infant misery, and quickly guessed the source of its hurt. I like so to believe, for after a little he returned to the carriage with a handful of prairie flowers.

'There you are, little one,' he smiled, slipping into my hands the first bit of loveliness for which my soul thirsted. Dear, thoughtful heart! What, to him, was a simple, kindly gesture, soon forgotten, was to me a precious gift, treasured throughout the years.

All the way home I hugged those lowly flowers to my breast – more sweet by far than any garden blooms, for the dreams of the great green fields enveloped them. In their little faces I read a thousand star-born mysteries, and in their faint perfume found something exquisite and fairy fashioned. They so absorbed me that I scarcely wondered why little brother had been left behind. It was not until we were home again, and mamma, grey and tired, had set the table for coffee, that the old anxiety returned to vex me. Dark questions flocked to my mind, a dozen unanswered mysteries. Something restrained me. I could only stand like a stick, clutching my flowers, ignored and forgotten, so it seemed.

Papa, rousing from his own painful musings, noticed me. He tried to smile, and the effort hurt me – as the sight of the sharp cold fence in that lovely green waste had hurt me.

'Poor little Lalla. Give me the flowers,' he said. 'We must put them in water, or they will die.'

They will die! They will die! The words shot through my child consciousness, tipped with terrible meaning. They will die! The words had been meaningless heretofore. Now I understood. Oh yes, I understood, and with a little cry I thrust my treasure into papa's hands and fled into a corner. I could not have said what hurt me so deeply, nor explained that the feeling in my heart was a darker sister of the odd pain that always assailed me when I watched the sun go down on golden wings in the west. I just knew that, whereas a moment ago I wanted to be remembered, to be asked to fetch a cup, or the spoons, or the bread from the pantry, I now wished to be left in my corner to face alone this strange new understanding.

But when I had gone to bed, and my prayers were ended, I pulled the sheet up over my face, and cried in the silent way I had. I cried for the flowers that were already dying when I hugged them to my breast. And I cried that little brother and I had not been left together in the beautiful quiet of God's fields. I cried until my old grey cat, being cold, came stepping softly over the bed, and nestled in my bosom.

12

Those child transgressions

My mother could never quite believe that I was not meant for the realms above. So sure was she of my early demise that I began to be a little impatient for the heavenly event. I used to imagine myself setting forth in great state in the Little White Hearse – for of course I was much too big to be taken away in a hack. After that I would flit about in a variety of wings, doing nothing in particular, for my imagination failed me completely when it came to a working programme in Paradise. It was really quite a jolly game, that helped me immensely when I was bored with living cooped up in the house while other children whooped and hollered around the village pump. My greatest disappointment centred in that pastime. If only I might have trampled that deli-cious mud, I felt that even death would not be too big a price. My second disappointment was God.

God kept a very jealous eye on wilful children. That I was a victim of this pestiferous sin I discovered one lovely morning when the sun was a bristling disk in the sky, and the local chil-dren especially merry, splashing through the puddles. Of course, I could not go out. There was a cold wind, my mother said, and if I caught a chill, what might not happen! It was all very sad. But, I thought to myself, just to open the window and hang out for a moment would hardly amount to a very heinous sin. It was a thrilling experience – I even yelled a little, just to show that after all I was not lacking in social graces. Perhaps I wriggled. At any rate, down came the window with a terrifying clop right on my wicked neck!

My screams brought mother on the run. No doubt she was frightened and envisioned who knows what injuries. When she saw that nothing much was amiss, however, her temper, always quick, rose to the occasion.

'Now you see how God punishes naughty girls!' she cried. 'Perhaps, after this, you'll do as you're told!'

Well, for the most part, I always did. My mother had a sharp tongue as well as a sharp eye. That I did not so much resent – mamma had so many soft moments. But that God should plunk the window down on my neck struck me as both ungentlemanly and unjust. From that day I had no use for the Deity. The angels were exempt from this condemnation – they seemed to be a cheerful lot with cheerful duties. And Jesus, the perennial Christmas Babe who later had to die for the sins of the world wrung many tears from my heart. I could never understand why God treated him so badly – except that God was just that kind of deity.

But though my mother was apprehensive that every season was my last (and who can blame her, when I was the only one of her babies born in those arduous years to survive infancy, and then only to fall prey to awful sickness) it was no excuse for ignorance. I had to learn a multitude of poems and prayers and scriptural verses. That was not very difficult if the words had a musical sound and a fitting rhythm. 'Lift up your heads, O ye hills' and 'Yea, though ye slay me, yet will I believe in Him' – such phrases had a fascination for me, entirely apart from any meaning. And of all the many sacred verses, I loved best the lyric passage:

> Dröttin blessi mig or mína
> Morgun kveld og nött or, dag,
> Dröttin vevji vaengi sína
> Míg um lífs of salar hag.

A beautiful conception of a divinity (which I never connected with an anthropomorphic God) that enfolded every living being in protective wings of love.

It was fun to learn these things, even if it seemed a little silly to roll them off so regularly every night. Where I rebelled, with sad consequences, was at the business of learning to read. Not that I was not thrilled with the general idea, but when my mother brought out the old yellow-paged family Bible for a text-book I struck for liberty and licence. I would *not* learn to read that musty volume. Besides, my mother's choice was sadly inept.

'And it came to pass after these things, that God did tempt Abraham, and said unto him, Abraham: and he said, Behold, here I am. And he said, Take now thy son, thine only son Isaac, whom thou lovest, and get thee into the land of Moriah; and offer him there for a burnt offering upon one of the mountains which I will tell thee of.'

Slowly and seriously my mother read, her slender finger tracing the words for me. Simple little words that brought a curious chill and as swift rebellion to my mind.

'Now, child,' said she, 'see how far you can go. Spell out the letters, and it won't be hard.'

Bleakly I looked at her. Well, let the heavens fall and all dark doom swallow me up – my mind was set. 'I won't read,' I said. 'I won't read a single word, mamma.'

I think she would have been less surprised if I had bitten her.

'You won't read?' she repeated helplessly, and, snatching at saving reason, quickly asked, 'Are you sick? Does your head ache?'

'No, mamma, I am not sick.'

'What's the matter with you then? Stop being silly and do as you are told.'

She might as well have spoken to a stone: neither argument nor reprimand moved me. I was wicked, I knew, and resigned to an evil fate, but not to reading such mischievous stuff. That fate, in the guise of a dark cupboard under the stairs quickly befell me. It was frightfully black, and I was sure that a thousand mice were nibbling in the corners. I sat there with my sins and waited for eternity to pass. I did not cry. I just sat there listening to the imaginary mice, and wondering how long it would be until they had eaten everything else, and would begin on me.

At least a hundred years had dragged by when I heard my father come home, and the next moment found myself hauled up before him in all my dusty iniquity. Said my indignant mother, when the chronicle of my unconscionable revolt ended, 'Now, young lady, perhaps you'll think differently, and obey like a sensible child.'

To which I instantly replied – quite as though she had pressed a button and released a prepared answer: 'Now I'll never learn to read, mother.'

It may have been her unfailing sense of humour which saved me from further pressure, which undoubtedly would have had a serious psychological effect. Or there may have been something in my strained white face that actually frightened her. She was never one to understand mental complexes or straitened emotional states. So now, rather than cope with something at once ridiculous and incredible, for I was usually obedient and completely ruled by her influence, she left me where I was, disgraced and contemptible, and hurried to the kitchen. Father said nothing, and quietly slipped out of the house. When he returned there was a whimsical smile on his face, and in his hand a small pink book. Quite as though nothing unusual were afoot, he exhibited his purchase so that I should see in all its shining wonder the fine frontispiece. There, bold as you please, stood a chubby little chap with a bundle on a stick jauntily perched over one shoulder. His cap sat crookedly, and his round face beamed. He was utterly adorable, and I promptly fell in love with him.

'This is Master Neils,' father told me. 'A gay young fellow, with adventure in his soul. He is setting forth to see the world. Now, how would you like to join in the journey, little miss?'

I was already upon his knees, my eyes glued to the charming creature. I was speechless for the thumping in my breast.

'Ah, I see that you do,' said papa. 'Well, then, you must learn to read. That, my dear, is the very best way to journey about the world.'

Thus was I saved, and, needless to say, I loved that little pink book above any other. It was not only my key to dreams, but a passport into a kingdom of understanding that has to do with charities to which the Marthas of this world remain for ever blind. I was to remember that trifling incident many times, and out of it grew the perception that, like liberty, true benevolence is a quality of mind.

That my mother had assumed the role of a commanding executive in our household was not exactly her fault. By nature she was gay and instinctively averse from conventional strictures that loom so all-important to the average woman. There was no sacred order in her house. If the weekly paper arrived in the midst of washday she would let the water cool and read the serial with no qualms whatsoever. Water could always be reheated, but enthusiasm, once cooled, was stale as a dry herring. We had our meals at the prescribed hours, although, for herself, she cherished no such boresome ritual. No one ever had less interest in food. How she managed to keep so healthy on such sketchy fare is still a mystery. 'If I'm not hungry, why should I eat?' she would say, and sit down with a cup of poisonously strong coffee and her endless knitting. It was the same with clothes. Now, why should she bundle up against the weather, when she never took a chill? In zero weather she hung out the steaming wash, dressed in nothing warmer than a cotton gown and undergarments made from carefully bleached flour sacking. 'Well, what of it?' she would parry. She never caught cold, and, besides, was immune to all diseases.

For her children, it was another story. I, at least, was swaddled in clothes, made to eat when I had no appetite, and, it now seems to me, actually was coddled into the invalidism she meant to avoid. Indeed, it became a kind of sin for me to even think of behaving like other children – a frightful challenge to evil fate even to dream of being well. I suspect there was a wide streak of jealous possessiveness in her character which fixed upon the one thing the world could not snatch from her – the affection of her children. Yet even in this she was not altogether successful. In my case, at least, it was papa who figured actively in my infant brooding. For no matter how gentle and kind mamma might be, and everlastingly concerned for my health, I knew quite well that it was papa who came nearer to understanding me. That this incipient understanding was not permitted to grow and outlast childhood was, I think, my mother's fault. In the end, she weaned me completely away, made an alien of the parent whose vagaries I share, and, as I now know, diverted my normal instincts into channels of activity for which I had no natural talents.

None of this my loving mother meant to do. She was always pathetically eager to plan some happiness for us, to join in the gaiety, however tired she might be. Those early years of unrelieved privation had concentrated into one unbearable memory. Her small son weeping out his heart because on Christmas Eve, when he had set out so stoutly through the storm to attend the church concert, there was not even so much as a red apple on the tree for him. She had not wanted him to go, but he had argued so defensively out of his child's high faith. He had been so good – and did not God love good children? He had watched little sister while mamma worked and tried his best to wait on papa, who was sick in bed. Oh, there would be something on the Christ Child's lovely tree for him – he would not be forgotten because he was little and shy and so very poor.

So now, when things were a little easier – when there was sometimes as much as seven dollars in the weekly pay envelope – why, she naturally was determined to make the most of every festival. My birthday was always a great occasion. I think it marked a sort of conquest over the fear that dogged her mind. I might be doomed, as one doctor had hinted to perish before I ever reached the teens, but each birthday was a milestone conquered. There was one particular birthday I shall never forget. I think I was seven or thereabout. Years did not mean so much, nor do they yet. At any rate, on this occasion mother had set her mind on a big party, a real Icelandic splurge. How hard she worked, God love her. What piles of her paper-thin and widely famed pancakes she made. How fine her fig cake looked in its gleaming brown frosting with the golden flecks winking gemlike on its proud head. What delicious odours teased my curious nose when the Icelandic coffee-bread came from the hot oven. Oh, it was a gallant time, let me tell you!

Nor was that the whole of it. Deep mysteries were brewing. I was sent to bed and enjoined to stay there on pain of severe displeasure, while mother remained in the dim secrecy of the dining-room. She was sewing something I must not see, that I quickly surmised, and squirmed and tossed with curiosity. As a rule I was not given to snooping, for I had scarcely any interest in the events of the common round. The world of my own imagination was much more intriguing and thrice as real. But this was a time of testing for which I had no strength. There came a moment on the day preceding the party when, black guilt on my soul, I decided to break the stern commandment. I actually opened mamma's bureau drawer!

If my heart sank in sore disappointment over what I then discovered, I quickly acknowledged that I probably deserved it. I had been very, very wicked, and wickedness brought its own reward. What I discovered was a huge doll, dressed in a marvellous creation of old rose and yellow silk. Yes, there, before my guilty eyes lay the treasure my mother had been creating. A doll!

How little I wanted a doll! I had hoped it was a dress, or even a new pinafore – but a doll! With tears of mortification and shame streaking my face, I fled back to my corner. Oh, how was I to meet the horrible experience that awaited me? Mamma would expect me to be so thrilled. And at the moment it seemed to me I should never be happy again. Dolls were such stupid things. I had no mothering instincts whatsoever. Never, in my entire childhood, did the game of motherhood enter my head. I had squads of paper dolls, it is true, but these were amenable personages. Sometimes they were a congregation, harangued by a fat brown fellow who reminded me of a country preacher I had seen. Sometimes they formed a company headed for adventure. They were, in fact, characters that acted out my fluent tales. They were people, and I loved them, but what was I to do with a huge yellow-headed thing of sawdust and porcelain?

Another horrid thought assailed me. Mother might expect me to keep the creature in the little wicker carriage I had received last Christmas. That would be the end of everything. Almost since the beginning it had served as a bed for my two cats. They had been dear, fluffy kittens when it arrived, and had quickly learned to sleep stretched out like little gentlemen, each on his pillow, one at the foot, the other at the head. Now much too large to share the coveted bed, they fought for its possession, the victor still taking his siesta stretched full length and purring loudly. Cats were the joy of my life. I loved them for their grace and independence. I respected them because they brooked no discourtesy and gave their affection only where it was deserved. They were my unfailing confidants, and I never doubted they understood me, and thoroughly appreciated the yarns I spun for them.

One of the cats seemed especially addicted to solemn philosophy. He used to sit at my knees, his green eyes fixed on the middle distance, and purr in a professional rumble as I gabbled on. 'Yes, yes, that's a likely tale, my child,' he seemed to be purring, 'but oh, what glamorous mysteries my inner vision beholds, to which you, poor dear, are blind as the blindest mouse!'

Naturally, it was to Gráni I now poured out my woeful confession.

'I have been very, very bad,' I told him, rubbing his elastic back. 'I have been snooping in mamma's bureau – a thing even papa hesitates to do. And what did I get for my courage, do you suppose? A doll! A stiff, wretched doll!'

Next morning I slept late, and was wakened by the entrance of mamma and a woman friend who was helping with the party. They came in smiling, and mamma, bending to kiss me, said, 'God bless you, dear, on this and every birthday.' Then, with tender pride, she brought from behind her back the big blonde doll in all its silken splendour. It was the moment I never forgot. I was so utterly ashamed I could only gaze at her speechless. Which fetched the coals upon my head. With the happiest expression, mamma turned to her friend.

'Bless her little heart – she's absolutely overcome!' she said. 'Dear little soul – she never had a pretty doll before.'

What a worm I felt. How dearly I should have loved to confess and cry out my wickedness. Instead, I hugged the beastly doll, and stupidly blinked my eyes. No doubt I looked a stolid simpleton. I was so often accused of letting the cat get my tongue that I have no doubt whatever that my queer silences were usually interpreted as a lack of intelligence. I sometimes think I must have been rather stupid in those years of recurrent illness. I remember so little of the actual daily happening around me, and yet I was always acutely aware of moods, and while I sat so stolidly in my place I never missed a single oddity of behaviour in the occasional visitor. Voices, gestures, a colourful phrase even though meaningless at the time, these stayed with me. So, too, I might be in the grip of some undefined emotion, and, like the wind out of a clear sky, thoughts undreamed before would swoop across my mind. So now I suddenly perceived with incontestable reason that truthfulness was not always a virtue. I could not now hurt mamma's feelings just to give myself the relief of confessing what I had done and how mistaken she was in her good intentions. Mamma was a great stickler for truth, for speaking her mind, and not giving any false impressions. Just the same, I knew now what papa meant when he argued that kindness was much more important than the conceits of a Puritan conscience. Not, of course, that I put it to myself in those words. I just decided that I would do as papa often did – say nothing, and let truth take care of itself.

How I scowled at that yellow-headed doll when the women moved off, cheerfully satisfied, as adults generally were with all their mistaken efforts on behalf of children. How I hated the smiling beauty. How disgusted I was to have to parade it as my dear treasure before the guests that night. Truly a time of hemlock retribution. Still, truth compels me to admit that everything was not gall and wormwood. In fact, delicious excitement triumphed so soon as the odious courtesy was off my mind. So many little gifts were showered upon me – even a bright new dollar, which I was permitted to hold for a minute or two. Later it would go for cod-liver oil, but now it was mine, and how rich I felt. Indeed, everything went off remarkably well, until Mrs

Swainson, mamma's best friend, brought her young son Johnny, who, quaking but obedient, handed me a mysterious package. Now, Johnny was a very nice boy, for whom I had a deep, though secret affection. He was almost as easy to play with as Gráni, my cat. We were really the best of companions, and therefore understood that our attachment was not to be flaunted under adult noses. Yet, here he was, made to hand me this gift, with every one looking on, and I must open the package. When the paper came off, my eyes nearly popped out of my head. Dear me! here was a treasure. I simply couldn't credit my vision. Think of it! There on the rustly paper lay a silver-plated belt such as Icelandic women wear on their national dress, and it was set with my blue birth stones.

'Now, picture that!' a laughing voice exclaimed. 'The little lover brings his dear the bridal belt. Now, surely he gets a kiss for it!'

Gracious goodness! Kiss Johnny – kiss my good friend! Frantically my glances swept the grown-up faces. Oh, were such fools ever! How could they ask me to do such a thing to a decent little boy! I did not have to look at Johnny to know how horrified he was – how he would hate me if I let him be thus humiliated. A stout female with a determined expression edged closer. I did not wait for the mischief I knew she contemplated. With a muffled squeal, I bolted from the scene. Laughter pursued me, horrid peals of merriment that brought a nervous dew out on my skin.

Thanks to mamma, who, at that moment, announced that the table was spread, I got away. With no thought to the fine feast I was missing, I tore up the stairs, my one conscious desire to hide away for ever. Mamma's room had a big closet, and I would creep into that, I thought, and then it occurred to me that such an obvious place was worse than none. There was no other hiding-place – but wait! There was! After all, I wasn't very big, and that old-fashioned washstand of mamma's stood waist high. I could easily squeeze into that.

When I wrenched open the double doors, I saw something that so astonished me and enthralled me that every fear fled. It was a blue paper box, parading four full rows of fat chocolate pigs with beautiful pink eyes! No need to tell me whose gift this was. Only papa would have thought of such a delightfully useless present. Why, I didn't even eat candy. I could play with my darling fat pigs, and in due course give each away as the sacrificial spirit moved me. I was so thrilled at the rosy prospect that I forgot Johnny. I forgot the party I was missing. I just sat there in utter bliss, twelve pink-eyed porkers on the floor before me, happy as a herdsman on a sunny hill, when papa himself came to find me. 'Dear me, whatever have you there?' said he, his eyes twinkling. 'Now, why should any one give sweets to a child that doesn't eat them?'

'Because that's why!' I shouted. And, somehow, we perfectly understood each other.

There was another time when papa turned disappointment to joy. It was Christmas, and mamma, still convinced that her birthday gift had been a huge success, gave me two little dolls – one dressed in the Icelandic national costume, the other like a sailor. As often happened, she was much too busy to notice my lack of enthusiasm. Anyway, she had taken such pains with the little dress, how could any child be other than pleased? And now she was making the Christmas chocolate. My sister Anna was there, now a pretty teen-age girl who sang in the church choir and seemed to me a paragon of all the maidenly graces. She had brought her guitar, and very likely would sing a duet with brother Minty in the course of the evening. Every one was very gay, and made a fuss over my novel presents. And no wonder, for the little dolls had each a tiny chair with a real plush bottom! Yet I hung about with a sober face, saying nothing whatsoever.

'Well! Well!' papa suddenly exclaimed. 'I don't wonder you look thoughtful, Lalla. A bride and groom on your hands, without a moment's warning. Now, what do you say to a wedding?'

'A wedding! But, papa – what to do for a minister?' I queried, eager enough, now that a game was to be played.

'Tut tut! Fetch my frock coat, and you shall see,' papa answered. Sure enough, when he had donned the old Prince Albert and set his face in a serious mould, papa might easily have passed for

'His Reverence.' Unless, of course, you caught the sly twinkle in his eye. But the dolls never guessed. Very eloquently, he read them the marriage service, with every one gathered round, and when all was done mamma's Christmas chocolate did double service. We toasted the bridal pair in the first cup, and drank the second to celebrate a happy Icelandic *Jule*.

It was all very jolly. The dolls were set on a shelf near the little tree, and when we had sampled every one of mamma's culinary marvels, we drew up our chairs in a ring while papa lighted the candles. The coal-oil lamp was dimmed and while the little golden flames leaped and flickered upon the sweet green branches, we sang the old old songs of the dear Christ Child and his holy maiden mother. And, sitting there in utter quietness, mamma's face was somehow changed – as though in this moment of blessed peace all the tenderness she hid in her heart were shining through the flesh. I should like to have told her how radiant she seemed, but for that I had no words. I could only cling to her hand when she came, that night, as always, to wish me good rest, to say, with old-world grace: 'God grant you good night!'

13

Tales strange and varied

It is undoubtedly true that human perceptions are not only widely different in their accuracy and acuteness, but that even in the case of each individual the growing awareness of the world is far from being an orderly process of development. In my own case, for instance, I seem to have been relatively untouched by the daily bustle round me, forming no faintest idea of even the most commonplace happenings, whereas I was always peculiarly sensitive to varying moods, and read into gestures and the odd high-sounding phrase all manner of provocative meanings and possibilities. Which is only to say that, so far as my fundamental characteristics were concerned, I was potentially a true Icelander. For the Icelander, tempered by centuries of cataclysmic disasters that have taught him the impermanence and inadequacy of material possessions, is more likely to be keenly engrossed with problems of time than of space. The ancient Norsemen set great store by pomp and circumstance, like the Greeks, to whose classics the sagas are comparable, they delighted in physical prowess and beauty, in everything that pleasured the five senses. But, as time rolled on and all these things were senselessly destroyed by senseless nature, their descendants came by degrees to fix the quest of their restless souls on imperishable concepts. Less and less they coveted and prized externals, and embraced instead beauties of the mind and heart.

This, I suppose, is the reason why so many Icelanders of the older generation were seemingly oblivious of their lack of trimness and taste in their houses, although they might discourse with understanding and deep insight on the elegance of literature and philosophy. As a matter of fact, most foreign visitors to Iceland find it necessary to comment upon what strikes them as most singular: that not infrequently some uncouth-looking farmer whose entire days have been spent in the fields, has, upon the least encouragement, launched into an animated discussion of subjects of this kind. The simple explanation is, of course, that the Icelander prizes intellect as other nations prize money, and that his true solace lies in spiritual abstractions. Consequently, he is not religious in the conventional sense, for religion is rooted in materialism. In its final analysis, it is a doctrine of me and mine, a sanctifier of property, patriotism, and war, and its ultimate glory is a triumphant entry into paradise. Perverse though it may seem, the thinking Icelander has, whether he knows it or not, reverted to the old common sense of his Viking ancestors, whose gods were merely symbols of abstract qualities, and to whom the creative force of the universe remained the Nameless One, unconditioned by time and space. In this scientific day the terminology has changed, but the idea is the same. The old Vikings spoke of death as a passing to 'The Other Light.' The modern Icelander thinks of dissolution as a return to the elements. And, in both instances, the obvious, the tangible, and concrete were recognized for what they are – perishable symbols of an imperishable power flowing on towards some dim, undivined fruition. For which reason, causes, rather than acts, engage our interests, and our standard of values is based upon lasting reality. No doubt these pleasant conceits will be wiped out of us in this enlightened country, Canada, where everything from a baby's bonnet to a literary masterpiece is conscientiously gauged by dollars and cents. But, as yet, those of us who were conditioned in old-fashioned homes cling to the delusion that what a man has is of less importance than what he is. For, say we, in the height of our folly, it is even conceivable that an unfortuitous series of circumstances might annihilate one or all of the Ford plants, but less likely that Mr Ford himself should be knocked on the head. Moreover, we are hideously sceptical of any art which is worn like a mental bustle to lend a bump of importance to an otherwise undeveloped space.

That I was a victim of that sort of conditioning there seems no doubt. Even as a child I was bored with the familiar and commonplace, and sought to escape into a weird world of fabulous imaginings. Because I could not attend school for reasons of ill health, this silly habit of dreaming became a sort of obsession, so that I walked about with my head full of imaginary people, whose perplexities and peccadilloes became my own. I talked to myself in several voices, and argued at length the destinies of hypothetical sprites and spirits. When, on rare occasions, I enjoyed a real companion, I naturally tyranized the show, for how could I play like other children when I had never been permitted to risk my precious skin in such happy pastimes? But if I knew nothing about pom-pom-pullaway, drop-the-hand-kerchief, and puss-in-the-corner, I could quickly improvise a dramatic situation with nothing better than a shawl, some chairs, and a pillow or two. I could walk about, imitating the wrath of God slaying the Egyptians, or, less thrilling, adopt the dignified mien of the good old homoeopathic doctor, and save, one by one, the suffering pillows from the vapours, biliousness, and lumbago.

There was nothing particularly clever or remarkable in these fabrications, but they served me well as an antidote for boredom on those sunny days when I must watch the antics of happier children from the prison square of my window. If my immediate world was confined to cough syrups, mustard plasters, and turnip soup, I could, at least, forswear these horrors in the jealous kingdom of my imagination.

So, too, if adult conversation centred upon sickness, struggles, and want, I drew back into my shell of cultivated inattention. Yet, so soon as the topic swerved to less familiar subjects, my ears were keen enough. I recall one hushed conversation to which I should have been deaf. A flibbertigibbet woman had deserted her two-year-old son and a husband who adored her, to run off with a scallawag paramour.

'He just a smooth-tongued wastrel!' exclaimed our informer, unctuously. 'An unholy rascal! The wretched woman has no sense at all – the soulless wench. To desert her own child – *Herra Gud*! If that were the end – what's to become of the little —' and she crossed her arms over an ample bosom, rocking to and fro, developing suspense with unconscious delight, while mamma, coffee-pot in hand, waited for the conclusion.

'Ja, ja,' sighed my parent, sympathetic but impatient. 'Out with it, Kristine. What has the poor man done, for I take it that's what you're coming to?'

Kristine groaned, her eyes accusative and wet. 'Ha! What could he have done, God rest him, loving that frivolous creature, as men will, the fools! Yes, what? What, but died of a broken heart!'

This final bit of acting was so mournfully sepulchral that the flesh wriggled on my bones and my stomach hitched itself into a hard knot under my breastbone. To die of a broken heart, I at once perceived, was indeed a terrible business, and the cause of it no better than a Jezebel. For our visitor further related how the maddened husband, in the dead of night, had wandered into the vicinity of the hospital and shot himself. 'And his brains scattered on the common walk!' sobbed Kristine, between bites of doughnut. 'You may call it death by a bullet,' said she, 'or suicide, more like, but that's not what the Day of Judgement will call it!'

Sure, and even I could guess that much! It was the flibbertigibbet wench killed him. Long after my bedtime I lay awake, with a hand to my breast, trying to suffer, as that poor man had suffered, speculatively awaiting the first indications of an acute internal eruption certain to end in a broken heart.

Thereafter, I used to watch women on the street, trying to distinguish the incipient Jezebel from her commonplace sisters, the light hussy from sensible females who trundled babies and trailed their voluminous alpaca skirts in the mud. I fared rather badly at the game, however, for the drabness of our neighbourhood was only surpassed by its virtue, and even my tolerant imagination balked at attributing glamour to the straight-haired,

firmly corsetted females who billowed by. Yet, fortunately for
my weavings, our house was a centre for all sorts of odd characters. Some one was always popping in from the country, or
near-by villages, with tales strange and varied.

There was Rosa, for instance. A pretty Icelandic girl, so the tale
went, but giddy in the head. So giddy, in fact, that she took up
with a Frenchman – and he a Roman Catholic. Yes indeed! The
silly girl met him at a picnic, and proceeded to beguile him to
such an extent that, by New Year's Day, he was ready, and even
eager, to take part in the Elf Dance. Now, as every one knows,
the Elf Dance should be conducted by intimates and lovers, for
the Little People are most particular that way. Their morals are
shocked by frivolities of the heart. Besides, it is undoubtedly a
pretty sight when sweethearts, arms linked, and lighted candles
in their hands, go dancing down a frozen stream on the peal of
midnight. For, as you must guess, the stars are then reflected in
smiling youthful eyes, and the greetings they shout to the Little
People are as warm and sincere as their heart's devotion.

Dear me! Poor Rosa seems to have thought more of showing
off her paces and a new red bonnet than of the custom itself, or
of the consequences of wheeling through the starlight with a
romantic Frenchman by her side. So, of course, they fell in love,
but under the ban of the offended Little People. Which may, or
may not explain the blight that fell upon them. For, can you
believe it, when little Rosa, red as a peony, and simpering like an
infant brook, told her papa the glorious news, the good man was
horrified. Never, in his wildest nightmares, had he suffered such
a shock! A Frenchman, and an idolator! Why, he refused point-
blank to give the creature house-room, let alone his daughter.
Nor was Pierre's mamma one wit better. Passionately, she
implored the saints to strike her dead if ever she consented to
such a preposterous union.

Goodness me, how the Little People must have snickered up
their sleeves, as the mischief grew from bad to worse. Never
dreaming that boastful mortals, who aspire to vanquish the
earth and rule the seven heavens, wouldn't find a happy solution for a little problem in random love. But there it was: the old

folks thundered, and the young folks sulked. When flesh could bear no more, Rosa stole into the fields to weep on Pierre's shoulder, and he, poor lad, shaken to the marrow, threatened heaven and earth – but not mamma.

Of piety and paprika there can be too much. Poor Pierre was seasoned too highly to withstand the boilings and bubblings of carnal passions. He hanged himself in the cowshed. 'Oh well, virtue is its own reward,' papa commented dryly, and added, 'That pious old beldam should be satisfied – her son chose Purgatory, rather than bliss with a heretic!'

As for Rosa, softly fashioned for a man's arms, and unburdened with brains, she took the blow philosophically. To be sure, she wept for a week, and wore a black ribbon on her sleeve for the rest of the season; but in the fall she cheerfully married a gentleman who possessed a good team of oxen, a quarter section of ploughed land, three cows, and her parents' admiration was unbounded because he played the harmonica and was a God-fearing Lutheran.

There were other tales, no less interesting, though without romantic connotations. Tales of quiet heroism, enacted by quite ordinary people. Gimli pioneers were fond of telling how a certain farmer, with little to commend him by way of concrete accomplishments, had, none the less, saved his daughter's life by a spectacular feat of endurance. The family lived near Sandy Bar, isolated from neighbours, and, even when the lake froze over, it was an arduous trip to Gimli if the snowfall was heavy, or the winds raging. But when the child was stricken with high fever and symptoms terrifying to the parents, the lake was far from safe. Yet the father set out in the teeth of the storm, determined to make the passage. He was a famous sprinter, and, in his speed, half-blinded by the snow that clung like frozen tears to his eyes, he fell into a wide fissure. Weighted with heavy clothes and cowhide boots, he thrashed about in the water, dodging moving ice, and finally, when almost prostrate, reached safety on the other side. By the time he reached the doctor's house, he was literally armoured in ice that had to be chipped from his clothing.

The doctor admired his courage, but not to the point of emulating such a crazy venture. He prescribed for the child to the best of his ability, furnished the required medicines, and with that the father was well content. For it meant he could return more swiftly, unhampered by a stoutish gentleman with no taste for berserk exploits. Nor would he wait for the dawn. Not he! A quart of coffee and a shot of rum were all the support he needed.

It is pleasant to know that the small daughter recovered, and that her father's devotion became a tale told with honest wonder for the edification of a softer, sophisticated second generation.

The laurels were not always for the sterner sex. There was Great-Aunt Steinun, as brave a little lady as ever faced the wilderness. She came to Canada in the first immigration, as we called it. That is to say, with that group of twelve hundred settlers who arrived in 1872, destined for the Gimli and Icelandic River settlements. Through the negligence of the immigration officials in Montreal, these poor, weary home-seekers were made to spend the night in quarters that had housed some Indians polluted with small-pox. Consequently, the immigrants had barely reached their destination when the plague broke out. And, for eighteen months, homeless and helpless, without medical supervision, they were quarantined in the swamps of Gimli.

Now that Gimli has become a favourite summer resort, with railway flier service to Winnipeg, it is difficult to conceive of a time when all the surrounding country was a fly-infested quagmire, through which, in rainy seasons, you had to wade knee-high. Homesteads were often under water for weeks in the spring, the wretched inmates clinging to the damp shelter of their miserable log huts until the water invaded the firebox of the stove, thereby routing the last shreds of comfort.

Great-Aunt Steinun's first shelter in Gimli was a roofless log enclosure, so full of water that her husband had to build a raft on which to lay their beds. A foolish sort of arrangement, you may think, but, to quote the little lady: 'It broke the October winds and kept us from floating all over the field.'

In such surroundings, the travel-worn immigrants had to meet and suffer the horrors of small-pox, alternating their labours of burying the dead with felling green timber for huts to house the living. Great-Aunt Steinun, though fond enough of reminiscing, did not like to dwell on the epidemic. It was too painful to think of the sodden graves that marked the end of so many fair hopes – and more painful still to remember that one hundred and twenty-five babies literally died of starvation. Poor innocents! How desperately their mothers tried to keep them alive on fish broth and bean stock, the only substitutes available for the milk which could not be had. The Government had intended to supply the settlers with cattle, but all such worthy plans were disrupted and long delayed by the raging pestilence. It was hard enough to get staple foods to the people, to say nothing of livestock and luxuries. Every few weeks the Mounted Police rode up to a specified zone with rations of salt, pork, and beans, food the Icelanders had never before tasted, and, consequently, found indigestible fare in their enfeebled condition.

Terrible though these trials were, the sorest weight upon great-aunt's heart was the uncertainty concerning her eldest daughter. This girl, about fourteen years old, had been sent into service by the immigration authorities, it being their thought she was well able to support herself in the city. In the general confusion of settling so many people, they had, however, omitted to leave the girl's address with her parents, and when the plague set in it was, of course, impossible to communicate this or any other information to the immigrants. During all those frightful months, Great-Aunt Steinun was haunted by the thought that this dearest of her children might have contracted the disease, and perhaps died among strangers indifferent to her suffering and loneliness. Nor was she relieved of this worry when the quarantine was lifted. By that time no one in the immigration bureau even remembered the girl, and it was not until three years later that the family was reunited.

What I like best to remember about Great-Aunt Steinun, however, has to do with an incident which, to my mind, surpasses all others in her hard experience and throws a revealing light upon her forceful character. It happened that, while raising his permanent house Mr Haldorson, her husband, cut his foot rather badly, yet continued his labour, giving slight heed to the wound. An infection set in, which, as the days passed, grew steadily worse, until it was no longer possible for him to keep on his feet, and, as the fever mounted, it was obvious that his condition was rapidly becoming critical. Their homestead, like so many others, was isolated, far from any neighbour. They had no means of conveyance, no draft beast of any kind, and Winnipeg was sixty miles away.

Great-Aunt Steinun was not the sort of woman to sit weeping, waiting for some miracle of grace. What they did possess was a crude hand sleigh for hauling wood. Her mind made up, she poured water on the wooden runners, affixed a rude harness, and, overruling Mr Haldorson's dismayed objections, pronounced herself ready to take him to Winnipeg. But when the sick man had been made as comfortable as the means permitted, Steinun was momentarily panic-striken. She realized suddenly that she had not the slightest idea, beyond an indefinite direction, how to reach Winnipeg. Her husband was no better informed. They had only made the journey once before, in the company of the other immigrants. Besides, the poor man by now was half delirious with fever.

'I thought for a moment that no one had ever been left so helpless,' she used to say. 'Then I was ashamed of myself. What was the good of having a God you wouldn't trust as well as your neighbour, I asked myself? So then and there I started, and, at the edge of the lake, put it up to the Almighty. Whatever thought He put in my head, I would take for guidance. And that's what I did.'

There, according to Great-Aunt Steinun, the tale rightly ended, for she was always loath to delineate personal hardships. Sometimes, however, especially if the listener were sceptical of divine provision, she might supply the remaining details. Drawing that cumbrous sleigh, with its human burden, was in itself a task beyond the normal strength of a little woman scarcely five feet tall, worn with vigils over the sick and dying, and in all probability under-nourished. Yet she trekked on bravely, over the lonely waste of ice, only pausing to rest when the heavy pounding of her heart made her dizzy. Hours later, a wind sprang up, with driving puffs of snow – not the gentle flakes of a milder climate, but the dry, powdered concomitant of a gathering blizzard. No one who has not experienced this phenomenon of the prairie can possibly imagine how quickly a peaceful landscape is changed to an inferno of lashing wind and whirling clouds of snow that sting the eyes and stifle the breath, and obliterate every familiar object.

'Oh, it was a bit of a struggle, to be sure,' she admitted. 'What of it? I had put myself in God's care. Humanly speaking, I was lost, I suppose, and the strength flowing out of me like water from a cracked crock. But again, what of that? Before I was overcome, an Indian found us, and took us home to his tepee.

'That was a lesson, let me tell you. The young squaw massaged my frozen feet with a mixture of bear's grease and some sort of herb. She fed us from the family pot, and, before I set out once more, dressed me in deerskin leggings and moccasins lined with moss. Ah, they were good, those two brown people. They shared all they had with us and when the storm was over that fierce-looking brave saw me off on the right trail. So you see if my husband was saved, it was not all my doing, but a miracle of God's mercy, working through the simple heart of a savage.'

Sometimes these homespun yarns had a humorous twist, even when the undertones were sober. I remember the hair-raising experience of an old charwoman whom the young wags loved to terrorize with tall tales of Indian atrocities. She lived alone in a tiny shanty on Point Douglas, and though her days were devoted to monotonous labour she was always exuberant in praise of her many blessings. Had she not a cosy shelter for her old bones, food in the larder, and good Manitoba spruce cut to fit her carron stove laid in against the winter? What was more, had not the blessed Lord given her a knack with the little ones, and more than enough strength and patience to struggle with spotted linen and pine boards, so that, whatever the ladies in their big houses required of her, it was always well and respectably done, and she paid with a cheery heart that often expressed itself in a cast-off petticoat or a queerish bonnet, in addition to wages?

Blessed she certainly was, and, except for that menace of red-skins, found the New World all that one might have expected, since the good God made it.

There came a chill October evening when this fixed obsession was especially rampant. It was cold, with flurries of snow, and shadows long and black on the river bank. A night for evil deeds, thought poor old Ellen, and quickened her stride, despite the crick in her back. On such a night it was good to have a secure shelter, a bit of a place that kept one safe from savage eyes. The sight of her tar-paper shack, hidden in a windbreak of ragged poplars, drew a sigh of happiness from her heart. In no time at all she would be toasting her toes by the stove, and the cat purring his gladness.

She was an orderly soul, and always laid the fire before she went to work in the morning. She had only to drop a match on the kindling to start a cheery blaze, light the wall lamp, and set the kettle on for coffee. This done, she usually called the cat, removing her wraps while Thomas took his time responding, and then shut and barred the door for the night. But now, chilled and blue from the biting wind, she thought of the woodbox, and frowned to discover that she had forgotten to fill it. Well, thought Ellen, that's what comes of sleeping in for fifteen minutes! Now she must fetch and carry, though nineteen devils plagued her back. Grumbling, she flung wide the door, 'Thomas' framed on her tongue, but neither that nor any other sound came from her lips. As stricken as Lot's sinful wife, she stood there, her horrified eyes fixed upon the road. God and his angels help her! Plain as the nose on her face, the doom she dreaded marched upon her. Three dusky, buckskinned knaves were striding towards the house, snow whirling round their horrid heads, a long lean hound loping at their heels. She was so frightened, so certain of the inevitable end, that it never occurred to her that she might shut the door, and, by this simple act, escape an unwelcome visitation. Instead, she stood there, too petrified for speech, while the strangers, who, politely enough, asked for shelter, filed in, and with grunts of satisfaction seated themselves on the bench before the table. Evidently they wanted food, as well as shelter, thought the old woman, dim stirrings of rising anger minimizing her fear. The scallawags! Why didn't they kill her and be done! Why must they prolong the agony, the murdering villains! She supposed they would scalp her as a matter of course, for she had long, yellow hair. Just the sort of hair braves love to dangle from their belts, so the wags had assured her. Just the same, there they sat, hungrily, eyeing the kettle. Well, thought Ellen, gathering what wit she had, and hurrying to the cupboard, if she must so shortly meet her Maker, she might as well do it without the sin of inhospitality on her soul. As glumly silent as her company, she laid the supper, which was eaten in typical Indian stolidity, and at its conclusion the trio plunged down upon the floor, prepared to sleep. Even the hound had dropped in a weary loop before the glowing stove.

Ellen was now completely mystified. Was it possible she had misjudged the wanderers? Or were they, perchance, waiting some prescribed ritualistic hour for their evil purpose? Whatever their designs, she had not the heart to let them lie on the cold, bare boards uncovered. Gingerly, she crossed behind the human huddle, and from an old wooden trunk fetched two patchwork quilts for their comfort. A grunt, thoroughly unnerving, was all the thanks she received.

There was nothing more that could be done. She dared not even call the cat. Poor Thomas must take his ease where he found it. Grieved for her pet, whose place was usurped by a smelly mongrel, she restocked the fire, and, musing upon the uncertainty of life, decided that she might as well snatch a wink of sleep to support her through the ordeal to come. With shaking fingers she removed the lamp from its bracket and bore it to the home-made table beside the bed, which occupied the far corner, and was neatly dressed in a cretonne cover and long, frilled valance. Being a modest female, she naturally meant to lie down fully clothed, howsoever her stays pinched. But the fine spread and valance must be removed. This done, she lay down, and then, the breath rattling in her throat, cautiously leaned out and extinguished the light.

Almost instantly hell broke loose. With a savage scraping of nails upon the floor, and hair-raising snarls from a cavernous chest, the great hound came hurtling across the room and dived under the bed. The sleepers sprang to their feet. Some one relit the lamp. Then, to the quaking woman, it seemed that men and dog were inextricably mixed in a heaving, howling *mêlée*. A nightmare of fury too swift to follow or comprehend, until the din of battle died away, and there was stamped upon her mind the ineradicable vision of a hulking negro who had been dragged from under her bed, and now hung limply in the iron grasp of the Metis.

Thereupon, realizing the miracle of her deliverance, poor old Ellen promptly fainted. When she regained consciousness the house was sheathed in silence. The red eye of the stove blinked beneficently through the dusk. The dog breathed like a cheerful bellows, and the angels she had entertained unaware snored in solid comfort.

Oh, but she was sore ashamed! Never again would she believe those tales of evil – never, never! In the morning she would open a jar of strawberry jam and fry a batch of flatbread. Other things as well she planned, and, in the midst of it, fell sound asleep – for fear may reign an hour, but old bones require rest. When she wakened the fire was crackling, and the kettle sang, and the bright prairie sunshine was a sunburst of joy on the window-pane. What happiness it now was to hustle up the meal. How glad she was that her bit of cooking was always a matter of pride – her flatbread golden-brown, and her tea hot and fragrant.

This morning she would have welcomed a little chatter to open the way for the question that burned her mind. But the visitors ate all that was set before them in unbroken silence. Not a murmur out of any of them. Not a single reference to the terrible incident of the night before. They behaved just as though nothing out of the ordinary had happened – just as though they had not saved her life.

Not until they were leaving was a word spoken, and then it was an irrelevant question, flung out with a sudden dazzling smile by the youngest of the trio.

'You like moose meat?' he asked. Yes, yes, she did, Ellen acknowledged. 'Good,' said he, and the others nodded. They would bring her some on their way back from the north.

'But — but —' stammered Ellen, 'I want to know – I've got to know —' And there words failed her.

It was then that the nut-brown ancient whose wrinkled face had struck the deepest terror to Ellen's heart spoke for the first time. Drawing himself up to his full, fine height, and swinging his arm in a majestic curve toward the Red River, he said, with proud finality:

'Heap much gone hell!'

As I think of it now, it seems to me that, despite the general hardship of our existence in those vanished days, life itself supplied us with sufficient interesting drama. We were rich in characters. It was not so important then as now for every one to be as like his neighbour as two rabbits in a taxidermist's window. Even quite fine ladies went in for little mild eccentricities. They strove for the unique, rather than the popular, and prided themselves on certain delicate, cultured reactions. As a rule, these ethical distinctions were a challenge to the flesh and the devil. One virtuous female, for instance, went about in nine petticoats. Another boasted, discreetly, of course, that never, in the entire course of her married life, had she disrobed in the light! This was the more remarkable, since the lady was reasonably good to look upon. Another good woman saved the morals of the neighbourhood by hanging her personal wear in a shed, out of sight. These excellent creatures were, in their opinion, delicacy personified, and had the same claim to virtue as the good Queen, who still graced the throne of England. Indeed, they fainted at the least hint of coarseness, and upon occasion, had to be helped from the meeting-house if the Pastor chose too sulphuric a topic. This was always a telling act if an attractive male happened to be near. Next to the dainty swoon, poetry was a genuine asset to any unattached female. An enduring asset, I might add, for, years later, when my small world had been greatly extended, I met a pathetically plain spinster who recited 'The Sonnets From the Portuguese' with such passionate abandon as would certainly have annihilated poor 'Ba.' The poor old girl was an exponent of culture, garbed herself in grey and leaf-brown, and never, under any circumstances, clipped her words like the abominable bar-

barians across the border. Commonplace as a sparrow, she was fond of quoting that beauty is only skin deep, and swatted every attempted argument on the social inequalities by murmuring that God was in His heaven, and all was right with the world. But, in those older days, there were ladies of equally fixed principles who were gifted with sufficient genius to inflict their preferences upon less admirable mortals. Such a one was old Rebecca. Her fetish was temperance, and her affliction a wayward spouse. Reason failing to cure the culprit, she sewed him up in bedsheets, administered a sound whipping, and promised a similar correction upon all or any occasion when his pleasant vice reduced him to helpless slumber. What was more, if he misbehaved in the near future she would leave him sewed up in a bolster until the minister saw fit to release him, for she herself wouldn't raise the scissors on his behalf! The threat was so effective that Rebecca's Cure became a byword among the less valiant, who envied, but dared not copy, such admirable measures.

The lordly male had other weaknesses, I was led to infer from guarded gossip and innuendo. The fine-whiskered creatures had too keen an eye for slim ankles and soft bosoms not theirs under divine contract. What was worse, the rascals slipped from grace without any appreciable shame or evil consequence. They carried on as shamelessly as Solomon with Sheba, secure in the knowledge that wives were by law and common acceptance little better than chattel, and that, to boot, the Holy Scriptures upheld the dominance of the male, in everything from petticoats to predicating piety.

This pleasant state of affairs was, none the less, not always maintained at even keel. There were rebels even in the Victorian harems – wives, if you will, who tired of the holiness of unquestioning submission and, with the vindictiveness of less fortunate females, sought redress for their long-suffered slights.

One gentle-spoken lady, whose tragic tale I have approximated elsewhere, once turned the tables on her philandering husband by installing his enamorata in the guest-room of her house. To say that the master was rudely shaken infers too little.

The poor man exploded. Shocked to the depths of his Victorian soul at the sight of his wife and the glamorous hussy chatting amicably over the breakfast table, manners flew windward, and his righteous indignation boiled over. What the devil did his lady mean by such scandalous behaviour? Had she lost her senses? How dared she invite such a – such a – well, such a person into the same house with his children? To which the maddening woman merely replied that, so far as she knew, *her* friends had always been perfectly safe companions for the children, and would so continue to be. What could you do with such a wife, I wonder – what, indeed, but build a new house, and henceforth curtail, within reason, those enchanting primrose pastimes.

True, grown-ups were a queer lot; that I perceived, as the small years lengthened and these tales were stored up in memory. At first I had expected unalloyed wisdom from my elders, for were they not swift and eager to point out the stupidities of a child? To confound what seemed the straightness of truth with complexities of conduct beyond my understanding, and which I must of course accept as right and proper? Unhappily for me, I discovered too quickly that adult reasoning was a curious process, as often as not quite divorced from common sense. For example, it was surely common sense not to eat what made you ill, but all the same the rule did not apply to whatever article of food the doctrines of the moment held to be most nutritious. So, however your stomach revolted, you swallowed what mamma or papa decided was good for you, simply because mamma or papa said so. The same was true of moral and religious mendacity. Every decent child must learn to be truthful, modest, and obedient, and under no condition to interfere with the rights and privileges of others. All of which, high sounding and splendid, was tremendously appealing, until it dawned on me that almost every act of my own life was interfered with by somebody, and without rhyme or reason. In matters of faith I fared much better than most children, as I was to learn much later. I was never forced to accept as literal the external word trappings of mythology, nor was I encouraged to feed my own conceit by the happy supposition that every one who adhered to another faith was at least a fool, if not actually predestined to everlasting damnation. In other words, although I had to accept as right and proper the superficialities of human conduct, I was not hedged about in my thinking by any orthodox strictures, and, therefore, in my own childish way, I began very early to form judgements and estimates of those happenings that stirred my imagination.

There was one tale above all others that captured my heart, and which to this day seems to me more eloquent of goodness than any organized charity. It had to do with a young Icelandic doctor, whose passion for the poor and the outcast was only equalled by his enslavement to liquor. He was too sensitive to suffering, and resented too deeply the inequalities of a social system that admitted of no practical cure for the miseries of the many. Old people who still remember him with affection shake their heads that such a brilliant man should have ruined himself with drink. With the untroubled judgement of mediocrity, which never sounds the heights or depths of profound emotion, they deplore what they consider to have been the weakness in his character, never suspecting that, without his vulnerability of spirit, the tenderness they admire could not have existed. For it was an excess of sympathy, weariness, and tortured nerves that drove him to luckless oblivion.

It is said that, toward the end of his ill-starred career, his colleagues would hunt for him through the taverns and saloons of the town, and literally carry him back to the hospital, where some serious operation required the magic they all conceded to his skilful fingers. 'Get him sober, damn it, no matter how!'

Faced by an emergency, by the sight of a poor, tortured creature crying for relief, the man had an almost superhuman way of snapping back to instantaneous efficiency. So the legend went.

He was a stormy soul, too swift in justice for the stone mouths of Victorian mercy. One incident, out of a meteoric career that leaves one a little stunned by its brilliant warm-heartedness, leaves all others outclassed. Or so it seemed to me. It had to do with a wretchedly poor woman who, like so many others of her kind, had established a home of sorts on the 'flats' – the lowly portion of the Red River banks which now have been filled in and built over with wholesale houses. As so often happens with the poor, this woman had refrained from seeking medical aid for her ailing child because of poverty. There was scarcely enough to eat. How then should she pay a doctor?

Besides, was there not God, to whom the miseries of the outcast are a special charge? Surely the Divine Ear must heed and comprehend such dire necessity? Surely her prayers would be answered, for had she not always been told that faith, though no larger than a mustard seed, would remove mountains? Night and day, her prayers went up to the Lord of Hosts in trusting supplication that knew no doubt. Yet the child grew worse, and on the rounds of his duty among the miserables the young doctor heard of it. But not until it was too late. The little thing died, and the distracted mother found herself facing even more piteous circumstances. How was the child to be buried? To whom could she turn in this sorest of afflictions?

Himself without funds, the doctor could offer no better solution than a plea to the city. The civic authorities must, he supposed, have made some provision in their laws for just such pressing emergencies. He was wrong. With admirable dispatch, his appeal was heard and dismissed. Such things were not within the province of the city administration, an impeccably polite individual told him. It was not their business or problem to adjust domestic difficulties, however tragic – they were not a charitable organization.

Fury eating his heart, the doctor studied the bland face of the imperturbable clerk, thinking how typical the little man was of the dead-in-life, who worship the letter of the law and let the spirit go hang. How worse than useless to expect intelligent, not to say sympathetic co-operation from such wooden heads. Nothing would have pleased him more than to air these and other similarly impolitic sentiments, but instead he replied with disarming, almost humble politeness:

'You've set me right about my paupers. Now tell me – for a doctor meets up with such unexpected problems – how would the authorities act toward a suicide – say, an unclaimed corpse in the street? Would it be left to the mercy of the elements?'

Certainly not! The civic mouthpiece was moved to indignation. Anything that endangered the public health was an immediate concern – the law provided for the removal of all such nuisances. Really, the little man was wounded to think that the doctor could harbour even the faintest doubts of the hygienic zeal of the city fathers. To which pained accusation the offender listened with a mounting gleam in his sombre grey eye, and a swiftly shaping plan forging in his mind. 'Well, that's gratifying information,' said he, slamming on his hat, and striding from the room.

An hour later he was back at the city hall with a large paper carton under his arm. Dark as a thunder-cloud, he stalked into the mayor's office. His worship had left for the day, so he was told. No, there was not the slightest hope of his coming back before to-morrow. 'What a pity!' exclaimed the visitor, with malicious politeness. 'Then I fear I must leave this bequest to his worship without comment.' With which ambiguous statement the mad young doctor deposited the poor little infant corpse in its paper coffin on the mayor's desk, and, highly pleased with himself, dashed out of the building. Well, that's once blood was squeezed from a stone!

The impetuous doctor has gone the way of the storm, forgotten save by a few. Yet I think that the ghost of his wreckless courage still walks the night, jousting with fears and injustices in the old, free-handed manner; yes, and that the fine passion which consumed him like a fire burns as brightly still in some medium of mind, stuff for the inspiration of susceptible hearts.

14

Vignettes of a private world

But memory is a democratic jade, and no respecter of persons. Many inconsequential characters, whose distinctions were neither praiseworthy nor remarkable, exercised a fascinating spell upon my imagination. There was 'Kattar Issi' for instance, a gawky, tow-headed youth, not the brightest, who derived a sketchy livelihood by exterminating surplus cats. Considering my unbounded passion for felines, it is not surprising that the mere mention of Issi made me sizzle with plots of dire vengeance. Vindictive as any prophet of damnation, I vowed to haunt him when I died, in company with all the innocent pussies he had heartlessly dropped into the muddy waters of the Red River. He was, I felt convinced, the worst of ogres, and ought himself to be tied in a sack and duly drowned.

In reality, poor Issi was an inoffensive youth, afflicted with a hare-lip, which made articulation difficult, and doubtless was largely responsible for his seeming stupidity. This handicap, far from arousing pity, only strengthened my displeasure and suspicion. He hissed, so what more proof was needed to establish his true kinship with trolls and ogres?

Issi's last visit to our house made an indelible record upon my mind. To begin with, I had not seen him for a long time – the sex of my pets having liberated us from murderous proclivities – and I thought we were for ever rid of his dark shadow. It was a double shock, therefore, on walking into the kitchen one morning, to find him sitting at the table, grinning crookedly, and shuffling his huge feet as he waited for the customary cup of coffee. Chills ran up and down my spine, and a host of doubts soared up like startled birds in my protesting heart. The creature wore the cheerful mask of hired villainy! I could read it in his eye that pleasant business was afoot. Nor was I mistaken, for his evil genius had actually been sought by my own mamma. Yes, she had sent for him, and, pert as a cricket, unfolded a horrible plot.

It seemed that an eminent physician – heaven forgive him! – had just discovered the electric qualities of cat skins. Electrotherapy was yet undreamed, it is true, yet here was a pioneer who imagined that the vibrations of such supercharged skin, if applied to a weak chest, would benefit the patient. Well, who was mamma to doubt the great man? Never let it be said that she refused to co-operate with science – that her precious child continued croupy for lack of a cat skin!

Speechless, I could only stand there, a helpless accessory to the plotted crime. The skin must be found at once, said mamma. And when mamma spoke in that firm, clipped manner, even the angels would hesitate to tarry. The grisly deed was as good as done! Yes, utterly oblivious of my sick displeasure, mamma shooed me into a chair and went on with her instructions. The skin must be sun-cured and properly dressed – it ought to be as soft as a chamois. And it must be black!

'Well, now, ma'am,' Issi scratched his unkempt head. 'I can't exactly promise that for sure. Not for certain sure, anyhow. Black cats ain't being discarded just now.' As a matter of cold fact, he hadn't a single dusky puss in prospect, and, being an honest soul, that factor presented an insurmountable hurdle. Of course, he would comb the town with might and main, and fetch the desired article at the first possible moment. With that, mamma had to content herself – although, I'm sorry to say, I inferred from her impatience that, in a case like this, she might have winked at a weaker brand of honesty. Why, for instance, should not a grey mouser serve a housewife as well as a black? In the end, however, it was a dark grey feline that surrendered its most precious possession for my unhappy benefit. A compromise not altogether pleasing to my hopeful mamma – yet I, forsooth, must wear it!

For years the sin weighed upon my soul. It used to haunt me, first as sheer wickedness against the dearest of pets, and later as a hateful reflection upon the intelligence of my otherwise highly capable parent. It was not until years later, when I met a charming French girl in Saskatchewan, and learned that she too had been subjected to the cat-skin cure, that I realized how widespread this ridiculous notion must have been. It had even penetrated into the Territories. So far as either of us could recall, however, the only apparent results were a fine frenzy of itching and an equally fine frenzy of revolt. How many innocent cats were offered up on the sacrificial altar I shudder to think, but, in justice to our mammas, I hasten to reaffirm that it was done at the behest of a high priest of science. The nonsense cannot be laid at the door of some unlettered housewife, nor to the commercialized guile of the now discredited homoeopathic doctors whose pills and plasters once served us not too badly.

One such genuine helpful and extremely courtly gentleman I well remember. His bearded face had distinction, and his eyes twinkled with perpetual good humour, as though, in the sum total of his being, he refused to accept the actuality of the aches and pains he worked to alleviate. His voice was pleasantly cultured, and his choice of words would have rejoiced Queen Victoria. Where his medicines failed I am confident that the positive quality of his personality flowed to the rescue, for he had what so many modern doctors lack – a natural sympathy with human frailty and a fixed faith in the divinity of nature. The old black bag he carried on every occasion, with its array of tiny bottles of every hue, was a fascinating receptacle. Words cannot describe the conglomerate smells that eminated from its yawning depths when the brass latch flew open: aromatic Hoffman drops, volatile substances that reeked of camphor, eucalyptus, sassafras and cinnamon – and, lustier than all the rest, a colourless fluid that shrieked of a million murdered onions!

Plasters there were, as well, black and red and white, some perforated, and others cut in cunning strips for quick application to the various angles of the human anatomy. Pills, like seed pearls, in small blue and green bottles, sang of relief for a dozen ills, and as many pastes promised ease to cramps and crimps of ageing backs and limbs. Whatever these things were, they doubtless acted in proportion to the faith held in them, and very seldom I think, caused any harm.

The old gentleman was devoted to me, for had he not brought me into the world, and he loved to tease me about my insignificant appearance. 'Why, my chick,' he used to say, 'you were such a scrap of a thing that your poor mamma refused to believe you were born until I held you up for her to see.' Then, fearing that maidenly vanity was wounded, he would add: 'Just the same, there was nothing wrong with you. No indeed. Four pounds of fat, and – hum, I cannot say just how much vociferation. That was you, my love.'

This piece of news never failed to charm me when I was small, for, like every other child, the mystery of my own appearance on the world scene was a fascinating miracle. Papa generally helped the old gentleman by adding other, even more thrilling details.

'Yes, and what is more,' he used to say, 'you had no will to be put upon, my lamb. Although you were so small that a shoe-box could easily have been your cradle, you understood perfectly how to scare the life out of papa. You see, here was I, all unwarned that a daughter had come to the house, and, in my surprise, sank into the old rocking-chair. *Herra Gud!* What a squawk came from the little bundle I had nearly sat upon! That was how we met, my little dear – and I don't mind admitting I've had no desire to sit on you ever since.'

'A child without a temper is a ship without a sail,' the old doctor supplemented, stroking my hair with a soft, white hand.

'That is so,' papa nodded. 'I wasn't inferring that the little miss yelled out of turn. No indeed. On the contrary, she knew from the start how to conduct herself. I'll confess I had some qualms when I took her to the baptismal fount. Now, thought I, will the midget startle the angels with her howls, and shame her poor father? It was an unjust suspicion. Never was there a better chick. When the holy water touched the small black head – oh yes, my love, your hair was as black as an Indian's – you would have thought the child understood here was something she must support with dignity. It may have been a cramp, of course, but I really think she smiled!'

Well, whatever it was, it seems I made a good impression in the Lord's house; that, after the ceremony, every one had to have a look at this littlest of human beings, newly entered into the congregation of just men and true. It was my long hair, mamma said, and no wonder, for it reached to my shoulders, and made me look like a Japanese puppet, and not in the least what one expected a sprig of Viking stock to be. It was this reference to my coal-black hair that pleased me most. For a few days, at least, I had shared this distinction with papa, whose hair had the polished sheen of a blackbird's wing. Now mine was yellow as corn tassel, and gave me no feeling of superiority, though it was so long and abundant that even mamma boasted about it in her weaker moments – weakness she bolstered up by explaining that, after all, it was not remarkable, since all the women of her house were noted for their long hair. Yes, even that wicked wretch who refused to give a lock of her tresses for the mending of Gunnar's bow, when it might have saved his life!

The logical inference to be drawn from this horrid incident was that handsome is as handsome does. What if I could sit on my hair? Was that something of which to be puffed up about, when, at any moment, the evil blood of my ancestress might lead me to undreamed mischief? Clearly, it was much more profitable to remember that only the mercy of God had preserved me to be a sort of witness to the power of His hand. Oh, I understood that perfectly. I had not been much of a baby. I could well believe that I must have been a surprise to poor mamma. Her other babies had always measured above the average in size and beauty. Yet those sturdy little creatures had not survived. They came and departed. I was so used to it that its sole effect was a kind of fearful distaste for all babies. They were such unstable entities, predictable in nothing save the certainty of their sure departure. Their cries disturbed us for a little, and then these plaintive protests were stilled, leaving only my brother and myself in the house.

It was not until I was eight years old that a more determined being made her appearance. My sister Dora was a beautiful baby of sufficient hardihood to withstand the shocks of existence, and her happy advent seemed to break the evil spell that heretofore had darkened the house. By this time sanitary conditions had everywhere improved. Barns and livery stables were still plentiful, and the disposal of middens haphazard, but, to borrow the jargon of the day, the citizens were becoming fly-conscious. Lectures were given on the sins of the bluebottle, and frightening pamphlets on the subject descended with increasing frequency upon the heads of the people. To be discovered without screens became a graver offence than to lose one's petticoat on Main Street, and it was a common sight to see whole households armed with papers and rags, wildly whisking the unwelcome blue swarms from kitchen doorways. The milk supply was better handled, and even the water was under such grave suspicion that no sensible mother dreamed of offering an unboiled drop to her baby. All this was something gained, and doubtless accounted in no small measure for the drop in infant mortality.

Many unrelated incidents crowd into the memory of those years: individual pictures that, for some obscure reason, remain clear-cut and defined, even though I have no way of fixing the actual time or place. Oddly enough, it was not the concrete and more spectacular of these events that most impressed me. For example, it must have been rather jolly when the band came to practise at our house, especially when the 'boys' were rehearsing for Victoria Day. They made a tremendous noise, I know, and mamma beamed upon them impartially, and fed them with pancakes and coffee. I thought them remarkable creatures, and was filled with elation if my brother let me hold his horn for a moment. Yet I was much more affected when, one evening, papa led me into the front room to inspect a new picture of Laurier and the Cabinet. Quite as though I were his equal, and not a fat little girl in pigtails, father named the various gentlemen, defining their importance, and in conclusion pointing out the handsome figure of the great Frenchman, saying: 'There stands an earnest man. Remember that, little Lalla – for it is only through the earnest heart that God works justice on the earth.'

The words meant nothing, but the serious inflection of papa's voice, which was always gentle and warmly human, sent a thrill through my whole being. Although I could not understand my own swift reaction, I had a lovely feeling of being caught up into something vital and important; as though papa and I shared a beautiful secret which made us heirs of untold riches beyond the stars.

A darker thrill concerns another picture, and is associated with mamma and my visit to the Borgfords, where sister Anna lived. I remember very little of the house, which was bleak and scrupulously clean, and where the goodness of its gentle mistress fought bravely against the stern overtones of a harsh house-father. Mr Borgford, it was said, prided himself on being a good provider, but one instinctively felt that this generosity did not extend to any marked degree to the innermost needs of his wife. Small though I was, I sensed something tragic in Mrs Borgford's eager defence of her domineering husband, for it was so obvious that her affectionate nature, though starved and denied a natural outlet, shrank with almost physical pain before the least suggestion of blame. Somehow, I never could form any definite image of Aunt Malfridur, possibly because of her great contrast with my firm little mother, whose characteristics were so knowable and fixed. There was nothing vague about mamma, nothing apologetic or uncertain. She knew her own mind and its limitations, and let it be clearly understood that in this and any other life, she would sail under her own colours upon her own charted highway, with utmost efficiency, and with that the world and her God would have to be content.

With equal honesty and without blame, she recognized the limitations of others, and neither defended nor condemned them – with this exception: stupidity and hypocrisy tried her patience. What was the good of fools, she wondered, and how could any human being embrace the cult of Judas without shame? Mamma was, I sometimes used to think, very like her old ancestors, who put to sea in their little ships, nothing daunted by the pounding waves, for their attitude to life was wisely impersonal; their indifference to danger the result of an inner feeling of kinship with the stress and storm of nature.

Mrs Borgford, on the other hand, gave one the impression of perpetual uncertainty, as though she lived in secret conflict under the shadow of fears that drove her this way and that, irrespective of her ardent desire to placate and please. Children form queer ideas that on the surface seem to have small relation to the truth, but, when I grew older, I learned from my father that this aunt of his, whom he deeply respected, was not so far removed from my childish impression. It was his opinion that ironic destiny had chained a dove to a hawk in that household, to the complete subjection of the one without marked benefit to the other.

At the time of our visit, however, I was only conscious of Aunt Borgford's fluttering kindness. I have not the least idea what the coffee conversation was about that day, nor what I did to amuse myself. I knew that mamma was waiting to see my sister when she came home from school, and I remember that, when she finally arrived, bright-eyed and merry, the bleak old house seemed to relax its austerity, stretch and yawn, and settle down with a sigh. Anna was then a young girl in her 'teens, too tall and thin for beauty, but with the lively charm and handsome eyes that characterized father's people.

To my thinking, Big Sister was a marvellous being whom I secretly envied, for it was a source of grievance to me that no one ever said I resembled papa. Nor could I really blame them when I looked in the glass. My familiar face was round as an apple, ridiculously grave, and not even my best friend, Nonni, would have perjured his soul by claiming I had 'Irish-grey eyes' like my father. No, the oftener I gazed at myself, the more surely I knew how unkind the fairies had been at my birth. There was no good fooling myself. I was just the sort of fat little girl an ogre might like for his pot, and whom no king's son on shining steed would ever break his neck to rescue.

So here was my lively sister, with her dancing grey eyes, chattering to mamma with an ease she must certainly have inherited from our father. I could only hang over mamma's chair and hope that no one noticed how stupid I was. And when I heard Aunt Malfridur telling sister she ought to do something to amuse the dear child. That was I, of course, worse luck! Now I should have to bore Big Sister, for what could I answer such a paragon?

'Why don't you show your little sister your collection of handkerchiefs?' my aunt went on. 'That would be nice, don't you think? And better, if you gave her one. You have so many, my love.'

Here was another manifestation of adult ignorance! Why, for goodness' sake, should my sister show me her handkerchiefs? Why should I see them? Had I not seen a thousand in Yes-mam's bundle – handkerchiefs with roses like cabbages and birds with stiff wings and stomachs rounder than my own? More reasonless still, why should sister give me something against her will?

Well, there was no help for it. When big folk made up their minds to be kind, it was as hard to dodge the assault as to slip through a snowball fight. As bored as myself, sister told me to come along, and out came the handkerchief box – and there were the scraps of silk, exactly as I knew they would be. Like a little owl, I stared at the fine pile, marvelling at the fleetness of sister's fingers as she leafed through it.

'Here is one you can have,' said she, kindly enough, glad to be done with the job. No doubt it was a pretty handkerchief, but I really never saw it – as I never saw anything I did not want to see in those wiser infant days. I'm sure that I received it with a shameless lack of enthusiasm, and, quite possibly, might have further disgraced myself if I had not, so to say, in the nick of time, discovered the awe-inspiring picture which instantly changed the face of the world.

It was a common print of Joan of Arc at the stake – a grim representation of the Immortal Maid in her final agony, the black smoke writhing upward from the faggots at her feet, the makeshift cross of twigs uplifted in her tortured, supplicating hands.

A common enough picture in those days, when popular taste was not yet freed from Calvinistic sadism. To me, however, it was not a framed print upon a cottage wall in a mundane prairie town. It was a living experience so profound that everything else faded out of mind. What happened after my senses were caught up and swallowed in that awful scene I cannot say. I cannot even remember going home. It was just as though the centuries had fallen away, and that every act of that piteous drama were being enacted anew, with only my eyes the unwilling witness and my heart the centre of deathless pain. I was no longer my comfortable familiar self, the fat little girl with an apple face and yellow pigtails. I was a point in consciousness, where the repercussions of that long-stilled torment registered with incredible intensity.

Horror clamped down on me with an iron hand, and I could not even scream, for my lungs were filling with smoke, and my limbs held fast in burning bands of steel. I stood there like a stupid sheep, hearing nothing that was said to me, lost in an eternity of suffering I could not even understand, and would never in the world have dared to mention. Even papa would have been displeased with such exaggerated emotion, and mamma, I knew, would have doubted my sanity.

Of course, I had often suspected that I was queer, for my moods tended, at times, to objectify in pictures, with which I liked to amuse myself. But here was something that leaped at me unawares, unprovoked by imagination, and therefore terrifying. And that abominable experience pursued me. In the dead of night the picture came rushing out of a thick grey cloud, and no sooner recognized than, bang! went frame and glass, and there were the billows of fire and smoke which hideously enveloped, but never obscured, the tortured martyr.

I hated these intense reactions to painted atmosphere. I hated them, as every child hates anything that marks him as different from his sensible little companions. No one could have dragged the confession from me. If I read all sorts of absurd nonsense into the most ordinary pictures, and in my dreams saw the most amazing people engaged in utterly unfamiliar pursuits, I decided that, for decency's sake, I could at least keep the weakness to myself. One had to have his senses about him in this world, for the Lord had no patience with people who could not tell substance from shadow – so mamma said on many occasions, when the porridge was thin, and papa's gaze too ardently fixed on some invisible paradise.

Still, there were exceptions, she admitted, with her usual, unswerving honesty. Poets were bound by no common rule, yet even they, poor dears, more often than not, found it hard to buy a shoe-string with a dream, to say nothing of the shoe itself. I could not doubt the wisdom of these observations, and therefore piously vowed on all ten fingers that, by the help of the holy saints, I would for ever forsake the vainglory of dreams. No, there was no question of doubt, for even I could see the difference between papa's old Prince Albert and the glossy black coat worn by a brisk gentleman who sometimes whisked past the house behind a pair of high-stepping bays, on his round of inspecting the ugly row of cottages his foresight had built for trusting foreigners. Certainly, no concrete good came of dilly-dallying with dreams. And yet, I have come to wonder if my queer obsession with that harrowing picture was not largely responsible for the curious, fraternal feeling I have for the past. A feeling deeper than interest, swifter than insight, and not at all dependent upon written history – a feeling inseparable from the conviction that human experience, translated into mind-stuff, is timeless with eternity; that, in the eternal, the past is co-existent with the present, and the future; that everything that ever was, or ever will be, lived out under the chiming clock of the years, is nothing but the slow unfolding, incarnation by incarnation, of the Divine principle seeking expression in matter. Whatever this living, all-sustaining, and all-inclusive medium of being really is matters nothing, it seems to me. But to perceive that all creatures, now and for ever, are extensions of it rounds the sum of existence into a crystal sphere, wherein whosoever has eyes to see can read a fascinating epic.

Even without much vision, it must be clear to most that the past lives in us – that we are not products of one generation, and limited to the peculiar attributes of a sole set of parents. We were forsworn in the loins of the remotest ancestor, and shall continue until the last living form is extinct. Is it so strange, then, to imagine that man's emotional nature, which is just another expression of universal activity, may, in moments of great stress, somehow register its patterned feeling upon the living ether – if one may use such a term – in which we have our being? Is it beyond the bounds of reason that a sensitive mind may upon occasion react to such heightened vibrations and be moved by them at least to similar feelings, resentments, glooms, or exaltations, even though the experience go no further? If not, what are inspirations, and what better explanation has been offered for the strange visions of many honest men and women? Were they all epileptics and fools? Were all the mighty prophets, whose impassioned words still ring down the dark arches of the years, and all the star-enamoured visionaries, whose dreams, once despised, are now realities, were they all ignorant victims of egomania and hallucinations? How pitiful then is the lot of the blessedly sane! How little reason for envying the proudly practical, who live and breed and perish like mice in cheese, without so much as a single enraptured glimpse of the golden moon!

Alas, none of these pleasant conceits comforted me at the time of which I write. Joan continued to haunt me with her smoke and fire, and other ghostly personages joined in the tireless sport. Seemingly, I was just a round little human sponge that eagerly sucked up every drop of emotion that splashed from the crock of life. It was a queer sort of ingrown existence for a child – the sort, in fact, that would make a modern psychologist swoon with horror – and yet I survived those unhealthy fevers, just as doggedly as I survived the onslaughts of measles, scarlatina, and the cat skin. And, somehow, by scarcely perceptible degrees, the narrow limits of my confining horizon spread and widened.

One beautiful, warm evening, as in a trice, the boundaries of the world, which had been so comfortably snug and small, sprang apart, and there I was, suddenly face to face with undreamed vistas of incredible space. Mother and I were sitting in the back-yard, when papa came out, full of excitement, a newly opened letter in his hands. It was from his sister, who lived in some mysterious place called the United States.

'Can you believe it!' papa began, visibly stirred to deepest excitement. 'Little Finny has joined the army. He is going to war!'

Clearly this referred to my cousin, whom I remembered as a leggy youth full of fun and mischief. By some miracle, he had become a different creature – the sort that pranced through the pages of history books with sabres and swords and such commotion that one felt the yellow leaves of the books groan and shiver.

'Heaven help us!' exclaimed mamma, frowning, and not at all thrilled. 'Why must people kill each other to settle arguments? At least we have learned better than that in Iceland, thanks be to God!'

Papa brushed this aside. 'He will make a good soldier, never doubt it,' he said, staring off into the sunset, quite as though the yellow streamers of the sun were the proud banners of a conquering host of heroes. So, naturally, I too must plant myself at papa's side, and strain my weak eyes in the hope of catching a glimpse of the gallant company. They were marching into a land called Cuba, where the Spaniards were misbehaving.

This was certainly a shock, for heretofore I had only thought of Spain in terms of señoritas with rings in their ears, and twinkling castanets in their supple fingers. Then, too, what were they doing in Cuba? A horrible place, full of swamps, papa said, where something infinitely more dangerous than bullets awaited the American soldiers. Swamps were the breeding-place of fevers, which I could easily enough visualize as a burning sort of sickness that shrank the skin off your bones, and left you a yellow skeleton, only fit to scare bad, bad children. According to papa, a good clean war was not so intolerable, for its dangers were predictable, and a quick death was nothing to fear, but who could strive against pestilence in a barbarous country? No, he had no doubts whatever but that little Finny would acquit himself with valour, if only fate kept him out of the swamps.

'Well, then, why doesn't he stay home?' demanded mamma. 'That's what's wrong with you men – you talk sense for amusement, and when it comes to action, you behave as though the good God had forgotten to put an ounce of brains into your heads. I'll thank you not to be talking war in this house. I was reared a Christian, please remember.'

'Tut! Tut! A lot that means, my love,' papa grinned, his grey eyes lighted for combat. 'Who were the bloodiest fighters, if not the Christians, I ask you? Yes, my love, I seem to have read somewhere that even to our small country protestantism came at the point of the sword.'

'Poof!' Mamma rose with a swirl of cotton skirts. 'What does that signify, Lars Gudmundson? What else could you expect of the Danes, no matter what they called themselves. What I'm very sure of is that nowhere is it written that the Icelanders rushed up and down any country shaming their Blessed Saviour. I'm going in to put on the coffee-pot. If little Finny comes home again, it's more than your sister deserves – God forgive her! – if she writes as foolishly as you are talking.'

Of course, papa said no more that night, which was rather a pity, since my skull was aching with all sorts of questions I should like to have asked. The following weeks brought more letters, fortunately, and though mamma refrained from voicing any sinful curiosity, she never objected when papa read these communications at the supper-table. The same was true of the weekly papers, which more and more featured the fortunes of war, and very soon, it appeared that papa had been right about the swamps. The soldiers died like flies of yellow fever, many of them without the glory of firing a single shot for the grand myth of liberty. Still, the conflict went gallantly on, piling up profits for the meat-packers, who were selling rotten supplies to the army. When papa expressed this opinion I was rudely shaken, whereas mamma seemed to soften, and listened more patiently to the scandalous articles. It was just as though her silence were shouting: What can you expect? Is it surprising that people who countenance murder should be thieves and liars as well? Is it harder to cheat your neighbour than to take his son to be the target of hate in which he had no part? Come, come, Lars, use a little sense!

So here was I, all of a muddle. The gallant company whose banners I had seen in the sun were somewhere wallowing about in a dirty swamp, eating rotten meat. Was that the fate of heroes? Was it, then, the patriotic duty of little Finny to stuff himself on musty beef, so that the meat-packers, whom I imagined as whiskered monsters stirring a huge cauldron full of carcasses, should get rich as the terrible giants in folk-lore? Moreover, there were other surprising angles to the war business. Every American child was made to purchase a shining button for its righteous breast. The button had on it the picture of a furious-looking battleship, with, over it, the provocative caption, 'Remember the *Main*!'

What a lucrative idea that was! How stimulating to the hearts of innocent children. My good aunt sent me one of these precious emblems, which, alas! mamma promptly threw away, almost as fiercely as she had flung out the wild rabbit papa once brought home. 'So!' she had ejaculated that time. 'It is not enough to bring us to a savage country, but you must introduce heathen food? Well, my man, you won't get me cooking cats, let me tell you!' And out went the rabbit, flying through the door like a startled shadow – nor have I ever had the courage to sample that particular food.

The climax of thrills came when Lieutenant Hobson sank the *Merrimac* under the very noses of the Spanish command. Dear me, he, at least, must have eaten better fare than the poor lads in the swamps, thought I, swelling with vicarious courage.

'Humph!' sniffed mamma. 'Let's hope he lives to use his wits more profitably.'

Poor lieutenant! How little he suspected at the time that the barrage of Spanish gunfire he so cheerfully braved was only a bagatelle in comparison with the deadly battery that awaited his homecoming. In short, the enraptured ladies of the victorious republic fell upon him with such violent manifestations of affection that the undignified spectacle led to his being demoted in rank. 'Well, of course!' sighed papa, 'only kings and cardinals, and bespangled admirals, can make fools of themselves to good effect.' Which is doubtless very true, and therefore makes it something of a miracle that the dear, discredited hero was eventually recompensed for the furious kisses of the ladies when his constituency elected him to congress.

For me, be it confessed, the glory of the Spanish-American War was not epitomized in Hobson and Dewy, but in the amazing fact that cousin Finny, marching home under flying colours, showed himself a 'true and gentle knight.' He had saved his wages, and bought his mother a fur coat! There were tears in mamma's eyes when she heard that. The darling boy! She had always known he had a heart of gold. Didn't we remember how kind he was to dumb animals? God love him. Think of it! Now my aunt could make her rounds among the sick, even in the coldest weather, as proudly warm as the fine ladies on Broadway for whom she once scoured and scrubbed. Sometimes one got a whiff of justice here below! Nor was this all. My generous aunt must share her good fortune, so what does she do but send me five dollars! Gracious goodness, what a shock we had when the bill fluttered out of the envelope like some strange, heavenly bird. How my eyes popped. How utterly beyond my wildest imaginings was the conception of such an enormous sum! When the pin-pricks and heart-thumping eased a bit, I began to wonder if I couldn't buy a horse and carriage – or, at least, a house. But no. Mamma had instantly recovered her composure and all her good sense. The money must go for a winter coat. Obviously that was the inference to be drawn from the letter. Dear Aunt Haldora wanted me to be as comfortable as herself.

If such had only been the case! Instead, the bitter truth must out. Never in the world was there a little red coat more hated than that which mamma made for me – never a little creature more miserable so attired. Oh, it was warm enough – warm as a fiery furnace, and red as blood. A perfect Santa Claus coat! A little red horror trimmed in white fur and with a silver buckle. On a small, rotund miss, it shrieked for attention – bellowed to high heaven for all and sundry to behold this roly-poly, female miniature of Father Christmas. To say that I loathed this beauteous garment, which my mother prized so highly because it was of pure wool, and trimmed with real fur, is a gross understatement. Why, even now, when I think of that woollen nightmare, I find myself wishing that the hero of the *Merrimac* had never been born – that Randolph Hearst had died of newsprint in the cradle, and that Cuba had never sprouted sugar-cane – which is wickedly to wish that the glorious Spanish-American War had never come to pass, with its sweet bonus of five dollars to me!

15

Selkirk interlude

It must have been about the time that our new baby was six or eight months old that papa experienced one of his many lapses from common sense. He was fed up with 'The Saddlery'! He was so utterly sick of the soulless grind that he warned us in a loud voice he was done with such drudgery for ever. He had made up his mind we should all be better off on a patch of land near Selkirk. It was ridiculous to go on shivering and sneezing, never warm enough, and half-fed, in a dirty prairie town, when we might be basking in sunshine and fresh air, and eating the produce of our own fields. He was done with such foolishness, and let no one imagine his mind could be altered.

Mamma said nothing. She seemed always to understand when opposition to papa's dreams was futile, and, to reconcile herself to the scheme in hand with exactly the same inescapable forbearance one has for an act of God. Papa was like that, so what could you do about it? This admirable acceptance did not, however, extend to whole-hearted co-operation, for mamma had not a flexible mind in matters concerning the practical issues of life. She was, despite her romantic marriage, too much the daughter of a family whose habits and behaviour were fixed as the bounds of the sea, and which bounds of sensible behaviour nothing less than a major catastrophe could induce them to disregard. It was part of their tradition of loyalty that mamma should, as a matter of course, bow to the periodic folly of her husband, without in the least lending moral support to such silly aberrations.

When I was a baby she had followed papa to Minnesota, where they were no sooner settled and the owners of a neat little house, than the wanderlust struck again. This time it was the sheep ranch in Dakota that lured my poor father from the path of virtue. Once again she had followed without complaint, and now that I realize how incomprehensible these vagrant ways must have been to my dear mother I marvel at her generosity in so seldom referring, in other than a half-humorous vein, to these wretched experiments. Yet I sometimes suspect that papa's failure in these ventures was foredoomed by the powerful undercurrent of her unexpressed displeasure. There was always an unconscious contest of wills between them. If mamma appeared to bend and obey in any given circumstance, I quickly came to realize that the ultimate humiliation would be father's.

Now it was tacitly agreed upon that a piece of land on the outskirts of Selkirk was to be the pleasant solution of our tiresome penury. Almost at once the exodus began. First of all brother Minty was sent ahead with the cow – for believe it or not we now had such an animal. This seemingly simple chore proved an onerous business. The cow, true to her sex, quickly revealed an amazingly recalcitrant and mischievous nature.

On the face of it, naturally, that twenty-five mile pilgrimage through a primitive country struck my light-hearted brother as a most thrilling possibility. There was no telling what dark dangers lurked in the leafy bend of the old Red River road! So many ragged half-breeds wandering the countryside lent themselves so handily to the tricks of imagination ... For of course every one knew that the devil himself could not predict what a red man full of whisky might do! Fortunately considering the brave hazards, brother had an equally high-hearted friend who readily agreed to lay down his life if need be for our darling Bossy.

With ample lunches of rolled pancakes and brown bread done up in bundles attached to stout sticks, the barefoot heroes started off at dawn with the fat red cow bawling behind them. All went merrily for the first five or six miles. Then Bossy developed temperament. Her real nature came to the fore. With astonishing caprice she rebelled against the promised land, resisting all endearments, urgencies, and arguments. Switches and prods and high-handed tyranny had some effect, it is true, but the upshot was that Dame Bossy lay down, militant resolution in every fold of her thick red hide. Hot and disgruntled, her frustrated champions made camp.

Well, that was fun after a fashion. Until the night came down in a rush of mantling sable. Then how quickly were the youngsters disillusioned! The 'stilly night' tenderly depicted in rustic verse was, it seemed, nothing of the sort. Sheer deception, that's what it was! No sooner was the dusk settled about them than a million mysterious noises leaped up from every crook and hollow. Worse still, something at first only felt in the bones, which may well have been the rhythmic snoring of overburdened Mamma-nature, assumed distressing audibility. Louder than Gabriel's Trump, it sounded sharp warning: Look here, my lads, this is no time for napping; the hounds of mischief must have their run now and then. Oh very plainly it was a time for extreme discretion, to say the least. Even the frivolous wind had folded its wings and, done with capers, crept through the land on cautious feet. The river sobbed in its long brown beard as it slipped past the shuddering red willows ...

Quickly the boys built a shelter of green boughs which, alas! was no meet cover in such dire stress. Nodding in the midst of a gory yarn, down came a knotted branch with the explosive crack of a pistol shot! Oh, say what you will, grey ghosts were abroad that night. Nor they alone. Things that sniffed and snuffled scurried by. Rabbits, said Reason ... But then in such a wild place might it not have been bears? Indeed there were awful moments when the boys wondered if a werewolf wasn't hanging about waiting for the first sound of their helpless slumber. However, even the most ghost-ridden night comes to an end and all her dark hounds are chained to the farthest star. The gayest sun came bounding up over the tree-tops; birds sailed into the yellow air, singing at the tops of their voices; the wind, freshened with dew, went scampering among the leaves, pinching their small green faces and babbling nonsense in their little ears.

Everything was drenched in goodwill. Even Dame Bossy showed a change of heart and jogged along, patient as a lamb, and only now and again breaking out into hoarse and melancholy mooing.

That same morning mamma, baby, and I set off by train. Father for whom this rendezvous with nature was to have been a source of healing inspiration, remained in Winnipeg. Oh, it wouldn't be for long, said he, gaily kissing us good-bye, and feeling really thrilled to be bundling us off on a real journey. Just a few more months of the old grind and with careful saving he'd be able to add to our dozen chickens, lay in groceries for the house and feed for the cow. That done he would stamp the Winnipeg gumbo off his feet for ever, and happy as a harper come and join us in good time to cut the winter's wood and bring in a nice fat Christmas tree. Poor papa! His face beamed with joy as these jolly plans came tumbling from his lips. In his grey eyes there shone a happy light that oddly enough made me want to cry. But of course one did not cry on a fine train full of strangers with bundles and babies and bags of food. So we all kissed papa the second time and I at least hoped his dream would come true ... Oh well, he did join us for the occasional week-end – which is perhaps all that dreamers deserve in a world such as this.

By nightfall we had reached our patch of land and were scarcely through inspecting the house when the bellowing of the cow announced the safe arrival of the weary pilgrims. It was a pleasant spot papa had chosen. The house, though bleak and grey and forlorn as a spinster in its patch of prairie, was far better than mamma had expected. Soap and water and our united energy would soon put it into fine shape. The first thing to do was to get the stove up and the kettle on for coffee ...

Except for mamma's incurable aversion for the country, I think we might have been truly happy there – fared more decently than was possible in the city. To me it was a delicious interlude. Here at last was a green field I might have for my own – wide and free and unsaddened by cavalcades of crosses as was that other in which I once had longed to try my feet. Here I might wander at will, wheeling the big yellow baby carriage, with my old grey tomcat for company. Gráni was a haughty creature who sometimes paced along with the dignified mien of a stout grey friar absorbed in metaphysical abstractions. At other times he stalked the tall grass low-bellied as a hungry tiger, and fierce as the jungle killer leaped sidewise, hissing furiously, as with unsheathed claws he pounced upon some unsuspecting prairie flower. Bless his bold heart! It was a rare game for the mighty hunter, and not infrequently I sat down by the mangled corpse with kitty on my lap while each of us in his own way sang a proper dirge. With so much that was new and delightful all about me I had no difficulty finding amusement. Neither then, nor ever, have I been lonely, except in crowds, where the tangled moods of humanity press in like jungle creepers. I can still recapture with a pleasant glow the effects of those long-gone Selkirk sunsets; how they transformed the low marshes in the foreground, turning every rusty blade of coarse grass to spears of gold; the little pools of bog-water to shields of polished bronze. Best of all were the bullfrogs. How I loved them! How eagerly I waited for the sound of the first hoarse voices that heralded the tireless chorus of unbroken passion to follow.

If I could only sing like that! I used to sigh enviously; sing and sing and sing, with never a pause for breath – nor need to wheeze and cough! It was simply impossible to think of sleeping without a stolen rendezvous at the window. Cautious as pussy when he crept upon mamma's bed, I used to steal across the floor, and safely perched in the window-sill I'd sniff the delicious fragrance of the night and feel my heart contracting with the same joy that rumbled up from the tiny breasts of my little marsh choristers. There were so many of them that not for an instant was there a break in their fervent vocalizing. From breast to breast the rusty music beat, calling, calling, calling – until at last even the brooding Night unfurled her smoky pinions, to weave a stately minuet beneath the smiling stars.

If I tired of the marshes I had only to shift my gaze to the dark bluffs north of the house, where, through the thinning ranks, low stars twinkled like knowing eyes and a baby moon sometimes climbed the sky, branch by branch, the little sweet! and then with a wink at the helpful trees, sprang clear into the blue. As a matter of fact, however, I kept the woods for daytime speculation – their shadows were too long at night. Besides, mamma had given them a dual character. That they were beautiful she did not deny, but in a land like this who could tell what dreadful deeds they harboured?

I should have liked nothing better than to romp through those leafy stretches all day long, for, dreadful deeds or no, I felt at ease with the lovely slender birches, the black poplars, and the friendly maples. Mamma shook her head. I must confine my play to the open fields, where she could keep an eye on me – and where I could wheel the baby.

There was some justification for my mother's caution. The country was full of restless half-breeds – homeless malcontents who had been overtaken by the evil fate that good Father Lacombe had laboured so long to avert. A new way of life had robbed them of the only livelihood for which their restless souls were fitted. The day of the buffalo hunt and the river brigade was done; Father Lacombe's attempt to settle 'his children' on the land had failed. Now they were derelicts, debauched by the white man's whisky, enfeebled by the white man's disease, drifting aimlessly before the deepening storm. These unhappy vagrants were not by nature vicious, but continued drunkenness made them quarrelsome, and their pastimes, more often than not, were wildly orgiastic. I have a vivid recollection of more than one such revelry, for, as we were shortly to discover, the marshes round our house had long been a favourite bivouac of the Metis. There was something uncanny and a little frightening in the way they would suddenly materialize out of the night. One moment the plain was silent and dark and the next filled with noise and confusion and the red glare of leaping fires.

From my bedroom window I had now a very different chorus to follow, with my heart in my ears; a very different scene on which to feed my eyes. Instead of the Night, dancing to the stars, dervish figures swooped and circled round the fires; tossing their arms and writhing like creatures in torment. Their songs, gay at the start, quickly gave place to shouts and shrieks and blasphemies – as their tortured dancing was followed by indescribable obscenities. How glad I was to know that mother always pulled the blinds the moment the noise began and, determined to lend no single thread of consciousness to such ribaldry, retreated to her rocking-chair, book in hand. I know that she always hoped that I had fallen asleep, and she would have been thoroughly ashamed of me had she known that I was happily ensconced on the window-sill. 'Did you sleep well, my child?' she often asked over the morning coffee, her own eyes strained from lack of rest. 'Yes,' I hastily replied – which was true according to the letter, even though the spirit of honesty was somehow betrayed. I really had slept – but I knew quite well that that was not the root of mamma's anxiety. She was afraid that such sounds and sights would corrupt me, coarsen the fibres of my mind, and cause me to disgrace the august ancestors.

She need not have been troubled. I was totally unaware of any sinister or sinful significance in those savage antics. To me they were simply part of the deep mysterious night. I accepted the noisy clamour as simply as I accepted the rolling thunder, and the white lightning stroke which splits the heavens apart. Yet I think there was a sense in which these midnight revellers deeply affected my growing perception of life. Their strange behaviour made me see normal folk in clearer light by reason of the sharp contrast. It made me prick up my ears more avidly than before when some gossip dropped in for a cheering cup. Which was natural enough when you stop to think of it. For, I said to myself, if the drab, lifeless half-breeds who squatted for hours in the village street were suddenly transformed into howling dervishes defying God and man, why, who could tell what sort of demon might not lie curled in the breast of even the mildest mortal? At any rate it was a charming speculation to which I owe many an amusing vignette that leaps to mind at the slightest provocation. For instance, whenever any one uses the silly phrase, 'a fallen woman,' I am instantly reminded of a dark-browed young woman, furiously sweeping a cottage floor with a bright new broom. Another paradox, you see. Whatever I had expected as the true and proper occupation of such a sinner it was certainly not wielding a broom. But that's what my Magdalene was doing, and not in the best of tempers, either, the day that mamma and I came to visit the old people. 'God pity their wretchedness!' our only neighbour groaned, in telling the story. Ella was not the first daughter to fall by the wayside; there was another who had scarcely doffed her confirmation veil and laid aside the catechism than she forgot that man is a miserable worm not to be trusted by a Christian female. 'Well, picture to yourself what it means to be the parents of two fallen women!' our neighbour exclaimed in such a tearful chesty tone that I was not at all surprised when mamma, who rarely visited any one, said with a sigh that she guessed it was her duty to visit the poor old souls.

As we trudged along the rutted lane, pushing the baby buggy by turns, I kept wondering what kind of disease made one a fallen woman. Was it a blight, like Issi's hare-lip, that gave his honest face a dishonest leer? Or was it a misery in the bones, such as old Yes-mam complained of, and which bent you double as a bowstring in a robber's ready fist? Reasonable assumptions, yet I somehow felt that neither one fitted the case. Our eagle-eyed neighbour would not have given a second glance to Issi. Plainly here was something too deep for superficial discernment and the simple mind of a child.

'Mamma, what's a fallen woman?' I finally demanded breathlessly, and, knowing my parent, resolutely added while yet there was time: 'Is that what made Ella a ruined character?'

Mother was always a bluntly truthful woman, averse from all hypocrisy and dilly-dallying. Nevertheless, for a wavering moment, she was obviously tempted to forswear her good angel. Then she said:

'That's a hard thing to say of any one, dear child. Remember that. And remember this, as well: if Ella is ruined, she has herself to thank for it. She ought to have known better than to trust a man. Now the poor creature will have a baby on her hands, and not a penny to her name!'

Here was a pretty puzzle, forsooth! So there were babies and babies! The harmless sort, referred to in whispers as just another mouth to feed, and this other kind that made one a fallen woman. Dear me! It was all very difficult. One of those queerer than queer vexations that big folk appeared to hug to their breasts as jealously as jewels. All I could do about it was to study Ella. But that also failed in any way to enlighten my darkness. Ella still remained just a woman with a broom. A tall, angry, awkward figure, sweeping out the kitchen, as no doubt, she would have liked to sweep away the ugly past. She was so fierce about it. Something sticky evaded the broom – it looked suspiciously like a crushed raisin. 'Papa, you might watch where you step!' cried my Magdalene, attacking the offending object with broad toe. Then she reddened and laughed, a chilly ripple of sound that reminded me of hail, and, seizing the broom more firmly, swept and swept and swept.

Thinking it over, that night, as I hung out of the window, harking to my frogs, I reached the conclusion that a fallen woman was nothing but a girl who had lost her laugh – as I had once lost my voice – and made such ugly noises to ease the fright in her heart.

Other, more pleasant, fancies, dated back to the Selkirk scene. It was there I heard my first light opera. I suspect that the amateur performers were neither good nor beautiful. They were all like angels to me! Brilliant beings, whose every gesture and burst of song lifted my heart a little nearer the gates of a glorious heaven. The theme, ever popular with Scandinavian scribes, depicted the amours and adventures of a pair of wandering students on the trail of romance. In his everyday existence one of the heroes was the village baker, but, striding the stage, dressed in spotless white and with a flowing cravat under his chin, I thought the archangels would have to look to their harps and haloes when he applied for a role in the celestial choir. Many fine singers have shattered my ear-drums since then, and not one of them can hold a fig to my little baker, who keeps right on carolling on some tiny stage tucked away in the cockles of my heart.

Another sort of play affected me profoundly. The terrifying dream world of the mad. How I came to be picking flowers in the field outside the insane asylum I cannot remember. Even the children who took me there are misty and unreal. All except their voices.

'That's the crazy house!' some one bawled, pointing to a huge building enclosed by a high iron fence. 'Where they put the people with no sense in their heads.'

Followed then the hair-raising tale of the lunatic who tried to make a soup of his doctor. Huddled in the high prairie grass, with tiger-lilies like flaming swords at our backs, we listened to the story.

'You see it was this way,' Tommy began, swelling with importance, as became one whose aunt worked in such a dangerous place. 'This here man wasn't crazy, except in spots. That's the kind that works round the kitchen and laundry and such. But shucks! Aunty says you can't ever tell when they'll go off like a rocket. Anyway, this here guy sees the doctor coming into the kitchen, looking for some one, just as he was filling a big pot with boiling water. Just like that, it happened. The luny looks at the doctor, and back at the pot. "See here," he said, "there's gotta be better soup. The stuff we've been getting has no flavour – no delicate flavour!" That's exactly what he said,' Tommy interrupted himself to assure us. 'You can ask Aunt Sigga if it isn't. Well, I guess it was worse, because the doctor was kind of fat. "Ha! ha! ha!" laughed the crazy man, "I see you're a bright fellow, and understand the situation. Be so good as to climb on a chair. I don't want to be rough. Would you rather be peppered or salted?"'

It would, it seems, have been useless to appeal for help to the only other inmate of the kitchen – a feeble-minded woman whom the least excitement sent into fits. The doctor used his nimble wits.

'The idea is splendid!' he approved. 'Absolutely remarkable!' And he cheerfully agreed that, very likely, his plumpish person would flavour the soup to a king's taste. There was one thing against it, however, a really serious thing, which, if not remedied, would easily spoil the broth. He reeked of medicine! Nor was it just his clothes. The nasty stuff had penetrated to his very skin. The only safe and sensible thing was to tub himself thoroughly from top to toe in a special solution which he kept in the bathroom.

The lunatic heard him gravely. 'You won't run away, I suppose?' he suggested, a worried gleam in his eye. 'It's time we had some decent soup, you know.'

'That's why we must make sure,' the doctor attested impressively, and thus made his escape.

Skin a-prickle, we crept to the fence, hoping to witness some untoward happening in that topsyturvy domain, while Tommy regaled us with still other astonishing incidents.

'What makes you crazy?' a shrill, girlish treble inquired, after we had shuddered to hear how a woman had leaped from an upper window because she thought she could fly. 'What makes you crazy, Tommy?'

Tommy answered with pious scorn. 'Huh! There's things you shouldn't understand – especially girls!' said he. ''Tain't good for you, see?'

No, I did not see! What possible benefit could any one derive from the existence of things forbidden to the understanding? Tommy was a little fool I thought, little guessing how often, in the years to come other pious souls were to express a similar predilection for a spineless moral code. I was cross with poor Tommy for taking such a lofty stand – he was just a silly boy showing off! Yet I found myself thinking of his infuriating logic, when, some weeks later I saw a child with hideously crippled feet, and overheard a woman speaking of the infirmity as 'an affliction of God, too deep for human understanding.'

Selkirk was not destined to contribute much more to my slowly growing store of understanding. Like every other attempt to transplant us to the land, it was never more than an abortive effort. Two disagreeable incidents which happened in quick succession hastened our departure. One afternoon, when mother was winding a skein of wool from my unwilling wrists, we were startled by the sound of angry voices. Hurrying to the window, we saw that four men were thrashing about in the marsh, filling the peaceful air with shouts and curses. A drunken brawl, thought mamma, and, telling me to hold out my arms, went on winding the yarn. A brawl it certainly was, but as the minutes passed it began to assume a more serious aspect. It began to look like the assault of three determined brigands upon an innocent wayfarer. Mamma was horrified.

'God help us, what can we do?' she cried. 'They are beating the man to death ...'

Whether dead or stunned, it was a nasty sight to see the poor creature dragged away into the bush by his erstwhile companions. Yet I think mamma would have dismissed the whole thing as just another Indian roughhouse if, fifteen to twenty minutes later, she had not seen the same three men emerge from the woods and rush pell-mell down the road.

Brother was working in the village; there was nothing for it but to trail baby and me to our next neighbour in the hope that that eccentric mortal might for once eschew his own peccadillos and go fetch the proper authorities. It was a vain hope. Flushed and excited, we arrived at the farmhouse just as another bitter conflict was approaching stalemate. Mr and Mrs Farmer were not on speaking terms. The house was in a state of siege, with madam loudly declaiming that God-so-witness she was done with male oppression and evil tantrums. Never in the world would she appeal to that creature she had married for anything whatsoever. Not though the blessed Queen herself were being strangled would she ask that toad for assistance. Not she! Moreover, mamma would find that all human appeals were unavailing in that quarter.

The prospect was cloudy, to say the least! No less determined than his fiery spouse, the farmer had retired to the hay-loft with his trusty pipe, resolved upon the first sit-down strike in the Dominion. If his wife refused to behave as a Christian woman should towards her lord and master, he had no intention of earning *her* bread in the sweat of *his* brow! That was the gist of the battle, or so we gathered from the angry lady. 'You needn't expect help from that mule,' she concluded her tirade with a sniff. 'He'll set in that barn till his stomach hits his teeth, so he will, the creature!'

Sharp humour lighted mamma's eyes. 'Jaja! That may be so, but on the other hand John may welcome a turn with the sheriff. Anyway now I'm here he may as well be told.'

So down to the barn we trekked, led by the militant housewife, whose shrill voice muttered anathemas upon God's masterpiece. The ill-conditioned hulks of passion! Well, she had warned us. If we came to shame begging help of that stubborn brute it was not her doing – she had warned us thrice three times!

'John! John!' mamma called, making her voice as cheerful and ingratiating as possible, 'I'd like a word with you friend. It is important and no doubt you will help me.'

Long seconds passed with neither sound nor sign of life from the loft. The baby cheeped and pulled at mamma's hair and mamma, stifling inward laughter, tried again: 'John, John, are you there?'

'Ha-ha! what did I tell you?' sneered the *husfru*, scooping up a handful of pebbles, which she flung with fierce delight against the gable. 'Now listen up there!' she shouted, 'I'm not asking you to talk, you cockroach. It's Mrs Goodman, with a tale of murder – you *might* act like a man, not a jackass, to a neighbour!'

A red, angry face, crowned with upstanding mouse-coloured hair to which bits of hay imparted a comical aspect, appeared in the opening above us. 'I ain't aiming to truck with no females!' roared the master. 'Murder or no murder – which ain't likely to be murder anyhow – I'm setting where I be. That's for any one to understand as has ears to hear.'

'But, John, a man was beaten into insensibility before my own eyes,' mamma appealed. 'Even if he isn't dead he was dragged into the bush and left there helpless. Surely something should be done about it. At least it ought to be reported to the sheriff,' she tried to reason with the human hornet.

'Master in my own house, that's what I'll be – no more, no less,' was his retort, 'you can tell that where you like, Mrs Goodman, MASTER in my OWN house ...'

Obviously there was no appealing to Caesar, so mamma decided to search the woods herself. The farmer's wife, who had broken into almost tender chuckles while her husband roared out his lungs, instantly pronounced herself ready to assist. But first we must have coffee, and the precious little baby a mash of sweetened bread! Of course we must ... If the man was dead he'd still be dead – if he wasn't, God would keep him safe if life was to be the poor creature's portion. Coffee we must have, and then she'd help carry the blessed infant. 'Ja, that I will,' she attested, 'for it ain't pants that make a man, nor a loud roar that gives heart to a mouse,' she finished, tossing the challenge like a brick back over her shoulder as the three of us made for the house.

Our search of the wood was not successful. We came upon a man's badly torn coat and battered hat, but no sign of the man himself. This was added confirmation that something really serious had taken place, so mamma thought.

As soon as brother had finished his supper that night she sent him post-haste back to the village to notify the sheriff. That worthy dismissed the whole affair as a lot of silly women's chatter. Besides, every one ought to know that half-breed squabbles didn't warrant troubling the Queen's Constabulary – they were common as fleas on a cur's back and no more important!

The second incident to hasten our flight was of a more personal implication. It happened on a drizzly afternoon some few days later. Mother, for once not occupied with some task, was sitting in the kitchen, which formed an 'ell' that gave out upon a long veranda. She had the baby in her lap and everything was peaceful and serene. Suddenly a heavy stumbling step was heard and simultaneously a cry from mamma brought me to my feet. Glancing from her blanching face to the open door, on which her startled gaze was riveted, I beheld a really terrifying sight. A tall, drunken half-breed, with a cudgel and a coil of rope in his hands, stood on the veranda steps, and as it seemed to me, completely blotted out the golden light of the setting sun with his huge menacing bulk. Fortunately for us, he appeared to waver uncertainly, as though he were wondering how he had come to this strange place and what to do about it.

'Lock the door!' Mamma's voice fell like a whip behind me. 'Quickly! do you hear?' I was accustomed to obedience – I would have jumped headlong into the bottomless pit at that sharp command. On legs that shook like jelly I streaked to the yawning door and just managed to shoot the bolt as the hideous creature pounced upon the screen, yanked the hook loose, and cursing blue rivers began a thunder of blows that threatened to rend the worm-eaten panels.

It was not a pleasant moment, yet I doubt whether it would have frightened me so badly if mamma's obvious terror had not turned my blood to ice. Never had I seen such a look of fear in her eyes or known her to sit in helpless inactivity. She was like a dead person endowed with frightening speech. I flew about at her behest, shoving knives into windows, barricading all the flimsy doors. All of which would have been useless if our visitor had been less drunk. As it was he went raging and roaring round the house, using fists and feet in blind anger, but mercifully never thought of breaking the unscreened windows. It must have been upwards of an hour before he wearied of his pastime, and muttering darkly staggered away into the bush, leaving us to a peace that henceforward would never be rid of his shadow.

This experience, which to my hardy pioneering aunts would have occasioned little or no distress, was so disturbing to mamma that it put an effectual end to father's utopian dream of Selkirk.

That same evening she wrote a letter which must have been a sharp decisive ultimatum. At any rate, the packing began in the morning, and I overheard mamma telling brother that she meant to leave so soon as the last cup was safely wrapped! Which we did – leaving the stuff to be watched through the night by Uncle Jacob. It seemed a rather silly and headlong flight, and yet it so happened that mamma's nervous foreboding was not altogether unfounded. Whether or not it was the same half-breed, with his cronies, who returned to rob the house, we had no way of telling. But the fact remains that Uncle Jacob, a huge amiable giant of a man whose wits were slow but his fists formidable, was roused from sleep by the shrieking noise of splintering wood. Uncle jumped to his feet and, seizing an iron crowbar which he had taken for a bedfellow, prepared to lay about him. Five exulting savages burst into the room, little dreaming that anything save welcome loot awaited their pleasure. 'Ja, well, I don't like to be cruel,' Uncle Jacob excused himself, 'that crowbar he hits pretty hard, I guess. In the dark you can't be so careful if heads get in the way. Ja, well, I dragged the poor critters out on the porch. Then I yust pull the stove in front of the door and sleep some more ...'

16

False security

Well, back we went to Winnipeg, to a colourless existence
bounded by narrow enclosing walls; back to the drab streets
with their ugly unimaginative houses and the dreary procession
of plodding humanity bent upon its furtive scramble for bread –
back to a leaden backwash of life where the one touch of beauty
was the remote, incorruptible sky. For the time being papa was
hopelessly beaten, outwardly humble and apologetic. However,
no rebuff of circumstances could quite obliterate the wanderlust
in his soul. His was not a circumspect heart. Never for its own
sake would he prize security. When he held forth upon the
merits of country existence he was merely arguing for a happier
compromise with the evils of material necessity. What he wanted
was leisure to develop his social instincts, for he had a genuine
interest in human affairs and a natural gift for friendly inter-
course. Like every other frustrated dreamer since time began, he
longed for the kind of life which permitted of individual expression and the full enjoyment of beauty.

That he should have associated such a happy state with the
country was not surprising. By now he had come to idealize the
easy-going life his own father had led at Ferry-Cot, wilfully setting aside the prods of less sweet memory. Upon which point
mamma was sometimes moved to elaborate with unflattering
inference. She, at least, had not forgotten those early years in
Iceland where the exercise of even a fragment of this new-blown

zeal for the land would have yielded reasonable fruit – nor had she forgotten Dakota, where the wolves were left to gobble up the lambs while papa exchanged courtesies and wisdom with some addle-pated neighbour. Not infrequently she drove home the shaft by adding: 'I've not the least doubt you'd make a capital farmer, dear Lars – if whist and toddy were the tricks of the trade.'

Yes, for the time being poor papa seemed utterly defeated. The old life was resumed, in a house that was perhaps, a bit shabbier, but otherwise not unlike the one we had left. Brother Minty, like so many other immigrant boys, although highly sensitive and eager for learning, was forced to leave school and find some sort of job to help out with the growing expenses. It was not merely a struggle but a genuine miracle that kept our humble home intact. How mamma managed to feed us even one satisfactory meal a day, let alone finding clothes which were always clean and reasonably neat, is an abiding mystery. She was, of course, an expert needle-woman and an indefatigable worker. Our garments were not only made and re-made, but turned and so often dyed that the Lord Himself would have been puzzled to know their original status. Skirts turned into jackets, jackets into pants, pants into bed-quilts, and bed-quilts into braided mats for the floor. All our mitts, socks, and stockings she knitted by hand; so, too, scarfs and mufflers. These were her pleasant pastimes! At such occupations she was not only a wizard of speed, but supremely happy. For thus engaged she might sit and spin a yarn for eager youngsters, or read a tattered book without the least guilt upon her conscience. Many were the tales she told to the lonely immigrant youngsters who adopted our open house for want of better pleasure. But then mamma was past-mistress in that ancient Viking art. Her yarning was not a haphazard narration of disjointed incidents but a colourful recital of vital events that progressed by logical stages to a fitting end. Nor were there any forgotten strands which she must arrest the tale to recapture. Mamma would have blushed for shame at such a stupid exhibition of muddle-headedness; 'Oh, I forgot, I should have mentioned so-and-so' did not occur in mamma's story-telling. Her memory was keen and unclouded and her sense of the dramatic almost perfect. She not so much told her tale as lived it, and she could imitate voices and emulate moods as expertly as an actress.

These sagas were our chief entertainment – usually topped off with hot pancakes (which mamma tossed together quick as a wink when the last tear was shed) and lots of coffee. These pancakes, made with flour and water, one egg and a dash of nutmeg, were, like the knitting, a source of joy and pride to mamma. They were thin as tissue paper and must be fried on a special griddle – to touch which for lesser purposes was a heinous crime in our house. They were greaseless, sprinkled with sugar, rolled into golden sheaves, and eaten red hot. They were justly famous, for after thirty years of prayerful attempt to create anything like them I acknowledge utter defeat! Other Icelandic housewives made excellent pancakes, with the help of several eggs and milk, but only mamma, to my knowledge, had the knack of creating this trickiest of titbits with water and one egg. 'Oh, well, you see,' she used to say, 'there is nothing to boast of in cooking a fine dish with everything to hand. A fool could do that!' The inference was plain. To this day I look with suspicion upon a two-egg recipe and with pity upon any one who succumbs to such a snare and delusion.

So these were our delicacies. The staple fare consisted of flat-bread, soup, rice, and porridge. Since there was never enough money for more than one substantial meal this had to be the soup. For as you may guess, then the pot boasted a joint of beef as well as turnips, potatoes, and an onion! Sometimes the stock was thickened with a dash of oatmeal – which seemed to me a crime against the soul of soup, but mamma held more with nourishment than aesthetic vapours. Except for prunes and dried figs, which at that time had not come into the popular cuisine and were therefore cheap, and might be indulged in on state occasions, I had not seen a bit of fruit in our house since the winter when dear Dr Chown used to leave an apple or orange in my sick hands. Well, with one memorable exception: I was bribed with an enormous orange to submit to vaccination. If I were good and didn't cry I should have this prize of the gods. But, alas, when the ordeal ended I found I was honourably bound to share my bribe with the unwounded members of the family!

On the whole we were rather cheerful, despite our draughty house and meagre fare. The gospel of balanced diet had not as yet been preached. None of us suspected that life owed us grapefruit and tomato juice. When in very bad times papa was too ill to work throughout the week, we did without eggs in the pancakes, turnips in the soup, milk in the coffee, and boasted that, after all, three dollars had done the work of six. Seemingly we were sublimely unaware that when toothache wracked us and colds kept us shivering beside the kitchen stove, a dash of calcium – like the nutmeg in mamma's pancakes – would have lifted the flat feeling and given us a more lively tang. Of course, we knew that good food was highly enjoyable – we might even have conceded that upon high occasions such as weddings, wakes, and christenings it was really essential – but if you could not have it on a budget of dimes you hid the fact behind a stack of flatbread, so to speak. You stuffed on starches and thanked your stars it was so filling. Besides, to quote mamma: food couldn't be so extremely important, since most of the human race had to get by on so little of it!

Well, as I said before, we had settled down to the old penny-pinch grind, moderately convinced that Winnipeg was our destined battle-ground. Mamma really appeared to think that the ghost of papa's dream was successfully laid. For weeks not a word had been said about the glorious inspiration of the rural scene or the necessity for man to be in close and loving contact with nature. Why, papa had suddenly developed such a streak of practical good sense that he had gone rummaging in a junk shop and found a sewing-machine which, because of various mechanical defects, he was able to purchase for three dollars – in two equal payments! It was a hopeless-looking object when it landed in the kitchen, but when papa had finished overhauling its insides and varnishing its outsides we all agreed that it gave the

entire house a flattering touch of scientific progress. This opinion was strengthened when the old machine went into action; it
ate its way through the thickest quilting as easily as the prairie
sun eats into a snowbank – even leather was no obstacle. And
what a voice it had! At its best, when mamma's busy feet were
racing up and down the paddle, it roared and thundered without
ceasing, setting up an awesome reverberation in every crook and
cranny. Papa had certainly redeemed himself! What was more,
his depressing humility had given place to normal wit and
humour. Once more we heard lively bits of gossip from the shop,
or sat with wrapt attention while papa read for us some article or
essay he had just finished in those precious Sunday hours. Peace,
if not plenty, reigned in our house; we began to have the smugly
settled feeling which goes with the firm conviction that the skillet hangs on the third hook behind the stove; that one's Sunday
dress hangs in a moth bag in the left-hand corner of the clothes
press; that the extra pair of sheets are in the second bureau
drawer, and that the bureau itself can be located even in the
dark.

Then the thunderbolt struck. Papa had made up his mind
again. This time we were going to the United States of America!
More specifically, our destination was Duluth, Minnesota, where
papa's sister was successfully established as a midwife, and was
already contemplating building a nursing-home. Oh, well, we
might have known that our domestic brig would never lie for
long in untroubled water. Moreover, we should have sniffed the
rising wind when papa turned from serious criticism to lively
satire – when, instead of a diatribe on the feebleness of modern
poetry and modern poets, he amused himself with a satiric
hyperbole on Napoleon's satin breeches. Indeed, we might have
been warned, for satire, contrary to popular belief, springs from
a cheerful heart. If papa made scathing fun of his favourite
adventurer it was because in his innermost being he was drawing closer to the beacon fire that feeds the quenchless hunger of
such avid souls.

As a matter of actual fact my incorrigible papa had been exor-
cizing his demon by writing passionate epistles to Aunt Haldora.

He had poured out his tale of frustration to such good effect that not only was his own heart purged of gloom but that of his sceptical sister filled with resolute pity. It was unthinkable that her dear brother should languish in such a wretched country for ever – especially when Ingiborg was so pig-headed. That's what came of having knights for ancestors. Thank heaven, the worst she had to live down was a lascivious friar and a musty bishop! Oh, she knew that papa had often acted like a fool, but now he must pull himself together and make a fresh start. He must not show the fleece of a silly ram and continue ba-ba-ing and bleating. There was no earthly reason why he should keep on killing himself in the service of a miserly money grubber! Canada wasn't much of a country anyhow. So far as she had been able to make out, not even the English thought of it in favourable light. It was nothing but the hapless hunting ground for misbegotten upstarts who dreamt of easy fortunes with which to dazzle other fools back home. Now, in the United States it was altogether different. Even the stupidest foreigner quickly perceived that his ultimate success depended upon a whole-hearted acceptance of American ideals and American citizenship. In other words, wrote my aunt, the United States was a self-respecting country – not just the tail-hair of the British Bulldog! What was more it availed you nothing down there to brag about Trafalgar Square, the Buckingham Palace Guard, and Queen Victoria's virtue. The United States offered you a chance to prove *yourself*, not what had impelled your ancestors at the siege of Malta, or in the golden age of the Vikings.

All of which, reduced to its ultimate challenge, implied that if papa had an ounce of initiative left he would at once set about returning to the Great Republic. Not to go mooning about coyotes this time, but to work like a sensible man at his decent craft, where decent wages were paid.

'And that's exactly what I mean to do,' said papa, waving his epistle in mamma's astonished face. 'You can say what you like, Ingiborg. Sister is right – I'd be a fool to let my children grow up in a country where the people haven't any interest in their national destiny – as a matter of fact I have sold the cow.'

Which qualifying statement, and not the national indifference of the so-called Canadians, was, I suspect, the decisive factor in mamma's swift surrender – or perhaps she had known all along that, cheated of his country paradise, papa must, inevitably, seek some palliative substitute.

PART II

17

The American scene opens

In due course we arrived at my aunt's comfortable house in Duluth and were well received, as was to be expected of that most hospitable of relatives. The house itself impressed me little at the time, for my aunt was such an overwhelming individual that everything else dwindled into insignificance before her. If ever a human being was magnificently clothed in her unique personality it was Aunt Haldora. Everything about her was large: her ungainly figure, which for all its bulk moved with dignity and surprising lightness; her head, with its fine broad brow and penetrating grey eyes, behind which one sensed a brain in keeping with this imposing character – and indeed in her thinking there was no room whatever for the petty meannesses and irrelevant trifles which constitute so large a part of the average female's mental gymnastics. For gossip and small talk she had no taste, and this indifference to insignificant details was extended to all those unimportant matters that clutter up most people's lives. There were no useless knick-knacks begging care in her severe house, which breathed wholesome comfort and cleanliness and an immense peace. I use the word advisedly; nothing else explains the feeling that swept away your preoccupation whenever you entered there – a feeling of being cut loose from cramped moorings and set adrift on a large quiet body of waters.

Presiding at her table, Aunt Haldora seemed to me a figure out of a Viking legend: impersonal, cold, but sincerely concerned with the fate and fortunes of her ragged, impecunious guests. She inquired after our health, thought we looked undernourished, and predicted that our starchy pallor would soon fade when papa had established us in this civilized country. She admired the baby, which had been named after her, and also predicted that, unlike myself, it had promise of good looks. I had nice hair, to be sure, but it ought to be cut, she said – so much hair on a puny girl ate up the vital energy for nothing. It was all well meant, but created in me an extremely painful awareness of insufficiency – made me feel that I was one of those unnecessary encumbrances that burden the earth. I did not resent this implied criticism of my worthless person, for it was so self-evident that never in this or any other world could I hope to attain to the magnificent stature of my aunt, or clutch for my own such unshakable self-esteem. I was ashamed to sit and stare at her in stupid silence, but what else could I do?

Every gesture of her really beautiful, well-kept hands fascinated me. The curt way she spoke, which brooked no doubts nor opposition, was a revelation in forcefulness. Everything she did and everything she thought and everything she expressed in words was so firmly fixed in a sense of absolute perfection, according to her lights, that even the most foolish person realized the futility of opposition. That she was an autocrat in every sense of the word is certainly true – but the sort of autocrat who rigidly abides by, and at all costs maintains a moral code predestined for a certain cast by an all-wise deity. She was utterly sincere and utterly without vanity. Her person, like her house, was dedicated to service. Her clothes were clinically severe; the only ornament she permitted herself was a velvet band that she always wore about her neck. I think she even slept with it. Her whole life was centred in her profession, of which she was justly proud. And, unlike most married women who dabble in professionalism, she had the good sense to leave the details of housekeeping to others. That was not her business. Often enough she was cheated in the kitchen, where a wasteful cook might happen to rule at the moment. Well, what of that? Such people knew no better! That phrase, more than any other, sums up my aunt's character. With all her heart she believed that 'the lower orders' were as God had made them. How foolish, therefore, to expect any sort of perfection from the poor creatures. She would as soon have blamed a crow for not singing sweetly as find fault with the stupidity or moral flabbiness of an individual whose racial inheritance was suspect. Conversely, she was critical and severe and alert for signs of shameful weakness in those who ought, in themselves and their behaviour, to be a credit to a decent family.

Naturally, I did not understand any of this at the time. But I certainly felt that, in addition to resembling my mother's people rather than her own, which she could hardly help thinking a sad misfortune, I was not a promising-looking shoot of an ancient, though somewhat sin-gnarled, branch. Fixing her clear grey eyes upon my abashed countenance, which had nothing whatever to commend it, she expressed the hope that I would take kindly to school, and brushed aside with a wave of her capable hand my mother's explanation that ill health, not dullness, had kept me at home so far. 'No matter,' said my aunt curtly, 'she will have to start now. She will be all the better for having something to think about beside these silly notions. I must say I am surprised at you, Ingiborg, coddling a great girl into believing she is sick! What do you say, child, wouldn't you really like to start school like a sensible creature?'

Indeed I would! I wanted to shout, but, instead, only nodded my head, turning red as a beetroot. It was a thrilling thought, which excited and scared me into a fever of anxiety. I wanted nothing quite so much and yet I shook in my shoes when I pictured in my mind what the experience would entail. I was nearly ten years old, and, except for a few words and phrases picked up from my brother, understood nothing of English. And I was so shy that even an innocent glance from a stranger threw me into such profound confusion that my mind seemed to go soft as putty. What was worse, I realized thoroughly what a fool I looked at such times – how utterly stupid my behaviour was to others.

The prospect of this much-desired, though terrifying, adventure seems to have absorbed me so completely that I have no recollection of just how or when we moved into a hideous barn of a house, one of a dozen project houses that occupied a block of treeless, unimproved land. Everything in the immediate neighbourhood was ugly, with the one exception of the big brick schoolhouse, which was handsomely situated upon the side of a sharply inclined hill. It was a fine modern building, boasting a square tower that stood out boldly against the grey skies, like the turret of some medieval castle that commands a squalid town.

Squalid in every respect was this American counterpart of the frontier town we had just quitted. There wasn't a splinter to choose between them! the same ugly, hastily erected houses offended the eye; the same unkempt streets and dirty alleys despoiled an otherwise decent plain. We still fetched water from a pump that rose like an iron-wraith from an oozy grave. The same sort of rigs rattled over the ruts and the same sort of humdrum humanity hurried by. Nothing in the adjacent environs enlisted wonder or inspired the imagination. We had not even the remote beauty of the flawless prairie skies on which to fix our searching hearts.

Here in the Lake Superior country grey clouds, gloomy and low-lying, obscured the sun hours on end, and by night spread a blanket of mist over the stars. The weather was cold and depressing; dank winds, like the breath of a corpse, blew from off the huge sheet of frigid water, congealing the marrow in my bones; rain pounded from the leaden skies, to rush in brown rivers through deep gutters. All in all it was a disheartening beginning to a decade which, as my aunt predicted, was yet to prove reasonably filled with contentment, and productive of the only security our wandering household was ever to know. But in those first trying months it was difficult even to dream of such an eventuality. To begin with, our resources were so straitened that I suspect mamma went to bed on black coffee most of the time. Father was still in Winnipeg, you see, working off our fares and saving for his own. What he could send us out of the pittance paid him at the saddlery was so incredibly small that to mention the sum would lead my dearest friends to suspect me. Not even a relief recipient would believe me! Yet the rent was paid. We somehow managed to buy oil for the lamp and slabs for the kitchen stove. There were no sugared pancakes, however, nor turnips to flavour the thin oatmeal soup. Still, mamma managed to be cheerful – very cheerful, let me say, when, on rare occasions, my aunt had the time to drive by in her neat buggy drawn by a stout bay mare, never stopping long, but always anxious to know how we fared, when papa was expected to arrive, and what progress I was making in school. Mamma was often lonely, I suspect, for now there were no Icelandic youngsters to run in for a yarn; no band-boys to bring down the rafter with rollicking marches. Brother had found a few young friends of whom mother had no high opinion, being as she was a very clannish Norsewoman who wished to know the history of your family at least to the fourth generation before she felt easy in her mind as to what your reactions to the possible temptations of this vale of tears might reasonably be expected to be. I was away in school, fighting my own peculiar battles; she had only the baby, her weekly letter from papa, and her thoughts, which she kept to herself.

18

New friends of novel fortune

There were only two other Icelandic families in West Duluth, the Halsons, and certainly they were odd enough to arouse any one's interest. Two brothers, as different as day from night, had married women of whom the same might be said without a figment of exaggeration. The elder brother, whom I shall call John, was a solemn priestly individual, who discovered too late that the Lord intended him for scholarly pursuits and not common ordinary labour. Much too late, one might say, for by now he was saddled with four hearty youngsters and a stout maternal spouse, whose natural destiny had nothing to do with books. John, unlike lesser men, however, had managed to strike a satisfactory compromise with his fortune. He had completely converted his little hostages and his big wife to an utter and passionate belief in his god-like qualities. Papa was much too good to sacrifice himself to crude labour. He had withdrawn from the rigours of life, and sat from dawn till dark in the warmest room in the house, surrounded by stacks of papers, magazines, and tattered, paper-bound books that lined the walls almost to the ceiling. 'The lazy creature has made a perfect firetrap of that dump!' my aunt announced unfeelingly, but with wisdom, as was soon to be seen.

Master John had another accomplishment. He played the organ, and so, of course, somehow or other, the family had scraped up money to buy him a little folding instrument, which was only used on Sundays and for family prayers. For John was as religious as he was learned – his head as full of salvation as it was overflowing with ill-assorted bits of information on all sorts of useless subjects. But what did that matter? Papa John was an oracle to whom the whole family looked with humble, adoring respect. They lived only to please him. The children hunted odd jobs, my aunt rustled up clothing to cover them, and the various hotels in the city gave them scraps of food.

Every evening Julie, the second daughter, or Johnnie, the only son, started off with a basket to gather up these scraps. Emma, the eldest daughter, was never subjected to these humiliations, because it was recognized by every one that she took after papa. She must be brought up like a lady, and therefore sat at home doing fancy work and assisting mamma in seeing to papa's comfort. There was talk of letting her attend a business college whenever the money should be found, and the inference was that my aunt would one day realize what an exceptional deed of virtue such an act would be.

A crazy household, some said, but, for all their queer ways, they were a kindly lot, and their poor cluttered four-room house breathed genuine goodwill and affection. There was not a mean streak in any one of them, nor was it ever known that harsh words passed between them. Of course, Mr Halson poked out his head from that holy-of-holies now and then if the youngsters got too noisy, and, like Moses on Mount Sinai, reminded his progeny that life was a serious affair – had they not better see to their lessons, the empty baskets, or the wood-pile?

Sunday was unique in that house. No matter if they ate scraps all week, on this Holy Day dedicated to God and papa there must always be hot chocolate and cakes after prayers, and every one must observe the sanctified proprieties. No smuggy faces, no wrinkled stockings, not a hair out of place. Even the patches on Johnnie's pants seemed to efface themselves and piously merge with the original cloth of the sabbath garment.

Since both Johnnie and the youngest girl were near my own age, I was eagerly invited to join these solemn Sunday festivals. I surmise that Mr Halson, knowing my father through his journalism, was really concerned with my spiritual health, and quite possibly thought to snatch me, a brand from the burning, by the power of these blessed moments under his pious roof-tree. How little he guessed the depths of my sin! How shocked he would have been to know that Fia, his dearest baby, and I, had a sort of sign language by which we communicated our restless thoughts to one another while we sat, meek as lambs, on the hard benches that served for chairs, waiting for the inspired prophet to be done with his sermon. On and on and on rolled the sonorous voice, unfolding the plan of salvation and the dark destiny of sinners. Writhing on our little sterns, Fia and I shaded our faces from the wrathful light of papa's transfixed countenance, and, under cover of hot little palms, mouthed a hope that the end was in sight – that soon we might escape to the creek in search of minnows, for which we had a passion, or up into the hills, where luscious patches of sauerkraut grass offered a delicious forbidden diet.

Yes, now the final stretch was come. 'Let us join in solemn prayer,' boomed Mr Halson. 'Let us bare our sins to the Father of Mercies, whose wrath is terrible, but His patience long-suffering.' So down we scrambled to our knees, Mrs Halson audibly creaking in every joint, and puffing like a weary camel as she settled her billowing petticoats neatly about her kneeling, corpulent form. An incense of sins floated up to the Almighty, sins of the flesh and sins of the mind and sins of the spirit, all properly seasoned with the spice of poetic humility. And not until we lay there exposed in all our variegated iniquity, not so much as a fig-leaf of vanity left to cloth us, were we permitted to rise and join in a gloomy hymn.

That final ordeal ended, Mr Halson rose from the organ stool and beamed upon the sinners, who, in turn, beamed back, like so many little starlets suddenly freed from a smothering cloudbank. Mamma Halson, glowing with pride, hurried forward to kiss the head of the house for his dear devotion, and then scurried into the kitchen, where chocolate was simmering in a black iron kettle at the back of the stove. All the young sinners followed suit. 'Thank you, dear papa! Thank you, dearest papa! Thank you, darling papa!' they murmured, and were solemnly kissed in return. No doubt I should have kissed the good man also, for he always waited patiently for my lame little gesture, for my limp little paw that hypocritically expressed the thanks I did not feel. Then, too, I was always in mortal terror lest Mr Halson, who towered over us in the awful dignity of his Sunday vestments, should address me in particular, and require an honest answer. From this nightmare I was always rescued, however, by the joyous voice of Mrs Halson calling from the kitchen: 'Come, my dear ones, be so good as to partake of a little refreshment!'

Dear Mrs Halson! How she gloried in that humble hospitality. How eagerly she filled the cracked cups with her thick, sweetened chocolate, smiling as a summer moon upon the harvest of love's labour. Not one cup, but two, we must have, and all the cake and cookies – made from the same batch with very little shortening – that our stomachs could hold. To refuse a second helping would have been a reflection, not only upon her cooking, but upon the goodness of her deeply maternal heart. All the week long she waited for this blessed moment – for the unspeakable joy of pouring out the best she had for those she loved, and whosoever these previous ones called friends. In her patched alpaca and spotless white apron, she stook at the head of the long table – which was made of pine boards on trestles, and covered with oilcloth and a centrepiece of cotton, embroidered by Emma – swelling with innocent rapture, waiting for her tithe of thanks, which was willingly forthcoming when we youngsters filed from the board and kissed her moist, smiling face. Yes, even the high-minded master soberly kissed his kindly wife, giving her a little pat on her thick, stooping shoulders.

The other Halson household was not presided over by the mistress, but by her spinster sister-in-law, a small immaculate female, as crisp as a baker's bun. The mistress was a semi-invalid, a thin little woman, with a great wealth of hair which she wore in braids down her back, and who limped about on a crutch, swinging her withered limb with a jerky, side-wise motion that gave her the air of a sloop tacking before the wind.

She was an intelligent woman, given to reading and needlework, and was always very cheerful, as perhaps she had cause to be, since both her husband and his maiden sister looked upon her as a delicate trust. Her husband, Einar Halson, was a short, apologetic person, of whom I remember nothing except his shy affection for the invalid, and that he had a bristling moustache which struggled vainly to impress masculine virility upon an otherwise hairless and extremely meek countenance.

Gossip waxed fat on this second household also. Mrs Halson was only half a wife, it was said – a statement which at that time I understood as applying to her withered leg. She had peculiar haemorrhages, which were spoken of in horrified whispers as a perversion of nature, for the lady was not consumptive, but had suffered this periodic distress every month since puberty. But, although Icelanders have no mock modesty about the human body and its functions, I was not much enlightened on the mystery, even when I overheard Stina, our Gossip (of whom more later), exclaim sympathetically: 'Poor creature! It's a cross the Good God laid on her for sure. The devil knows it's bad enough to be a woman when your insides work the right way round!'

Naturally, I was fascinated by Jorun Halson after that. On the few occasions when she paid us a visit, swinging down the narrow sidewalk with her swift, uneven gait, her neat black dress flapping against the clumsy crutch, the sun picking out the soft gold of her beautiful plaits of hair, I was all agog with excitement. Would the lady's insides maintain equilibrium or would they take this unhappy opportunity to display the curse of God? Would this ethereal being, whose habits were such a mystery, fix upon this moment to 'give up the ghost,' as Stina predicted that she might do without warning, 'between two breaths?'

Sometimes the sister-in-law, Helga, came with the invalid, and, by her tough brittleness, defeated my earnest hope. She was so attentive, so watchful, so practical, with her quick attention upon draughts, and her hand ever ready with a shawl for the tender shoulder of her charge, that even I understood that Death himself would have a tussle to steal away her beloved. Nothing would happen between the two breaths unless Helga had her head turned the other way! These visits had their own tang, none the less. Mrs Halson was delightful to look at as she sat with her little white hands folded in her lap, the profile of her delicate face traced against the sunlit window-pane, her whispering voice filling the room with an illusion of ghostly charm. For her talk was more often of marvellous dreams and forebodings than of everyday matters: of a misty borderland, where the spirits of men departed yet fettered to earth by ties of love or hate, mingled with the souls of questing dreamers. Nor was it difficult to imagine how readily the eager spirit, looking out from her clear blue eyes, would seek some such finer world, where the ills of the flesh neither stay nor hamper the flying wings of yearning. Her speech was gentle, all her manner restrained and resigned, yet even to a child, it was manifest that the undertow of her thoughts were fierce and earnest. Life had cheated her, but death would be kinder. In that far green land whose bounds were illimitable and eternal, the God of the Meek and Lowly would fully compensate each broken hope. Over the bitter coffee drunk to the accompaniment of this Elysian murmur, I found myself catching hold of the garments of Prophecy and soaring to fanciful heights. For I, too, dreamed dreams – was it because my own insides were ill assorted? – and who should say that I might not one day have visions, see the shining hosts that sing before God's face, and count the wheeling planets that form His living rosary? Who should gainsay that flaming possibility, when little Mrs Halson, who was scarcely a whole woman and only half a wife, spoke so unerringly of the winged powers of the deathless spirit?

Very different from the ethereal Mrs Halson was Stina Olson, who became a devoted friend to the family. She was a woman with a past! Hard though it was to believe it, when one studied her unprepossessing person, she had had a lover, of whom gossip said he was handsome, years younger than herself, and quite a dandy. What puzzled me still more was the added information that this lover was none other than the son of my dignified homeopathic doctor. How any one so scrupulously well behaved could have a scapegrace for a son struck me as a most unrighteous state of affairs. God was much too free with his afflictions, that I perceived, and shuddered in my bones.

Stina had worked for the old man, so it was said, and what could you expect of a spinster whose charms were flitting away as rapidly as a witch on a broomstick, when she suddenly found herself alone in the house with a fledgeling male as full of hungry curiosity as a mouse in a cupboard? No one was the least surprised, unless it was Stina herself, when the curse of Eve came upon her. But at that there were no tears. Stina was gaunt, almost toothless, and her hair was colourless as dried straw, but the springs of her heart were rich in humour and goodwill. What was a baby to growl about anyway? Goodness knows she hadn't expected so much of life. Without the least rancour she betook herself to other quarters and cheerfully waited the blessed event. She was well rewarded. The baby was a beautiful child – a dear son who never was to cause her a day's uneasiness. And she loved him as fiercely as only such a derelict can love.

Now she had drifted to Duluth, and if you please, had got herself a husband. A little bantam of a man, a perfect pepper-pot, always spilling over with indignation at the injustices of the social order. 'I'm a union man!' he would shout, 'I'm a socialist – ja, let them fire me, the dirty rapscallions! I stay by the union and starve, God help me!'

Fired he was, from job after job, and not always because of his devotion to justice. He had a weakness for the bottle that equalled his passion for the rights of man. 'Ja, well, I have to drown my grief like a hero. I have to bear up somehow,' said Sam, and shook his round head that was thatched with black and white patches of tenderly nursed hair. 'Sure, and what else,' Stina agreed cheerfully. 'It's a queer world, and that's a fact. Now try a bite of herring for your health's sake.'

So Sam continued to drown his grief periodically, never offensively, you understand, for he was a tidy little mortal with every pinfeather always neatly in place, and his peppery crowing was entirely without malice. Stina kept the pot boiling by one means or another. Sometimes she lent a hand house-cleaning or washing, but when we met her she was mothering another rudderless soul, a huge dock-worker whose past was one long friendless buffeting. If he had a surname I never knew it. Every one called him Big Tom, and big he certainly was, a mountainous creature who shuffled through the world in melancholy isolation. He rarely spoke, and what few words he uttered were monosyllables half whispered from the corner of his mouth. He gave the unhappy impression of always having existed on sufferance, and to be patiently waiting the next swift kick of fortune. Sometimes, when Stina was waiting at table, hovering over him with kindly anxiety, a sort of paroxysm would twist his rugged face, as though he were about to cry, so strange it seemed that any one should take the least thought for his comfort. Still, he never thanked her, unless these surprising grimaces and the dog-like devotion of his eyes, were meant for thanks. But on payday, when he came home from the docks, reeking with sweat and black as Satan, he dumbly handed out his board money the moment he crossed the threshold. 'Ja, sure, it is enough to make you weep,' Stina told my mother, weaving to and fro on her nervous feet. 'Out comes the money like I was waiting there with an axe in my hands. Now, can you tell me what devilry has done the like of that to a decent creature? No you can't! God Himself will scratch His blessed Head and that's a fact. For mind you, my dearie, it isn't just that the poor brute has no friends – neither kith nor kin nor even a hussy to steal his pay – it's like he was dead at the core. If you ask me, I'd say he was killed in the cradle – ja, I'm thinking he had no mother, the poor little poppet – more like she ran out on him, the wicked scullion, and left him to the Devil's jobbing!'

Well, now he had found a haven. Little Sam had discovered him one noon, sitting, lonely and abstracted, away from the gabbing workers who were taking their midday ease. Sam, bubbling with indignation over the inequalities that smirch the Lord's footstool, thought he might discover an attentive ear in that huge, silent figure. Nor was he far wrong. Little Sam bristled and barked, beat his fists together, and kicked up clouds of powdered iron ore, covering himself and the motionless listener with a clogging film of dust like pulverized blood. Never had he enjoyed such an understanding audience! The big man sat there, dim amazement slowly giving way before a vast admiration, as the bold little cockerel hopped and howled. Though he said nothing, it was plain this was an accomplishment for which he would gladly have exchanged a span of years. And when the little Union Man finally ran out of wind, Big Tom unscrewed the top of his round dinner pail and poured out a mug of brackish coffee, which he silently offered for the easement of the orator's palate. When the six o'clock whistle blew clever little Sam was on hand waiting for the amiable giant, whom he adroitly manoeuvred into the nearest bar, and, over twin mugs of foaming beer, learned all that ever could be learned of the big man's past. He was alone in the world; had always been alone in the world; he had a room near the waterfront.

'What kind of a room, my friend?' demanded Sam. 'Ha! I can guess what they think is right for a working man – especially for a fellow who isn't a union man. Now, my wife is that clean a fly has to wipe its feet to enter through a knothole. Such a nice room she has behind the kitchen, with a comfortable bed you could have for next to nothing. What do you say, Big Tom? Why don't you come home with me and taste the bean soup? You won't have to hunt for the beans in the pot water, I promise you!'

'Ja, that was the way of it,' Stina informed us, and giggled, as she was wont to do at the end of every sentence. 'He came slinking in with Sam, the big ninny, and, let me tell you, he took some feeding to get the green look off his bones.'

Stina was our most frequent visitor while we lived in that desolate, barn-like house near the school. Always out of breath from unnecessary haste, whatever the weather, her starched print dress billowing in the endless wind, she blew into the house puffing and giggling, her small son neat as a doll, trotting behind her. 'God give you health! How are you? Wouldn't you think the Holy One would quiet the wind! Don't tell me it was ever worse in Iceland ... Bless my soul is that the same baby? Now don't screw your mug up, my angel, its just old Stina taking note of the new inches. Kiss the baby, Valdi, like a good boy, and behave yourself, my rabbit!'

That was our Stina, The cheerful sinner who refused to be burdened with a sense of shame for her stolen escapade on the primrose highway. She was always welcome, but I remember one bitterly cold autumn day, with iron rain sleeting the windows, when her sudden appearance was nothing short of a miracle. For some reason, papa's slim allowance had not reached us, and all that day mamma had beguiled our hunger with tall tales of heroic splendour, washed down with cups of hot water. Stirring tales, to be sure, but somehow or other my spongy spirit kept veering, like a rudderless skiff, from the fine feats of the ancestors to the gratifying vision of flatbread and butter. Mamma grew a little sharp. 'Listen here, my lamb, there are worse things than an empty stomach! An empty head, for instance! Would you like to hear the story of the Twelve Wild Ducks?'

Well, of course that would be nice, I admitted, with a dampish sniffle. Though to tell the truth, I wondered a little that I should even have thought the tale fascinating. Yes, now it struck me that the queen whose woe it was to have twelve sons and no daughter might well have restrained her tears. The little princelings had all the pigeon-pie they wanted. But there it was – the silly woman moped and moaned, and finally pricked her royal finger, the red blood dropping to the white snow outside her window. 'Oh, that I had a daughter with cheeks so white and rosy!' cried she, completely forgetting the bounty of her bouncing sons. And instantly up pops an ugly creature from nowhere with previous comfort. 'Give me your sons,' says the horrid thing, leering like a drunken turtle, 'and you shall have your heart's desire – the fairest in the world.'

'Really?' cries the queen. 'Well, take the little brats! I'm sick to death of keeping tab on all their boots and buttons —'

So here we were, off to a good start, with the princess as good as born and knowing quite well what hardships she must endure to recover the twelve brothers so carelessly mislaid by the queen. But at that we never compassed the royal christening, for, all at once, there was a scraping of feet on the doorstep and the next instant in flies Stina, beaming her toothless smile, a mysterious bundle under her arm, and the small son tagging behind.

'God bless us, what dirty weather!' says she, shaking the rain from her ancient ulster. 'Valdi, did you wipe your feet, my lambkin? Well, well, off with your cap then and speak like a Christian.'

'My dear Stina,' said mamma, in a queer weakish voice, 'what on earth brought you all this way in such biting rain?'

'What indeed!' exclaimed Stina with a giggle. 'Well, then can you believe it, I got such an itch for a bit of a walk the divil himself couldn't have kept me from coming. What's more, thought I to myself, Stina you're a queer one if now and then you can't return a little cheer to them that always treated you to victuals with an open heart. So my dear, if you'll be taking it kindly, I've brought a loaf of bread fresh from the oven and coffee enough to drown a tom-cat!'

For a terrible moment I thought mamma was going to cry, her face turned so white, and crinkled so queerly about the lips and eyes as she swept Stina into her arms, kissing her on each windbeaten cheek. Instead, she said softly, almost gaily: 'Dear good Stina! I should have known when God gives us friends He foresees all our needs. Lara, put on the kettle and get out the best table-cloth.'

Well, there you are. What did we care about the lost princes after that? The kitchen hummed with merriment, the old stove crackled, and the kettle sang. The cat came out from his favourite corner and arched himself round Stina's leg as much as to say, Madam, even I worship before you. Out came mamma's finest porcelain cups, with the purple pansies and dabs of gold on the rim; and of course the huge newly baked loaf was displayed in all its glory on the very best cake plate. The coffee was good and strong and set our pulses singing with warmth and happiness, although Stina insisted on a thousand apologies for the brand.

'Arbuckle's coffee isn't the best,' said she, giggling. 'But for eighteen cents you can't expect a miracle – especially when you get a coupon thrown in for nothing. My Sam is saving up for a newfangled razor, and Valdi there wants to get a watch, the little sparrow. So you see, the more we drink the richer we get, and that's the holy truth, my dear!'

Oh, we were very gay indeed, but when Stina had departed in the drizzly dusk mamma stood at the window, watching the thin figure till it faded from sight. When only the thickening rain and the crowding shadows were to be seen in the desolate street, she crossed to the stove where the dishpan was heating. 'Now you see how foolish it is to listen to the grumblings of the stomach,' she said, smiling at me through a mist of shining tears. 'Put the rest of that blessed loaf away. It will do us till papa's money comes.'

Sure enough it did! We had scarcely finished the last sweet crumbs when the postman's whistle announced the safe arrival of the delayed letter with its sorely needed stipend.

'What did I tell you!' laughed mamma, a little shakily. 'Gracious me! An extra dollar! And papa thinks he may be coming in a week or two. That calls for a real celebration. What do you say to liver and onions for supper?'

19

The scene brightens

The leanest of the lean days was over; the larder was never quite empty again; and, after papa rejoined the family, life quickly settled into the old familiar grooves. As our aunt had prophesied, he had no difficulty getting a job at better pay and shorter hours than he could ever have hoped to enjoy at 'The Saddlery.' Mamma immediately began to set aside quarters and dimes, her heart fixed upon a stove that would really draw and not make such a mess of every batch of bread. Well, that was very fine, said papa, but why stop at the stove? Why not dream of a house in which to put it. A house with a garden and a chicken run, and a barn big enough for a cow and her calf?

These dreams were not much comfort to me, however. I had my own troubles to solve, and no time for such nonsense. I had started school with fear and trembling. How I lived through that first awful day I don't know. The principal looked at me helplessly. What was she to do with such a big child who scarcely understood a word? Heaven bless her, she understood what an ox I should feel among the babies – yet what was to be done? To the first grade I had to go, where a very young teacher received me with the kindest smile. However, I only stayed there for a day and was shunted off to the shoulders of another harried lady, who took me in hand with a firm, efficient grip. Whatever the cost to both of us, I must learn to read. To that end I stayed after four, and consequently dashed home on wings, full of vanity and wisdom. I had actually spelled out two magnificent words! Saucer! Altogether! They were honey on my lips, beautiful beyond every other sound. But, alas, when my practical mamma inquired into their splendid meaning, I was lost. Worse than lost when, days later, I discovered that saucer had no poetic connotation whatsoever, and was just the dish from which my pussie drank!

Nevertheless, I bore up under the disillusionment, I was so busy memorizing a host of other words, fixing their sound in my mind and translating them back to their Icelandic equivalent. That was not so bad, but how on earth was I to add the trick of spelling to this twofold exercise, when the sound had no bearing on the letters? Why was *c* sometimes hard and sometimes soft? And why, for goodness' sake, was fox spelled with an *f* and 'phrase' tortured with a harnessed *ph*? But, at that, the idiom was ten times more confusing. A hound was *fast* when he cornered the rabbit, and likewise *fast* when secured by a chain. You *were* cold when the winter winds buffeted your bones, and you *had* a cold when your flesh was burning with fever!

It was all very queer, and frightfully unreasonable, but there were combinations of sounds that from the first were music to my ears. I made up my mind that this language was my own – that I would struggle with its capricious parts as patiently as papa wooed his Icelandic phrases.

I should have had a miserable time of it, however, those first few months, if I had not been adopted, so to speak, by Katie Pepolenski. Katie was a big Polish girl who had all the qualities which I lacked. She was pugnacious, cheerful, and completely satisfied with herself, although she was poor and almost an outcast in the school. We were two curiosities; two awkward foreign creatures who made an easy target for the cruel humour of our small companions. Katie was a dirty Polack, and I a dirty Icelander! I, of course, was even more derided, because no other child in the entire school suffered from such a peculiar nationality. An Icelander! Ho, ho, look kids, she's an Icelander! What do you mean, Icelander? Eskimo, that's what! Hey, blubber, how do you like living in a wooden house?

So it went, and although I could understand well enough what was shouted at me, I had neither the courage nor the facility to defend myself. After one such attack, when I stood cowardly and affrighted amidst a savage little mob, Katie, hitting right and left with her hard brown fists, plunged through the crowd, and, tucking her arm through mine, out-shouted our tormentors. 'Leave her alone, you devils! You skunks! you dirty Swedes!' she shrilled, her dark face blazing with rage. And, to my unholy delight and utter amazement, she completed the rout by shrieking a blood-curdling curse: 'You filthy Cossacks, I'll spit in your eye! I'll spit in your eye and curse you to hell!'

'The skunks!' sniffed Katie, as the humorists dispersed, each after his own fashion, hooting, laughing, tongues pointing scorn. 'You don't know much, do you?' She beamed upon me. 'Well, come along. After this, you stick by me – Katie Pepolenski don't get walked on by no dirty Americans!'

Thus the queerest friendship began. Katie, it transpired, lived in a tiny two-room cottage half-way up the hill that began its ascent a block or two beyond our house. Her parents were Polish peasants who had come to America with an eye to making a fortune, on which they hoped to retire in the beloved homeland. They were doing very well, said practical Katie. Most of papa's wages went into the sock, for, by now, they owned the house, a cow, some chickens and geese. They sold eggs and milk, and raised their own vegetables. With the eggs and milk money Mamma Pepolenski bought flour and sugar and tea, papa's daily pork chop, and molasses cookies. This latter was almost a sacred rite, as I soon discovered. Every evening after four Katie dashed to the corner market for the chop, and, faster still, made her way to the little Scandinavian bakery for five cents' worth of the fat, newly iced molasses cookies. On the few occasions when the bakery had not the required six cookies left Katie turned pale. Why, she always came for them every day, to get them fresh! Why didn't the bakery missus remember and keep them? The bakery missus generally did, but sometimes in the busy season the extra help forgot about the Pepolenski cookies. 'Holy Mary! What will papa say? Mother of God, what to do!'

Katie's big freckled face turned helpless eyes on the equally helpless Icelander. 'Maybe a white cookie will be nice for a change?' I once ventured recklessly.

'A white cookie!' Katie shrieked. 'A white cookie my father would spit on! I should spend money on a piece of white dough? You're crazy!'

'How about a ginger square?' suggested the amused saleswoman.

'Six for five cents?' haggled Katie.

'Well, no, they come a little higher, but I'll let you have six this time.'

'How much higher?' Katie demanded, the born barterer's gleam lighting her eye.

'Four for a nickel.'

Katie peered into the glass case to make sure of the size of the squares and if they were frosted. Satisfied that no better substitute could be found for the customary favourites, she paid over the nickel, and, with a sharp request that to-morrow's purchase be safe-guarded, departed. 'Anyway, papa won't be so mad when he knows he's eating on the bakery,' she informed me. 'The frosting is just as thick too. It saves on the sugar when you dunk the cookies in the tea.'

My first visit to the Pepolenski domicile was an absorbing adventure. I had never crossed a foreign doorstep. For that was the secret source of our strange attachment: each of us thought the other a queer 'outlander,' although we stood together against our common enemies. The first thing that struck me when I entered the dim cool house was a peculiar smell – an unfamiliar odour that permeated the whole place. Yet everything was clean as a new broom, every pot and skillet scrubbed and scoured. To be sure, the small kitchen was cluttered – but neatly cluttered – with all manner of strange things to see. Strings of garlic and other seasoners hung from a frame above the stove; huge bags of sunflower seeds adorned the wall, and, in one corner, stood a big barrel of sauerkraut. The smells began to explain themselves.

Katie's mamma was a short, corpulent person, whom I never saw uncovered. Her head was always adorned with a kerchief from which her round, smiling face and dark, twinkling eyes peered out with candid good humour. She seemed always to be on the verge of bursting into chuckles. My advent was something of an occasion which called for a gift of sunflower seeds. 'Eat! Eat!' urged Mamma Pepolenski, nodding and twinkling. 'Much good, you see!'

Truth to tell, I was sadly deficient in the etiquette of seed-munching, and, besides, found the delicacy rather tasteless. But Katie saved my face by hustling me off to the front room. I must see their Ikon. It was from Poland and occupied a place of honour above a little shelf that was dressed with a crocheted fringe. Two tall candles in brass holders stood on either side and a bowl of paper flowers, blue and red, made a patch of gay colour in the centre. There were several lithograph prints of various saints upon the wall, and an especially dolorous representation of the Saviour crowned with thorns hung above the paternal bed. Except for this huge bed, and another smaller one at the back of the room, the only other pieces of furniture were some wooden chests and a big iron-rimmed barrel. The beds were like small mountains, so high they were with feather ticks and enormous pillows, all white as snow. Katie was immensely proud of the beds, on which not a wrinkle nor a ridge could be found. Their smoothness depended upon expert rolling with a broom handle after the feather beds had been shaken and fluffed into those proud, airy formations. 'It's a big job,' said she, patting a bolster with a loving, rough paw. 'But, you should know, to be careless with beds won't get you a good husband.'

The barrel inspired curiosity. It was the biggest barrel I had ever seen, and why it should stand there instead of in the kitchen proved too much for my limited culture. 'Katie, why do you keep the water in here?' I queried. 'Isn't that awful unhandy for your mamma?'

'You're crazy!' said Katie, amiably. 'That's not mamma's water. That's papa's bath – don't you wash in your house?'

'Well, not in a barrel,' I admitted humbly. 'How do you mean, it's your papa's bath?'

'Holy Mary! Don't you know anything? Oh, well, I suppose in Iceland it's too cold for a skin bath. It's like this: every morning papa jumps into the barrel, and then runs to the gate and back to get the air on his skin.'

'Katie! Not in the winter-time? Through the snow – with nothing on?'

'Of course. For the health, there's nothing better.' Katie explained, smilingly patient with my ignorance. In all his life Papa Pepolenski had never known a day's illness, which blessing, thanks to God's mercy, was due to the invigorating influence of cold water on the back, and snow on the feet. Yes, in winter Papa Pepolenski was even healthier than in summer, for, as every one ought to know, the sun sucked the health from the body through the sweating pores.

Here, surely, was something to think about. Perhaps all that ailed us was the lack of a water-barrel. 'Do you jump into the water too? You and your mamma?'

Katie threw me a pitying glance, her face reddening with shame. 'Holy Mary, it's good mamma can't understand much English. Should a woman run out naked – in *this* country? You're crazy! It's better not to say such things. Look here, are you a Christian? I'd like to show you my confirmation veil. At Easter I take my first communion.'

'I'm not a Catholic, Katie, but I'm going to be confirmed one day – my sister had a veil too, and lilies of the valley for her hair.'

'Come along then!' Katie pulled me towards one of the chests. 'I guess you're not the bad kind of Protestant.'

Mamma Pepolenski, who had been hovering in the doorway for some time, now hurried forward, and shoving her daughter aside with a cautioning rebuke, herself displayed the filmy treasure. Proudly she pointed out that the veil reached to the heels – it would do for Katie's wedding if the good God gave her a husband. It was a beautiful veil, bought with fifty quarts of raspberries! Fifty quarts picked in the early dawn, and sold in the broiling sun from door to door. That was the price of Katie's finery. 'And may the holy saints mark the sacrifice, that something comes of it!' said Katie's mamma, crossing herself.

All these things were marvellous to me, and were passed on to my own mamma with proper emphasis, but neither the sunflower seeds nor the health-giving barrel impressed that stiff-necked daughter of the Viking. In fact, my parent abjured me, on my oath as a civilized creature, to forgo the bird seed and think no more of the water-barrel. That sort of thing was well enough for Russian peasants, said she, but who ever heard of white people scampering about in their skins? It was disgraceful. 'If you can't find better friends, do without them,' was her heartless injunction.

'But, mamma they aren't Russians,' I pleaded. 'Poles are a different kind of people, aren't they, papa?' I appealed to my milder forebear.

'What do I care for all that?' mamma interrupted crossly. 'This Katie the child runs around with is a little savage. She shouts and stalks along the street like an Indian. Do you want your daughter to behave like that? Is it a mark of distinction to hop into a barrel and dash out into the snow, naked as the Lord made you?'

'Well, well, well, the Lord's handiwork is not to be sneezed at, my love!' papa rejoined gravely, that glimmer of familiar mischief darkling his eye. 'I'm neither for nor against such exhilaration, but I hardly think the child will come to grief because Katie's papa disports himself so bravely.' Then, to me: 'What does Katie talk about, my dear, besides her father's health and the blessed saints?'

Now I was cornered. Instinctively, I knew that mamma would frown upon our conversation about good husbands for whom one prepared by making soft beds. Nor would she relish the verbal battles so colourfully peppered with pointed curses.

'Oh, we talk about Poland,' I temporized, trying to remember something scholarly and impressive. 'It's a nice country. They have so many holidays, when they dance in the street — '

'And knife each other, I'll be bound,' mamma interpolated, crossly. 'Put your mind on your reader and forget such foolishness. That's my advice. And don't let me catch you shouting like a stable wench!'

Mamma could be very unreasonable, I thought to myself, and stole away to the window, hoping to cheer myself with a glimpse of the beautiful young man who lived on the next corner.

I was quite in love with him, and after Katie's remark about a husband my heart jumped like a startled mouse each time he passed. Of course, I knew to the exact minute when this glorious experience might be expected. He always fetched water from the pump at seven o'clock. That he was married, and lived in the same sort of barn we ourselves did, nowise dampened my ardour. He was tall and dark, and always wore a bright red sweater that seemed to me as beautiful as a breastplate of beaten gold. Above that blazing garment his bold black head rose with the proud lift of a warrior. Nor was it difficult to provide my hero with a mettlesome steed and a broad axe in place of the pail. Those daily excursions to the pump, told to the beat of my racing heart, were really the sublimest conquests, executed with romantic dash and daring. Imaginary enemies strewed the streets behind my darling as he whizzed back from the diabolic stronghold of the pump with his pail, converted into a casket of glittering jewels.

This rendezvous at the window was the most precious moment of the whole day, for which I waited with delicious twitters and bated breath. Each day the glorious creature drew a deeper sigh from my suffering breast as he swung past in his scarlet breastplate, cheerfully unaware of the sore havoc he was causing. But, just as I was at the point of confessing my hopeless devotion to Katie, I was happily cured. Alas, what should I see, one dreary November day, but my Beautiful Knight trundling a baby carriage! Now, that was too much. A wife was no obstacle, but a baby was definitely not in keeping with prancing steeds and heroic conquest. The wretch had deceived me! Never again was my nose pressed against the window-pane, nor my eye beguiled by the flash of a red sweater.

It was a sad disillusionment, almost as depressing as the weather, with its squalls and sleet and scudding, angry clouds. The eternal damp chill seemed to leap at my throat, choking my breath with clammy fingers that left me gasping and sputtering, to my utmost humiliation. Sometimes these attacks were so severe that I had to sit down in the street, with Katie keeping watch between me and any possible enemy. For this trusty guardianship, I was deeply grateful, yet it had its bitter alloy. Katie delighted, with all her rugged soul, in defending such a miserable weakling, but at times she lost patience, and banged me on the back with peasant thoroughness. 'Stop! Stop! You'll bust yourself? Holy Mary, you're blue in the face! Here, get on with you. Hang on to my arm. Do you want to catch your death in the gutter?'

Under the full steam of this righteous indignation we would stagger down the hill, Katie outshouting the lustiest wind as she laid down the law for my benefit. If I wasn't so crazy, I'd burn a candle to the saints. No telling but they'd hear me, though I was a Protestant. Catholic saints weren't limited in their miracles. Any way, I could eat raw meat and lots of suet.

'Katie! I couldn't – not suet!'

'Shut up – you'll choke again,' Katie admonished. 'You could eat a dog if you had to. Haven't you any sense? Do you want to bark yourself to skin and bones? What sort of husband would that get you, do you suppose?'

No, I had no fancy to become the sort of thing Katie painted with vivid word strokes and considerable relish. Katie's mamma had known such unfortunate baggages back home: pale wretches who shivered in their greyish hides; hacked and wheezed their lungs away, and, finally, to no one's regret, ended up in a pauper's grave. That last called for serious cogitation. Goodness knows, I was inured to the thought of an early, saintly demise, but this pauper angle gave an entirely new and sinister twist to the familiar story. I solemnly swore to Katie that henceforth my prayers would be addressed to the whole calendar of saints – for it seemed highly probable that if I picked one haphazard, the rest might take offence – and my sole petition, for release from the wheezes and the threatening shadow of a pauper's grave.

Katie thought it a capital idea, and called the Blessed Mother of God to witness that she would put a copper in the poor-box on Sunday, and add her sanctified prayer to mine.

20

Fresh misfortune

Strange to say, all this piety and fervour bore sad fruit. Instead of getting better, the misery increased, augmented by headaches that, after days of angry raging, left my head stiff as a board, and all my senses dulled. About these headaches I said no word. I had a dreadful fear of being taken out of school, where, if I met with much teasing, I also derived the greatest joy. I had jumped to the third standard, and was assured by the optimistic teacher that I should pass into the fourth at Christmas. That would place me among children of my own age, which, at the moment, represented the seventh heaven.

But, as I was to find out in the years ahead, even such a simple dream was not to be realized without obstacles. I went to bed one night feeling oddly limp and dizzy. The bed rocked under me, and the ceiling wavered and wheeling like a rift of clouds. There was a queer, sickening pressure in my chest which, when I drifted towards sleep, had a terrifying effect. It was as though some deeper wisdom inside me were warning me not to lose the reins of consciousness. But at last I dozed off, comforted by the sound of mamma's even breathing, enheartened that her big bed was no farther away than the opposite wall.

No words can describe the hideous sensation that shook me awake, sending me bolt upright with a strangled cry on my lips and a gush of something hot and crimson spraying my cotton nightdress. My impulse was to reach that other bed, but when I tried to move, the world went black. But not before I had seen mamma, who must have jumped at my scream, peering at me in the white moonlight with helpless fright in her eyes.

Poor mamma! For an otherwise intelligent woman, she was always sorely at sea where illness was concerned. She seemed as incapable of the simplest elements of nursing as father was of acquiring business sense. Her lexicon of healing consisted of stuffing you with food, rubbing you with goose-grease and turpentine, and rolling you in a hot blanket; where, the longer you smothered the better she loved you, and the more certain she felt of eventual recovery. Freely she showered her tenderness, had absolutely no fear of contagious diseases; but, young though I was at this time, I had long ago discovered that the sight of blood threw mamma into utter confusion. So now, fighting the most frightening giddiness, I struggled to slip off my gown – no doubt I was dying, but at least mamma need not touch that dreadful garment.

Somehow, the night passed, and a bright day dawned, clear and cold, and no sign of the golden chariot. I must have slept, for my first thought was that I must have had a nightmare. I was alone in the room, with the usual comforting sounds coming from the kitchen. Cautiously I slipped to the floor, and found, to my vast surprise, that except for a funny sort of hollow feeling in my stomach, I seemed no worse for the trying experience. Then a new fright laid hold of me. I suddenly remembered Jorun Halson, and her disorganized insides. I recalled, with rising agitation, all the muttered whisperings about that poor creature who was less than a woman and only half a wife.

My hateful doom was fixed! I studied my little carcass with apprehensive eyes, trying to find some outward sign of the topsy-turvyness within. So far as I could discern, my small flat chest and little white stomach exhibited no visible marks of villainous treachery. To all intents and purposes, I seemed to be intact; a bit wobbly in the knees, to be sure, and singularly inept with my benumbed fingers as I drew on my clothes, but otherwise unchanged. That was comfort of sorts, and yet I could not escape that room fast enough. I longed, as never before, for the warmth of the kitchen, the reassuring hum of the old copper kettle, and the welcoming purr of my precious cat. Mamma glanced up, startled, when I came stealing into the kitchen and slid my chair by the table.

'Are you better? Perhaps you shouldn't have got up,' said she, eyeing me anxiously, yet speaking harshly. As though, for once, she were weary to death of my ailing capers. Dear me, I had not expected any such reception! Cod-liver oil, and another cat skin, perhaps, but not an implied rebuke. Something cantankerous had come over mamma as well as myself – one of the evil visitations of which both Mrs Halson and Stina spoke with such deep conviction. It often happened, said they in old families which had a host of sins to their credit.

Yes indeed, cases of sudden madness sometimes broke out in the best of families; fits befell the sturdiest fellows, and pious mortals, who hitherto had lived by faith, and crossed themselves before and after meat, were, all of a twinkling, plunged into riotous iniquity. Cattle sickened; ewes forsook their lambs; the hay whizzed away on a withering blast, and ravens, by twos and threes, appeared upon the roof-tree, croaking doom and damnation. All this, you understand, through the retributive machinations of some drear *afturganga* who could not rest in holy bliss till judgement day because the evil wrought against it was still unrighted.

That there were more than enough sinners between me and Father Adam I was fully aware: not just the simple, ragtag transgressors whose sins were meanness of mind and mustiness of soul, but lusty brutes, who had cracked skulls as lightly as eggshells, and thought no more of stealing a pretty wench than of turning a nithing-verse against their enemies. Sadder still, there had been women with hearts no softer than flint, whose hands had more often caressed an avenging blade than a baby's poll. If Stina were half-way right, there must be a sizable company of moping spooks to pinch and pester me and mine for the sins of our fathers.

Quite possibly, I should not have hit upon this plausible explanation of the curse which had pounced upon me in the dead of night if now, in broad daylight, I had not been confronted with such strange behaviour in my parent. Astonishment and the sting of the hurt quickened my perceptions.

For the first time, I saw my mother, not just as my mother, but as a stout little woman with a pale mask of face behind which thoughts and emotions in which I had no part moved with vexed urgency. Standing there, stirring the porridge, a troubled frown knotting her brow, she seemed just as alien and much more remote than Katie's moon-faced mamma. In one of those lightning flashes that illuminate the darkness of the fumbling mind, I suddenly realized what made her so difficult, engaged in all her vital energies, and made me and everything else a troublesome hindrance. Mamma was going to have another baby again!

Heretofore, I had never thought about it. Some one was always having a baby, or burying a baby. It was a commonplace nuisance, that meant a row of bottles to be scalded, and diapers blowing on the line. It meant a smelly lamp in the bedroom kept burning all night in case the baby needed changing – it meant a hack at the door, and another small cross in the lone green field under the stars. But now, for some inexplicable reason, it meant a cleavage between me and mamma. It set up a kind of quivering horror in my whole being to have suddenly plumbed the alarming possibilities of the female body; to have forced upon me, unsought, the staggering knowledge that all the while that mamma sat quietly knitting and spinning a tale from *The Thousand and One Nights* for our cheer and amusement, her woman's body, like a creature apart, was pursuing its own creative mysteries.

But the thought terrified me much more than the threat of a legion of ghosts. Had I dared, had my legs not been like water, I should have run back to the chilly solitude of the bedroom, which, only a few months ago I had mistakenly believed was the only haunt of malicious magic. I buried my face in the cat's furry warmth, tearfully conscious of my own little miseries: that I had a horrid pain in my breast, a dull aching in my head, and was practically orphaned besides.

'Put the cat down,' said my strange mother curtly. 'I sometimes wonder if you don't get sick messing with those everlasting animals. No telling where they prowl. I declare, I'm at my
wit's end. You'll have to see a doctor. If you think you can manage it, you'd better go at once to your Aunt Haldora. She will
know where to take you. She knows everything – or so your
father believes. You'd better eat something first. Would you like a
boiled egg?'

Holy Mary! The exclamation dear to Katie flew into my mind,
but, happily for me, stayed there. An egg! Of all the foods that
soured and sickened my stomach, eggs were the worst.

'No thank you – I'm not very hungry,' I whispered.

'That's another thing! You won't eat. Even as a baby, you set
yourself against milk and eggs. How do you expect to build up
strength that way?'

I said nothing. Somehow, it no longer seemed important to
attempt to defend myself; to explain, to no purpose, how vio-
lently, and sometimes successfully, my perverse little stomach
dealt with those sainted foods. I really scarcely listened to what
mamma was saying, for I had unconsciously withdrawn into
myself to escape hearing the numbered list of ailments, past and
present, which I was supposed to trot out for the doctor's benefit,
so that he would know how to deal with me. I tried to eat, but
the bread stuck in my throat, and just to look at the porridge
swimming in milk was nauseating. The best I could do was to
dig up a spoonful or two under the white sea, and gulp down
two cups of coffee.

Yet, I would gladly have devoured a dozen breakfasts to put
off the business of starting on an errand that scared me to death.
There was nothing to be gained by dawdling, however. Nor the
slightest use in telling mamma I was such a coward. As quickly
as I could, I put on my things and left the house. The air, cold
and sharp, and for once blessedly dry, cleared my head a little,
but my feet and legs needed a deal of encouraging. There was a
queer, nagging pain under my left breast that increased as I
plodded on. Sometimes it caught me unawares, piercing so
sharply that I had to stop, frightened because the street, with its

familiar lamp-posts and heaps of dirty snow, grew indistinct and wavery, like water stirred with a stick. I was almost glad for these pauses, which furnished an excuse for loitering, holding back the difficult moment when I must show myself in this fresh humiliation to my majestic relative. For, to tell the truth, it was the thought of the coming interview, not the giddy weakness, that tormented me. My aunt had not thought very highly of me heretofore; how much more despicable I must now appear, coming with this fresh tale of peculiar iniquity. Moreover, it struck me as a sort of spiritual insult to both of us that I should have to inflict such an intimate confidence upon her. Why on earth should she be burdened with further details of my weakness? Why must I be driven to bare my shame to the one person whose good opinion I secretly desired above all others? For the first time in my life, I thought of mamma with angry bitterness, and a little seed of doubt and incipient enmity was sown in my heart. Then and there I resolved that, whatever further ills should come upon me, I would keep them to myself – yes, and not only disappointments, but my innermost thoughts, should be hidden, for I was beginning to realize that even a mother could be astonishingly blind to the emotional temper of her child.

But I need not have fretted so foolishly over my aunt's reception. When I ashamedly crept into her comfortable, quiet house, she looked up sharply from the book she was reading. 'My dear child!' she cried rising with amazing spring for one so heavy, and, before I could say a word, had me stowed in a chair by the glowing heater.

Gently, her hand stole over my forehead, my cheek, felt my pulse. 'Now, sit where you are – sit perfectly still,' she commanded, and sailed off to the kitchen for a glass of water, into which she put some spirits from her medicine closet. When I had gulped it down, holding the glass with both hands to keep it from shaking, her patience cracked a little.

'What on earth are you doing out, in your condition? Don't you know you're sick? Doesn't your mother know it?'

Miserable to extinction, I nodded. 'Mamma sent me. She thought – maybe you would take me to – to the doctor.'

'Sometimes your mother —' she began crossly, then checked herself. 'Well, well, it's not your fault. But no one with a grain of sense would send a child in such a mess into the street by itself! It's stupid! It's heartless! There, there, child, I'm not scolding. I'll say no more. Now, tell aunty all about it.'

Well, that was not so easy. The tongue clove to the roof of my mouth, and, where before I had been chilled to the marrow, I was suddenly bathed in scalding perspiration. No confession ever came more hardly, or cost more pangs of cutting shame. But at last it was done. After which, it was almost joy to sit huddled in my faded blanket coat, letting the peace of the quiet house pour over me in comforting vibrations, while aunt gave orders to the cook, and then hustled into her wraps.

We were not obliged to wait in the doctor's outer office, for my aunt had telephoned that she was pressed for time, and must ask an immediate interview. Consequently, we sailed through the waiting-room without so much as a glance at the other patients, my formidable relative a mountain of strength, with me clinging to her might like a fluttering sparrow, fearful of everything and everybody.

Fortunately for my shrinking spirit, Dr Keys was a soft-spoken, stoop-shouldered man, with a kind, greyish face, and grave, quiet eyes. Just to meet those eyes had the instant effect of easing my twitching nerves, and, somehow, simplified the business of slipping out of my frock and dropping the top of my petticoat. Then, too, I was spared from speech. My aunt did the talking, making short enough work of the necessary explanations. In conclusion, she charged the doctor:

'Give her a good going over. But don't go putting sickly ideas into her head. There's more than enough trash under her bonnet as it is!'

Dr Keys, who knew and understood my aunt very well, chuckled, and proceeded with his mysterious tappings. Obediently, I said my 'Oh's' and 'Ah's,' now loud, now whispered, and tried not to anticipate the forthcoming verdict – hoping against hope that Katie's holy saints would hide from this miracle man the ultimate dark doings of my perverse insides.

'It's the heart,' said Dr Keys, putting down the stethoscope, and turning to my aunt. 'Strained. Rather bad – have to be careful.'

'The heart! But doctor, that haemorrhage? The child has a terrible cough,' my aunt objected.

'Bronchial – not the real trouble.' Dr Keys, who apparently eschewed unnecessary words, turned to his desk and began writing on a little pad. Then, as in afterthought, he remarked: 'Violent cough seldom tubercular. Complicates things, though. Here you are, little lady!' he smiled on me, holding out the bit of paper. 'Get that filled. Mind now, that you do as I say: no school till spring; no running; never skip; when the queer feeling comes, stand still; count ten; better still, sit down.'

None of which mattered, except that injunction about school. Yet such was my relief at having escaped the fate of Jorun Halson, I dared not complain. No doubt at all but the saints had saved me! At the very first opportunity I must tell Katie, and, if possible, slip her a penny for the Saint Anthony poor-box.

Buoyed up by this glorious thought, which translated my escape into the nature of a miracle, I found the trip back home less difficult, although the street seemed bent upon upsetting me with its mischievous wavering. Then, too, I was rather proud, and vastly comforted to know that I had at last developed a really ladylike ailment. It was so very fashionable to suffer with a delicate heart! Mamma, much to my dismay, was not the least impressed.

'What next?' said she. 'What a country, where even the children get weak hearts! I never heard of such a thing. Never. Well, to bed you better go. I'll bring you something to eat.'

A cold reception, thought I, slinking up the stairs. Later, I consoled myself with the brilliant assumption that if I were slighted too much I might reasonably expect to go off in a fine burst of emotion, like the poor gentleman whose wife had spurned him for a useless gallant. Such romantic fancies were not of lasting compensation. The weeks dragged slowly by with monotonous weariness. Something vital had gone out of the house. It had the depressing atmosphere of rooms that have been stripped of the homely treasures that give them living personality. No doubt what I missed were those pleasant hours when mamma used to tell her dramatic yarns to the youngsters in Winnipeg. Here there were no youthful contacts, no companionship of the sort that mamma deeply prized.

To make matters worse, my cognizance of her condition had erected a wall of inhibiting reserve between us. However hard I affected to thrust the thought aside, she remained a stranger, in whom it was impossible to recapture the image of the mother I had worshipped as an entity untouchable as the angels. Strange though it may seem, my attachment had not been of the affections, but of the mind. Mamma was my unquestioned voice of authority, my inspiration and source of wisdom. I had not thought of her in terms of human weakness, nor expected from her the kind of easy sympathy I had found in papa. Consequently, I was completely dazed by the shocking realization that even mamma was not exempt from the arbitrary fates. For the same intuition which had quickened my first understanding left me in no doubt as to my mother's own secret resentment. She had had enough of babies. Yet, here she was, absorbed and utilized in the unwelcome business, and daily more oppressed by the approaching event.

It was all strange beyond believing, and aroused within me no end of confusing speculations. I had the gloomiest forebodings that nothing would ever be quite the same again; that I should never more feel certain of any preconceived idea or eventuality. Having reached such a melancholy solution, I was not particularly upset when I learned that Christmas would not be celebrated in our house this year. Nor was I greatly astonished when even the cat disappeared. Cats, I told myself mournfully, were independent souls, and not to be pressed into conformity with human gloom. No doubt, wise pussy would find herself a more cheery haven.

On Christmas Day, Aunt Haldora made a hurried visit, bringing a blast of icy air and a whirl of snow that feathered to the floor as she shook herself with characteristic vigour.

'Now then, woman,' said she addressing mamma. 'What do you mean by this dawdling? You might have finished with the business before Christmas. Yes, indeed, you might have managed better. Now I suppose there'll be no getting you to help me eat the stuffed goose.'

Mamma received the banter in good part. Yet, I had a distressing conviction that something sharp as a sword flashed between them. That the air quivered under the shock of clashing temperaments, whose differences were too fixed for words. I could not have explained the why or the wherefore of this sudden notion, but I knew beyond any possibility of doubt that it implied some sort of ancient antagonism, some ineradicable dislike that persisted in spite of their obvious respect for each other.

Mamma put on the kettle for coffee as usual, and I set out the china cups.

'Foolishness!' cried my aunt. 'I don't need any coffee. And I've got to rush. I'm expecting a call from my grocer's wife any moment. Ja, that's why I came up here. I'm wondering which of you is going to interrupt my dinner. Well, Lars, what do you say to joining me? If I know my dear brother, you're not much use around the house. Ingiborg will be just as well off without you.'

Well, papa hemmed and hawed a little. He ought not to leave mother alone, he said. There was no one to send in an emergency alarm. Brother Minty had gone off for the day with a group of boys, and there was no telling when he'd be home. No doubt the whole lot of them would be hanging around the harbour until sunrise – they talked of nothing but ships and the sea.

'At least, that's what I gather from Minty's chatter,' finished papa, and took a pinch of snuff.

'Yes, and you encourage him,' mamma spoke impatiently. 'You never say a word against all that silly talk of the sea.'

'Well, what's the use of talking when a boy gets that kind of idea in his head?' my aunt interposed defensively. 'You don't imagine I wanted Finny to rush off to war? But, at that, you've got to let the youngsters find their own legs somehow. One way's no worse than another. Well, I must be off. I'll expect you before six, Lars. As for you, my fine woman, if you've got any sense, go to bed and get some rest.'

21

Solitary Christmas

Even with this cheerful break and the little bag of sweets aunt left for me, that Christmas was a dreary experience. The chill of it entered my very bones. It was so much harder to accept the betrayal of an ideal than to suffer ordinary aches and pains. Even a bilious attack would have been easier to bear than the creeping coldness of a house where not a single candle burned to the glory of the Little Christ Child. True, papa had tried to offset the gloom by putting up a huge tree in the extra bedroom, which was cold, uncurtained, and empty of furnishings. After supper, which I ate alone in the kitchen, I put on my best dress, and, thus girded with the trappings of gaiety, I made a bold attempt to keep holiday vigil in that cheerless room. But, although I lit the brightly coloured candles, and sat myself, Buddha-fashion, under the festive tree, nothing remotely joyous came of it. The twinkling lights were bravely beautiful, but their tiny, heart-shaped flames were no match for the unfriendly shadows that filled the room. Even when I tried to sing *Holy Night* – under my breath, so as not to be heard across the hall – the darkness only deepened. The shadows assumed fantastic shapes in mocking opposition to my lame merry-making. Tearfully, I snuffed the lights, and went to the window, seeking, as I loved to do, the far distraction of the sky: that jewelled space, wing-spread above the small green stage of earth.

It was a lovely night. The ugly street had put on a gentle beauty. Feathery snow, drifting thickly through the windless air, thatched the houses in layers of shimmering down. On the slope in the foreground three squat cottages reminded me of old ladies in hoods of Iceland wool, their slits of eyes smiling goldenly upon the peaceful earth. The uneven road lay smooth and white as a winding sheet let down from the dark fastnesses of the hills in the background.

Not a soul could be seen, except the solitary dog that shot across the path, sniffing the ground, the plume of his tail hugging his flank as he bounded along. Poor dog! I hoped he was on his way to a house where laughter rang, and the spicy odours of Christmas filled the air. As for me, I glued my own nose to the black pane and, gazing upwards through the dropping snow, found the silent, silver stars.

Young and foolish though I was, I could not for long fix upon that splendid spectacle and not be quieted when I remembered the timeless history in their watchful keeping; when my mind opened like a window upon the past that was as thick with human souls as the blue above was thick with drifting snowflakes. Suddenly, I found myself thinking of the tales papa loved to tell of the great law-givers of Iceland: of sages and singers, and fearless men of arms; a mighty company, whose deeds lived after them to inspire courage in the desolate ages that lay in store for their descendants. Those tales had often bored me – they had seemed so far removed from the tiny orbit of my tiny life. Now it seemed to me that those resplendent souls were drawing near, almost I could see them in the ghostly Valhalla of the dreamy night; almost I could hear their voices shattering the silence of centuries, bridging the illusion of time and the cold chasm of dead yesterdays. A strange excitement thrilled me, for now I understood a little what papa meant by the immortality of right effort. That which people accomplished, whether good or evil, was the true substance of themselves, and could not perish. It went on and on, born in memory and the hearts of later generations.

To me, forlornly standing at that uncurtained window, it seemed a profound discovery, a revelation that clothed those historic figures in lovable humanity, that made them real and companionable. Why, thought I, how easily the years fell away, bringing us all together in unified existence, when I stopped to think that the same stars which now were my consoling inspiration had lighted those stormy souls upon their stressful ways. And how much that was terrible and splendid they had witnessed on even my ancestral heaths! Embittered Gudrid, plotting death against Kjartin, whom she loved; Olaf's harper, singing with the arrow in his breast; dark deeds and fair, repeated over and over under these selfsame stars that shone upon our shabby little house. Oh, and, most wonderful of all, these same white lights had guided the longships of Leif Ericson over the shoulder of the world!

Tears dribbled down my cold little nose, but whether for these lofty sentiments or my own returning loneliness, who can say? It is hard to sustain majesty when one is only just turned eleven. Shivering, and sweetly sad, I scuttled down the stairs to the front room, where, for the last few days, I had been sleeping, on an exceedingly slippery sofa. I do not know when my father came home, or whether my aunt returned with him. I only know that when I wakened next morning she was out in the kitchen, cheerfully drinking coffee and telling papa, in stentorian tones, that she hoped to heaven this was the last of his nonsense. Catching sight of me, she quickly changed the subject. 'Well, my girl,' said she, 'you better go upstairs and see what a fine new brother you have got. But mind, don't touch him – you don't look as though you could manage a mouse, let alone a baby.'

'I don't want to touch him,' I said. Which was perfectly true. I have always had a horror of new-born babies. Then, duty-bound to explain such a strange phenomenon, I added, 'I don't think there's much to see any way. They all look alike.'

'Well!' snorted my aunt. 'Well! Well!' And looked at me as though she really saw me for the first time – but whether in a good light or not, I had no way of telling.

22

The world enlarges

The winter dragged along, with little or nothing to break the monotony. An occasional visit from Stina was the highlight of endless days that seemed to me just an eternal round of stupefying washings. To begin with, you washed yourself, or were washed. Then your little sister was washed. Then the breakfast dishes. Then the baby, the baby's bottles, and the baby's clothes, including a million diapers to be hung in the sun, or the air, at least. The lamp chimneys had to be washed and polished. Then the kitchen floor. By which time the dishpan was full again, thanks to the noonday porridge, flatbread, or pancakes. Well, now one might breathe a little in dryness and comfort, you would think. Oh no! This was a fine time to wash out the new stockings that mamma had knitted, or to turn out the cupboard, or launder papa's shirts. After which, of course, one had coffee to sustain the spirit, and provide a bit more work for idle hands. Which left an interlude for taking in the diapers, to be folded corner-wise, and for scorching flour for the baby's buttocks. Well! well! now it was high time to wash the potatoes for supper. Just barely time, in fact, before the baby had to be washed again for the night, together with his bottles.

The only exceptions to these cleansing festivals were my half-hearted visits to Aunt Haldora. I had really no wish to go, because of shyness and a deep sense of my inferiority. But my parents seemed to consider it a sort of duty, and, doubtless to make it a sanctified gesture, the visits were generally made on Sunday. This sharpened the ordeal, for aunt always insisted I should join the family at dinner, which I consumed in thorough discomfort, convinced as I was that every one present must know me for a nitwit with a bobinjay heart.

At this time my aunt had not as yet converted her house into the cottage hospital, although the plan was formulating in her energetic mind. But, being eminently practical, she had let the two best rooms on the upper floor to the Baptist minister, who was considered one of the handsomest and most eligible bachelors in the town. Naturally, I stood in fearful awe of this paragon, and could scarcely attend to my dinner for watching his every gesture.

He certainly was handsome, and quite gay, but apt to be brusque in speech, and even caustic, for he was something of an intellectual, and doubtless chafed a good bit under the narrow restrictions peculiar to the prevailing order of piety. He had dark eyes of exceptional brilliance, that seemed to snap and crackle at odd moments. Consequently, if he so much as turned in my direction, if only to ask for the vinegar cruet, I shivered in my boots, and sprouted gooseflesh all over my shrinking carcass. That he was an exceptional person I concluded more especially from a strange little habit he followed. At the close of each meal he ate a glass of bread and milk – not out of need or preference for such food, but because he had established the habit as a kind of ritual, by which he honoured the memory of his parents, who had been devout Quakers, and whose fare had always been poor and meagre. This peculiar gesture amused many people, but to me, always eager to seize upon the unusual, the strange rite seemed exceedingly poetic and impressive.

In time, I am sorry to say, the awesomeness of the young minister somewhat faded. I had joined the Sunday school of his church, and there, much to my amazement, heard him discussed with reckless familiarity. It was said that his looks, not his sermons, of which many ancient worthies disapproved, filled the pews; that maidens young and not so young, who tripped up the aisles arranged in their Sabbath best, thirsted less for salvation than for the sight of his flashing eyes. The most persistent worshippers were two spinsters, who had, of course, to be tolerated, for their papa was a substantial citizen, and the younger daughter played the church organ. This gave her a tremendous advantage over lesser damsels, who could only teach in Sunday school, or sew aprons for the occasional bazaars.

That the boiling devotion of these two devout virgins was something of an odious pest I came fully to realize, for not infrequently, when the persistent ladies swarmed up the front steps of the house, the poor young minister would flee down the back stairs, to escape by way of the kitchen.

Once, grinning like a gamin, he said to the cook: 'I'm out, Lena – that is, I *shall* be out by the time you deliver the message, so neither of us need suffer a twinge of conscience!'

'He's the nicest young man. Too nice for the cloth!' Lena confided to me, happening to be there on some errand. 'Puts him at the mercy of every old scarecrow as pretends she has a sin to confess, or a soul to save,' said she, hotly, pulling off her checkered apron to answer the snarling doorbell. 'Blooming shame, the way those old maids chase after him.'

On this occasion it was the organist, who had come to discuss the Sabbath hymns with her pastor, only to find her way barred by a resolute and far-seeing cook.

'No use asking you in, Miss,' Lena's voice soared triumphantly, 'his reverence has gone for the day. Called away sudden, he was – fearful sudden. Like as not, one of them deathbed miseries. Leastwise, we ain't expecting him back for supper. I'll tell him you called, Miss, and thank you kindly.'

Returning to the kitchen, Lena beamed delightedly. 'That's once she didn't get her hooks into him, the minx!' said she. 'Now, mind, don't be misunderstanding me. I ain't saying that I'd set myself against nature. But it ain't nature for an old girl who's clean forgot the year of her dipping to fasten herself on a young man, even if he is a minister. The poor thing ain't all gospel! He's soft-hearted, he is. Why, when your uncle drowned that litter of kittens last week, the Reverend lost his taste for dinner, he was that upset about old Puss. 'Tain't Christian, says he, to be taking the poor thing's babies from her. That's what I call a soft heart. And more like it will be his undoing, the world being what it is, all pitfall and trouble here below!'

Naturally, this bit of touching information increased my admiration no end, and also my concern for the handsome pastor. In fact I began to watch the organist with a coldly critical eye. At first glance there was nothing formidable about the lady. She was small and mousy, and wore a brown poplin skirt that hugged her narrow hips and flared out below the knees, making me think of a tea-cosy marching up the aisle. Above the cosy, rose a pink shirt-waist adorned with a frilled neckpiece, stiffly starched, and so immaculate that, in contrast with her face, the latter, piously unpowdered and sabbatically grave, had the look of a discoloured mushroom.

It was, at best, an inoffensive, pointed face, trained to a righteous smile that never varied, except when her mild brown eyes were fixed upon her shepherd in glowing worship. Which I, of course, interpreted as the outward sign of a desperate mind hatching fresh and feverish plots for the poor man's undoing!

Fortunately for my own peace of mind, I was soon back in school, where, to my everlasting surprise, I found myself promoted to the fourth standard, and so, at last, among children of my own age. The wonder of it warmed me through and through. For, think of it, I was no longer the big lout among babies, but just another kid in the class, with nothing to mark me out for special torment except my yard-long pigtails and my peculiar nationality. And even that would only have to be admitted when teacher recorded our names.

When the midday bell sounded I found myself marching out of the building with two other girls, bursting with protestations of friendship. In one voice they offered to walk home with me. That was very nice, very gratifying, and I tried to say so, but, out of the tail of my eye, I could see the dark figure of Katie, hovering in the foreground, a deep frown on her stormy brow.

'I can't – I've got to go with – with Katie,' I stuttered. 'I – I guess she's waiting.'

'But you're not a Pollack!' exclaimed the small wisp at my right, whose face was guileless as an angel's.

'Well, I'm just as queer,' said I, resolved to face the music and be done with it. 'I'm an Icelander. Any way, she's nice – she picked a million raspberries to buy a confirmation veil!'

'Gosh, that's funny! I mean, it's the cat's whiskers, everybody thinking everybody else is queer!' whooped the other, a sallow girl with stringy hair but the liveliest grey eyes. 'What's the difference anyhow? If Katie wants to come along too – it's all right, isn't it, Tilly?'

An innocent question, yet the words implied a challenge bordering on a threat, so it seemed. The little wisp grinned sheepishly. 'I don't care. Did I say she wasn't nice? You're always jumping at me, Laura J.!'

'Rats!' snapped the grey-eyed one, and shot away to intercept Katie, now slowly moving down the hill. Thereafter, for a period of almost a year, we made a solid foursome, against which the battery of even the fiercest derision was as chaff. For, if Katie was a firebrand, Laura Johnson was a comet of destruction. Even in class it was risky business for the toughest boy to pull a face in her direction, let alone lodge a spitball in her ash-blonde hair. A new boy tried it, to his burning sorrow, one lazy afternoon, only to find a hellcat on his neck, a howling fury, who not only scratched, but bore him to the floor in an undignified, tangled mass.

'Laura! *Laura*! LAURA! bawled the stoutish teacher who ruled our destinies. 'What in the *world*!'

'The dirty rat spit in my hair!' shouted the Amazon, letting go of the scarlet culprit, and smoothing down her frock, the while she fearlessly glared back at the astonished teacher.

'Dear me! Dear me! I *am* ashamed of you!' cried the lady, helplessly. 'Willie, is that true? Were you blowing spitballs?'

'I said he was, didn't I!' Unabashed, Laura answered for him angrily. 'Do you think I'd bash him up for nothing?'

Any one else guilty of such an outburst would have been soundly strapped for the insolence, but, as always, there was something so engagingly honest in Laura's violent exhibition that all the punishment she received was a piece of memory

work after four, and the unbounded respect of the young rough-
neck she had pummelled.

Tilly Rhinertson, on the other hand, was such a mild little soul
that she invited criticism. Even the teacher was not above caustic
remarks, and on more than one occasion almost drew tears by
her cruel fault-finding. Why didn't Tilly straighten up? Was she
put together on a shoe string? What made her so inattentive? If
she hadn't slept, why didn't she stay in bed – school was no
place to slump about half asleep!

Tilly shrank into herself, smiling. But, to me, who, as time
passed, had come to understand the why and wherefore of
Tilly's stoop and tiredness, these jibes were hateful. So hateful
that I grew to detest the fussy, fuming instigator of them, and it
inspired my first resentment against all self-appointed critics of
outspoken opinions.

How Tilly came to attach herself to Laura was no mystery,
although they had so little in common, for, with all her tartness
and temper, Laura Johnson had a kind, generous nature. When
she ranted and raved Tilly stood by, smiling, no doubt unconsciously enheartened by an exercise of talent denied to herself. Not
that Tilly was either a coward or stupid. Far from it. But by
nature she was of a temperament that preferred any compromise
to outright battle, and if her speeches sometimes lent themselves
to hurtful connotation it was because timidity, rather than harsh
intention, made her blurt out what happened to come into her
head. In time she was to shake off all these weaknesses and more
than justify the affection she inspired in those who really knew
her.

We became extremely fond of each other – formed one of those
lasting, unalterable friendships which are rare among women-
kind. For neither distance nor altered circumstances had the
least effect upon our little threesome. We quarrelled like cats
among ourselves, but stood back-to-back against all others. Yet
not until death removed one of us were we really made aware of
how deep and true this childish alliance was, how much it had
meant in affection, and how impossible to replace.

The Rhinertsons lived in a ramshackle house, built under the
brow of the hill, upon which the Halson houses stood like hun-

gry cormorants staring bleakly into unfriendly space. To the critically minded, they must have seemed a shiftless lot. The house ran itself. Certainly, there was no evidence of human interference. Except on Sunday, when things were 'redded up,' and Mrs Rhinertson concocted a very good cake and a huge batch of waffles against the coming of visitors, I doubt if any one ever knew where a single object, garment, or staple of food was logically to be found. Ordinarily, some sort of meal was cooked, somewhere near the customary hours, and was eaten by those members of the family who happened to be on hand. If they were not on hand, or the meal had disappeared, the unfortunate ones rustled up a bite as best they could. Even the chickens, upon whose largess these delinquents usually depended, led the same, disorganized life, scattering eggs where fancy dictated, and thus provided a thrilling hunt for the hungry children.

In this clutter the family lived with supreme good nature and contentment. Exhibitions of temper were almost unheard of, as no one in the family even thought of seriously criticizing any one else. Mr Rhinertson, a tall, gaunt Norwegian, years older than his wife, was a master-carpenter, an occupation which at that time was both well paid and in constant demand. So far as I know, he was always employed, yet the net result was only a string of children and the old house, which kept sprouting editions to accommodate the growing brood. In her youth Mrs Rhinertson must have been an extremely pretty woman, of the delicate blonde type, which, unfortunately, too often fades into pale insignificance. At this time she was still comparatively young and slender, but reminded me of a weedy willow, precariously braced upon a crumbling river bank. She looked, in fact, as though the least wind could whisk her away, and that, upon the slightest effort, she would fall apart. Even her clothes hung upon her in a loose, disheartened manner, as if not at all certain that this was their rightful peg. Her hair, of very fine texture, had lost its former sheen, and straggled in cobwebs from under the knot at the base of her neck, and her voice, equally colourless, was faintly quarrelsome, though not ill-natured.

Yet, for all this seeming listlessness, Mrs Rhinertson was tremendously tenacious, and fulfilled her specific functions with marvellous ease. Dressmaking was her love and passion, and she much preferred to run up a new frock to laundering an old one. So, too, she seemed to bear new babies with less effort than was involved in keeping track of her former creations. Once born, the babies became Tilly's concern, and Tilly grew stoop-shouldered, bent as a little old woman, under these ever-present burdens.

These and many other quirks and peccadilloes peculiar to the Rhinertson *ménage*, I was not fully to understand, however, until we had moved into their neighbourhood and our association became more intimate.

That we did make such a move, and to that particular locality, came about through a combination of circumstances that require a somewhat lengthy explanation. We had no thought of moving at this time, for papa was desperately bent upon saving a few dollars out of each wage-packet, towards building some sort of cottage on the edge of town, and, of course, it seemed a very remote possibility. Then, in rapid succession, occurred two tragic events which, in aftermath, decided our course and fixed us in the hills for years to come.

To begin with, John Halson's house burned down. As aunt had predicted, the fire broke out in the good man's cluttered study, which, on the instant, was transformed into a roaring furnace. The family barely escaped with their lives. The children slept in a loft, which was reached by a trap door and a ladder that descended into the kitchen. This way of escape was cut off by the leaping flames and clouds of coiling smoke from below. Except for the energy of Julie, who somehow managed to bundle the half-smothered younger children through a tiny window, it is certain they must quickly have perished. As, indeed, they might all have perished in their beds if Johnnie's little terrier had not roused them with his furious barking. His last loving service. How we wept to see his tiny, blackened form among the ruins! How bitterly poor Julie berated herself because the blinding smoke had forced her to jump before she could reach and save the little creature.

However, the dire needs of the destitute family quickly eclipsed everything else. Not a scrap, except the night-clothes in which they fled, remained to them. Of course, they found shelter in

Einar's house, but three rooms could not for long shelter so many souls. My aunt was called upon, and rushed to the rescue.

She found a house, and paid the first month's rent, and then, with customary firmness, she approached the ladies of the Presbyterian Church, of which she was an adherent, and not so much asked as demanded that every one who had a stick of odd furniture, extra bedding, cooking utensils, and clothes, should do her Christian duty. She made the same appeal to her grocer, and to the coal company – and heaven only knows who else. Consequently, the Halsons became a sort of holy crusade, for whose deliverance the whole town was shortly rallied. In less than a week they were far richer in goods than ever before, and infinitely better fed. Nor was that enough. Recognizing that now was their day of destiny, my aunt so worked upon the emotions of the head of the business college that Emma found herself enrolled without cost. Aunt, of course, furnished her with the necessary books.

'So far so good,' said she to papa, who had been doing his bit in the rehabilitation scheme. 'The poor creatures are safe for a few weeks, but you know what public sympathy is. It never lasts. Something new pops up to claim attention. Nor am I such a fool as to expect that virtuous windbag, John Halson, to change his habits. He'll never work where he has found such easy bread. I tell you, Lars, we must ship the whole lot to the coast. It might be the making of them.'

'Bless my soul!' exclaimed papa. 'Where will you find the money to send six people to the coast?'

'Tch! Tch! Would it be cheaper to feed the whole tribe for years to come? Besides, there are plenty of people in this town who can well afford to give a few dollars towards helping to make something of those very decent youngsters.'

Which point she speedily proved, for I imagine it would have been as difficult to withhold a contribution when my aunt marched in upon a simple business-man as to evade a Government levy. She was not the kind of woman to whom one offered excuses. The glance of her penetrating grey eyes, and the slightly scornful curl of her firm mouth, was much too disquieting.

Moreover, even silly people recognized the absolute justice of her impersonal attitude. If she asked for anything it was because the thing had to be done, and the doing of it somehow acquired honour.

It was not my aunt's intention that the Halsons should be shunted into unknown waters, as it were, without the best possible preparation. Papa wrote to acquaintances he had made at the coast through his journalistic articles, sounding these men for information as to working conditions in general and the fortunes of the Icelandic immigrants in particular. A stone might have wept at his description of the Halson calamity, the inference being that John was another Job, supporting in holy patience the afflictions of the Almighty, confident that, in due season, a righteous recompense would be meted unto him. To have any part whatsoever in helping such a good man to realize the fruits of his faith must, as a matter of course, be a profitable undertaking, bringing dividends of personal satisfaction and well-being. After this philosophic preamble, papa was naturally inspired to interpret the glorious possibilities inherent in the Halson children, every one of whom became creatures of the highest genius and unsullied character, waiting the guiding hand of some good Samaritan.

In the meantime, Julie found a job in a restaurant, Johnnie ran errands, Emma struggled with shorthand, and their saintly father, having borrowed what books he could, enheartened his wife with high, unworldly thoughts as she scrubbed at the washboard. For the present, the family had settled, so much as might be, into the old family rut: the children bringing home the loaves and fishes; mamma cheerfully performing the labours of Martha so that dearest papa might be free to interpret the tortuous ways of the spirit. With this difference, however, that an eager, adventurous sparkle was to be marked in the young faces as the girls speculated upon the forthcoming wonders of the coast, and, as for Johnnie, he had already fixed his mind upon the sea. He meant to be a sailor and visit every sinful port of which he had ever read, ending up a captain of a great ocean liner. All of which (to anticipate the future) shabbly little Johnnie accomplished, to the complete vindication of seemingly idle dreams.

There were other and tragic results of the fire. Whether from the shock of witnessing the terrifying spectacle, or from the exhaustion of rendering help beyond her feeble strength, Jorun Halson fell ill, and took to her bed. At first her general weakness and the heavy cold on her chest were not taken seriously. It was by no means an uncommon experience for the frail invalid to suffer these bouts with bronchitis and fever. Helga flew about with poultices, delicate broths, and, by night and day, saw that there were hot flat-irons at the patient's feet. These ministrations had never failed before, but now, as the slow days filed away, a depressing doubt began to torture her. Dear Jorun was not making any sort of recovery. The doctor was called, but even his energetic, conscientious efforts brought no improvement. The little lady whose shining spirit had been such an inspiration to the two plain souls who worshipped her had reached the end of her weary pilgrimage. There was nothing to be done but watch with her through this last dark stretch of the journey.

Papa undertook to relieve the husband and Helga in their nightly vigils. It was the sort of duty for which his gentle, sympathetic nature was eminently fitted. He, who had so often been perilously close to the borderland, understood what sort of comfort the dying woman needed. Hour upon hour, her small, cold hand in his, he sat beside her; silent when her need was peace; or telling, one by one, as on a rosary the everlasting verities upon which her heart must fix.

To have known and recognized the permanence of beauty; to have understood, however dimly, the everlasting quality of love, which motivates and sustains the living universe; and to have supported sorrow with unembittered patience: these three simple concepts of the true nature of life and man's power to rule his own spirit were a sufficient augury of an irrefutable immortality. Whatever was good or beautiful was eternal, and to have shared in either was to have projected oneself into an everlasting medium.

Toward the end, Jorun's mind, as so often happens, sharpened, becoming lucid as a quiet pool which reflects with silvered radiance each glancing light ray. In her little whispering voice she recounted bits of loveliness from the long-lost past. How sweetly the shrike had sung on the green hills of Iceland! How liquid and full of song were the rushing waterfalls – living lace let down by an angel's hand to soften the hard shoulders of the old grey promontories – how she had laughed to see the small lambs frisking in the flower-strewn meadows.

'You remember our mountains, when the sun beat down on their mottled flanks, picking out all the glowing colours of their Joseph's coat? I could never climb to the top like my happier friends, who had no infirmities. Perhaps that is why they have remained for me, "The everlasting hills, whence cometh our strength." I could never catch a sight of the sea from their snowy peaks – but I think I saw God in their quiet shadow. Oh, I thought of many things – not the kind of things that my poor Helga would credit, for, you see, I would like to have done something in the world – it was not easy to accept the part of a useless, broken thing.'

No doubt a sensible soul would have stopped this flood of melancholy confidences, but papa was not a sensible soul, thank God! He had the tender heart of an unsuccessful poet, whose sensibilities have not congealed into sterile ink. He knew, with the wisdom of the dreamer, that drops of pain bear witness to the growing life of the soul. He knew that this tragic murmur was not so much a futile grief for those unrealized opportunities as it was a tender pleading for assurance that what she had forged for herself out of her own inner resources was imperishable and true. He let her talk, and only hoped that Helga and Einar, whose comfort lay in the belief that their faithful care had brought her happiness, would not waken to be wounded by useless regret. Good, practical souls, it would not be given to them to understand how this unburdening would release the spirit unto its own immortal joys.

'I don't know why I tell you these things,' she whispered on. 'I don't even know why I should think of it now – except that it surprises me to find that all of it is so clear. For, you see, I had tried so hard to bury my dead. It had been so long since I resigned myself to the dullness of an existence devoid of hope. Determined to hide from every one my consternation that you could go on living, knowing so well that the future held no surprises – that even death, which touched me so early, would neither ease my hurt nor end my secret questioning.'

'Dear Jorun, why not grasp that thought more firmly. Isn't there something wonderful in the realization that, no matter how hard we try to accept defeat, it comes to this: that, in the end, every smallest broken hope returns as full of vital yearning as ever it was? Is not that the greatest surprise of all, and reason to believe in the everlasting realm of thought? Death touched you, you said. Are you then so sure it was not Life – the only true life, which is the essence of all ideas – that chose you out of the stream of everyday toilers, to search out its mysteries in quietness and resignation?'

The dying woman's eyes shone with unearthly brightness. 'I do not know if I rightly understand you. I am such a simple, unlettered woman, but it is true that I have thought more than I might have under better circumstances. Not deeply, but earnestly, and still the thread of what you might say seems indistinct. Yet, how sorely I long to know!'

Papa grasped her hand with gentle firmness. 'My dear friend, what is there to know beyond what you yourself have discovered? That God reveals himself in every circumstance and experience. Yes, in the doubts of our hearts, no less than in our highest aspirations! Wasn't it all said, with moving simplicity, by a stubborn little man who had to be stricken blind before he could see the truth of anything:

'"For I am persuaded that neither death, nor life, nor angels, nor principalities, nor things present, nor things to come, nor height, nor depth, nor any other creature, shall be able to separate us from the love of God."'

That, in essence, is the story of Jorun's passing. That I should remember it more clearly than many a personal experience is not strange. Aside from the gift father had of recounting even the smallest events, so that they became as real as concrete pictures, this particular incident was rendered memorable by a peculiar phenomenon. I don't know what wakened me, but wake I did this night, and, sitting up suddenly, I saw that mamma was also awake, and staring intently, her face white and strained in the dim light, at something I could not see.

'Mamma!' I shouted, my skin prickling queerly, for no reason. 'Mamma!'

'Be still,' said my mother, sinking back upon her huge pillow. 'Go to sleep, child. I thought perhaps your father might be coming home.'

Well, that sounded reasonable enough, yet I could not stop shivering, or keep from searching the shadows with expectant eyes, and the dawn was creeping in at the window before I drowsed again. We were at breakfast when father came back; very grave and tired; he slipped in and hung up his coat and hat without a word. Mamma set out another coffee cup.

'So she is gone,' said she. 'You need not tell me. She died at three. I know. I saw her, God rest her sweet soul.'

'Yes, at three,' papa answered, without surprise, and began to sip his coffee. 'It was a happy death, my dear.' And so, the tale unfolded.

That mother should have seen Jorun gliding into the room, to stand for the moment, smiling, at the foot of my bed, occasioned no astonishment to either parent. Mamma saw such things, and took them for granted. She always knew when any one near or dear was seriously ill, and was always warned of a close death. It was just as commonplace as the clouds in the sky, or the white summer rain washing the street. Something so ordinary that to surround it with mystery and make of it a topic of dissention would have seemed to her the height of foolishness. In all her life mamma never revealed the slightest interest in any phase of an after-life. If it existed, well and good, said she. If not, also well and good. In either case, her speculation about it would have no appreciable effect. Death was as arbitrary as birth and what followed was equally beyond human control.

For so-called spiritualism, and for the quibbling spiritualists whose little societies were creeping up everywhere, she had an amused contempt – the same sort of contempt she had for the egotist who laboured so diligently at saving his soul from a problematic purgatory. She was a practical little woman, impatient of speculative theories, and would as soon have entered a cage of wild animals as a spiritualist meeting, or an orgy of holy revival.

She believed in God, for not to believe in a Divine Intelligence seemed to her a little silly. Surely human wisdom, faulty and feeble though it was, implied some source of fountain-head other than matter. But she had no bent for metaphysics, and, like her ancient forebears, dismissed the thought by saying that whatever the Power that had sustained her through the trials and tribulations of this world, it would do at least as good a job in the next. It concerned her no more than the manifestation of sunlight. You lived, you did the best you could with such talent and strength as heredity and circumstance provided, and you died. That was the sum and substance of existence.

For me, however, cursed with the same sort of imagination that plagued my father, this vision of Jorun Halson, smiling at the foot of my bed, was not so easily dismissed. Who could say that the little lady might not come again! And if I should see her, would I be so calm and unperturbed as mamma? Diving into my bed at nights, and pulling the sheets up over my head, I doubted it sorely. For what, I wanted to know, was it exactly that mamma did see? She glided in, mamma had said – what, then, of all that business of angels with wings? If you weren't an angel when you began gliding about visiting your friends, well, then, when did you become an angel? From which thought sprang a dozen others.

The Last Judgement, for instance. How did that fit into a scheme of things where the disembodied spirit was already flitting about hither and yon, as it listed? Really, it struck me as a decidedly silly parable, without much point, and a complete disregard of common sense. Even I would not bother to drag people back from heaven and hell to judge them, when the judgement merely sent them back to their respective habitations. The more sleep I lost about it, the more certain I grew that papa must be right – and mamma, too, up to a point. The sensible thing was to believe in the immortality of right effort, and to believe what one's senses revealed as credible.

Confiding these thoughts to Tilly was not a very fruitful effort. Goodness gracious! Whoever heard of nice people seeing ghosts, or questioning what was written in the Bible! It was a sin. The minister said so. The minister had as little use for spirit phenomena as he had for the doctrines of the Scarlet Woman. Which doctrines, I inferred, were the abhorrent centre of faiths not his own.

'But, Tilly,' I said, 'what's the sense of teaching people they have souls that don't die, and then telling them they are crazy if they see a ghost?'

'But a ghost!' cried Tilly. 'Goodness gracious, I wish you wouldn't talk like that. I wish you wouldn't – it *can't* be right. You don't want to go to hell, do you?'

'How do you know there is a hell?' said I, now firmly set on riding logic to the bitter end. 'How do you know any of those things are true, any way? Just because somebody said so doesn't make it so. You don't believe that devils give people fits do you? Now, do you?'

'N – no –' said Tilly, vaguely, but suspicious.

'There you are!' I crowed, with more villainy than wisdom. 'That's in your Bible! It's full of people full of devils. So there! Now, what do you say to that?'

'Oh dear – I wish you wouldn't talk like that, I really do.' Poor Tilly was distressed. 'It's safer not to think such things.'

Which maddening remark I had the witlessness to repeat to papa, and got for my pains a cynical retort.

'She is perfectly right,' said he, calmly helping himself to snuff. 'Matter of fact, not to think at all is a still safer plan. You will find, my dear, that all sensible people like to have everything nicely arranged for them: their little heavens; their little hells; their saints and saviours; all done up in neat compartments, for which pleasures to share they drop a coin in the collection plate.'

'Lars! That's enough,' said mamma, trying to look severe, though there was a twinkle in her eye. 'You are talking to a child, remember. Do you want to make her more muddle-headed than she is?'

'Well, fish or fowl —' papa replied. 'According to your excellent logic, isn't it better to be completely one thing or another? A perfect dunderhead, for instance, is a joy to behold.'

'Oh, go back to your scribbling,' mamma retorted. 'And you, Miss, since you're too lazy to do anything, sit down with a book. That will give you something better to think about.'

Well, thought I, perhaps it would, if I had not already consumed everything readable about the place. Everything, that is, except a dull and disheartening volume of religious homilies, dedicated to God, and designed, it would seem, to give the reader dyspepsia after his Sabbath meal.

I was, like every other sentimental soul, to take my plunge into religion by way of salving my wounded ego, but that was still in the future. Just now, I was wanting to be put right on ghosts. The happiest solution was to revert to the *Pjodsogur og Munnmaeli*, a compilation of folk-tales peppered with all manner of tasty superstitions. Ghosts reared and ramped in that cheerful volume. They dropped down chimneys piece by piece, and stood forth, none the worse for wear. They bounded and haunted sinner and saint alike, and, not seldom, some foresighted minister of the Word made use of a really forceful *aftur ganga* to plague his enemies. With a spirited command, he sent the lost wraith to poke about bedrooms, rifle butter butts, and bang around the cookhouse, sending kitchen maids into fits. It was all very hair-raising, but not particularly enlightening. I was just as much at sea as before, on the relative status of ghosts, spirits, angels, or whatever thing it was men called their souls, once they had quitted the crooked lanes of life.

23

Meeting destiny

But though such mysteries filled me with pleasant unrest, they were quickly forgotten in the new excitement that descended on our household. Einar Halson had persuaded papa to buy his house. He had not the heart to continue in this town, now that Jorun was dead. He, too, would try his luck at the coast, and papa might have the house on whatever terms he could afford. Well, think of that! It wasn't much of a place, to be sure, but it stood on a hill beneath whose stony breast ran a full-throated brook that tumbled over itself to reach the wide blue waters of the St Louis River. The land on which it stood was part of a sixty-acre tract, and under the agreement of rental you might put in whatever garden you pleased, and could, besides, pasture a dozen cows on the green slips of meadows that threaded through the hills. There were other houses built farther up the slope, where fat German women waddled about in the tangled fields, shooing flocks of geese and fierce ganders that made a furious din, hissing like angry kettles forgotten on a hot stove, and flapping their wings with incredible impertinence. Geese must be a paying proposition, thought papa. He had a good mind to buy a few and become rich.

'Frightful creatures!' cried mamma. No, the thing to do was to get hold of some leghorns and a cow. You knew where you stood with chickens, and the baby had to have fresh milk. Well, dear me, you can imagine how many cups of coffee were consumed before all this tremendous business was settled – how many pancakes mamma had to fry before the few dollars which had been tucked away in a handkerchief box were properly spent. None of us slept very much, for what was the use of spending time so dully when you could be repapering the house, painting the pantry, laying out a garden, and counting a harvest of hens?

Best of all, for me, was the knowledge that, for years to come – probably for ever and for ever, until our heads were grey, Tilly and I were to be honest-to-goodness neighbours! The idea was so delicious that, in representing it to Tilly, I found myself for the first time so eloquent that we were forced to sit down upon a stone to support the onslaught of so much tender emotion.

'For, think of it,' said I, 'every single morning we can go to school together. We can be blood sisters, Tilly. We can be faithful and true for ever and ever and ever. We could even read together, if you ever get free of the babies – and if I had anything to read,' I finished, on a gusty sigh, considerably deflated after my flight of fancy, and suddenly plunging into despair as I reflected that, although a cow and chickens would lend us an air of respectability, they added little to the glamour of life, and nothing whatever to my private happiness. And then it was that Tilly made the first and only spectacular contribution to my painfully unfolding consciousness.

'Why don't you get a card from the library,' said she, shaking her dear little blonde head, on which a veil of fluffy snowflakes had settled wetly. 'There's a nice children's section. I've read all the Dinsmore books, myself.'

'What!' said I, hopping up, and almost choking with excitement. 'What do you mean, get a card – do you mean, you can borrow books – anybody – just for nothing?'

'Sure, why not? That's what a library is for,' Tilly replied, looking at me with oblique suspicion, as she often did. Well, for once I did not resent it. How stupid I must seem – what a crazy foreigner.

'Dear goodness! Think of it, I didn't know. And I can read like anything, too!'

Never was there an adventure like that one, when, in my shabby brown coat, buttoned tightly against the wind and snow, I set out for the local library. It was not much of a place, to be sure, just a long, dingy room in a low, dingy building housing offices and stores, but the moment I opened the door to see before me row on row of books on the unpainted shelves that lined the walls, all to be had for the mere asking, such a flood of emotion filled me that I could only stand there rooted in wonder, my legs like jelly, and the heart in my breast beating like mad. What a sight I must have been in my queer, made-over coat and knitted toque, wet pigtails down my back, like yellow snakes, and heaven knows what sort of dumb expectancy convulsing my round, colourless face. For the shameful truth was, I wanted to bawl – I wanted to howl to the stars. It was suddenly so clear what I wanted most in life, and always would want. And I had wasted seven whole months. Think of it, I could spell out whole words, almost as big as inch worms, even that long ago, and I had not known there were books to be had!

From somewhere, at a seemingly vast distance, some kind voice spoke, jolting me, red hot and prickly, back to the present.

'You want a book, little girl?'

Want a book? What a question – and how to answer, with a lump as hard as coal in one's throat? Somehow or other, I managed to squawk that was meant for politeness, and thoroughly ashamed of myself, hurried toward the desk, where a grey-headed lady sat watching me out of kind, very blue eyes.

'There is nothing to be afraid of, dear,' said the voice. Such a kind, low voice. Not at all like most American voices, that even I knew mamma was right in pronouncing shrill and unsympathetic. But, even so, I could not answer because something very queer was happening inside me, some travail of spirit, that had no words for its pain.

'You have only to sign a card – you can write, can't you, dear?' And a soft hand closed on my faded sleeve, sending a thrill of happiness through my tangled senses.

Yes, I could write, I managed to mumble, and forthwith proceeded to decorate the precious card with round gobs that looked like tiny eggs strung on a wobbly string. But it made sense. That was the important thing. *Laura Goodman, Ramsey Street.* For the first time in my life, the funny characters had infinite meaning. They stared up at me from the face of the card, and seemed to say: Now you have really come into being. This is yourself, this string of wobbly ovals. This is your passport into the world of men.

'So now you want a book.' The small, grey lady arose, and the swift rising was like a little wind that blows away the perfume of delicate flowers. Silently, I followed her to the shelves, where the children's books were stacked. Books with rabbits, and strange-looking animals, and stranger children, disporting on the covers. Pretty books with coloured pictures, and big round print. 'Here you are,' said the lady. 'These are a good beginning for a little girl whose English is still young.' And she left me, with a smile, to look the treasures over and make my selection.

That was very nice, of course. But what did I want with rabbits, and pert little hens, I, who had been fed on papa's heroic narratives and mamma's proud tales? Little by little, I edged over to the other shelves, and came, at last, to a huge, blue volume, where a man's austere features arrested my wandering eyes. *The Conquests of Julius Caesar.* But here was some one I knew! I had wept when papa explained the perfidy of plunging knives into so true a son of liberty! Thrilled to the marrow, I opened the book.

The closely printed page danced before my eyes. Truth to say, there was scarcely a word that I could understand. Yet there was something here that I wanted, something vital, some proud defiance that captured my fancy. The written word was beyond me, but the pictures were of fighting men, of splendid palaces whose ruins were like broken music, or rare and graceful images, which, even to my child's mind, expressed the perfection of beauty: poetry of line and motion, crystallized in immortal marble.

These pictures moved me then, as, indeed, they were destined to move me throughout my bit of time – moved me to a passion to live in this splendid past – to suffer the shocks of turbulent fate, and thrill to those ancient dreams, that even now, refusing death, breathed from these dull pages an irresistibly stirring charm.

How long I was lost in these pictures I have no way of telling. Several children, and a man in a bulky coon coat, drifted in and out again. But I remained there, locked in a trance that was at once an exquisite rapture and a frightening melancholy. For I was suddenly overborne by the meaning and majesty of books, conscious, for the first time, of the truth of papa's statement that to be a maker of books was the greatest destiny. Again and again, lifting his tired eyes from some yellowed page, he had paused in his passionate reading to remark with worshipping envy that only a maker of books had the power to immortalize his age. For he it is who gives fame to the great, justice to the vanquished, doom to the traitor; and out of his own troubled hour of life he creates an imperishable fabric that reflects the torment and splendour of his age.

Yes, I had heard this said so often it had become commonplace, no more arresting than mamma's strictures about rubbers and cod-liver oil. But now I understood. I understood that even in this one small, unbeautiful room were a hundred empires and a gleaming host of immortals, into which mighty company I might enter at will, thanks to the makers of books. Thanks to the saga-man, who wrote on the walls of time.

It was more than understanding. It was a conviction that sprang from something deeper than any mental process. It was a feeling that spread like fire through my consciousness. Standing there, rapt as a sleepwalker, an odd figure, surely, in my funny, made-over clothes, I was face to face with my own predestined *Vafarlögar* – with those fatal flames that quicken desire, and feed upon human vanity and hope.

In the light of that consuming fire, I could see that nothing in the world mattered, except the faculty to see and to feel and to understand what went on in the world of men, so that it might be caught up at a centre, and called a book. And then, in a blinding flash of terrifying impertinence, the wild thought leaped to my mind.

'I too, will write a book, to stand on the shelves of a place like this – and I will write it in English, for that is the greatest language in the whole world!'

PART III

24

New worlds to conquer

In the ancient writings of China, which are so ripe in usable wisdom, there is a saying which I shall now confess I had meant to take as a lodestar to keep this rambling chronicle from falling into utter confusion. The saying runs something like this: 'Count not time by the risings and the settings of the sun, nor by the turn of the years, but by those events great or small which have left an indelible impression; for we live not by virtue of length of days but by the brunt of experience.'

It seems an easy guide, a most simple formula, but alas! like the perfection of most simple things, it requires art of a high order and which therefore now appalls me. And yet the nice economy of arrangement suitable to the novel does not lend itself to this sort of narrative. How easy it would be, and how flattering to vanity, if at this point I could make a tidy cleavage. If, having stumbled into the world of English books and formed in a rash moment a fantastic ambition, I could sail along like a resolute heroine, sure of myself and the future. If, having discovered this wonderland, I could even say that it had brought me nothing but profit and pleasure, how neatly I might patch my quilt of years.

But nothing could be further from the truth. And truth, permit me to interpolate, is not the same for all of us. No, not even any given circumstance or experience stands in the same relationship to what we call truth, for any one of us.

After all, there are so many truths, and all of them are fragmentary. Truths, let us say, of the geometric order, which give us the impression of necessity; truths of the physical order, of which we conceive they might be mended; truths of the natural order, more contingent, at a given point, at a given moment in time; and so on, through a thousand speculations. Obviously, we pass from one order of truths to another, and, equally obviously, the character of truth itself changes with the objects affirmed, the speculations dealt in, with the passage of time. Which is merely to say that not only are the most commonplace concepts subject to endless alteration, but even so-called scientific truths never stand still. Everything is relative and subject to the demonstration of evidence. Applied to ordinary beliefs and experience, their sum-total of truth as bearing upon ourselves is therefore nothing more nor less than what we can extract from these things for our individual unfoldment and expression. There is no other truth and it is fruitless and foolish to quarrel with any one's fumbling manipulation of such problematic facts and heterogeneous experiences as come his way.

We learn a little, I think, chiefly by reason of the intensity of our interests, even though our reasoning may be neither particularly intelligent nor profound. In my own case, it is safe to say that I had at least a healthy curiosity, and a genuine interest in human beings. The daily round had no meaning except in so far as some happening brought out a sharp reaction in myself or others. More especially in others, for, as I have already shown, when I was a child I had little amusement except to watch the behaviour of our friends and acquaintances.

But now, in the months that followed my discovery of the public library, a painful change took place in my scrambling mental processes. In proportion as I became absorbed in a new type of reading, accepting everything therein as grand and glorious, I began to suspect the austere old tales on which I had been fed.

More painful still, I began to suffer (what every child of an immigrant race must suffer, I suppose) a vexing doubt of my parents. Certainly they did not behave like the brilliant creatures in these books. What was even more appalling, now that I began to look about me with a searching eye, I soon perceived that in most part we were horribly different from our American neighbours. We had no style. Mamma was as indifferent to the prevailing fashion as she was unimpressed by the manners of Mrs Jones and Mrs Smith. When I rushed home in tears because the beauteous daughters of a small contractor snickered at my clothes, all the comfort I got was a thorough scolding for my own ill-bred sensibility. It must be the squire of Ferry-Cot in me! Silly man, he was always vain and wanting to be admired by every fool. One must be above such nonsense. Indeed, people of character were entirely unconscious of trifles of this sort. She was utterly ashamed of me, and set me to patching a flannel petticoat.

Well, there you see what a nut I had to crack! Why, to begin with, even Tilly did not have to wear flannel petticoats, let alone patch them. The prospect was dreary as a November drizzle. Our house was as un-American as our garments. There was no carpet sprinkled with glowing roses in the parlour. There was no parlour, in fact, but a common room where the slippery sofa, on which I slept, apologized for itself in a shadowy corner and where mamma's big black bureau, glowering from the opposite wall, defiantly kept the secret of our antiquated finery.

The chairs, which wandered in and out as the occasion demanded their services elsewhere, were not the sort of pieces visitors marked with awe. It is true that, when the house was paid for, a high-masted organ came to rest between the two tall windows that looked out upon a rather pleasant grassy slope and the tumbling brook, which was the one really beautiful thing in the whole district.

But the advent of the organ only strengthened my suspicions. It always quarrelled with the bureau, and, moreover, reminded me of Papa Halson's psalm singing. The contractor's daughter executed the *Black Hawk Waltz* and *Robin's Return* on a glittering piano that reposed on a bank of red roses.

There were no pictures on our painted grey walls. We had no vases with spear grass and coloured leaves; no wreaths of wax flowers lay under a crystal dome on our haphazard table, which held, instead, a trio of plants that bloomed the year round. Nor had we any bric-à-brac, cockle shells, or cupids – all that mamma's cabinet boasted were cups and saucers, plates and pots, and a berry dish with a plain green border. It was very disheartening. Wherever I looked, our foreignness shrieked at me. We were hopelessly Icelandic, and doubtless doomed to remain so to the end of time. Mamma was not likely to be influenced by what I told her of Mollie MacDonald's house, even though her papa had the contract for the new meat market on Central Avenue. Though I were to outbabble the brook, I could never convince my parent of the importance of conformity with popular fashions, nor make her see the horrid crime of being different.

Nor could I expect much help from papa. Novel ideas intrigued him, it is true, and he might have grown enthusiastic over a tortuous system of breathing, or a new heresy with regard to Original Sin, but to tatting on the towels and flying birds on the pillow shams he would have remained indifferent, if not totally oblivious.

Indeed, I had ample reason to suspect that dear papa attached so little importance to such things that you might have set the kitchen range in the front room, and the organ in the shed, for all he cared. He might have thought it uncomfortable, and a trifle queer, perhaps, but not half so queer as the doctrine of the Trinity, and the Plan of Salvation. Any such topsy-turvy arrangement he would have accepted quite cheerfully as the normal aberration of human conduct, which always ran to fetish and feverish worship of the ridiculous.

But that it was really momentously significant to hang curtains of Nottingham lace at the windows and perch a plaster shepherdess on a nervous pedestal he could never have seen. All this you may be sure caused me no end of bitter cogitation, for I had the gloomy intuition that I should have to fight alone for some semblance of modernity and American culture. And, to make everything worse, the books I read so avidly led me to suspect that all was not well even with the contractor's daughter –

there was something not altogether convincing in her superior attitudes, and though I should have greatly rejoiced over a green carpet with purple dandelions, I was not quite easy in my mind that such a choice represented the last word in perfection.

I still derived peculiar joy from the barren halls and long fires of the Norsemen. Nevertheless, I was determined to take myself in hand and, starting with the outside, make the best of a sad situation. The logical first step was to get rid of my frightful clothes. Here was I, bottled up in prim poplins, unadorned as an egg, while all the decent little American misses billowed about in frills.

My battle with mamma ended characteristically. If her dress-making did not please me, I was entirely free to do better myself, said she. In fact, there was no earthly reason why my superior wisdom and taste should languish unseen.

That was a bit of a dilemma, I must confess, and the best I could do was beg a few coins of papa, and, calling upon the angels, I let the scissors take their course through the spotted brillianteen which was to clothe me in grace and beauty.

Well, there is this to be said about that remarkable creation, it certainly puffed! It was so agreeably free-and-easy that in a high wind it might readily have been mistaken for a gay and giddy balloon.

But, sad to say, a floating garment does not make a free mind. It seemed that I had exchanged my prim poplin for a prudish spirit. I could no longer enjoy anything for its own sake – I was much too occupied with the discouraging business of acquiring respectable scruples. Where formerly, as I have tried to show, existence, even at its worst, had a romantic flavour, because I had accepted it as a series of astonishing events, life was now become a most confusing tangle of social commandments.

As may be imagined, my passionate desire to become an unspotted American would not permit any question of these things. The less sense they made and the more they conflicted with my natural inclinations, the more certain I was of their sanctity. Consequently I contracted a virulent and lingering type of the comparison mania. Everything I had valued and enjoyed underwent a dubious dissecting. I perceived, for instance, how scandalously unprogressive, inefficient, and disorderly the poor Halsons had been, and though I had wept to see them depart, I was moved to thankfulness that I should no longer be lured by the Sunday chocolate to endanger my own future. The same was true of Katie. I still loved her, but I shuddered to think how joyously I had joined her and Mamma Pepolenski in their last berry-picking orgy, for no lovelier reason than to peddle our harvest from door to door.

Heaven help me! So crude was my orientation at the time (and this only last year, mind you!) that I had actually thought it a capital adventure. Panting up the hill-side in tow of fat Mamma Pepolenski, whose agility was incredible, I had felt myself treading diamonds instead of dew and heading straight into the red eye of the rising sun. And, with two little pails strung from a cord round my middle, I had tasted the delectable thrill of competition, as I valiantly, but in vain, attempted to keep pace with Katie as we stripped the tall raspberry bushes of their glowing spoils.

Yes, I had even thought it marvellously enterprising to traipse behind her sturdy figure as she offered this sun-born gift to the haggling ladies of the town. Dear me, how fortunate it was that the Pepolenskis had gone back to Poland, where, it is to be hoped, Katie found the good husband for whom she had prepared herself so well, and laid away in tissue her ankle-length veil.

Now all such robust vulgarities had come under a fearful ban, for I had come to a point where I innocently imagined that the hurdy-gurdy going round in my head was solemn thinking. I had reached the trying stage where I no longer reacted naturally to the common scene, but must, forsooth, listen to the carping of a timid, inner mentor. I no longer enjoyed, as once I had done, the cheery spectacle of old Mrs Scheider, as she came waddling over the brow of the hill, shooing her pearl-grey geese before her, as shrill a scold as her fiercest gander. Oh, no, I was much too conscious that her tough old feet were bare and her high round stomach unrestrained by a respectable corset! The kindly old world was no longer just an interesting place full of queer people who behaved with enchanting idiocy – it was fast becoming an appalling problem, which, in spite of its 'orneriness,' must be solved on strictly American lines.

For this brilliant assumption I had, of course, a perfect authority: my beautiful, slim-waisted, pompadoured school-teacher.

Perhaps it was the pompadour that made her seem so high-minded, as though she kept a bolster of wisdom tucked on top of her head, ready for all eventualities. Certainly, she did her best to elevate the assorted savages under her discipline. We hailed the flag with less indifference under her shining example, and never doubted that in the land of liberty for which it waved in the breeze we were all free and equal. In a vague way, I recollect that our easy conversion to this pleasant myth had something to do with the Pilgrim Fathers. Nor was this surprising, for, whenever Miss Brent found occasion to orate upon this remarkable set of fathers, her smooth pompadour seemed to swell with golden satisfaction, and something very like a purr crept into her exultant voice.

Even I, who thus early thought but little of the domestic virtues, was carried away with wondering amazement at their peculiar accomplishments.

Never before had I even imagined that such a sober lot of men could have left behind them anything faintly glamorous. But, somehow or other, Miss Brent created this happy impression as she recounted their exploits with bated breath. They had subdued The Wilderness! One saw the forest melting away like snow before their determined tread – simply whisking away into nothingness, and civilization in the shape of meeting-houses, stocks, and gallows popping up in its stead. Piety was the mainspring of all these miracles – indeed, it left me gasping. The Pilgrim Fathers not only bore with equanimity the struggle for daily existence, but gladly supported the chill of the meeting-house, where they praised the Lord from morning to night. Now, that was something! I tried it, and failed abysmally before the day was half spent.

Other wonders they accomplished with equal facility. They converted the Indians, and invented pumpkin pies. Yes, even jack-o'-lanterns were their idea, said Miss Brent, a trifle apologetically, and hastened on to more impressive examples.

Under Pilgrim guidance, the skittery female somewhat redeemed her sex. Abigail, Mary, and Mehitabel applied themselves to the loom and the distaff, and cheerfully filled the cradles and the graveyard, thereby leaving us the imperishable precept of righteous mothers in Israel. Naturally, wantons and witches were dealt with as beseemed a godly people who had left the sinful shores of England to plant the flag of liberty on the rock-bound coasts of Maine.

Of course, these concrete examples only served to show that Divine Providence had predestined the moral tone of the future republic. Even the most backward and barbarous among us must realize that the Pilgrim Fathers had stamped their sterling character upon the fabric of the nation. They had laboured as instruments of fate for those who were to come after them – yes, for even those of us who, like Ishmael, were of doubtful origin. And how they had laboured! Pretty Miss Brent folded her arms across a dainty bosom and transfixed us with luminous blue eyes. Why, think of it, with only scratchy chicken quills, the dear old things had penned reams of homilies for the uplift of the colony and females in particular. In the midst of subduing the wilderness, they had actually found time to settle the line of my lady's dress and fix the number of bows on her bonnet! In the same humble spirit they had studied the ways of the heathen and thereby learned the secret of planting the yellow maize, and the fine art of eating corn on the cob. They had tamed the wild turkey – tamed, too, the obstreperous spirits of the young by inventing the courting trumpet. Such mundane matters out of the way, the fine flower of their genius was free to concentrate upon a multiplicity of rules for human conduct, to the ends that even a fool should have found it difficult to err, bounded by so many safeguarding prohibitions.

Well, well, it was all most remarkable, and we were certainly glad that the sturdy little *Mayflower* survived the bounding billows to fetch such a cargo of piety and wisdom to these darkened shores.

To be strictly truthful, however, there were dark moments when I saw quite clearly my thorough unfitness for adoption into such a meritorious fraternity. My ancestors, remote and near, had never shown much humility, and I had the horrid feeling that any Norseman who might have dared to dictate his lady's shift would have found himself among the shades of Helja's halls in no time at all. Obviously, as a race, we not only laughed at laws, but were woefully lacking in modesty. Even mamma, with her stern rectitude, never dreamed of washing her intimate garments in a hidden pool like the pious matrons of old Boston Town. Not she! They flapped in the sun for all to see, and something told me that even the passage of the President would have given mamma no alarm. On the contrary, she would have expected the August Eye to brighten on beholding such a fine example of sun-bleaching.

Other offences stared me in the face. Heretofore, I had suffered no qualms when mamma poured a nip of brandy in papa's coffee on a frosty morning, nor realized the enormity of growing merry over a bottle of port on New Year's Eve. But now, of course, I must mend my ways – eschew, as far as possible, the reprehensible manners of my mistaken forebears. Whatever the cost, I simply must become an upright and useful member of the Great Republic.

Tilly sympathized with my ambition. The problem was, to find a logical starting-place. With so many perverse notions in my head, she suggested that the Elsie Dinsmore classics might help me to see the light. Elsie, she assured me, was exactly the kind of girl the Pilgrim Fathers would have approved. Why, even the Lutheran minister, who frowned upon all novels as inventions of dissolute and idle minds, found no fault in Elsie.

I flew for the book, and got for my speed a blighting experience. The sweet little darling of that tremendously popular series affected me like cold porridge. With the best will in the world, I simply could not see any particular virtue in dear little Elsie's sitting on a piano-stool until she fainted, rather than play the waltz tune her worldly papa demanded on a Sunday. To tell the truth, when the wicked man repented of his folly and was duly converted at the bedside of his pale angel, I lost heart completely. There was not the slightest use fooling myself any longer that such tender sensibilities were within my spiritual province. I must watch for something less dainty on which to feed my hungry ego.

The glorious opportunity fairly leaped at me when the village drunkard slit his throat – from ear to ear, mind you, and no halfway measure. Now, there was something to tickle the nerve ends and try moral fibre.

'Heaven save us! What a sight to see!' giggled Stina who brought the news. 'Just picture it, Mrs Goodman! Lying stark and stiff in his own gore, and not a soul to care! To think what some of us come to in this wicked world.'

Good old Stina had by now joined the hill community, and each evening she came floating down the stony path that led to our door to fetch the quart of milk mamma always set aside for her, and rarely did she fail to bring some morsel of gossip. As might be expected, the milk required a preliminary drop of coffee to spur her up the hill again with the green lard pail. But this was more than gossip – ja, sure, it was life at its worst, and the devil's doing! So there she sat, chirping away in the tone – slightly chill and breathless – she thought suitable to sorrow and tribulation. In so far as was possible to such a happy human magpie, her mien was sternly serious.

'Sure, it's a terrible thing,' said she, shaking her head and reaching for a rolled pancake, 'a terrible, terrible thing, even for a sinner bereft of his senses by alcohol, to lie forlorn, and lost, with not a soul caring – with none to shed a pitying tear.'

There was the gallant mission for you! Something more commendable than pining away on a piano-stool. I must shed that pitying tear. In fact, I could feel the moisture pressing upon my eyelids the moment the thought was born, for you must know I instantly saw myself drooping above the dead, shedding the soft, benignant tear. It was a very moving idea.

But, alas, hard on the heels of the beautiful vision came the chilling recollection that here was no ordinary death. On sober reflection, I saw the feasibility of a little moral support. I still wanted to weep for the lone, lorn sinner, but after all, the deed would be doubly glorious shared with another. There was no use offering the opportunity to Tilly. Something told me that Mrs Rhinertson would frown upon any connection with suicide. She was a respectable church woman. No one worked harder at a rummage sale, or baked better pies for the thanksgiving festivals. She, nor her offspring, had little need to rush into the alleys of life to perform an act of grace. Laura J. was a better prospect.

To begin with, the Johnsons were a funny lot – so said the neighbours. Mr Johnson was a noisy, virile woodsman, who literally blew into the house on his infrequent visits, roard at Laura (who was a step-daughter) in good-natured bluster, tossed his own progeny about like balls, and drove his poor wife nearly crazy. How such a morose and melancholy female had ever captured his fancy was a complete mystery. In the five years of my close friendship with Laura I never once heard her mother laugh, express a cheerful opinion, or even agree to anything whatsoever. She moved about the house in a perpetual miasma of irritable gloom, attacking every bit of work with a kind of suppressed fury, and saying nothing until some inner geyser erupted, and brought a sharp staccato reprimand to her thin, colourless lips.

Between mother and daughter the queerest of relationships persisted. A sort of honourable undeclared warfare. In everything save mutual stubbornness, they were poles apart. Young Laura was tender-hearted, erratic, gay. The mother affected you like a cold vinegar compress. The warmest emotion shrank to zero under the chilly sting of her mere presence. Yet the poor lady must once have possessed some fatal charm to acquire a double dose of husband and five boiling progeny.

Laura had her own peculiar method of attack. Bouncing into the kitchen, she announced stentoriously: 'I'm going to L.G.'s, ma.'

No sound from ma, but the banging of a pot lid, or the thumping of a swishing broom.

'Ma! I'm going to L.G.'s, I tell you – I'm going for supper.'

Still the screaming silence.

'Ma! Ma! —'

'Am I deaf, *crazi ungi*!' ('Crazy youngster.')

'Well, I'm going! Do you want me to do anything first?'

'You are not! Fetch some kindling, and be quiet!'

'Sure, ma, but what's the matter with that lump, Ole? Can't he do something?'

No reply, naturally, nor did Laura expect it. Blythe and bouncing, she filled the kindling basket, and then, instantly assuming her embattled expression, returned to the attack.

'Well, I'm going, ma.'

'I said not. Be quiet.'

'Ma – I'm going.'

Valiant sniff from the corner of the room, where ma was angrily kneeding a mess of bannock.

'Goody-bye, ma!' shouted her daughter, straightening her tam, which was always shifting to one ear. Not a word from ma, only a perceptible thickening of the atmosphere.

'*Good-bye, ma!*' roared the persistent child, bounding for the door, and rattling the cracked knob. 'GOOD-BYE, MAMMA!'

Then, in final, but honourable surrender, ma returned the roar: 'Good-bye – *crazi ungi*!'

This curious method of procedure never varied. The silent, soured woman always said no to every proposal, and never once succeeded in keeping her *crazi ungi* from doing exactly as she pleased. The moment the door shut behind her, Laura beamed upon the world, cheerful as a cricket. For the moment she was the victor, and all was well.

In the end, this everlasting friction, gloom, and struggle, bore a bitter harvest which, unfortunately, neither the acid mother had wisdom to foresee, nor the victim of her perverseness sufficient guidance to escape.

But that is to borrow from the future. At the present time neither Laura nor I took the daily round very deeply to heart. We were much too busy with our own emotions, and a new and sharpened awareness of the world. When I gave any thought, beyond a half-alarmed wonder, to those curious scenes, it was to reflect that Mrs Johnson was like thunder, noisy, but ineffectual, whereas mamma was like lightning – and pity the poor object she wished to annihilate!

Well, you will see that the neighbours had some justice on their side. The Johnsons were queer enough; which, for my present purpose, was rather an asset. I had only to suggest that Mamma Johnson would undoubtedly disapprove our charitable excursion to be sure of Laura's passionate support. Otherwise, knowing her to be full of morbid notions under her surface gaiety – screaming with terror at the sight of a dead gopher, and thoroughly convinced of the reality of ghosts – even my best persuasion might utterly fail me.

So that was the unscrupulous line I followed. Laura gave a sharp yelp at mention of the suicide, but the moment I mentioned her mother's possible objection, her mind was made up. The idea was crazy, but of course she'd go. She had as much right to make a fool of herself as I. So far so good, thought I. Yet it would never do to take along such a sceptic. Besides, my romantic instincts were cruelly wounded. Was it foolish, said I, to show ourselves merciful towards this forlorn sinner who lay forsaken and forsworn in the undertaker's parlour? How would she like to be left like that without so much as a single flower on her breast, or a solitary tear shed above her bier?

Laura wept as easily as she raged. 'Gosh! I never thought of that. You say the darndest things, L.G.' Whereupon I strained my noble efforts, drawing upon Stina's touching vocabulary to such an extent that we both sat down on a boulder behind our barn and wept deliciously.

Our better natures thus firmly to the fore, we finally resolved to scour the neighbourhood for posies. White asters would be most fitting, we thought, with just a touch of scarlet to strike a tragic note, and a background of asparagus fern to give our bouquet a professional touch. Old Mrs Scheider had a huge asparagus bed, and a bank of sweet-william under the kitchen window. She was rather a nice old lady, even though she walked about in bare feet the colour of baked mud.

Mrs Scheider received us with beaming enthusiasm. *Ach, Himmel!* So we felt sorry for the poor man who cut his throat? Good hearts we had – we should have a handful of fresh pretzels for such a pretty thought. And all the flowers we wanted. Oh, but weren't we scared? Such a corpse was not a pretty sight?

The pretzels were nice and salty, the flowers all we could have desired, yet it must be owned that a chilly gravity descended upon us when we left the Scheider yard and turned our steps towards town. By the time we reached Recktor's Parlours (which was a gloomy, one-story building appropriately opposite a flourishing saloon) neither of us dared to look at the other. The same, horrid expectation shook us both. Left to individual inclination, we should have bolted, but pride is stronger than cowardice. There was nothing for it but to turn the clammy knob, and plunge into the dark terror behind that dreadful door.

What was this? No dead strewn about? No miles of coffins? Just a pleasant, tidy room, with varnished chairs in rows. Two healthy ferns beside a table, and a little folding organ in the dark corner. Not even a cavernous clerk. A curtained window at the back let in a stream of white autumnal sunshine. There was a scent of incense in the air! Quite an ordinary little man, with a mild blue eye, tidy fringe of hair round the pale pancake of his scalp, and neatly waxed moustache, materialized suddenly to ask us in mildest tone the nature of our errand.

Exactly what tumbled from our stiffened lips I cannot say. Some sort of trembling duo about the poor suicide and the posies, which I thrust forward in great haste.

'Oh —' exclaimed the little man, with, I thought, an unbecoming humour quickening his glance. 'How very thoughtful – you will want to place them yourselves, *of course.*'

O Vision of the Pitying Tear, how far and fast it had flown. 'No! No!' I wanted to shout, but that sly twinkle, for now I was sure it was a derisive twinkle, decided me.

'Of course,' I repeated, with what I imagined a perfect imitation of mamma upholding the honour of her ancestors.

Believe me, it was a bad moment. Glancing at my gallant partner, I perceived that her habitual sallow hue was now peculiarly vivid, as though some elemental sprite had poured pea-soup under her skin, and the glassy stare of her eyes was anything but enheartening. However, I had always a mean sort of tenacity, which, early and late, has stood me in good stead.

'Come along, L.J.,' said I, grabbing her arm, and making after the little man, whose very back, it seemed to me, quivered with challenging amusement.

At the threshold of the terrible door he suddenly fell back, and, moving aside, motioned us to enter. Well, there was no escape now. None whatever. Unless the angel Michael did us a swift and saintly favour, we must go on with the bluff, and drape our garden flowers on that hideous breast. For, of course, we must have expected, and, perhaps, in our savage soul, really secretly hoped for the worst.

So how to explain our mingled feelings when the poor dead lay at last before our wild young eyes, I do not know. For here was no ghastly sight, but a quiet, most painfully respectable gentleman. Not a hair out of place, his greying moustachios sprucely turned, and a gleaming expanse of starched shirtfront, on which I hastily laid my floral token. He might have been the Lutheran pastor lying in state, so well had the city, which let him starve in the gutter, made amends now that it was too late.

Outside, we frankly bolted, running like a pair of frightened hounds back to the comfort of our shaggy hills.

'Gosh!' wheezed my faithful sidekick, as we clambered upon a good grey boulder, where we could swing our legs and look down the shining runway of the creek that skirted papa's turnip patch. 'Gosh darn, I *never* was so scared! And to think it was all for nothing – they must have sewed him up neat as a sock!'

Which ended the matter, for we discovered that we had a cent between us, and decided that a couple of liquorice sticks would soothe our rumpled nerves and set the world to rights.

25

Adolescent conditioning

This put an end to our pretensions towards charitable grief. I think we all fell in love – and not only our threesome, but every other girl in the class. The object of our passion was a new student who, in addition to having a fascinating profile, played the piano with dash and tremendously impressive gestures. His name was Simon, and all I now remember of him with tenderness is, that on Valentine's day I was the happy recipient of a pinkish card that bore flattering erasures testifying to our hero's romantic struggles. Patently, it had first been intended for Laura J., but wound up with my initials instead. I am glad to say that I had the fortitude to refrain from drawing attention to this amazing fact, although, quite naturally, I slept with the precious missive under my pillow for at least a week. After which, I am sorry to confess, we had an unholy scrap about Swedes and Norwegians, which ended all heart throbs. Simon was a Swede, and not unnaturally, took it amiss when I quoted Olaf Trygvasson's opinion of his Swedish enemies: Swedes, said the great king, were not to be trusted, for in guile they were almost the equal of Danes!

Well, poor Simon might have forgiven me even this if, to clinch my argument, I had not reminded him about the erasures on the Valentine. Even in love you could never tell which way a Swede would jump, said I, and flounced off, leaving Simon to the softer graces of Molly MacDonald.

What stings of conscience I may have had were soon forgotten. The complex business of growing up was too engrossing for any one twitter of emotion to hold the stage long. We three inseparables, Laura J., Tilly, and I, held many a counsel on the good old sun-baked rocks in our back-yard, tackling everything under the sun with sublime confidence in our ability to hit upon the right solution. Mostly, these orations had to do with the shining futures we meant to carve out for ourselves, and our individual reactions to what we mistook for a precocious grasp of life.

Foolish though we were, and buoyed up by all sorts of sentimental trash, we none the less understood quite thoroughly that none of us would have an easy time attaining our simplest ambitions. Laura wanted to go to a business college, but where on earth was the money to come from? In a household where there never were enough decent shoes to go round, and a joint of meat had to serve for six different stews, was it likely she'd get any help from that quarter? When she finished grammar school she meant to go to work. The match factory paid five dollars a week, and even after paying board she hoped to save towards her ambition. Tilly wanted to go to work too, but not to save money, but to spend it fixing up the house. To get a carpet, and curtains, and new chairs – and a girl had to have some nice corner to entertain her friends. Tilly's idea of perpetual bliss was founded on the Dinsmore myth. Mine was the most fantastic dream of all.

I, if you please, wanted a college education. It would all be very simple. I had only to finish the ninth grade, take a year of Normal (possible then), and teach my way to glory and renown. It was a dream I kept bright, as I washed the kitchen floor of a Saturday, shined the lamp chimneys, and renewed the pink rags in the fat belly of the parlour lamp. Yet there were weak moments when I wondered if being a fairly good student were all it was cracked up to be.

Molly MacDonald was such a dud in class that she couldn't conjugate a verb without choking on her teeth, but she was going to finishing school next winter to fit herself for the kind of profession Tilly coveted, and would never embrace. Not because Molly had a sweeter nature, or the maternal heart, but because

Molly's papa was now in politics, and, consequently, picked off the biggest civic contracts. I understood that clearly enough – as clearly as I understood how surely Mr MacDonald attributed his successful chiselling to the grace of God.

It would seem that nature, by way of compensating for many deficiencies had generously sprinkled my natal dust with the wholesome salt of scepticism. Which might have served me well, had I not betrayed the gift and followed instead the foolish lure of impossible ideals. Even at this early stage I suspected the weakness of the pretty sentiments peddled out for our edification – be good, sweet maid; kind hearts are more than coronets; virtue is its own reward, etc., etc. Nevertheless, I wanted to believe in this nonsense, and tried, therefore, with amusing silliness, to emulate the Sacred Monkeys, seeing no evil, hearing no evil, speaking no evil.

Destiny and desire are not always compatible. The comfortable blinkers that most sweet souls wear throughout life, to the exclusion of distressing realities, were not to be my portion; nor yet the soothing cotton wool of indisputable conviction that shuts out all contrary thought. Whatever my predilection, I had to see and experience no end of things that the average individual knows only by hearsay, or not at all.

There came an unforgettable day that was to leave an indelible impression. Mamma, who had always great pleasure in sharing anything she had with others, sent me with a quart of Jersey cream to my aunt, who, by now, had transformed her house into a cottage hospital. She was getting on in years, and found it arduous to continue her rounds in every sort of weather. Gone, naturally, was the handsome minister, and gone, too, the former atmosphere of intimacy. The homeliest place was the kitchen, where a variety of housemaids presided, untroubled by snooping interference.

But, on this day, when I stepped into the cheery room out of a golden autumn sunshine, I was instantly oppressed by a feeling of freighted tension. The cook was nowhere about, nor were there, at the moment, any sounds of activity. Thinking the girl was busy upstairs, I put the cream in the pantry, and then, every nerve jittery, tiptoed through my aunt's private quarters. I was just on the point of mounting the stairs when a sudden piercing shriek rooted me to the spot.

My impulse was to flee, but my feet refused to move. What followed was so hideous, I felt as though my own flesh were riddled and torn with a battery of javelins. The sudden assault upon the nerves was nothing compared with the subsequent shock of horror when the significance of these ghastly cries flashed upon me. Everything in me revolted, every quivering sense rebelling hotly against this obscene anguish at the roots of life. Yes, now I understood what was going on up there. What, my terrified mind told me, was going on and on and on all over the whole wide world. A shambles of suffering, senseless and cruel. And, I thought with fierce loathing, no life was worth such a trial of suffering.

I wanted to run, to hide for ever from such hideous reality. But to save my soul, I couldn't stir. I sat there paralysed in shameful misery and vicarious pain. Oh, would it never end, never, never be over and done!

Why didn't my aunt put a stop to those unspeakable wails! Oh, I was soon to learn how much more insufferable the sounds of spent and dying energy can be. The poor, tormented voice lost all its human quality, changed to hoarse, inarticulate, animal groanings, that made me long to howl in horrid sympathy. Then, in a wild burst of reviving consciousness, the hateful sounds shaped to piteous clarity:

'Dear Jesus, save me! Save me! Jesus! Jesus —'

Almost simultaneously, the door opened, and, dreadful to behold, there stood my aunt, slumped against the edge of the door, broken, beaten, such a look on her face as I shall never forget.

O God, I thought, now all was lost! When that tower of human strength hung there, defeated, what hope remained for the pitiful sufferer. But Haldora Olson was not the kind of woman to support defeat. Only a moment or two, she steadied herself, breathing heavily, summoning all of her flagging forces with eyes shut, with lips a ridge of drawn purple in a strong, out-jutting chin. Then, with a quick lift of the shoulders, as though to unseat weariness and fear, back she marched to the grim battle.

I cannot say, for time had lost its meaning, how long thereafter it was that Berta, the cook, came streaking out of the room with a bundle in her arms, and the tears streaming down her face. I don't suppose anything could have surprised her after such an experience. A fainting youngster cringing on the stairs occasioned no concern. Catching sight of me, she fairly yelled in triumph:

'She pulled her through! She saved them both! Dear Lord, I never saw such a woman!'

Feeling very small and insignificant I crept out into the mellow twilight, but with a warmth of pride about the heart – a beat of stirring happiness in my frightened breast.

I had plumbed the ugliest fears in an overwhelming realization of menacing death. Those awful moments were often to infest my dreams, awake and asleep, but always the sturdy figure of my aunt came to the rescue. Life was full of terrors, that I perceived, but courage, plain human courage, was a force that worked miracles. And now, too, I could appreciate the answer my aunt once made to a pious dame who was taking her to task for laxity in church attendance.

Said the lady: 'Surely you have some thought for the afterlife? Have you not considered that you must render an account at the judgement seat?'

'Sure,' said my aunt, with jovial patience. 'If old Peter gets obstreperous at the Gate, I'll wave my forceps under his nose. That, I think, will silence the old fellow!'

But to go on with my tale. That experience seemed to usher me into an entirely new world – a world I frantically sought to dodge by burying myself in books more deeply than ever. I found my escape in the nature poetry of Bryant, and used to go mooning about the hill-side, or sit for stolen hours in some cranny of rocks overhanging the brook, mumbling *Thanatopsis*, and *The Ages*, growing sweetly tearful over some noble savage in chains. Yet even this device could not for long stop or stem the natural curiosity that prodded and pricked my mind.

The rhythm of verse was an enchantment less fascinating than the mystery of life. I began to see human beings in a different light; for the first time I was conscious that the really interesting thing about any one is not what he seems at any given moment, but what he represents in the sum-total of his experience. I was still very much of a child, and thoroughly enjoyed the surprise parties that were the order of the day, but, in the midst of such a lark, I would suddenly find myself worrying about Mrs Peterson and Mrs Berg, and even Simon's antics at the piano would lose significance. And again fate conspired to feed my curiosity. In quick succession a number of events befell, each one contributing its lasting impression.

To begin with, that case at the hospital became a sort of village wonder, discussed everywhere with varying emphasis. It was commonly agreed that my aunt had performed a miracle, but that it was rather a pity the effort had not been expended in a better cause. For Olga was an unmarried mother, you see, and, as a woman of thirty-eight, should have known better.

Which was doubtless true, yet neither the sinner nor my aunt seemed to think the situation called for sackcloth and ashes, although Olga had not a cent to pay for her care.

'Oh, I expected that,' said my aunt. 'Look here, my girl, can you cook a decent meal?'

'God love you, how do you suppose I got myself into this mess!' exclaimed the beaming miscreant. 'Sure, it's the black truth, you can cook yourself to what a man calls his heart. If it's a cook you want, Mrs. Olson, I can pay off a dozen babies in no time at all.'

So Olga remained, not only a month or two, as so many others were to do, but for three years, presiding with energy and dispatch over the big kitchen – cheered to the marrow, as she used to say, by the sight of her little Stanley tumbling about the floor. A more amiable creature never fell from grace. In the end, aunt got so fond of her that she gave way to occasional grim forebodings.

'I can't think why the Lord made a woman like that!' she'd say angrily. 'No hips at all! I hope the creature has sense enough not to marry.'

Which was asking too much of an optimist like Olga. One day she met a farmer from northern Wisconsin, a very decent man, who accepted little Stanley without comment, and Olga thought herself the luckiest of women to have found a kind father for her nameless son. Two years later she died in childbed.

But that is stealing from the future. At the time of which I write, Olga was just entering upon her long service, and I had yet to learn, by contrasting her kindly behaviour with that of many another self-righteous mortal, that so-called sins of the flesh are perhaps the least of evils. I, naturally, was not much of a character analyst, but neither was I so stupid as not to perceive that Laura's mother, for example, managed to make herself and her daughter thoroughly miserable, and her whole house a forbidding place to enter, although she was doubtless free of the cardinal sins. Yes, and despite the fact that she meant well, and really thought she was spending herself for the good of her children. This thought, no less than the more arresting events I have been leading up to, gave me many a fretful hour. For I had the tidy sort of old-maid mind that wanted everything fitted into neat little pigeon-holes.

The two happenings which now transpired in quick succession, to give me still another slant on the peculiar workings of the human mind, have to do with Stina, our dear old gossip. She and her Sam had a tiny cottage on the brow of the hill, above our house, and, though the place was small, she had made room for Big Tom. What is more, she surprised every one by having another baby. A little girl, now nearly two years old, of whom she was immensely proud.

Milde was a sweet little creature, with wide blue eyes, and the kind of sunny hair that looks like wisps of summer cloud. It was more than touching to see how tenderly the plain, hard-working mother waited upon this tiny human being – the little flower of her old age, as she used to say. Marvellous were the ambitions Stina had for the pretty child, and, of course, poor old Sam prized her even above his sacred unions.

Then, one Saturday morning, just as we were sipping the ten o'clock coffee, in burst our neighbour, wild-eyed and distraught.

Milde had taken sick! But the sickness wasn't natural, said Stina, sinking into a chair and staring at mamma helplessly. She was sleeping now, the wee angel. But all night she had tossed and cried out – sometimes gasping as though ghostly hands were tormenting her, choking the breath out of her little body.

'My dear Stina! It may be a touch of the croup. Children are subject to such things,' mamma calmed her. 'I'll come at once, if you like, and perhaps we should send for the doctor.'

Stina started to cry. No, Milde was quite all right now. She breathed easily, and had no fever, but, the fact remained, something evil hovered over her. That Thing in the Night was a Visitation!

'Now, Stina, be sensible. Drink a bit of coffee and put such notions out of your head. Very likely the child ate something that disagreed with her.'

Stina obediently drank her coffee, bolting it down like a bitter medicine. Then she said: 'It's no use denying these things, Ingiborg. *Isafell's Mori'* (Ghost of the Mountain) 'is after my child!'

So there it was. Sam, it seems, was a member of a family afflicted with a ghostly follower, a malignant creature who, in each generation, took vengeance for an ancient wrong done him by a cruel employer. Nothing that mamma found to say could in the least comfort Stina. She knew in her heart of hearts that Milde was the chosen victim.

To satisfy herself that the child was not seriously ill mamma immediately set off for Stina's house, and, so far as she could judge, the little girl appeared quite normal. In the afternoon she was playing about as usual, and so we thought no more about it. In fact, Stina and her ghost were the subjects of affectionate derision that night at supper. It was all nonsense, said papa, but added: nevertheless a lot of intelligent old-timers firmly believed in *Isafell's Mori*.

Whatever it was, we were sufficiently shocked next morning when Sam, almost beside himself, tore into the house to tell us that little Milde was dead. She had died at dawn, in the throes of some sort of violent convulsion, with no other signs of sickness, and no warning of the attack.

Poor Stina! There was little enough we could do for her, except to share, with all our hearts, in her bitter grief. To listen, days on end, to the pitiful tale, not even daring to dispute the justice of the sins of the fathers being visited upon the children. But at last Stina comforted herself with the thought that little Milde was safe in the heavenly country.

'Ja, maybe it's best,' she sighed. 'My little love won't break her heart as women do in this world.' After all, she herself was lucky to have Valdi, who was such a good boy. Smart in school, and always so cheerful about delivering the washing she did for the ladies in those fine city houses. A handsome boy, Valdi, and never a nasty word out of him, thank God.

There was another shock in store for our good neighbour. One day Big Tom came home from work, and, for once he had something to say.

'It's early, I know, Missus,' said he, apologetically. 'I ain't feeling so good – in here.' And he tapped his broad chest.

Stina left the wash-tub, and flew for the coffee-pot. 'Man, dear, you're green about the gills! Now, Tom, don't perch on that hard chair. Take the rocker by the window. You'll soon perk up with a nice hot drop. You hadn't ought to work so hard at your age.'

Tom accepted the chair in silence, but when Stina brought the cup, he made the first speech of his life:

'You're a good woman – I – I – well, good!'

Telling us this afterwards, Stina covered her face and wept. 'Such a look in his eyes, poor man. It made me ashamed, Mrs Goodman – me, that was so often so short, what with my sore feet and all.'

His speech made, Tom had drunk his coffee, and, a little later, went out in his silent, shadow way. Stina finished her washing, and began to make supper, before she realized that her boarder had not come in again. He was not on the porch, nor in the yard, where he sometimes did a bit of weeding. Then, suddenly, she knew, and came rushing for papa.

Big Tom, always the butt of malicious fate, had died in the outhouse. To Stina, this was an almost insupportable misery. Ja, it taxed her faith in Almighty God! It was so unseemly for a decent man to die in such a place – as though it were meant as a final insult.

Kind soul, she did her best to make amends, and nothing would do but that her few acquaintances should honour the dead man by gathering round his coffin in her small front room, before he was taken away. As might be expected, these friends were humble women, none of whom could speak English very well. They came in their Sunday best, their plain scrubbed faces eloquent of honest sympathy. They had not known Big Tom, except as a plodding, inoffensive toiler, coming and going upon his dull rounds. But they knew death, as all the poor know death. Their solemnity was sincere, and their faith earnest.

When they had sat in respectful silence for a woeful interlude, and then suddenly realized that no pastor was present, that, in fact, no other rites were to be held for Big Tom, one good old soul rose to the rescue. Tears streaming from her faded eyes and her hands weaving nervously, she addressed the solemn company.

'It's not fitting to say nothing. What's in the heart should come out. Big Tom, now – God knows, we are sorry – Big Tom – ja, poor man – p-poor man —' tears choked her, and, with a heroic rush, she concluded: 'He lived like a dog – and he died like a dog. Lord Jesus receive him. Amen.'

Thus, luckless to the last, Big Tom departed our ken.

This same year mamma began to worry about my Christian education. I use the term advisedly – my possible ignorance of the Scriptures, not any fear of moral obliquity, troubled her. Mamma was a firm believer that decency was inbred, not imbued. But she held firmly to the notion that respectable people should pass their religious examinations like any other. That I knew the contents of the New Testament almost by heart she was well aware. Papa had given me an English Testament, which I still treasure, and which is marked from cover to cover. I was to learn English by reading it, and read it I did, every night for many years. Now, however, mamma wanted this reading to bear some tangible result. I must be confirmed like every other child of decent, Episcopal Lutheran faith.

But how to do it was a problem. There was no Icelandic church in Duluth. The only solution was to attach myself to the Norwegian church which Tilly attended.

It seemed a timely thought. The church in question had called a new minister, a young man full of zeal and fervent ambitions. The old church was to be completely renovated, the basement enlarged, new pews installed, and a pipe organ was to replace the rheumy instrument which in former days defeated every musical effort. And to start the thing off right, the official opening of the reborn church was to centre around the pastor's first confirmation class. Well, you could hardly ask for a more auspicious entrance into respectability. Still, if I were to be thus favoured, I decided that Laura J. must share the good fortune. Laura's mamma naturally objected.

Crazi ungi, how did she think Papa J. could find a confirmation dress, and goodness knows what other nonsense? *Crazi ungi* raised her voice for righteousness and rectitude, and won, with breath to spare. So Laura, who understood as little of Norwegian as I, read the English Catechism with me.

The class was large, and we two were forced to sit through all the tedious examinations of the others before our answers were required. The Reverend Bjerke was a serious young man, determined that none of his sheep should go amiss. In addition to the Catechism, the wider sanctities were impressed on us. The Virtuous Life eschewed all frivolity, such as card-playing, drinking, dancing, skating to music (for some reason incomprehensible to me, it was commendable in the open, but not under a roof, where you were comfortable), the theatre, wordly books, unseemly companions, immodest language, foolish mirth, and, above all, the dangerous pitfalls of spurious religions.

For the first time in my life I became intimately acquainted with Satan, and all his works, and the sulphuric terrors of the yawning pit. It all had a dreadful sound on the Pastor's grim lips, and yet, to tell the truth none of us lost an ounce of weight. As a matter of fact, we were all very fond of Pastor Bjerke, for, despite his fierce recitals, he meant to be kind, and certainly his earnestness was above question.

He had married just before taking the charge, and as soon as his wife was established in the modest manse, he celebrated by giving us a party. Dear me, what a serious business it was! How impeccably modest and self-effacing was the lady of his heart. Except to shake us by the hand and play the organ for a brace of hymns, and to pour coffee in smiling shyness from a high silver pot, Mrs Bjerke discreetly kept the peace.

This humility made me thoroughly uncomfortable, for the women of my family were by no stretch of imagination gentle doves. They did not look to their husbands for approval before they cracked a smile at the mildest joke, nor defer the faintest opinion to their lordly sanction. Which was, I soon discovered, the appointed ritual for young Mrs Bjerke.

No doubt this was good and beautiful, but, somehow it left me as unconvinced as the precious prattle of Elsie Dinsmore. So too, much of Reverend Bjerke's lusty thunder passed over me with small effect. His vitriolic blasts against other forms of faith, for instance, only served to sharpen my critical senses. I had spent three years in the Baptist Church, and, so far as I could see, there was little difference between that hapless congregation and this little flock. And if there were a difference it favoured the Baptists, whose hymns, at least, were cheerful, and their minister a joy to the eye. Also, for a brief while, I had attended Sunday school in the Presbyterian Church, of which my aunt was a member, but fled in consternation when a lady tapped me on the shoulder, and, in dripping piety, inquired if I were saved.

I had been led to believe in the mercy of God, but not in the practice of boasting of grace. Moreover, I knew quite well that mamma would have been amused at the notion that an infant of thirteen had as yet anything to be saved from, anything at all to brag about. However, these ventures furnished me with courage to contend that other denominations were as concerned for the souls of men as Our Saviour's Lutheran Church.

For the most part, Bjerke confined his barbs to the Catholic heresy – for the Scarlet Woman who had set up her Abomination of Abominations in the Holy of Holies. Idolators! Deluded mortals, steeped in superstitions. A betrayed people, who fixed their faith in signs and symbols: for example, the sign of the cross.

Well, at that, I pricked up my ears. Believe it or not, I still crossed myself when I said my prayers, nor could I see why the moral effect of such a practice was any more superstitious than setting up the cross on the altar of the church itself. Moreover, when Bjerke waxed oratorical, painting the glories of the church as the Bride of Christ, I was tempted to ask if he had not stolen a leaf from the pages of Catholicism. To be truthful, I not infrequently plagued the good man with outrageous contention, all of which he bore with patience although he seldom permitted the little Norwegians to say a word. If any had wanted to say a word!

Perhaps the novelty of my impertinence amused him. Or mayhap he may have realized that honesty, and no desire to be smart, was my defence. Or perhaps it was simply that, as yet, he had not hardened into the unyielding jelly of infallible bigotries.

Be that as it may. Whatever good I derived from this experience, it had nothing to do with Bjerke's instructions. In all those months nothing except questions of doctrine, and various chosen passages from the Scriptures, was discussed. All of which stressed the moral of implicit obedience to a God who thereupon smote your enemies, and made a jolly bonfire of the miserable upstarts who questioned the rules of the game.

This Germanic ideology might have appealed to me – it is so tremendously flattering to imagine one's self the chosen elect of an all-powerful dictator – if I had not read the New Testament in the same spirit applied to any other book. If I had not formed a picture of Jesus of Nazareth as a man above all bigotry and hatred, a man clothed in the righteousness of a tolerant mind, sensitive to beauty, compassionate of weakness; who loved the birds of the air, and the lilies of the field; who spoke in parables, which is the language of poetic hearts; and said of the Sinner: 'Neither do I condemn thee.' There it was, simple and direct, a sword of truth, against which all this sectarian thunder must surely die.

For the moment, however, I was bound over to the dusty rituals, and must acquit myself creditably in the pastor's eyes. I must stand forth fully equipped on confirmation day. And let no one imagine I had not my own earnest desire to make something of this experience – a confession, not of religion, but of an honest desire to respect the precepts of decency and justice.

Pastor Bjerke did not spare us, bless his heart. With the conscientious patience of an inquisitor, he plied his questions, gravely heard the answers, and ponderously elaborated upon the meanings therein, and the seriousness of the step we were taking. And there we stood, in our new-found finery, solemn little owls, growing hungrier by the hour, and foolish with fatigue.

My good aunt had come out for the occasion, dressed in her Sunday satin, but, when, almost two hours had dragged by with no signs of weakening on the pastor's part, she picked up her reticule, and, indignation in every rustle, stalked away, nothing caring how many saints she shocked.

Greeting me later over the celebration dinner mamma had prepared, she said: 'My dear child, does the man go on like that all the time? Assaulting thought with Biblical brickbats? Heavens above! Well – well – did you like the muff I gave you?'

Certainly I liked the muff. Liked all the new regalia, which, I fondly hoped, gave me a very smart appearance. The cashmere dress, with its overlace yoke and shirring, was nothing to sneeze at, believe me. A competent dressmaker had made it, and proudly declared that the puffed sleeves were copied from the dress of a society queen. I had a new coat, too, of slate grey, form fitting, which added years to my innocence. Indeed, I could almost believe my hated plumpness was easing up a bit. My face would never launch a thousand ships, or even a single frigate, but the rest of me wasn't so bad. An opinion which seems to have seized upon the fancy of a very nice young man in the congregation, for, a couple of Sundays later, he very properly saw me home.

Goodness me, that was a twittering occasion. Nor was he to be got rid of so easily as Simon. He was not argumentative, which was a terrible handicap, and he loved books, which made it impossible not to be interested in his conversation. Moreover, it was very flattering to be asked to the next basket social.

But the fly in the ointment was my passion for another fascinating creature, a beautiful thing called Manfred, whom I worshipped from afar, had never spoken to, and should very likely have died of ecstasy had he so much as glanced my way. And there was still another complication. Never mean with my affection, I had a really soft spot in my heart for Arne, one of the boys in the confirmation class. All through that fall Arne had steered me safely past the terrors of the homeward path. It was difficult, to say the least. Tilly thought it very romantic, for Carl was quite the best catch in the church. She said she and no end of girls were angling for him. Even Mrs Bjerke's niece had her eyes on him. If I had any sense, I'd nab the poor dear before he changed his mind.

This excellent advice had a startling inference. 'But, Tilly,' I yelped, 'I don't want to nab him. I don't want to nab anybody. I'm going to school for years and years and years.'

'Just the same, I'd hang on to him,' she retorted, with admirable logic. 'To make safe. You'll never find any one nicer.'

We had reached that certain age, it seemed. A delightfully silly age, where, for a brief interval, we played with emotion, walking in rosy light, and forgot reality. It was all very harmless and innocent – a statement which will be suspected in this day of Freudian preoccupation – nevertheless, true. I shall come to more serious attachments, but, at this time, our romantic attachments never exceeded the charming business of holding hands at a sleigh ride, or on the doorstep under the stars, and, strange though it may seem, it was very, very thrilling.

To be sure, I had enough to keep me occupied in school and at home. I was still subject to bouts of bronchitis and everlasting migraine headaches. There was scarcely a week when the latter did not steal a day or two from my classes, and I had therefore to work the harder when my senses cleared. Then, too I read an unconscionable lot, made all my own clothes, helped with the children's clothes, did the marketing, and not infrequently the Sunday baking. Carl, and the odd social, were the least of my concerns.

What did intrigue me, far above any flutter of romance, were the pathetic cases that drifted to my aunt's hospital. From all over the State, and sometimes from Ontario, these girls and women came to be eased of their unwelcome burden, and to hide from society. That so many strange human histories unfolded before me was not due to any persuasion on my part. I popped along to the hospital, and aunt, perhaps looking up from some bit of reading, would push up her spectacles, eye me soberly, and say:

'So there you are! Well, run up to number eight. There's a poor creature needs cheering. But, mind you, take no stock of what she says. They're apt to lie, poor souls.'

Up I'd go to number eight, or ten, or two, or whatever it was. Not much wanting to be a perambulating confessional, but nobody, in his right senses, crossed my aunt lightly. At first I nearly perished of fright, as I entered these little cubicles, so overcast with tangled emotions. For always, the *feel* of a room communicates a great deal to me, and the vibrations of spiritual anguish are a terrible force. After a bit, however, my very shyness and stupidity inspired confidence – as though each of those unhappy Magdalenes said to herself: there's no harm in telling my troubles to this idiot, no more harm than talking to the clothes-press.

26

Tales out of time

It is not my intention to run through the whole, colourful catalogue, but I hope I may be pardoned for retelling two or three of these stories: the two or three that really exceed fiction in melodrama, needless tragedy, and twisted humour.

There was Bessie, who, for several weeks after her baby was born gave me music lessons, because my aunt thought it would settle her mind, and that I might as well benefit by the healing process. Bessie came from Port Arthur. She was a fragile, soft-spoken young woman, with fair hair and the wide blue eyes which are supposed to be so appealing to men. She had a fairly good education, and was an excellent musician. Her people were the sort we usually call the salt of the earth. Decent, respectable, hard-working people. Bessie's story reads like something out of Dickens at his most lacrimal inventiveness, yet it was impossible to doubt her.

Bessie was the only daughter in a family of several sons. Her father worshipped her, and her brothers, who had paid for her musical instruction, were immensely proud of her. Yet it was they who unwittingly paved the way for her tragic experience.

One day they brought home a mining engineer, a young fellow to whom they had taken a fancy, and who wanted lodgings in some decent house. He came on a visit, and remained over a year. That he should have repaid the kindly regard of the family, and Bessie's affection, as he did, is nothing new in human affairs, but the way he made his escape deserves mention.

Employed as he was, it was not unusual for him to be away for several weeks at a time. After one such absence, Bessie, in fear and trembling, confessed her predicament. But of course there was nothing for her to fear! Certainly not. Was he not her lover?

How ashamed she was, to have doubted him! How she wept in his comforting arms! Once again, all was well with the world. Even when, a few days later, he left again, she accepted his smiling reassurance in perfect faith. He had a job to finish, but when that was done they'd be married, and go away somewhere. Twice he repeated his flying visit, each time augmenting the golden promises. Then, silence.

Weeks of silence, while fear turned her blood to ice, and every night to sleepless misery. What was she to do? To whom could she turn? To her brothers, who were so proud of her? To her father, in whose eyes she was still a little child? To her mother, who would suffer the most, believing that she had failed in maternal guidance? Night after night Bessie struggled with her terror, not quite believing the dark intuition of her heart.

Then, one morning, she stole up to her lover's room, where some of his clothes still hung in the closet, and his trunk stood under the north wall. With rising alarm, she thought, perhaps the trunk was empty? For a glance told her that the clothes in the press were discards. No, the trunk was not empty. When she shoved it, in sudden anger, it didn't budge.

'And that,' sobbed poor Bessie, 'was what frightened me out of my wits. It was too heavy! Even before I pried the lock, I seemed to know what was in it. Oh God, I don't know how he could do it. I don't. I really don't —' And then she fixed me with her wide child's eyes swimming in tears. 'The tray was full of stones! Stones, from the fields where he made love to me.'

So now those flying trips were explained: trips to remove his valuables, without arousing suspicion. The rest of the tale came out in broken phrases, both of us frankly crying. There was nothing now to be done except to tell her mother, and the mother, of course, had to inform the father. Poor Bessie could hardly go on from there. Her father had been so crushed, so utterly broken, and then had flown into such a towering rage.

He would set the law on the scoundrel! He would have him tarred and feathered! Oh, any number of mad threats fumed on his lips. But, in the end, the poor parents knew that none of this would benefit their daughter. What they did decide upon, was to send Bessie away, before her brothers discovered the truth. And here she was, presumably visiting a relative. When the baby was born, a good home was to be found for it, and she herself would return to pick up the broken pattern of her life. Oh, yes, she was sure that that was best. That nothing else was possible under the circumstances.

What she failed to consider, what they all had failed to consider, was Bessie's unspoiled, normal instincts. The moment the baby was born, she refused to be parted from it. The very thought made her clutch it to her breast in wildest agitation. She refused to give it up. Rather than part with it, she would never go home, but somehow would fend for herself where she was.

My aunt wired for the mother, not to dissuade Bessie from a natural course, but to give them the opportunity to hatch a fresh scheme. And, pathetic enough it was. Bessie's mother was to pretend she had adopted the child of a relative, who had just died in Wisconsin, and Bessie herself was not to come home for several weeks. (Since becoming acquainted with her home town, I've often wondered if anybody was fooled.)

Well, that was better than nothing. The baby would be hers to love. 'Oh, my sweet!' she wept, hugging the little creature. 'I can't ever be your mummy – but I'll love you – love you.'

The baby had to be weaned, and that night Bessie cried herself sick. It was after this that my aunt decided she should give me music lessons. To take her mind off the child. But the baby had only to send up a thread of sound, and away Bessie flew, nothing caring how I murdered the scales. How vividly her memory lingers. How often have I longed to know the end of the story.

Then there was Catherine, whose story not only touched me at this time, but was to unfold yet another chapter some years later. It is not an easy tale to tell, for the rock on which Cathy's happiness grounded was religious prejudice, always a touchy subject.

And I should like it understood that my rambles amongst people of all shades of faith have convinced me that the score of kindly people is the same in all of them. That the thoroughly unreasonable person is so, not because of his faith, but by nature.

Cathy's father, a prosperous business man, was the sort of household tyrant we have come to associate with the Victorian age – a paragon, with no lovable weaknesses. The kind of man who neither smokes, nor drinks, nor lets himself believe that he ever cast a lingering – not to say lascivious – glance at a pretty ankle. He was a pillar in the Presbyterian Church, blessed his bread before eating, and, quite naturally, expected his wife and daughter to render thanks to Almighty God for such a flawless husband and father.

He was liberal with money, and maintained a good home. In other words, he had all the easy virtues, but not an ounce of actual charity, not even a glimmer of spiritual grace. Everything he did was right, and whatever he believed was beyond a single point of difference. His church was his God.

Until Cathy met Jim no occasion had ever risen to threaten the sway of that Presbyterian authority. Jim was a Catholic, and Jim had the audacity to love Cathy with a most unreasonable tenacity. But what really threw papa into violent fits was the discovery that his own child, his flesh and blood, his pretty, carefully reared Cathy, returned this outrageous affection. There were tears and battles, and more tears and battles. Cathy's mamma, the meek sort of woman such men always choose with unerring good sense, tried a little mild argument.

Jim was such a nice boy. Indeed, there was nothing the least wrong with him, except his religion. And, after all, was he responsible for the delusions of his parents? Well, what of it? roared papa. If a man had small-pox, he was not responsible, yet one did not endanger life by contact with him. Was Cathy, the apple of his eye to risk even worse infection? No more arguments, *please! Not a word!*

Love is no respecter of religions. Cathy simply flew to Jim in secret, and the hopelessness of their case increased their need of each other. That they reacted unwisely is no reflection upon their innate decency. They were both very young, very much tormented by a multiplicity of emotions. For Jim was just as judiciously steeped in his particular brand of loyalty as Cathy. He was a devout Catholic, and his sisters, much older than he, were equally devout, but, as the final sequel will demonstrate, had also a sense of duty that Cathy's father could not have exercised.

It was a thoroughly miserable mess. The kind of mess good people provoke and doubtless will continue to provoke so long as their goodness is tangled in sectarian creeds. When the inevitable consequences of all this useless struggle had to be faced, Jim very sensibly decided that they should be married at once. Cathy confided in her mother, and then the real battle began.

It was impossible! Quite impossible, moaned the thoroughly frightened mother. Papa would never survive such a shock. Only last year they had lost their elder daughter, and all papa's affection centred in Cathy. It would kill him if she married against his will – and, moreover, how could she think that this – this other horrible thing, wouldn't be just as insupportable, even though they did marry?

I must confess that, if Cathy's mother had not herself repeated this part of the tale in an agony of grief and self-reproach, I might have come to doubt it. For, quite frankly, I have never been able to understand this, how human beings can believe that God, the Spirit of Life, can possibly be served by the destruction of his creatures. But the mother so worked upon Cathy that she consented to be sent away. They told the father she had an offer of a secretarial job in Duluth. So, here she was, in one of my aunt's little rooms, eating out her heart and whiling away the endless hours writing to Jim, and, of course, to papa, who had to be told how the job progressed. Jim paid her expenses. That's another thing I've noticed about piety. It seldom quarrels with the sources of money.

Cathy was a handsome, robust-looking girl, but appearances are seemingly deceptive. In the sixth month she began to develop serious symptoms. Aunt called in a specialist, who diagnosed her trouble. Diseased kidney, said he, which was the worst possible report under the circumstances.

Aunt at once decided that Cathy should be taken to the general hospital, where she would receive the necessary supervision and treatment. But, in spite of every care, she grew steadily worse, and before the month was up her condition was so critical that my aunt, who was still the go-between, sent for the mother and notified Jim he might expect a wire any moment.

A few days later Cathy died, giving premature birth to twins. Now, thought my aunt, indignantly, the wretched father will realize the enormity of his wrong-headedness. The poor young things might just as well have had a happy year or two. But, she was wrong. Overwhelmed though she was with her own loss, Cathy's mother thought first and foremost of papa. Never, never, must he discover the circumstances of his daughter's death. It would kill him. He felt so intensely, and his heart was so bad. Cathy's death he could accept, as an act of God – but not – not the image of Cathy as the mother of illegitimate children! Utterly disgusted, aunt let her weep. Weep and pray.

The practical details she attended to herself, helped to some extent by Jim, who bore the brunt of all the expenses, though so numbed by grief it was pitiful to see.

The end of it was that Cathy returned home in solemn state, to be buried from the Presbyterian Church, and the little scraps of humanity were taken over by my aunt. What a fight she made to save them! Tiny, blue, under-developed, they had no more gotten a lease on life than they developed a severe cold that every minute threatened to cut off breathing.

Night and day, she watched them, in the end applying artificial respiration, and I don't know what else. Futile, said the doctor, utterly futile! But one of the children survived, and grew to be a pretty little girl for whom my aunt formed so deep an attachment she wanted to adopt her.

But that was not to be. And here I must borrow from the future to end the tale. Jim, who obviously could do nothing about the baby without casting reflection upon the memory of

Cathy, compromised with his conscience by sending the odd donation for little Ruby's maintenance. Of course, my aunt acknowledged these gifts by reporting the child's progress. Now, as fate would have it, Jim had received such a letter from her just as he was leaving on a visit to his elderly maiden sisters, who lived in Seattle. As spinsters will, the sisters decided to renovate their brother's wardrobe while he was with them, and, in emptying the pockets of a coat, before sending it to the cleaner, they came upon a letter with a mystifying return address: 'Haldor Olson, Midwife, Private Hospital, Duluth, Minn.'

What on earth could Jim be doing with such a letter? The temptation was too much for them, they opened the letter, and discovered Ruby. What their reactions were, or what sort of struggle ensued, I cannot, of course, say. But what their final decision was, I know only too well, for by the time all this took place I was living with my aunt and doing her correspondence. The sisters wrote that it was clearly their duty to give the child a happy, proper home.

'Now I like that!' cried my aunt. 'A couple of old maids understand the needs of an infant better than I! Especially a baby like Ruby, whose emotions are bound to be unstable. Tell the good women all I want from them is permission to adopt the child.'

Letters flew back and forth. But again the vexatious question of faith popped up. The aunts refused to relinquish the child they had never seen, and could not possibly love, because my aunt, who thought the world of Ruby, was a Protestant. No, they could not think of it. They were setting forth at once, to fetch their little niece. It was a matter of conscience, of Christian duty, against which the lesser claims of materialism were of no avail.

'Religion!' snorted my aunt. 'The stupid women! Well – no doubt they meant to be kind. Oh, my poor little Ruby!'

But now to go back. Fortunately, these cases had not always a purely tragic flavour. For instance, a tall, dazed-looking individual presented herself at the hospital one wintry day. She wasn't so well, she said. She had a tumour, she thought, some kind of swelling, anyway, that gave her a misery. So? Well, there were other hospitals for such ailments, explained my aunt, as seriously as she could. Oh, sure, but Jenny had taken a fancy to come here. A bit of rest might be all she required. To get off her feet, and be quiet.

Then she started to cry, in a soundless way. 'Now, now! That won't do!' boomed my aunt. 'I expect I can handle that tumour, all right.'

The tumour, in due course, made its appearance as an eight-pound boy. Even then, Jenny clung to her defences. It was most astonishing. It was that. She really couldn't understand it – unless it was that the son of the house slipped up the back stairs, one night.

'Well,' chuckled my aunt, 'the thing to do now, is to let the son of the house slip down to a lawyer's office, and sign a cheque for the tumour's maintenance.'

27

I discover drama

To return to more relevant matters. My young friends, no less than I, had reached a point where the impressions crowding upon us so swiftly made a sort of crazy-quilt of our thoughts, each patch of experience highly coloured and distinct, but without sequence or tangible design. The only thing any one of us was clear about was our dissatisfaction with the cramping circumstances of our lives. Laura was thoroughly the rebel. She hated gloom and growling and the unrelieved dreariness of her home. At the first possible opportunity she meant to get away – it didn't matter where, or how she managed it. Anything would be better than that endless round of stupid chores and bitter complaints. Tilly seldom expressed any violent opinions, yet she, too, dreamed of something better than the dull service to which she was enslaved. Not with envy, but a sort of bated admiration, she sometimes spoke of the carefree existence girls like Mollie MacDonald took for granted.

As for myself, although I ranted freely enough about things I disliked, I was secretive with my dearest ambition. Ever since that day in the ugly old library, my dream had never wavered. I wanted to write. Goodness knows how many arithmetic lessons I had flunked because the fever to scribble something refused to be denied. Reams of verse, principally in the Bryant strain: mournful requiems to the weather, the woods, the timeless stream, and what not. About which beautiful silliness I was secretive as the grave.

And secretive I remained about anything I really prized. Although I have ridden many hobby horses, I never had the courage to hie me forth like Lady Godiva, stripped to the skin. If one must make a spectacle, it might as well be in plumage of sorts. After all, very few people, I soon discovered, care a fig about the natural complexion of your hide, or what you believe or hunger after for your innermost heart's desire. Every one was equally preoccupied with his own crying want, which made it ridiculous to expect passionate concern for something which to him seemed a remote and alien abstraction. Even your own family seldom showed much sympathy for the quirks of temperament which set you apart. And since it was my misfortune to be over-serious and ridiculously sensitive about the things I deeply prized, I kept them to myself.

For instance, like most Icelanders, I was a confirmed bookworm, and what is even worse, had a natural taste for stuff that either horrified or bored my friends to death. What in the world made me want to weep over yarns like *The Necklace*, and work myself into a frenzy over the horrors of the Inquisition, they couldn't imagine. It was crazy! Things that had happened ages and ages ago didn't matter now! What did matter were pretty clothes, and a boy friend to take you places. Certainly, I agreed about the clothes. I should have liked nothing better than to slink about arrayed like Anna Held and Lilian Russell. But you couldn't get wearing apparel at the public library.

This all-important question did begin to worry me. Perhaps I thought that Carl might tire of trotting me about in my confirmation dress. At any rate, when I chanced upon an advertisement by the *Mack-Leon Players*, for extras, I borrowed a dime from mamma and took the car uptown. The mere sight of the old Lyceum Theatre sent me into a dither. I'm sure I circled the block ten times before I had the courage to creep into the dark passage beyond the stage door. Pitch-black and empty, the tunnel seemed, and beyond it an equally black, yawning space.

No one was in sight, but just as I was screwing up courage to explore this strange pit, a gay laugh sounded from somewhere.

'You do look a ghost! Come on in – it's a grand place for spooks!' a voice informed me.

Then I saw her, sitting on a keg, under a mountain of scenery. My eyes, adjusted to the gloom, I could see that she was young, though not such a chit as I, that she had a merry face, and curly, blonde hair. 'I'm Hedda,' she went on. 'Just another stage-struck nanny. Where does it hurt most? Comedy or Tragedy?'

That was the start of a friendship and an interlude of pleasant excitement that was the happiest period of my life. Hedda was a graduate of a Chicago school of drama and oratory. What its specific name was, I forget, for it seemed of little consequence. Hedda herself was such a remarkable discovery. I had never before met any one whose entire heart was bound up in these arts.

She had real ability, and was wonderful at characterization, which was what she longed to do, and for which she had a perfect voice, flexible, sympathetic, and beautifully modulated. I think, too, she realized she had not the slightest sense of dress, and could never in the world represent a dear young thing in fluffs and billows, although she was shapely and good-looking. This may seem a curious criticism for me to make, whose knowledge of such glories was solely derived from the buxom beauties on cigar boxes. Still, it does not necessarily follow that, because you have no money to invest in fine feathers, that you cannot wear such trappings with a certain dash if they are provided.

In the months to come both Hedda and I had many an opportunity to strut in borrowed plumage, and the first and dearest compliment I ever received from Miss Leon was upon my management of an Elizabethan court dress. In farthingale and train and elaborate coiffure, Hedda made anything but a stately appearance. She looked so robustly dowdy that nothing but an elderly make-up saved her from outright comedy. I doubt that Svengali could have given her grace to walk.

However, these limitations were an asset to the kind of roles she coveted. Any kind of old harridan, any dialect, any mood, from the most tragic to the utterly ridiculous, was her dear delight. That Hedda gave up a predestined career is one of the many unsung sacrifices to which countless women give themselves for the so-called good of selfish relatives. But that was still far in the future.

At this time Hedda was in constant demand as a public entertainer, and because she was waiting for a chance to slip into the legitimate theatre she was on call for small parts. Thanks to her liking for me, I had the same chance, and, what was even more gratifying, she managed to teach me something about voice, and the necessity to create from within any characterization.

During the school holidays I spent many precious hours with Hedda, poring over all sorts of oratorical stuff. Most of it was cheaply melodramatic for, that, said Hedda, was the best possible medium to give one emotional control. But we read good poetry as well; charming lyrics, for music; Bobby Burns, for tenderness; and, of course, Shakespeare, who is every actor's last word and testament. These readings, over which we had the greatest fun imaginable, with Hedda performing in a dozen voices, and the two of us often reduced to tears, or uncontrollable laughter, were, I think, the true incentive for the course I mapped out for myself some time later, when my own dream of a classical education turned to ashes.

Deprived of so much, I none the less made up my mind to form the habit of constructive reading, of setting myself subjects to cover in honest fashion: history, philosophy, art – of these one need not remain ignorant in this day and age, no matter what the state of the purse. Yet, perhaps I might have failed even here if I had not, by great good fortune, found an elderly, retired schoolmistress who sometimes did a bit of coaching. I wish I had the power to depict this gentle soul, as I remember her in my heart of hearts. Her whole life had been one unselfish service to the kind of mother who sits like a spider in the centre of the family web, devouring, one after the other, the vital years of her progeny.

Consequently, Miss Rudd looked exactly what she was: a little lost lady, who fed her emotions vicariously. No doubt she was a capable teacher in her generation, but even in my comparatively unsophisticated youth her romantic susceptibilities seemed faintly foolish, and I shudder to think how dangerously decadent she would have found the smart young things of the post-war generation.

She had a most amusing way of darting off on remote tangents, caught up on some far-winged thought to which she had drifted while her supposed students plodded through laborious passages.

For example, reading *Richard the Third*: King Edward replying to Stanley, pleading the boon of his servant's life:

> Have I a tongue to doom my brother's death,
> And shall that tongue give pardon to a slave?
> My brother killed no man, his fault was thought:
> And yet his punishment was bitter death.
> Who sued to me for him? who, in my wrath,
> Kneeled at my feet, and bid me be advised?
> Who spoke of brotherhood? Who spoke of love?

Miss Rudd, dreamily: 'Ah, human passion! Poor, distraught, human passion. So many hearts rent with bitter, bitter regret. Everywhere. Yes, everywhere. Even among the most tender lovers – do you remember that precious lyric in *The Princess*?

> As through the land at eve we went
>   And plucked the ripened ears,
> We fell out, my wife and I,
>   We fell out, I know not why,
>   And kissed again with tears.
>
> For when we came where lies the child
>   We lost in other years,
> There above the little grave
>   Oh, there above the little grave
>   We kissed again with tears.

'Go on – go on: "Who told me how the poor soul did forsake —"'

Not the most scientific treatment of Shakespeare, I dare say, but a pleasing introduction to the tender vagaries of the mind. Since that far day I have been privileged to listen to many erudite mouthings, and to worry through much admirably compiled material, yet none of it inspired a more earnest desire to rightly appreciate the riches of letters than those winsome vagabond asides. For I came to see an underlying unity of purpose in those queer flights and turnings.

Time! Time! She had so little left of time. And in those kind, faded eyes that smiled on me so mistily, I seemed a likely subject for what she found most worthy in a sadly harassed world. Her goodness gave me attributes beyond desert, motives beyond fulfilling. If only I could have told her how dearly I treasured her foolish faith in me! Youth is not given to honest speeches. If only she could have known how often in the days to come that cherished faith drew out of the dark a solitary star which refused to doff its light.

But Hedda waits, in the dressing-room of the old theatre. It is a night I recall with especial vividness, because of a bit of comedy that took place in the wings. Or such it seems now, although at that time none of us, extras or company, saw much humour in it.

Willard Mack was a man of tremendous energy, and somewhat overbearing enthusiasm. Whatever the company undertook, he required that every detail should be as perfect as their combined talents and properties permitted. He demanded unreserved co-operation, and expected implicit obedience. He detested any signs of levity off the stage when a serious play was progressing. As a rule, even the extras were properly solemn, and sufficiently impressed by the subject under way not to crack a smile, much less to laugh.

But this night, the unforgivable occurred. Some one laughed, and that some one no irrepressible youngster, but our grave and stately heavy. And at the ill-starred moment of an impassioned speech by Willard, down stage near the wings. The last word uttered, out the gentleman catapulted, thunder on his brow, lightning in his eye.

'Laugh! Damn you, laugh!' the outraged artist roared, his fist crashing into the handsomest face in the company.

What now? Our pounding pulses throbbed. Would our handsome villain, measuring his elegant length on the dusty floor, react as actor, or mere man? Would the play go on, or a backstage brawl make history?

The play went on. With the same inscrutable composure that he faced death and damnation with in a dozen plays, the gentleman picked himself up, brushed his dishonoured trousers, and, without a word, sauntered up to his dressing-room to calcimine his eye. Which was the end of the incident, except for a lingering, purple bruise, and an increased quiet in the wings.

I should not want to give the impression that Mr Mack was an irascible tyrant. Forceful, volatile, brilliant, he was impatient of perfection, but not at all a fearsome individual. A splendid actor, with a really fine voice, he possessed to a marked degree those qualities of interpretive invention which were to make him famous as a playwright – famous far beyond the dreams of the thousands who revelled in the production of the old Mack-Leon Stock Company.

Miss Leon was not fated to create the same stir in the world, but there must be many a sober middle-aged woman in the range towns and Duluth who remember with sentimental fondness the beautiful roles she created for their youthful enjoyment; roles as divergent as Sappho, and simple trusting Gloria; remember, too, her vivid beauty and sympathetic voice.

Less important members measured up to the best traditions of the stage. There was an *ingénue* who grimly finished the week, though she was coming down with a serious illness that required an operation; and her successor, a slip of a thing who took the boards on the following Monday, with less than twenty-four hours' preparation.

I worshipped them all for the enthusiasm they radiated, the zest they had for life. They were the first group of people I had ever seen actively engaged in the pursuit of happiness. Whatever their individual difficulties, faults, and failings, they really lived. Even our stage-manager had a redeeming sparkle, although his morals were a bit blotchy. He had a fondness for the bottle and buxom wenches. Yet, he it was kept a fatherly eye upon Hedda and myself, and, on one occasion, fired a young chap whom he thought too fresh. No saint, but a fierce old watch-dog when the

need arose. Nor was our romantic lead a Sunday-school hero –
which was not surprising, considering the horde of temptresses
that hung about the stage door.

I loved it all. The miraculous transformations, the dark clutter
of jumbled scenery translated into romantic splendour: gay
gardens, devoted to lovers murmuring of immortal devotion;
pillared palaces, where strutted lords and ladies, glamorous and
brave; classic heaths, where the grand cadences of Shakespeare
wrung the heart. I loved the yawning black of the empty house
at rehearsal, a fretful, dark expectancy that hung upon each nervous word like a creative challenge. I loved the musty smells, the
swift irritabilities, the lightning moods, the hustle and haste and
eternal anxieties; everything, from the reek of grease paint to the
rosy arch of the footlights. It was a world in which to lose the
mean and the commonplace, a world of noble sentiment, where
the written word was clothed with living power.

There it was. That was the source of my worship. The theatre
revealed, as nothing else ever had, the force and beauty and persuasion of words. That was why I was happy to warm myself at
this magic fire, yet never thought of the profession as a possible
vocation. Words I meant to acquire, but that I now possessed any
marketable attribute had never dawned on me.

Small wonder I could scarcely believe my ears when, one
night, the stage-manager rushed in to say that I could sell my
legs. My legs? My legs?

'Yes, yes, your legs, you fool! Don't you know you have a perfect pair of legs?' he roared. 'What's wrong with you? Here – let
me show you! There you are! There you are! That's something,
let me tell you,' said he, beaming down upon my startled knees.

Yes, and there was I, staring idiotically at familiar, yet utterly
strange extremities, for which it appeared I could collect real
money from a vaudeville house down the street. How they
laughed at me, standing there clutching my skirts and eyeing
suspiciously the objects under discussion. Legs, it seemed, were
not always just fatted bones to cart one about. Perish the thought!
There were as many kinds of legs, and to as many themes conjoined, as bungled sonnets. Legs that filled the really sensitive

artists with fretful despair: too long, too short, too flabby, too muscular; yes, even shapely legs that rudely leapt from rough knees, utterly blasting the poetic promise. To put it bluntly, most of the beauties prancing the boards had to wear 'hearts' to hide the nasty little hollows that ruined otherwise perfect show-pieces!

From such a sour calamity fate had saved me. Just think of it, I was neither knock-kneed, bow-legged, nor afflicted with those curious blemishes that give nightmares to the sensitive connoisseur of female legs. It seemed that I could click my ankles and knees together without inviting mirth. Hence this remarkable offer from down the street. My would-be benefactor, who had caught sight of these rarities in a rough-and-tumble mob scene, was instantly filled with the milk of human kindness. No matter what sort of face went with the legs, he would overlook it.

Here was my chance, said the stage-manager – and let me not imagine I'd get any other. If I had an ounce of sense, I'd thank my stars and grab it. Dear me, how lightly promises flourish, and how uselessly. Even with the best of sense, to which I lay no claim, there was still mamma to be reckoned with. Mamma, and the ancestors. The mere thought of persuading the daughter of a long line of dignified clerics that her child should gamble about in pink tights for the entertainment of dispirited business men, put me in a perfect funk. Gracious goodness, if that was my one hope of immortality I might as well resign myself to a nameless grave.

Hedda reasoned with me. So did the benevolent gentleman. If my conscience was so tender, I could wear a mask! The implication, not exactly flattering, ruffled my temper. Then and there, so to speak, I committed myself to rectitude, and a plain face. Thirty dollars a week was a fortune to be sure, but in that day I had not realized the significance of money, and certainly never dreamed how cheerfully virtue may starve, for all that any one cares. It could not be done, quoth I, little thinking I should shortly rue it. So Lady Luck simply shrugged her shoulders, and forthwith passed me by.

28

Darker reason

The season closed, and almost immediately I found myself in the thick of domestic calamities. And what maddening calamities they were to us girls! In reckless autumnal burgeoning, our poor mothers produced a new crop of babies. To no one's joy, that we could see. It was nature, and the will of God and had to be endured.

Nature be damned, said we, fierce as fishwives. If other laws of nature were circumvented and controlled, why should generation be the one exception? Why indeed, thought we, glaring at each other helplessly. Tilly always mild, demurred a little at such brazenness. It really wasn't nice to talk about such things, perhaps we might not have been born if people had been too wise.

'So what?' demanded I. 'What difference would it make?' Of all the crazy things peddled out to us, the craziest, to me, was the feeble twaddle about being grateful for the gift of life. Who could be grateful for bleak existence full of misery and deprivation? My own lot was beside the point. Before human beings could be expected to render thanks for the burden of life, it should be something better than the miserable scramble we saw all about us. Something less cruel than history portrayed. What was more, said I, waxing furiously oratorical, if that kind of craziness hadn't been stuffed into people's heads they wouldn't have made themselves paupers by having children they couldn't decently feed! Even children who weren't fit to live!

Whereupon I could have bitten my careless tongue. Tilly looked so crushed. The Rhinertson baby, which, fortunately had died – some said it was mercifully permitted to die – had been hideously misshapen. Scarcely human. And other whispers had revived ancient scandal. Mrs Rhinertson had herself to blame, the wise protested. What could you expect, when you married your own uncle! It was no wonder the children were puny –s why, every one could see that the little girl who preceded this – this mishap – wasn't normal. The child was nearly four, and couldn't speak a word! Buzz, buzz, buzz, wherever two or three gathered. Poor Tilly, meanwhile, creeping through her duties like a timid little mouse, her soft blue eyes apologetic and ashamed.

Laura frankly raged, a state of mind I understood quite thoroughly. Whatever hope she may have entertained of financial assistance was completely blasted. Doctor's bills and a new baby were hardly the sort of inducements which would persuade her stepfather to invest in her education.

'It *is* crazy!' Laura shouted. 'Nobody wanted that baby – least of all, mamma. I can't stand it! Everything gets worse and worse. Somehow, I'll get away. I'd rather starve trying to make something of myself. There's nothing for me at home. Nothing, nothing, nothing. It's a holy mess, and I'm getting out. What's more, if I ever get ahead, I'll see to it little Elma gets a chance.'

Minnie Nelson, though less bitter, was just as resentful. Theirs was a happy, moderately comfortable home, where goodwill and a natural love of music created a cheerful atmosphere. They were all good-looking, and good-natured, and even the littlest tot sang as gaily as a wren. Just the same, there were too many of them, Minnie contended, as dourly as her blithe soul permitted. 'The kids are smart, but what good does it do if they can't even get music lessons.'

None too cheerfully, I mulled this over as I sewed the tiny garments for our own prospective blessing. Sewed them well, since sew I must, for mamma's eyesight was seriously affected. No angel of mercy, resentment worked like yeast in my mind.

Whirling the old machine, I thought of the millions of women committed to this sort of thing, world without end. To drudgery, and pinching, and those niggardly economies that stifle the spirit and slay all hope.

To what conceivable end, I wonder. Was it so important to perpetuate this dreary existence? If so, important to whom? To the churches, that they might have these miserables on whom to practise humiliating charity? To the State, that it might extort tithes and services? To the 'Big Bosses,' whom little Sam hated so fiercely?

Oh, I had listened to his reviling with attentive ears, despite my seeming indifference. Something of the hope he placed in his sacred unions was at least partially clear. But how effective could union protection of labourers hope to become, with the market glutted with unskilled workers? It was all very confusing, and beyond my depths, yet one thing was certain: all that fine balderdash about the glory of motherhood could stand a bit of cool dissecting. All that mother-child glorification that ended in the cradle. It was time, it seemed to me, that the serious thought should embrace the future of those hallowed infants. A kiss or two in infancy was meagre compensation for a lifetime of bitter bread!

I had seen many broken creatures, had heard so much that was woeful and sad. I thought of Big Tom, sitting of a summer night, watching the sunset with brooding, lustreless eyes, his whole expression so darkly withdrawn as to put me in mind of a passing hearse. What did he mourn, sitting there? What once fair dream lay dead in his heart?

That was the tormenting thought that drove me for comfort to the quiet hills, to the small, green coulees, where the sun dappled the tender grass with dancing motes of gold. It was there, and not in any church, that God became a reality, a living, healing influence, that eased my troubled mind. Here, in the quiet hills, where little swift creatures sped on soundless feet and the whirr of tiny wings ascending conspired to create a sense of joyous purposes, it was not so hard to think, with Tennyson:

> That nothing walks on aimless feet,
>   That not one life shall be destroyed
>   Or cast as rubbish to the void,
> When God has made the pile complete;

not so hard to apply to my own small need, the poet's fine dreaming:

> The hills are shadows, and they flow
>   From form to form, and nothing stands;
>   They melt like mist, the solid lands,
> Like clouds they shape themselves and go.
>
> But in my spirit will I dwell,
>   And dream my dream, and hold it true;
>   For though my lips may breath adieu,
> I cannot think the thing farewell.

How many errant tears I wept into the tender grass on those quiet slopes, stirred to the quick by so many illusive images that teased the mind, carried far beyond my own fears into the wider sea of universal experience. For that was the queer thing in me no one understood. I could never free myself from the tentacles of the eternal years. I wanted to be happy, but demanded a happiness that had some deeper meaning than creature enjoyments that die on a breath, leaving only dull ashes behind. I had seen too much of ash heaps!

Where to seek such an excellent state was a mystery. I only knew that life without purpose, joy without meaning, was a betrayal of those inner impulses of the soul that linked all mankind, living and dead. It was not an intellectual concept, nor any idea gleaned from prose. It was something that flowed through me when I lay on the grass on that old hill-side, watching the tangled clouds, or the low, winding valley that unrolled to the dark blue water of the bay. Something out of the elements themselves, that seemed to carry my thoughts backward into other times, where the forgotten dead had joyed and sorrowed. Always the one thought I carried away, the one abiding determination: to keep, against the world, my own little fragment of that mysterious quality in man which gives him the power to dream.

Something else I discovered. These thoughts of mine were unwelcome and annoying to others. It was queer, and definitely boring, to speak of anything so vague as a haunting feeling of kinship with ages past. It was sheer affectation to utter anything save moth-eaten commonplaces. Yet people read, I supposed; suffered, without complaint, the homilies of scribes. They went to church, and, apparently, listened to scriptural passages that rolled like grandest organ music. Yet none of this coloured their speech, dignified the structure of their mental images. And for any one else to attempt a poetic phrase, however spontaneous, was as shockingly out of place as to breathe the name of God.

Oh, I had more than enough to learn. Much that was paradoxical and depressing to the eager thing in my mind, enhungered for intelligent revelation. Consequently, I burrowed deeper into my protective shell, adopting as best I could the facile insincerities that pass for thought and feeling.

Fortunately, the business of living devoured so much time that these moody speculations were hardly more than an occasional luxury. A new baby makes more work than a dozen adults. It seemed to me that I was always rushing about buying nipples, bottles, lime water, peppermint, and goodness knows what not.

The buying of groceries, every sort of errand, had to be done, all of which ate up the precious hours. Hours I needed for study and the important business of making my graduation address. Believe me, that took a shred of ingenuity and anxious thought.

Papa had given me two dollars, with which I was determined to uphold the family honour. Fortune favoured me. I found some dotted Swiss marked down to twenty-five cents the yard. With five yards safe in the crook of my arm, and three spools of thread in my pocket, I raced for Woolworth's, to purchase a fearsome tangle of lace and insertion. Thus committed, I must, forsooth, treadle miles and miles of intricate stitching, mostly by lamplight, to the tune of many a headache and sundry crimps in the erstwhile valuable legs. The dress eventually emerged, flatteringly, and mightily pleasing to vanity. Thought I, triumphantly, how proud mamma would be of me. Why, even my aunt would take no shame, and perhaps my cousin would think me less the gawky lout. Unless the cloudy mirror lied to console me, I really looked quite nice.

When the brave day dawned, however, not a single relative was present to commend me. Not a soul. Though long since I had meticulously peddled out my five tickets. To further deepen the hurt, what I had most set my heart upon, for which I had striven to reach the highest standing – the valedictory – was denied at the last moment.

It chanced we had a singer in the class. So Gladys represented our school by warbling, 'Go, Pretty Rose,' and the world must wag along without my painstaking wisdom. To make everything quite perfect, I developed an infection in my right foot, and thought I should never squeeze into my adorable new slippers.

By the time I reached the high school the pain was so intense I wondered how I should drag through the ordeal of endless speeches, endless chatter, of girls whose parents beamed enraptured from the benches. Endless exhortations to youth, standing at the portals of a rosy future!

What did I care for those fine-sounding words just then! How could I believe in a rosy future when not a soul cared a fig whether I had acquitted myself well or ill. When every nerve in my body ached with longing for some tiny gesture of pleased affection, how should I credit the goodwill of the fortuitous world, painted so grandly by glib little gentlemen vestured like penguins?

I was not quite alone, I discovered. Where my own failed me, a friend came to the rescue. Carl was there to pilot me, sweet and kind and patient with my limping. For that I must always love him! For being there; for understanding, without comment, the source of my depression. And if I cried a little when I stole to bed that night, it was less for the hurt in my heart than the dear knowledge that a good friend is sufficient unto any ill day.

29

Again green pastures

Life broke in strange and complex patterns. Papa had the wanderlust again. He had been receiving glowing letters from my eldest brother, who, after knocking about the sea, had settled in the south. I suspect that, like dear papa, this light-hearted brother saw everything in brighter colours than is given to more cautious souls to see. At any rate, papa took such a fancy to the picture he painted of life in Mississippi that, against every one's counsel, and to mamma's heartbreak, he sold the house and everything else that mamma's economy had made possible, and off we went on the mad adventure.

What was to become of my higher education? What of the normal course my hope was set upon as the first step to glory? Oh well, there were schools everywhere, said he. If not, I might find a rich husband. Anything was likely to happen in the paradise he envisioned. Mamma, a little grim, devoutly hoped that, at least, we'd find something to eat, and a roof to shelter us.

The journey down the Mississippi valley was not without interest. Those interminable miles through black plains vast as the sea; through strange cities and towns, so different from anything I had seen before, stirring the liveliest speculations, and somewhat reviving my sinking hopes. Perhaps we were not heading into sheer disaster, as mamma predicted.

When we crossed the Mason and Dixon line, coming to a stop at a station where hundreds of coal-black faces stared up from the station platform, I lost sight of worry. What a spectacle that was! Never had I dreamt that so many black people could congregate! Never had I seen so many wide grins, such gleaming teeth, such multi-coloured, billowing skirts, and bright turbans. While at every window, black hands offered snowy baskets of fried chicken, golden brown, and irresistible.

What supersedes every other memory, however, was our first view of an immense cotton-field. Acres of bursting cotton, that seemed to float in the coral light of a setting sun, like so many millions of ghostly roses. Of all the beauty to come, the most beautiful, thought I. Yet when the field lay at our backs we found ourselves streaming through a pine forest that must have stood tall and stately when the world was young.

I had thought the Minnesota pines grand beyond dreaming. I had watched them felled in a lumber camp with a constriction of the heart as each giant fell, so convinced was I that something superlative and irreplacable was being stripped from the earth. But here were trees that soared up into the blue with the proud elation of creative thought. Pillars of living grace, to bring the heart of man to the dust in worship of the lovely earth that bore such beauty in her breast.

But, at last, the long lap of the journey ended. We came to a stop in the midst of what seemed empty wilderness, and, stiff and dirty, piled off bag and baggage. Not quite empty, we perceived – some yards away stood an unpainted shack, the station, towards which we stumbled in quest of information. Entering the gloomy box, I looked around, perplexed. Where was the station-master, I wondered.

Whereupon, a panel slid open in the dirty wall, and a rusty voice barked at me: 'You-all can't stay there, Missy! Come round, Missy, come round.'

'I only want to ask —' I began, and was interrupted sharply.

'Cain't you-all read?' the worthy ancient queried indignantly, pointing to a sign I had failed to see in the murk: 'COLOURED WAITING-ROOM.'

Meek as milk, I trotted round to a twin cell reserved for the exalted white race, and forthwith was informed that a jitney would come in due course barring acts of God or other violence. 'Bout an hour, he guessed. The freedom of the field was ours, and right welcome we were in these parts.

Mamma settled down on a box with the baby. The children scampered off like kittens. Papa strolled sedately, inhaling with audible relish the remarkable air. Such fragrance! cried he. Such soft, sweet ozone! He felt another man. How warm it was! Warm as a summer's day, and this October. Imagine how we'd feel stranded in the open at such an hour by the shores of Lake Superior!

Our jitney joggled into view, and, with the patience of Griselda, set off again through the wood, fetching up at last before a rambling, unpainted structure in the village of Buckatunna. We had arrived.

This dusty road, solitary building, and a gloomy bulk beyond a clump of trees, was all the town we could see. Mamma's face set in a bleak mask that not even my brother's fond greeting could melt.

We cheered somewhat after a good wash, and the dinner Minty's southern wife had thoughtfully prepared. In the evening we drifted to the porch and tried to get our bearings. In the white moonlight the road turned silver, and the shadows cast by the great trees were more purple than black, except where huge masses formed midnight banks against the sky.

The town, we now perceived, was a scattering of houses on either side the most crooked river in the world. Houses all alike, tossed up for temporary use in this temporary town, which depended on the mills for its living. A few homes on the other side of the Chickasahay had been built with some better end in view, but those on our side were nothing but ugly boxes, without conveniences of any kind. There were no industries, nothing but the mills, and, beyond the town, small planters, who lived from hand to mouth. Not a promising prospect for papa, who, I imagined, had laboured some hope of starting a harness shop.

There was charm here for the poet. A sort of sleepy grace enfolded the ramshackle town. At midday the sandy road which was its main artery lay softly golden in the glittering light, and over it ambled many a darky wench in bright green petticoat, and basket on her head. Strings of oxen slept before the store – long teams of them, with sometimes an old blind beast for leader. Now and then a horseman cantered by, raising a fine amber cloud, and making scarcely a sound in the soft dust. And everywhere were fierce razor-back pigs that streaked along on incredibly nimble legs from one unseemly rooting place to another. Built in an hour, destined for a day, the village had something primeval about it. Something old as time, and imperturbable as the trees whose death song hummed all day long from the greedy mills.

Of the people I shall have more to say by and by. My first impression was confined to the strict divisions imposed. The same division of sheep from goats everywhere accepted as right and proper, but here more noticeable, because more honestly and openly avowed than in sophisticated society. It seemed that quite respectable but less highly paid mortals lived on our side of the river; the gentry of the mills on the other. At a nice distance from the respectability sprawled 'Hell's Half-Acre,' the dubious district dedicated to the misfits and the disreputable. Beyond that, again, lay the Negro quarter, where some two thousand cheery black folk disported themselves in their own fashion. I think, if I remember rightly, that the white population numbered about eight hundred.

Of course, I got into trouble right away. Always accustomed to ramble about the hills at home, I set off one late afternoon on a tour of discovery, only to reach home long after dark to find mamma almost in tears, and my brother in a nervous rage. He had always been very dear to me, this brother who had cared for me so often when I was little and mamma was working elsewhere. His anger was prompted by genuine anxiety. A sound riot act he served on me!

Women did not run about the woods down here. They went nowhere unescorted after dark. Only a few days since a negro had been lynched for a brutal assault upon a white woman! I was to behave myself, henceforth, and if I must traipse about the countryside I should have to wait until some nice young man offered to satisfy my curiosity.

My next misdemeanour was to offend such a nice young man. There was a good band in the village, led by my brother, and one of the boys very courteously sent me a note by a little black messenger proposing a drive through the country. Well, we youngsters back home were not very formal. Certainly I'd like to go, said I to the piccaninny, and left it at that.

The young man did not arrive. He was deeply insulted. I should have replied in kind, not trusting such a personal letter to a coloured boy.

I was rescued from the threat of oblivion by a personable individual who was bookkeeper at the general store. Which, in a manner of speaking, brings me to my first serious love affair – never an easy subject. Complete evasion of intimate experiences would scarcely be honest. On the other hand, there is an element of unkindness in exploiting the feeling of others for which I have little taste.

However, a casual survey of the women men presumably love and marry, poor darlings, reveals an amazing democracy and forbearance – sufficiently astonishing to lead one to believe that any female clothed in a whole skin must have had a lover. Toss in a bit of whimsy and humour, and the possibilities are boundless. This precious fact must serve as my defence. My relationships with men have been extremely fortunate. For which I thank a plain face and a sense of humour. Safe as a salt block from the purely predatory male, I should, none the less, fall short of truth contending that masculine charity had passed me by. Life is not so cruel as that!

To continue: Bob duly presented himself, and carried me off to some sort of party on the elect side of the river. He was an amiable sort, and took no offence when his best friend whisked me off his hands. This high-handed individual had an impish eye, devilry all over him, and a most engaging manner. Not handsome, except for those brown, mischievous eyes and a lighting of his face when he laughed – the kind of laugh that puts you in mind of music, and moonlight, and spangled Christmas trees.

Every one grinned at the mere mention of Gordon Bannister. A likeable rapscallion, said the villagers. A rapscallion, none the less. Unconscionable flirt, he spent his money like water, had no serious thought in his head, and for all that any one knew he might have a brace of wives in Mobile, he flittered thither so often. What was even more reprehensible, not being a native of these parts, but a suspect product of Little Rock, Arkansas, he was callously indifferent to the hopes he raised in palpitating country bosoms.

This charming plague took it into his head to herd me out of that party into the silken treachery of moonlight and leafy lane, so dear to the heart of poets brewing doom for guileless females. As if that were not enough, the mad young man raved like a book, expertly exploiting every shade of sentiment and all the gradations of a fluent voice. For a mile or more I stood the strain of it without breaking. Then, I'm sorry to say, the humour of it ran away with me.

Midways of a most romantic bridge that spanned the sleepiest of serpentine rivers, I – to quote the wounded gentleman – threw a fit: shrieked with laughter to the shuddering skies, and to the disquiet of every self-respecting water snake and slumberous alligator. Presently, we were both hanging helplessly over the rail, poor poetry dead as a smoked herring.

'You're a nasty creature,' said the young man, when breath permitted. 'Nasty, unfeeling little friend. How about it – shall we be friends, you monkey?'

'Why not? I want to see the country, and I can't run about with my shadow.'

'That's what I call a noble spirit,' quoth he. 'But what a disappointing audience! Here I strain my heart putting up a good show, and what do I get for it? Not a gentle twitter! What was wrong with it, pray?'

'Just everything. A good show works up to the climax – or hadn't you thought of that?' said I, glad of the chatter. There would be more than enough of monotony when I got back to the cluttered rooms we called home. It was lovely, being there, where the moonlight played whitely over the opaque waters of the slow, coiling river moving soundlessly under the black shadows of the heavy trees. And what girl of seventeen can fail to be a little thrilled at the pleasant lies of a gay young man with the gleam of devilry in his eyes?

'Oh, I see,' he retorted. 'You have a nice taste in conquest. Well, I shall mend my manners, I promise you. I'll map out a plan in easy stages before asking you to come for a drive. Now tell me, what on earth brought you to this God-forsaken place?'

That was not for me to explain to a stranger so I changed the subject, switching to my curiosity about the country, the mills that were devouring a sea of timber, the little sprawling village, and the people, whose way of life was so strange. So we hung there, upon the splintered rail, for how long only the stars knew, while Bannister told me how northern capital was financing the timber operations in this most backward of southern states. Poverty and inertia were the curse of Mississippi, said he. The last state to be laid waste by the Civil War, it had not yet gained a normal rhythm of existence – quite possibly would never gain its former peace and security.

Some day, he would take me to see an old ruined plantation that would tell the tale better than words. For himself, he was here for the time being, because he made a good living. When he had saved a little money he was going back where he'd never see another confounded mill, and where you could think of trees in better terms than so many feet of boarding. If it wasn't for the occasional jamboree in Mobile, that kept him from going crazy, he'd never have stuck it this long. Why, the highlights of existence here were wakes and christenings – and of neither enough to wear out a pair of shoes!

Hardly enheartening, yet when I slipped into the silent house it was not to envision wakes but to wonder if I should hear again that easy voice juggling truth and fancy under the stars. He was going to Mobile for the week-end, he said, but promised to redeem a bad beginning when he came back. What was a promise to a lunatic young man who lied like a poet, and cheerfully admitted the fact, thought I gloomily, braiding my hair for the night. Was it conceivable that nothing more entrancing than city lights prompted those weekly flights into Alabama? No, not likely, I told myself sensibly, and decided to make my peace with Bob.

30

Magic moonlight

The next day I had little time to worry about Gordon Bannister, although, as might be expected, mamma demanded a character sketch. What sort of person was this young man, she wanted to know? Did brother know anything about his people? Brother thought they were sound in mind and marrow, but Gordon was a fickle wretch, and I'd be well advised to remember that he was not a kid like myself.

'I don't expect my daughters to be fools!' snapped mamma. With which remark Bannister was shelved, and a real grievance presented. We were short of milk for the baby! The folk from whom we had purchased the vital supply had lost their cow. That is to say, it had wandered away, and no one had sufficient energy to hunt for the beast. Cows, like pigs, were free souls in these parts, and usually paraded whither they listed, companioned by nudging calfs. Cannibalism would have shocked mamma less. Fancy fighting with a calf for your milk each evening! Was ever such thriftlessness? And what to do? The baby couldn't digest condensed milk, nor could he wait upon the whim of a cow making an infrequent social call.

Oh, it would work out somehow, papa comforted, nervously helping himself to a pinch of snuff. The cow was sure to turn up sooner or later. If he knew what the creature looked like, he'd hunt for her himself. My sister-in-law had a more concrete suggestion. The Wilmots, on the far side of the river, had a good milch cow on which they kept a sharp eye because of their own brood of young ones. They might spare us a pint or two, she imagined. In any case, it would be a pleasant trip for me. Betty Wilmot was about my own age, and quite a nice girl.

This enheartened mamma, who fetched another difficulty. There were no decent washing facilities. Just a huge, black cauldron in the back-yard. How on earth was she to struggle with the laundry under such circumstances? Oh, that was nothing, shouted my little sister. All you did was light a fire under the pot, fill it with water and soap, pitch in the clothes, and stir with a stick. She had seen it done in the next yard, and it looked awfully jolly. She was sure she could do it herself. She'd prove it by doing the baby clothes. And so she did, making a better job at eight than I at thirty.

The problem was not so easily settled, however. No self-respecting white woman did her own laundry. Whatever the pinch of the purse, a negress must do the wash and save our face. Heavens above! Mamma sank down weakly. Here was a pretty tangle of thistles! Imagine being above a healthy tussle with the washtub, when everything else was primitive as Noah's Ark! Nothing irritated mamma so much as vanity, unless it was a dishcloth that could not hold its own with a summer cloud for cleanliness. She had nothing whatever against coloured people – the Lord must have known what he was doing when he made them – but that was no reason to trust them with the few bits of household linen that doubtless would have to serve for the rest of our lives.

Small wonder I should forget Mr Bannister and his blandishments when our very sheets were threatened! Small wonder I should gape like a ninny when, about sundown, a tattered little messenger staggered up the steps with a huge basket of fruit, bedecked with tissue paper and bow knots. It was for me, the beaming black midget assured me. But that could not be! There was some mistake. Who on earth would be sending me a carload of fruit?

'Don't stand there arguing with the child!' Mamma's voice was faintly amused. 'Suppose you try looking inside. That might tell the tale.'

Sure enough, there was the card, with my name on it, written in a beautiful, flowing hand, and something else, which, to read under mamma's scrutiny, turned me red as a tomato.

'Well, don't be foolish – who sent it? The dangerous young man, I'll be bound!'

'Yes, he did,' I mumbled. 'Mr Bannister, I mean – he didn't seem so dangerous to me.'

'So that's the kind of a lad he is!' twinkled mamma, and, laughing for the first time in days, she resumed her interrupted task.

That was the beginning. Two days later, another mysterious package found its way to the house. Then three days went by, and along came little Moses with a huge box of candy. This time, a note was tucked under the wrapping.

'A discreet opening, don't you think?' it said, and I could almost hear the letters laughing in every loop and line.

It was enough to give any girl palpitation of the heart, especially when another week-end went by without a sign of the mischievous sender. By midweek I could have scratched his eyes out. He was making a fool of me, I felt sure. Why, every time I went to the store Bob, now grave as a bishop, asked after these odious parcels, their assembling having been left to him. But he studiously avoided recalling that he had promised to show me some of the places of interest.

Mad as a hornet, I laid myself out to flatter a susceptible cornet-player who came to practise with my brother, and was rewarded with an invitation to go driving the next Sunday night.

All a-flutter, and carefully arrayed in the second best of my two good dresses, a violet-coloured garment which I had made with great care, there I sat, in the gentle dusk, triumphantly waiting the carriage wheels. Eight o'clock came and went, and minutes slowly ticked off another hour. By half-past nine I was in a pretty dither, and by ten o'clock I was so boiling mad that I could have kicked a cat. There was nothing I could do about it, however, except to demonstrate contentment whenever mamma came to the door for a whiff of air. The night was so beautiful, the moonlight so lovely, I could sit there for ever! Which, thought I viciously, was exactly what I'd have to do for the rest of my natural life, if this kept up.

Then, materializing so suddenly that I could scarcely believe my eyes, Mr Gordon Bannister spoke out of the dusk:

'What a waste of fine weather! Surely you haven't been sitting here, alone, all night?'

'I'm not such bad company,' I snapped crossly, wondering what had become of the clever things I had meant to say, completely forgetting to thank him for all those suspicious presents.

'I'd never have guessed it,' he laughed at me. 'You have such a nasty way of hiding it. I could have sworn you were cursing your poor grandmother, just now. Or was that rapture on your innocent brow?'

No use fencing with the amiable wretch. Whatever I said, he'd make hash of it. And, besides, if I were rude, mamma would be sure to hear it through the open window, and upbraid me soundly for lack of manners. I parried with a question in my nicest voice:

'Why aren't you in Mobile? I thought you went there every week-end?'

'Oh, tastes change. I got tired of red hair. Look here, couldn't you enjoy your own company just as well, down the road a bit? Perambulating meditation is so good for the soul.'

'I'd like to see Hell's Half-Acre,' said I. 'That's the kind of mood I'm in.'

'Don't doubt it,' he laughed. 'Just the same, you'll get the opposite direction, my sweet. I want to show you something to touch the heart of a stone.'

What we went to see was a glorious old oak that stood by itself at the crook of the river. A tree so perfect it might have been the model for all sublime poetry. Covered in trailing Spanish moss that looked like silver veils in the moonlight, it had an unearthly beauty, as of something seen in a vision, full of mystery and significant beyond immediate comprehension.

I have always been susceptible to such impressions – quickly elated, yet as quickly depressed with a feeling of limitation. A finer spirit must sense so much hidden from me: draw so much closer to the heart of beauty. There is always an element of sadness in deeply moving loveliness. It was so now. Speechless, scarcely conscious of my fumbling reactions, I could only watch the sweet wizardry of the moonlight playing upon the lovely shoulders of the bridal oak; stand there, faintly sad in a silence that pressed upon consciousness, forcing the heart to quicker rhythm, the mind to subtler comprehension. Here, if anywhere, are all dreams gathered up. Time loses its relative meaning, and the ghost of all treasured desire blossoms with life.

From across the woodland the melancholy cry of the whip-poor-will thrust its little sword of sweet complaint; a tiny, troubled sound that shook the silence. Apprehensively, I glanced at my unknown companion, and saw, with relief, how still he was, stripped of the smart mask that grinned at the world. Then, snapping back to the familiar, he said impatiently:

'It's too easy to lose one's self. Come away, before we forget how bright we are.'

Back we went to the little bridge, and now I remembered how cross I was with this cheerful imbecile, who, I somehow felt, was responsible for my frustrated evening's pleasure. As though he caught the changing mood, he forestalled with able strategy my boiling accusation by calmly telling me that poor Jim had had some trouble with the buggy. That's what he had really come to tell me – that, and, of course, to offer Jim's apology.

Thought I, whatever the mischief, you are the cause! But I realized there was no use charging the gentleman with grappling-irons. However, I wriggled in my skin – knowing that he was laughing at me, I doffed my spleen before a seemingly impenetrable armour. Nevertheless, there is always some vulnerable space even in coats of mail, I reminded myself, and devoutly vowed to find it. Somehow, I'd make this charming creature squirm. He was so sorry I should have been disappointed. It broke his heart to think of my anxious hours on the porch watching the moon flirting through the tree-tops! 'Well then,' said I, sweet as carbolic acid, 'while you're so full of pity, why not offer to show me that plantation you were talking about.'

A bright thought, he agreed, his brown eyes crinkling at me, but naturally, he would have to sleep on it a week or two. Since I refused to be tormented, he tacked round to current gossip and local history, all dressed with ironic humour. So we parted in amicable spirits, and, said he, if I really behaved myself, I should see that forlorn reminder of a glorified myth.

But I did not behave myself. By midweek I was full of nagging aches and pains, sudden waves of fever, and gripping sensations in my midriff. For a day or two, I kept to my feet, then, in a surge of fury, the fever mounted, my head hummed like a hive of bees, and nothing but pain had any meaning. I had malaria.

31

Deep interval

Of the first horrible siege I remember little: interludes of ague, hard on the heels of consuming fire, when the sweat froze on my body, the muscles jumped on my bones, and no matter how many covers were piled on the bed, the cold of the grave shook me to the marrow. Half-hour interludes when I was conscious that a million devils plucked my brain, beat on my skull, pricked my eyeballs, and chewed along the edges of my spine. Then, back to the hell of flame, where the only reality was the shrieking voice of an everlasting thirst. A tortuous, inescapable frenzy, that nothing quieted. Whatever liquid passed the lips dried on the swollen tongue; boiled away with the boiling blood that hissed in the writhing veins and threw up a sickening odour more hideous than all the rest. This nauseating reek that clung to every breath was what finally drove me nearly crazy. It is no exaggeration to say that the thought of death seemed a blessed escape without terror of any kind.

Swift as its rushing crisis, the fever broke, one strange morning. The sunlight streaming under the lowered blind was sweet to see, comforting to follow on its wavering quest through the ugly room. There, like old familiar faces, were the few sticks of furniture mamma had salvaged. The sober bureau, in whose mirrored eye I had measured the progress of my graduation dress; that had so often witnessed the struggle of putting up my hair. The battered chair, that seemed to give back mamma's voice reading some ancient tale. Even the stiff enlargements of infant pictures were welcome sights. When mamma herself stepped in with a bowl of steaming soup I could have wept with happiness, only, somehow or other, I had no tears. I felt as dried up as a withered stalk of corn. And what a sight to behold!

Yellow as a hoe-cake, the skin on my bones like sandpaper; even my hair a lustreless mop! It came away in dead tufts under mamma's gentle fingers. Secretly grieved, she comforted me. It would grow back in no time, beautiful as ever. She had lost all her hair when she came to this country, and mark what a decent recompense she had.

That was the least of my worries, my hair. Hairs I could spare by the millions, but oh, what a face to bare to the merry glance of the spruce young doctor who came to dose me with quinine and cod-liver oil! How on earth should I venture past the door with a complexion like a cracked egg?

La, what a dither! All forgotten in a twinkling, the sunny day I shamedly set forth with smiling Mr Bannister to see the famed plantation.

It was a sad old house, sitting disconsolate amidst neglected fruit trees, dead as joys long fled; cotton-fields slipping back to wilderness; sagging slave quarters settling to ruin. The sole survivor of the family was in Mobile, penniless, as lost in the new world as the ghostly house in this kingdom of decay.

Other scenes, though less romantic, raised a host of questions in my mind. The small tenant farms with primitive cabins that often lacked even window-panes and the furnishings of which reminded me of the makeshift equipment of the first Icelandic settlers. The more thrifty had a grist mill or a cotton gin to supplement the meagre living, for meagre it must be, despite the fertile soil and semi-tropical climate, if appearances might be trusted. I had seen more hope in the faces of Norwegian women hoeing their bits of field among the tree stumps of northern Minnesota, than here, where listlessness and apathy seemed to have reduced every one to the same ageless antiquity. A dry rot of indifference cast a blight everywhere. And this was the Eden of papa's hopes!

If such cheerless thoughts intruded upon my happiest hours, what must mamma have suffered, shut up with despair for ever-present company! With not even a house of her own to occupy her restless energy, and utter ruin ahead, what chilling anxiety she bore with silent fortitude. How good she was to urge me out into the sunlight, to the small gaieties that came my way!

Simple pastimes. A visit to Bannister's sister, whose house was a little oasis of comfort in this comfortless place. Walks through the woods, pungent with the scent of pine after the sheets of rain that washed the world clean. We spied on Hell's Half-Acre; hung on the fringe of the Negro quarters, listening to plaintive spirituals and old familiar hymns jollied up to revival glee. Sometimes we went to the meeting-house, where an earnest mortal exhorted us to forgo the flesh and the devil. Nothing unusual or startling, except the wake to which I went, with a jumbled feeling of curiosity and distaste.

From the look of it, all the village was there. Every Jack and Jill in Sunday best and blameless humour. How carefully they kept the proprieties: turn and turn about, gravely keeping watch with the dead, then back to the moonlit porch to whisper discreet nothings to the enheartening thrill of clinging hands.

Queer, thought I, and hypocritical. Others besides myself were strangers to the dead man. Then why were they here? To relieve the family, Bannister informed me, a little shortly. There was no hypocrisy in shouldering this responsibility for the worn-out family who had to face the terrible to-morrow.

How soon and sharply this truth was borne home to me! Without warning of any kind, my little brother Stanley woke one morning with a strange, restricted feeling in the throat. Poor mamma, who had herself just come down with the fever, was terrified, her thought flying back down the years to that dark morning when I had suffered a similar experience.

The doctor was instantly called, but neither he nor his young assistant could do anything. In spite of their frantic efforts, the child was dead at four o'clock. Of all the cruel blows life had dealt my dear mother, this was most insufferable: to lie fast to her own bed, watching her little one die in frightful agony.

Then it was we came to know how much beauty of human kindness dwelt in this ugly village. Women whose faces were strange and names unknown to this day were suddenly in quiet possession of our shattered house. Without question, or a single futile word these gentle Marthas set about the sad task that must be done. With the deftness of long experience they cut and fashioned the shroud from a length of soft white flannel. A young woman, with a sweet, sensitive face, cut lacy patterns into borders with which to line the small coffin their men were making. Others, dim shadows in my mind, washed the little tormented body, now so terribly still.

Every detail of the funeral was assumed in the same devoted spirit, with the unaffected manner of folk steeped in golden deeds. Except for this inestimable kindness, I cannot think that mamma would have survived. She had lost so many children in the starved days on the prairies.

It was like a paralysing dream to be standing in the depths of a pine forest, remote and still as some land of tragic allegory, watching the small casket lowered in the earth; seeing papa weeping; knowing that now the mainspring of his heart was broken. The spirit of hopeful yearning that had kept him young, his eyes on the far horizon, no matter what the blows of circumstance, dead, with the dear, small son whose death lay on his conscience. Terrible to feel these things, to know them without shadow of doubting, and to have no ease of tears. Bitter beyond telling, to read in papa's grieving glance a hurt rebuke for my hard indifference. How insensitive! How poor in spirit! This, his thought. This the thought of others, whose tears fell lightly to the rhythm of volatile emotion. Ills that shake the roots of thought link themselves with an eternity of human woe for which no redress is possible, have always frozen my heart, turning inward the shock of feeling, so futile in the face of endless pain.

32

Forced decision

Mamma rose from her sick-bed with only one thought, fixed and clear. We must go back! But where to get the money for our fares was a humiliating problem. For a time we pinned our hope on the tragic possibility that Stanley's insurance would save us all. The company repudiated the claim. The last payment on the premium had reached them too late. My cousin, to whom the money was sent, had forgotten to mail it in time. A lapse of three days!

Papa swallowed his pride and appealed to my aunt and my half-brother, a struggling young musician with cares enough, and his name to make. While this correspondence went forward, our few bits of furniture, everything, except our clothes and bedding had to be sold.

I had the melancholy satisfaction of persuading Betty's mother to buy our fairly new carpet and some decent tea-cups. I knew how badly Betty wanted to 'pretty up' the parlour, a cold-looking room where comfortless chairs were lost in a sea of sanded floor. All the house was cheerless as an empty barn, yet there must have been a time when the wide hall and high-ceilinged chambers breathed of happiness and comfort. So much had I guessed when I paid my respects to Mrs Wilmot, lying in with another infant, none too willingly, judging from the mood she was in.

'Declare there's no end to misery,' she greeted me, freeing one hand from the infant she was guiding to her breast, to indicate a rocker near by. 'It kills you to have them and it kills you to feed them. Declare, it's misery all around!'

The lobster-pink infant was only two days old, and the frail anaemic mother was suffering stubborn after-pains. With each new baby, they got worse and worse. If this kept on, it would get so that the after-pain met the pain of labour. Nothing but misery, that's what marriage was, yet look at Betty, honin for a man!

Whilst thus enlightened, I had time to observe that the bed in which she fretted was of polished rosewood. So too, the bureau, which, together with the rocker, completed the furnishings of the room. Enough to make me see the house in better days; to make me wonder if the querulous woman with her small, impatient face and inadequate hands, was not designed for softer living.

As a matter of fact, the lady neither toiled nor spun. The house might be empty, her progeny arrayed in a single cotton garment, and nothing in the larder save a fletch of bacon, hominy, and rice. A negress came to cook the evening meal. Mrs Wilmot rocked in the shade, grumbling at the everlasting babies, and calling desultory orders to poor Betty, who was as soft and ineffectual as herself.

Yes, Betty was thrilled to have the carpet and the cups. To the best of our combined ability, we enheartened the room, washed the windows, gathered greens, lit a fire in the grate, and celebrated her triumph and my coming departure. Gordon Bannister was the supporting spirit of the occasion, as he had been my sole comfort in the terrible days just passed. Something I had taken for granted, without much thought. Adolescent blindness, due for a rude awakening!

There came a day when the skeleton of our poverty was dragged into the daylight – bone by bone, as it were, tossed upon the dining-room table. A pitiful heap of greenbacks that no amount of faith could strengthen to our need. Not nearly enough for all of us, said papa. Of course, he had been counting on me, which was doubtless foolish of him, if I had elected to marry Mr Bannister. The young man had asked his permission very decently, and above board, etc.

You could have heard my heart across the street! I was scared out of my wits. Frightened to death to hear papa disposing of my precious future in such terms as these. For the moment I didn't think of Bannister at all. Neither he, nor any one else had figured in my secret programme. And papa, who should have understood the bent of my mind, calmly and even a little eagerly suggested that I had *elected* to get married!

Anger that was nine-tenths pain succeeded my astonishment. How could my own parents wish me such a humdrum fate! Why did they stare at me with grave patience, as though expecting me to justify their mean opinion! What did they want me to say? That I was too dumb to realize that a man was in love with me? That the crazy idea gave me a hollow feeling under the breastbone, but not a single flutter of the heart? Oh, what was the use of saying anything, thought I, bolting from the scene, and setting off on an agitated ramble. In the quiet of the wood I began to think of Bannister – to feel horribly ashamed of myself to have been so selfish and unseeing. The innumerable kindnesses I had accepted rose up to accuse me, and all the agreeable characteristics of the young man himself ticked off in my mind. I could have wished myself wings, and a hole in the moon. All of which added up to the remarkable wisdom that, if I must marry somebody, it might as well be Bannister!

Mamma promptly nipped the noble resolution in the bud. If I had only shown some sense, and not run off like a rabbit, I should have heard her laying down the law for all of us. Naturally, she had been waiting to hear what I had to say for myself, if anything. But never for a moment had she dreamed of leaving me behind to make a fool of myself, like – like, well, so many people did who couldn't distinguish between fact and fancy.

So mamma, at least, had not been content to sell me into bondage to save a railway ticket. That was something gained. The young man himself was still to be reckoned with, and not so lightly, it transpired. A bee in the bonnet was nothing compared to the hornet that that erstwhile mortal had under his hat. We finally compromised on a promise, to be redeemed or cancelled next summer, when, presumably, my youthful mind was to have come to its full senses.

Off, then, on the long back trail, with Bannister keeping us sombre company to Meridian. Thereafter, it was one interminable nightmare of weariness, dust, squalling children, overlaid with the sickening reek of orange peel, ham sandwiches, and rancid clothes.

33

The north once more

But even the longest journey ends. In the evening of a bitter, blustery day the train rolled into the grey, familiar station, and there, in the lee of the wind, stood my aunt, in her fur tippet and cap, solid as the Rock of Gibraltar, and scarcely less formidable.

She received us kindly, however, rushed us home, and, when we had washed and changed to clean, though wrinkled, garments, she fed us a sensible, nutritious meal. It can't be said that joy abounded. None of us had much appetite, though papa did his best to wax enthusiastic over the roast. Fresh meat was the luxury in the south, said he, and thereby precipitated the storm. A nice mess we had made of our lives! Now what in heaven's name did papa intend to do? Quite likely, he had been too immersed in his dream to read the papers intelligently, and foresee what now had the country tied up in knots! Industrial panic! That's what it was! Jobs scarce as mercy, and here we were with nothing but the rags on our backs!

Maybe so, said papa, rallying for conscience' sake. He was sure to find something in the shop that had known him so long as a competent, reliable worker. There was something to be said for skill, you know – to be sure, he'd find something.

From then on, the conversation disposed of us like sheep. We would spend the night here together, but in the morning mamma and the younger children were expected at Uncle Jacob's. He had a large house now, not far from our old home. Naturally, papa would remain with his sister for the time being. Nothing was said of me. I might have been the Ghost of Christmas Past, for all the part I had in the painful proceedings.

What was to become of me, I wondered, as I peeled off my clothes in a chilly slice of room that gave off the upper hallway. Why hadn't I spoken up myself, like a sensible being, instead of sitting there with the face of a mummy and the indifference of the dead? Why was it so hard for me to express vital hopes and fears, and so easy to say what was furthest from my earnest thought?

Miserably, I told myself that unquestionably I should have to ask my aunt to solve the riddle for me. Perhaps she had it solved now. Perhaps that was why nothing had been said. She had helped so many strangers, done so much for other nieces not particularly deserving. After all, what I wanted was not so very much. A year in Normal. After that, how simply everything would adjust itself.

Before I went to sleep I had almost convinced myself that such a sensible procedure would appeal to my aunt. It was something of a body blow, therefore, to have her transfix me with a cold glance at breakfast, saying:

'Well, young woman, you, of course, will go to work.'

Yes, of course, I mumbled, glad of my shell; glad that the sickening disappointment did not show in my empty face. Too occupied with the need to hide my hurt even to wonder why she was so hard. Never suspecting until years later, that papa, doubtless anxious to prove that something had been gained by our southern flight, had told her about Bannister. That I would be married in the summer!

Yet, had I known it, I question whether I should have explained myself. I was too much like mamma, which, no doubt, was something else she held against me. Bless her heart, she had her own fixed, iron pride. But a sensible pride, not the chilling reserve that cannot even bend to lighten its own discomfort.

Somewhile later mamma called me to her room, where she was packing the grips. She handed me two dollars – all the money she had – and her best black skirt. I could make it over for myself at Uncle Jacob's. It would make me look older, and had a little warmth, besides. The next day I set off job hunting. It seemed to me I trotted endless miles. No one wanted the services of an inexperienced youngster.

By noon I was half frozen, and hungry, and glum as a raven. The Bon-Ton Bakery offered the warmth I needed, and I knew that hundreds of underpaid clerks went there for soup and a bun at the lunch hour. How good it was to slip into the hot little room smelling of fresh bread and teasing spices! How wonderful to see, in the corner towards the back, Laura Johnson, the old, familiar, half-quizzical frown on her pale, high forehead!

'For heaven's sake!' she greeted me. 'What the dickens has happened? You look awful!'

Just the cold, I told her, and cowardice. I had no talent for netting jobs. Well, I'd get nothing in the stores, she informed me, stirring her soup viciously. Not a darn thing. Every last one of them had cut the staff, whittled the wages, and handed the responsibility of starving clerks to the Lord God Almighty! Fortunately, a few favoured souls still ate ice-cream. That was how she came to be drinking soup and had a bed to sleep in.

'Gosh, L.G., and we are the smart little girls that had such Big Ideas!' she finished, glaring at a silver blonde who whisked by our table with a sizzling steak. 'See that? Now, there's a wise virgin. But don't ask me how she buys a sirloin on three-fifty a week – you wouldn't like the answer! Guess I'll blow you to a cream puff for the good of our souls.'

Over the cream puffs we tried to push out of mind the spectre of jobs, wintry weather, and virtue. Some of our old crowd had run to luck. Carl had a splendid position, and Arne, whom I had bullied into attending night school, was determined to go in for law. Minnie played the church organ like a wizard, led the choir, and sang better than ever. If she had any sense she'd study singing.

'But she won't,' Laura sniffed. 'She is too darn satisfied being the shining light in the Lutheran church. That's another funny thing, L.G., you can kill yourself being satisfied.'

Clarice, another confirmation classmate, was married, which put an end to her fine chatter. Tilly had a job taking care of a couple of old people. Nice change from babies.

The lunch hour passed too quickly. I dreaded the thought of the snowy streets and the thankless business before me. Wise with experience, Laura tried to warn me. As we separated, she gripped my arm in the old affectionate manner.

'See here, I know what you are up against. I know what a romantic fool you are. Oh, don't I remember the high-flown bunk you spilled over Tilly and me! It's so much birdseed in the wind, dearie. Not that I ever got the drift of what you wanted, it was so mixed up with Jean Valjean and the Piece of String. Dam fool stuff, used to make me roaring mad when I got home, where ma was grousing, and the house stank of socks drying by the stove. Well, I'm warning you, those fancy thoughts won't save your shoes. When you reach the stage of cardboard insoles, go to the Employment Bureau. They'll get you a *dear* little job, in somebody's *darling* house!'

Never! thought I, heading smartly into the wind. Even our leanest days had not prepared me for such an eventuality. I'd rather pick rags and keep my self-respect! Unfortunately for me, I had not been taught to accept poverty as an act of God – as one's portion, to be borne with humility. Mamma counted her blessings not in terms of meekness and the World-to-Come, but in the strength of inner fortitude, bequeathed by generations of self-respecting people. And self-respect was synonymous with creditable deeds. How often had she intercepted papa, riding the gale of some lofty sentiment:

'Oh, yes, you talk beautifully! But, to my way of thinking, the ills of the world won't be mended with tender sighs. I have no stomach for Pauline doctrine!'

Nor had I. 'Servant, be obedient unto your masters, as unto the Lord your God.' What a glorious whip that had been in the hands of pious exploiters! I had reached the stage where mamma's practical wisdom overrode all papa's idealism. It would be years until I should see any possibility of compromise between such extremes of opinion. At the moment, I could only see that, in any crucial period it was mamma who saved the situation; mamma who exhibited the virtues she thought it beneath dignity to frame in words.

Yet the gist of her teaching summed up briefly. God was not confined to creeds and a book. That was something to remember when confronted by injustice enacted in His name. Right action sprang from a right heart. That was something not to be forgotten when temptation urged you, against the decent instincts bequeathed by your ancestors.

Nice thought, that! Just how, I wondered amusedly, would the decent instincts of dignitaries in ruffs and crosses conspire to solve the problems of a green servant! The humour of it kept me insulated against the cold for a mile or two; kept my benumbed feet marching smartly; stiffened my resolution, as place after place gave me the same answer.

At last, it seemed as though this determined prowling was to be adequately rewarded. I was actually hired, by a fierce-looking little man, whose topsy-turvy establishment was holding a three-day sale. Think of it, I was to be privileged to flit up and down this dim lane of miscellaneous merchandise, where socks and shirts and feather boas dangled from a clothes-line as gay as any pennants of an ancient tourney. I really had a job – if only for three days. The blissful knowledge sent me home on wings. An elation that was ill-founded, however.

I was sacked the next night. Not because I had failed to make the sales. Oh, no, I had done rather well, as a matter of fact. But, in making out my sales slip, I used the dollar sign and decimal point. This affectation I was guileless enough to explain as something learned in school.

'In school! Abie, she thinks she's in school!' roared the irate little man at the cash register.

'There's nothing wrong with it,' I tried to explain, which was an even greater error.

'You should be telling me! Young lady, here we got us cent signs, understand? Cent signs! Maybe you go back to school and learn some more monkey business!' my indignant employer shouted – and that was that.

Oh well, there would be other sales, I told myself, as I pocketed my dollar-fifty, and faced the dusky street. To-morrow was Sunday, and perhaps I might visit the Rhinertsons and find Tilly there. To-morrow, I could be happy for a few hours, at least. Mamma Rhinertson would be sure to have piles of potato cakes and a fund of gossip with which to regale her visitors. And I had my letters to write to Gordon Bannister.

Sunday was a cheerful day. Tilly had not changed very much despite her longer skirts and piled up hair. She had a better colour, but otherwise was the same, self-effacing, smiling servant, flying about her multiple tasks: whisking the house to rights, setting the table, making coffee, one eye always on the little tots. She liked her work, she said. The old couple were very nice to her, and she had a comfortable room to herself. Best of all, she could save her wages, and one of these days she meant to buy a couple of stuffed chairs, and a Brussels carpet for the front room.

Going home that night I passed our old house, and stopped under the big poplars where I had so often sat reading my books. It was queer, meeting the yellow eyes of the old house this way – the eyes of a stranger, indifferent to my wanderings. I had always hated its ugliness, but now it seemed to me that something inseparable from the strong, stony hills at its back had put its mark on that house. Something that had given me courage, and that I had not sufficiently prized.

I stole down to the creek bed, and listened to the old familiar voice of the water, grumbling to itself under the pearl-grey ice. Suddenly my eyes were wet. I had so loved the little brook. So loved the brown water that rode so boldly over the shoulders of the hills. Now its brave voice reached me through a shroud, unreal as the voice of a dream. That was it! The little brook had all my fondest, fiercest dreams down there, under the cold, grey ice.

34

Trials of a job hunter

Came now the long, dreary days I would rather forget. Days measured in aimless, endless tramping, through sleet and snow, frigid winds, and sub-zero weather. Each morning forcing myself to believe that to-day the miracle would happen. To-day, all prayers would be answered. To-day, I should find a job. An old, old experience, to which every one is thoroughly indifferent, except the wretched novice in the economic scramble.

Not a pleasant, or particularly elevating experience, yet to be highly recommended as initial training for the righteous snobs who play at redeeming mankind. It instils lasting pity for the slattern and the beer-bibber. It so quickly reduces all high-flown necessities to the common denominator of shoes and soup. It bares the bleak bones of mutual dependence as nothing else can. For the painful side of this begging is not its direct effect upon yourself. It is the coming back to those who wait upon your success or failure. I came to loath the last block home. It was torture to sit down to supper, where I felt a burden, and thought all eyes condemned me.

Down to the last quarter, I pocketed pride, and bolted to the Employment Bureau. Yes, there was a job I might try. Mrs H. on Third Street East wanted a second girl. The wage was small, but the work easy. The house was one of those three-story, brown-stone buildings popular in those days. It seemed a prison. I thought I should never muster up the courage to approach the dark door.

A small, sharp-featured woman in black answered the bell, eyed me coldly, and told me to go up a flight of stairs, turn right at the second chamber. Mrs H. was not very well, and was still in bed.

Mrs H. was not the least terrifying. From her mount of pillows and eiderdown she smiled genially, and her voice had the soft, unmistakable slur of the south. She had no objection to my inexperience, which I freely admitted. The work was not the least difficult. I was to notify Hattie – the prim woman in black – that I was hired. Hattie would make a place for me in her room, and explain my duties thoroughly.

No doubt a sensible, pious soul should have rejoiced, grateful in every hair that board and bed was forthcoming. On the contrary, I could have howled with misery. To my jaundiced thinking, this was the end of everything. Laura J. was right – high-flown thinking got you just exactly nothing.

For girls like us the dice were loaded from the start. The ensign of the mop and the dustbin hung over our cradles. No wonder thousands of us married any old fool! Bed and board! Was that the answer? Was that all of life? Was there no room in this iron world for the quickened sensibilities? For the white fire that raced along the edges of the mind at the beautiful, swift soaring of a bird? No meaning to the strange, insistent yearning for a deeper fulfilment of purposes? Just to eat and sleep, propagate your misery, and die!

By the time I scaled the hill to my uncle's house I was in a pretty dither. Mamma, seemingly, understood what ailed me, and applied the pertinent remedy. She did not, as papa might have done, launch into a moving lamentation about the mischief of poverty; the necessity to support with the courage the slings and arrows of outrageous fortune. Somewhat grimly, she watched me dourly packing my few belongings, then she said:

'There is one thing left. One precious thing. Keep yourself to yourself. To those people, you are nothing but the means to get things done. Do it well – but keep yourself to yourself.'

At any rate, now I should see how the folk on the right side of town moved and had their being. That was something by way of interest and compensation. As a matter of fact, there were many compensations. Mrs H. was an easy-going individual, seldom fault-finding, and never unjustly. Following mamma's advice, I effaced myself so much as possible, and followed Hattie's instructions to the best of my ability. Fortunately, I never found it hard to employ my hands, no matter where my thought wandered. There was plenty to do, with three floors to keep clean. Seven bedrooms, carpeted to the baseboard in the good, Victorian style, all to be swept with a broom, the vacuum-cleaner being yet unborn. Two master bedrooms, with lounges attached, filled with a clutter of heavy furniture, heavy drapes, stuffed cushions, and dust-collecting knick-knacks.

Only two floors had bathrooms, which meant that water must be lugged to the top floor. I had charge of the linen, and must remember that some of the family abhorred soft towels, and others swooned at the sight of anything harsh. One of the rooms was occupied by a friend of the family, a member of a law firm and son of a senator then at Washington; a very dainty gentleman, whose bed must be made with extreme care.

His stomach was as pernickety as his hide, and Hattie had always to concoct especially mild dishes for his sustenance. It used to amuse me that this six-foot American masterpiece suffered insomnia from a wrinkle in the sheets, and indigestion from a whisp of steak. I hasten to add that, on high occasions, when the social obligations so demanded, the gentleman laid down his comfort for the sake of his country, and ate anything from oysters to nuts.

Hattie was not given to conversation. For several days she scarcely spoke, except to direct the work, and heaven help me if I failed to understand, for nothing short of the Archangel Gabriel could have induced her to repeat herself. Even that first awful night, when I crept upstairs, too miserable to sleep, she calmly said her prayers to the whisper of her rosary, climbed into bed, and, without a word, turned out the light, leaving me to my moping by the window.

Oh well, there were the stars. Bright and clear, and far removed from human flurries. If I cried myself to sleep, there was no one to see; no one to hear; which was just as well. Neither Hattie nor any one else could have comforted that young creature by the window. Nor did she herself understand the exact source of her exaggerated misery, or why she was suddenly more afraid of losing touch with the stars than of anything tangible and real.

35

Readjustment and the righteous few

I had served a tolerable apprenticeship. I could be trusted with the beds, trusted not to rattle the cutlery, or spill the soup down sensitive backs; I could even be trusted with madam's breakfast tray. All of which, to Hattie's way of thinking, argued that now I might also be trusted with the family honour and glory.

Hattie had been with the family for eighteen years, which in itself spoke volumes for their indubitable superiority. Hattie was not merely a jewel of a cook, but a flawless pearl of rectitude. Saint Peter himself would hesitate to question the credentials of her favourites. Well, *her* family, though not rich, had something of which to be proud.

Mr H., a notable lawyer, was a Virginian. The eldest son was attending the University of Virginia, as had all the eldest sons for generations. The second son was at some military college, and I gathered from the sudden fluster of Hattie's manner as she pummelled her pie-crust that Master Jim had need of discipline. The two daughters, she felt sure, must have impressed me with their exceptional promise of beauty. Madge was a dashing brunette, and Vera such a demure little blonde! A lazy baggage, I would have said, and fat besides! Of madam, no need to speak, said Hattie. I must have judged for myself what a splendid woman she was.

So I had, and had long since suspected what Hattie's loyalty sought to suppress. Amiable Mrs H., with her feline sensuality and self-complacent comfort, was not quite the social equal of her saturnine spouse, whose ancestors may well have snooted peg-legged Stuyvesant, with his cow and cabbages and petty leases in New Amsterdam. According to Hattie's conviction, it was my solemn duty to be thoroughly grateful for the privilege of standing in the shadow of the Lord's elect. She had no doubt I was properly impressed.

How scandalized she would have been to read my thoughts! How shaken to the roots of her religious soul to know that every beautiful thing in that house intensified my resentment against the cruel inequalities of life. It was not that I coveted any of these domestic trappings. Things in themselves meant little to me, for all my yearning centred in the world of books. It was the atmosphere these things created, the sense of security and well-being, that made gracious living a matter of course. It was the contrast of this home as against Laura's dead dwelling that set me thinking. Laura had brains and ability and a burning desire to better herself. To what good? She was starving in a cheap little room, for the sake of peace! Exaggeration? Well, I wondered how Miss Vera would manage her placid graces on ten dollars a month, six of which went for a bed, a patch of hall carpet, and a pine bureau! I wondered then, as I wonder now, how the fine moralists expect a girl to feed and clothe herself on ten dollars a month, in honour!

I love the picture the assembled family made at dinner, every one self-assured, even in displeasure, all so beautifully groomed. I admired the picture, but often enough, as I cleared away half-eaten food, I had a fleeting vision of the Rhinertson children watching with big eyes as the plate of potato bread went around. I used to see, against my will, thousands of similar tables, where the so-called respectable poor stoked their bellies with meagre, starchy fare, and, in spite of clinging faith, I was revolted. There was something terribly wrong in attributing such contrasts to the dispensation of the Almighty Providence. Something blasphemous in preaching a religion that laid such evils on the shoulders of God. Not so long as I had wit to judge for myself of the boundless riches of the earth should I be persuaded to believe that these natural resources were solely designed for the enjoyment of the few who invested their money, which, without the labour of the disinherited, would have been as worthless as charity.

Solemn sermons on the merits of thrift and virtue and wisdom should not alter my conviction that these things were wrong and iniquitous. None of these excellent qualities are the fruits of poverty. Even to practise the thrift of a squirrel requires a surplus over and above the meanest needs of the body. But neither the squirrel nor the prosperous individual knows anything about the vicious sort of thrift to which the very poor are shackled more ignominiously than was any African in irons.

In a vague, tormented fashion, these things simmered in my mind as I slipped about with choice cheese, fruits, coloured ices: foods I had not known to exist. Yet, how fortunate I had been compared to many! And these people thought themselves cruelly pinched. As they doubtless were, compared with the wealthy clique in Lakeside.

These rambling resentments did not effect my interest in the family. Mrs H. was kind, as many indolent people are kind, chiefly because it administers to their own comfort not to disturb the *status quo*. She did nothing from morning till night, and accomplished it perfectly. She was never bored, seldom irritable, and rarely ever sorry for herself.

At nine-thirty I brought up her breakfast, for which she had a good appetite; which amazed me, who hate the sight of food at that hour. For the rest of the morning she played with her complexion, her hair, her finger-nails. Failing an engagement after lunch, she occupied first one soft chair, then another, toying with a book or a piece of embroidery. The same books lay on the table when I left, three months later, that were there on my arrival; the same piece of needlework beside them. What her thoughts were, only heaven knows.

She had the virtues of the lazy. She never questioned the progress of our work. If Hattie was satisfied with my efforts, that was all she cared about. She made a point of inquiring after our comfort. She had heard me coughing in the night, and wished to be sure that nothing serious ailed me. I was thin, she thought. Perhaps I didn't eat enough. One morning she told me to sit down. She had been watching me, she said, and had decided that I was not the sort of girl who usually applied for housework. Why had I not thought of something better? I had a nice voice, a quiet manner, and I spoke very well indeed.

That shops were not hiring help astonished her. How queer! People still bought things, and prices were outrageous. Only yesterday she had paid seventeen dollars for four little doilies. They were not worth it, but when your finances were embarrassed, you had to put up with inferior stuffs. Why hadn't I kept on at school, if things were so difficult in stores and offices?

I had no desire to dramatize the situation. But, I admitted how much I had wanted to attend Normal; that for the present it was impossible, since I had neither home nor other means of livelihood. How unfortunate! Well, in the spring, everything would improve. Business always picked up in the spring, for some reason or other. Meanwhile, she would ask her dressmaker and the milliner if there wasn't an opening. It must be fun trimming hats – and so respectable. Then, which was very kind, she handed me a book, and told me I might read whatever I liked in the evening.

Mr H. seemed little more than a dignified figurehead in the house, coming and going about his business in grave, absorbed silence; asking nothing; saying nothing. Now and then he brought home a gift of flowers for his wife. The girls were good-natured and amiable, like their mother: troubled with nothing except clothes, skating parties, and sorority dances. They lived in a world distant as the moon.

For the most part, I gave little thought to any of them. I had my own problem to solve. On my day out I felt like a thief, stealing into the street from the narrow back alley, and thought I must surely die if, by some mischance, a former friend saw me. I still had all my vanity intact. That Tilly and Laura should know of my predicament did not matter, but the thought of meeting Carl, or Arne, or fortunate Mollie of boarding-school glamour turned me faint with shame. Then there were my letters from

Bannister – dear, charming letters, that made me feel a horrid impostor. Impossible to believe that the queer creature who lived by grace of mop and broom had any right to these pages! And it scared me to death, being constantly reminded that not later than July he was coming to Duluth.

That must not be! Until I was out of the mess, and had some sort of home in which to receive him, he must not come! Not for all the romance of earth would I meet any man at a kitchen door! Fool or not, I had not sufficient faith in male affection to believe that it could survive the shock of meeting the object of its dream attired in a cotton uniform, and popping out of an alley!

Perhaps I did not want it so. To love me was to love my pride. What a headache it was! What endless hours of frantic worry it created. The prospect of a home was still a misty vision. Papa had temporary employment, and was planning a lecture trip through the Icelandic settlements of Manitoba when the job was done. He had some hope of locating something better in Canada, which seemed less effected by the general depression.

Mamma was hoarding the pennies. She was the proud owner of two chairs and a kitchen table. In a month, she hoped to buy a stove. So far, my contribution was only the payment of the two dollars squandered in job-hunting. The most sainted thrift falls short on three dollars a week. Out of my first week's salary (bless the word!) I had to pay the employment bureau, and buy blue percale for two dresses. I would look so nice in blue, Mrs H. thought. I was much too young to go about in a black skirt and blouse.

A pair of shoes ate up the next week's earnings, then I paid my debt, and now I had only to wait six weeks to get a spring coat. All providing the devil did not tempt me to think of a hat, or some wickedness like a lace collar, or the book of Aldrich's poems, marked down to twenty-five cents in a near-by shop window.

Satan won, to the extent of the poems, I am glad to say. Virtue has brought me such small comfort. The little book was an oasis of joy in the dull monotony of stupid housework. For everything about housework is a stupid repetition, with the exception of cooking. The book of verse, and Hattie expertly assembling a beautiful meal, were the highlights of existence. Hattie's cooking was a fine art; not an idle gesture, not a single, superfluous spoon cluttered the table. Everything was accomplished with ease and dispatch. Because I watched her intently, asking no worrisome questions, she tossed off a priceless hint now and then which I tucked away in the crannies of my mind. Many years later, when I had to feed thirteen pernickety boarders, I had reason to bless Hattie, and be grateful for a memory that retains and easily calls forth whatever it really fixes upon.

36

A kitchen-view of society

Three unrelated incidents of those otherwise uneventful months stand out in my mind. Not that they were spectacular, or of particular interest in themselves, except as they sharpened my understanding of certain mental concepts that form an impressive guard between the sheep and the goats.

Mrs H. informed us one morning that she was expecting a house guest: a very dear friend. There would be no fuss. A dinner and a tea, perhaps. Nothing elaborate, for the lady was unwell, and desired a quiet rest. The visitor arrived next day, and to my astonishment, for I had been anticipating a delicate, dainty female, the lady looked about as fragile as a mountain lion. Tall, stout, with a square, though not unhandsome face, she was anything but the type one associates with condiments and cushions. Yet, within the hour, this heroic bulk, eased of its stays, was gracelessly overflowing the softest arm-chair in madam's lounge.

Then it was, against intent and inclination, that I overheard an illuminating shred of dialogue. Entering with a tea-tray it was impossible not to hear the delicious chatter:

'Of course, it's impossible at your age, Edith. You couldn't be expected to submit to such a thing, darling!' This from Mrs H.

'I certainly cannot. A baby would be too ridiculous!' the lioness rumbled.

At which awkward moment I perforce set down the tray! Bless their buttons, I dare say neither one thought I had sense enough to follow such erudite reasoning. I can't say that I was shocked. Long since, I had reached the conclusion that accidental and undesired parenthood was no great blessing. That this square-faced Amazon rebelled, albeit tardily, at the beautiful boon of Eve, was not so startling. I had heard a deal of grumbling in the hospital. What sent a wave of hot resentment from head to heel was the quick realization that in her case the attitude was accepted as eminently practical.

I remembered a rag of a girl, pleading vainly for help in a similar situation. How horrible that was! How wretchedly sinful! The folly in either case is beside the point. What struck me like a blow was the obvious injustice of a society which exacts the letter of the law only from the less fortunate.

The incident had its humorous aspect. Next morning Mistress Edith hasted away on her pertinent mission, and shortly thereafter returned in a somewhat shattered state. The bell screaming shrilly, up I flew, hot-footed, to the lady's chamber. What a sight to see! A helpless giantess in distress, the poor woman, half stripped, stood amid the clutter of discarded garments, tearing at her corset with shaking fingers.

'For God's sake, help me out of this,' she yelped, 'I'm dying. I'm dead! – I've got to get a cup of tea!'

Easier said than done! However, at the cost of great groaning, frantic fumbling, and desperate hauling on miles of laces, the feat was finally accomplished, and the victim tucked into bed.

The rest of the day devolved into a marathon between the kitchen, where I was helping Hattie prepare for a formal dinner, and the bedroom, where I supported the guest of honour towards a better lease of life.

The dinner was set for eight o'clock. Little dreaming the fortitude of socially ambitious females, I kept wondering how the patient expected to attend her own party. At seven the bell rang peremptorily, and off I bounced, to receive yet another enlightening shock.

Draped in a blue wrapper, Mistress Edith was up, seated at the dressing-table, calmly applying blobs of cream. On the bed lay a bell-shaped moiré underslip and a shimmering, white satin

Princess dress. Beside these the wicked corset, with its multiple straps, clasps, and strings, looked a fearsome strait-jacket.

I could guess the pleasant job before me. What hectic pinching, pulling, and alarming breath-holdings it required to jockey the unruly flesh into proper mould. How the wicked laughter chortled in me as the fat rolled up under the thick, unlovely arms, and down upon the heavy thighs in order to achieve the fashionable wasp waist which, presumably, gladdened appreciative male eyes.

Then, panting but triumphant, on with the moiré slip; on with cream and powder and perfume; on with the resplendent gown, fortified with whalebone and its thousand and one safeguarding hooks and eyelets.

At eight o'clock the lady swept down the winding stairs, three-foot train rustling majestically, and the saints alone knew at what cost she stepped so lightly, laughed so blithely, in response to the greeting of the gentleman who led her in to dinner.

Throughout the many courses Mistress Edith maintained her gaiety, which, happily, hid her total lack of appetite. The following day she spent in bed. The cold had settled on her chest, you understand. When she finally took her joyous departure she generously presented me with a fifty-cent ribbon for my hair – which I ungenerously dropped in the ash-bin.

Shortly hereafter, I inferred from Hattie's apologetic murmur that the younger son of the house was coming home to digest some indiscretion. As not infrequently happens, he was his mother's idol, and Hattie implored the Holy Saints to smooth the way of the transgressor. It would be so terrible for madam if the father were too harsh.

Nothing daunted, the young man arrived, and, apparently, had no difficulty in squaring himself with his parents. Certainly Mrs H. glowed with pleasure to have him home, fluttering and fussing over the darling boy's every whim and foible. For several days he behaved with admirable docility, perpetrating no greater mischief than driving his sisters into abortive rages.

Then, one afternoon, as I was pottering about the second floor, I heard the vestibule door below open with a crash, and, simultaneously, the sound of some heavy object striking against a chair; a smothered yelp of pain, then uneasy steps on the stairs.

It was Master Jim – a very groggy Jim – listing windward, a nasty, greenish pallor in his youthful face. Catching sight of me, at the stair head, the gallant waved a cheery fin, but the effort of supporting both equilibrium and charm was disastrous. The poor thing clutched his midriff and, with a brave bound concluding the stairs, dived for the bathroom.

Mrs H., enjoying a pleasant nap, had rudely wakened. What was that noise, she demanded irritably, though unsuspicious. What on earth had I done out there, making such a clatter? To which I answered nothing, trusting that indolence would outbid curiosity, and the scapegrace find cover before his mother aroused sufficiently to quit her easy couch.

Which he did, though by so mean a margin I had barely time to obliterate the stains of iniquity. Mrs H., accusative and cross, confronted me as I emerged from the bathroom.

'What *is* going on —' she began, and faltered uneasily as a malodorous whiff struck her offended nostrils. Something bordering on consternation showed in her face for a fleeting moment, then she broke out crossly: 'What was that – that noise?'

'Was there a noise, madam?' said I, no muttonhead more dumb.

'Of course there was a noise! It woke me,' she carped, obviously on the horns of a dilemma, wanting the truth, and fearing the confirmation of her suspicions.

'I was putting the linen away. The door often slams,' I offered, which was true – up to a point.

Whatever she may have thought, it went unspoken, for suddenly she remembered the gentleman with senatorial connections.

'Mr K. will be here any minute! And the wretched drains are smelling!' she gasped. 'For goodness' sake, open the window, and ask Hattie what to do!'

The episode had its anticlimax some days later. It happened I was hurrying down the same stairs, and found my way barred by gallant Mr Jim.

'See here, can't you be a bit friendly to a loving young man?' he demanded, wearing his most fetching expression. 'You can't be such an icicle,' he pursued, improving upon invention in fine, histrionic style.

Oh well, a sturdy, bovine stare is more effective than a million words. The loving creature dropped his arms, and off I went about my business. Keeping myself to myself. So far as I was personally concerned, the incident had no significance. I had no taste for backstair flirtation, and lacked the vanity either to be flattered or insulted. I simply chalked up another score against a class which has such scant respect for the sensibilities of those whom ill circumstances confine to humble service.

I had my own, specific temptations, less easily dismissed. Sometimes I spent my Sunday with Laura in the tantalizing folly of window shopping. Spring was almost upon us, and everywhere a hundred pretty garments teased our eyes. There were so many things we needed, so many more we should have been delighted to wear.

In the case of myself, none of this was so urgent. But for Laura, who was expected to look smart, the situation was distressing. Yet how distressing I was not to understand for several months. That she was pale and nervous, so that the slightest noise made her jump, I could see, and I had the uncomfortable feeling that to dress herself she went without food. And she was always fastidiously clean, which meant that, however hungry she was, the laundry had to be paid.

She suffered from loneliness, too, for, unlike myself, she had no interest in books. It made her jumpy trying to read after working hours. It made her boiling mad to follow the impossible successes of the bright mortals spun out of the heads of comfortable nitwits who thought that life was an angel cake. And the stuff I mooned over gave her the jitters. Imagine getting a kick out of *The Laughing Man!*

But when she saw me wistfully eyeing a wine-coloured suit in Freeman's window, she understood me. It was exactly the sort of thing I should wear. It would go so well with my dark brown hair and show to advantage my only attribute, a very decent figure.

I had not thought of the tempting thing in just those terms. I simply pined for it as I never before nor since pined for any scrap of ornament. It seemed to me that its mere possession would clothe me with magical virtues, and restore all my battered self-respect.

For three nights running I stole out after dark, just to look at it. And then I received a letter from Bannister that tried me sorely.

Said he, in effect, that I should remember that, whatever he had, it was mine for the asking. That he imagined things were not too easy for us, that he wished I would have faith enough to let him help me.

Dear goodness! With the letter in my pocket I marched to that window once more. I could have that precious thing. It was mine, for just a word or two. Why not? Surely that was the sensible procedure. Yes, I would do it! I would go straight up to that attic room and write the letter —

But when I had the pen and paper before me I froze with shame. I sat there, staring at the slanting walls, seeing for the first time quite clearly what I must write. Something sharp and final, that put an end to all these devoted letters. And that something must effectively break Bannister's idealized image of me.

Well, I had always some gift of words, when it came to putting them on paper. I wrote my letter, and promptly mailed it. Then I took a farewell squint at my precious suit, and scampered home to cry myself to sleep. By return mail, I received a cryptic note. Three short, angry lines. He was leaving for the north, May 13th. He would not see me; and ending:

'We Bannisters keep our word.'

That night I took a long walk up into the hills, where the dark lay thick, and the heavy silence, full of healing wisdom, quieted the ache in my troubled mind.

A few days later the last of the three illuminating incidents to which I referred leaped at me like an angry cur. The eldest son had come home for the Easter holidays. He was a humourless prig, filled with his own importance: as certain of success as fools were sure to give it. I had been dusting out his room, and, perhaps an hour later, was peremptorily hauled upon the mat.

He had left a cheque on his desk. It was gone. What had I done with it? There was no use lying. No use stealing it, either. It would do me no good.

Perhaps the decent instincts of the ancestors did support me then. At any rate, I had the grace to say little, and say it calmly. It was he who raged in undiluted, proletarian fervour, ripping through papers like a whirlwind, and bringing his mother on the jump by the precious clamour.

Kind soul, she was distressed. I was free to go on with my work; she would help Master Jack find the cheque. No doubt it was merely mislaid.

It was found in the book he had been reading. Mrs H. came to tell me the glad tidings. She was sorry: she hoped I had not taken the little storm to heart. One had to be careful with money.

I was cleaning the silver, and kept on cleaning it. To be called a thief is not exactly pleasant, but it has its sharp merit. It jogs your little ego: makes you see very clearly what the poor really look like to the respectable people who save the heathen and pack such lovely Christmas hampers.

Not long thereafter Mrs H. decided to dispense with the services of a second girl. The sons had gone about their business, her daughters would soon be leaving, on their summer holiday, and she herself was thinking of a trip east. Hattie could manage by herself, but now she wanted me to realize how pleased she had been with my behaviour. If I could find the books, I was welcome to come back in the fall and work for my board while I attended Normal School.

What was more, she had a job for me. Mrs C., a connexion by marriage, was going to Chicago for an audience with a famous singing teacher. She expected to remain for two or three months, and wanted some trustworthy girl to take charge of her little

daughter, Bea. Mrs C. was – well – a trifle exacting and tempera-
mental, which was to be expected of an artist, but it would quite
likely prove an easy place once she had left. There seemed nothing else to do. Business was still just as slack in the stores, and
the only hope on the horizon was the promise of a job at
Kugler's drug store, where Laura worked, when the fountain
trade picked up. Until then, I might as well turn nursemaid.

The new household was a revelation. Mr C. was an eminent
eye-ear-nose-and-throat specialist. A dry stick of a man, years
older than his india-rubber wife, with the coldest voice and eye
that ever I encountered. The very first morning he fixed me with
a microscopic glance, hoped I had a shred of sense, and would
see to it that not a drop of water got into Bea's ears.

'Wipe them with a dry towel – a *dry* towel, do you understand?'

The lady rattled off the rest of the instructions, standing at a
safe distance, as though afraid of contamination. She never
passed either the cook or me without pinching back her skirts.
Nominally, I was supposed to watch young Bea, but until the
lady's departure I might as well make myself useful, doing the
upstairs work, waiting table, and wiping the dishes.

Quite a chore, since there were seven ill-assorted individuals
in the house: a crotchety doctor; his tempestuous wife; an infant
of three; and, in addition, the lady's widowed brother-in-law
and his three half-grown children. It certainly gave promise of
more than interest! The house looked like a junk shop above
stairs. In every conceivable nook and cranny were dismantled
beds, antique chests, high-boys, and tables, all yelling for dusting. These treasures, I learned from cook, were being purchased
to furnish the grand new home the doctor was building in Lakeside. A home to properly house this lady, and hold her voice.

Cook had other things less complimentary to tell. Mrs C. was
so mean she counted the eggs every morning! She peered into
the tea canister, the sugar-bin, and the bread-box, and never in
the three months that Annie had been there, had she tasted a
chop, or a sliver of steak. Madam ordered exactly seven pieces,
and then carped about the shrinkage.

All of which was perfectly true. We were lucky to get a scraping of vegetables and left-over bread. One night, there was a delicious row over the number of potatoes required for a creamed dish. Annie insisted upon four. Madam decided that two large ones were quite sufficient.

'What!' croaked cook, mournful as Hamlet's ghost. 'Two potatoes for nine people?'

Which was no way to speak. There were only seven people – and two servants. But this little scrimmage was nothing compared with the comedy of a later night.

All that day madam had regaled the angels with soaring rhapsodies, and not for her soul's sake would cook have dared intrude with questions of food. Consequently when the family sat down to dinner, it consisted of a meagre blob of salt cod, riding the crest of an immense platter, and a tray of brown bread.

What a feast of joy that was! Dr C. glared at me with his microscopic orbs. Well, was that all? What was I standing about for – where were the vegetables?

Sweet as the Paschal Lamb, I said there were none.

What, roars he, and why not? And, to my unholy glee, he ramps into battle with the undaunted prima donna.

'Gertrude, what's the matter with you?' demands he. 'Have you lost your senses? Do you expect me to put up with this – this beastly mess!' And more of the kind.

To which the great lady replied by blaming the cook. This was the sort of thing that happened, if one trusted to the intelligence of menials. Annie was such a fool.

He would see about that, replied the master, and forthwith, bounced up from the table and out into the kitchen.

But Annie, cheerfully swishing out the solitary pot, simply waved her hand towards the pantry.

'Have a look for yourself, Dr C.,' said she.

The shelves yielded a bag of prunes, and nothing else.

'Damnation!' muttered the indignant lord, grabbing a fistful, by way of ammunition for the final round with his wife.

After that, the vegetable bin was never empty, although everything else was whittled to the nicest fraction. But now I was to see the shining side of all this stupendous thrift.

Madam gave a dinner to celebrate her forthcoming departure, and to properly impress a well-chosen few. Food poured into the house like an avalanche. From morning until night, Annie and I struggled with an incredible variety of greens, shell-fish, chicken, ham, plain and fancy vegetables, condiments, ices, and small cakes. Boning crab, blanching almonds, stuffing dates, to say nothing of preparing hors-d'oeuvres, kept us hot and hopping.

By nine o'clock I had served this feast of fat things to the joyous crowd, for, of course, as madam explained, there was no sense hiring a waitress when I had proven myself so apt at my former place. In a white dress, borrowed from Cook, who, fortunately, was a small, trim Swede, I should look well enough.

The kitchen was a sight to see, with dishes and glassware and tumbled food stacked in every conceivable corner, even under the table. It was one o'clock before the mess was cleared away, and we small fry had a cup of coffee and a chicken sandwich.

It was the following week that Mrs C. took me to task for inefficiency. There was no reason for wasting an hour on the upstairs. Why, she herself could make all the beds, dust, and sweep, in half the time. It was scandalous. Bea must get out into the sunlight. Unless I improved, she would hesitate to leave the baby in my care. To put it bluntly, I was not earning my wages.

'Very well,' said I, quite calmly, 'in that case, I shall not take it.' And, much to the dear lady's indignation, away I went.

37

The working world

Kugler's would not take me for another month, but I put in six weeks working for a jovial Norwegian woman who ran the Lakeside pavilion and dance-hall. The season was not started, although there was plenty to do; but, as Mrs Gunderson was as amiable as she was frankly fat, the work was a pleasure.

It was fun, watching the rolling gait of her walk, and the agility of her huge, red arms beating up immense cake batters. Always fond of cooking, the family dinner fell to my lot, and that was a nice change from sliding about with a duster.

An occasional dance stepped up the trade, and added to interest. It amused me to watch the proletariat having a fling at fifty cents a couple.

The following month mamma moved into a tiny little house, far back in the hills: three small rooms, with a wide, secluded meadow for a yard. Not much, yet how glad we were to be under a roof of our own! So now I had a bed at home, and, shortly thereafter, was busily serving the dear public with ice-cream sodas, sundaes, and what-not. It was wonderful, feeling free! Wonderful, working with Laura! Wonderful, being roared at by a fussy Greek, who never meant a single word of his angry abuse.

A new sort of life unrolled itself before me. A sort of pageant of gay pretence: little stenographers playing at being ladies, flirted bravely over mounds of sickly stuff; frizzled sales girls stomped in with the boy friends after the show; middle-aged housewives eased themselves from shopping, and placated their cranky youngsters with five-cent blobs of vanilla. Not infrequently, some sour-looking gentleman crept in on his way to work to ask Tony for something to settle a rampaging stomach.

There were acres of offices over our heads, and some of the medical men had a habit of dropping in for Coco-Cola and a bit of badinage with us girls. One incorrigible old duffer, whom I had met at my aunt's hospital, delighted to plague me by hauling on his rubber gloves when his glass was drained:

'So now to visit my gallant ladies,' he would twinkle. Said gallant ladies being housed on the waterfront behind us.

There was a young dentist who always raised our temperatures, a really beautiful creature: clean-limbed, shapely suave, with not a care in the world, that we could imagine. He was always fascinatingly gay, and almost broke our hearts when he popped along with some pretty girl in fine feathers. And then, one morning, there was a shot – a terrible sound that ripped the air, for a moment, leaving a dreadful silence. Our handsome doctor had killed himself. He had no debts, no unhappy love entanglements, no threatened ailment. He just thought the show too trivial. On his tidy desk lay a scrap of note:

'The game isn't worth the candle.'

Laura wept amid the ice-cream cans in the storeroom, and I suffered something very near panic. I understood too well the queer despair that had lain behind those easy smiles, and I did not want to see so clearly.

'My God!' Laura kept moaning, 'my God, fancy killing yourself, with so much to live for!'

Tony slapped our backs with a broad paw, and uncorked a bottle of pop.

'Musta been nuts, poor nut!' quoth he.

Threading my way into the hills that night, I wondered. I sat down by the old brook, singing to itself so contentedly, and thought: now he had the answer; or the tale was told; and, in either case, life went on as before. Some one else would do his work, some one without that hunger for an inner satisfaction compatible with intelligence and reason. Some allegedly normal young man, who could thrill to a bank account, embrace heaven in the Ten Commandments, and be perfectly content with a world that met his own physical needs.

The weeks straggled away uneventfully, except that, now, I could patronize the library in my free hours. There were no amusements; anything of that nature within my means would have bored me to tears, so I stuck to my books. I had always loved history, and now I could scamper over the bleaching bones of the past to my heart's content. It kept me from worrying too much about unco-operative nickels and dimes, and the shadow of the winter coat I should have to buy eventually.

Racing about in the store, and reading myself silly, kept me blind to Laura's increasing fatigue, though now and then I used to scold her for eating nothing. Nonsense! She ate heaps of ice-cream. Every one knew that ice-cream had lots of nourishment.

Then, one day, she came prancing in with a little brown fur slung from her shoulders. Heaven knows how many dinners it cost. And then she found a suit and a smart pair of shoes.

Finally, a young man, quite a nice-mannered chap, a book-keeper somewhere – attached himself; and so I gave up worrying about the pinched look and the dark rings under her eyes. She had her beau and I my books. We were working different shifts now, and, by degrees, saw less and less of each other.

In September I left Kugler's to try my luck in the tent and awning department of the Marshall-Wells Company. Not a dainty job, but it paid six dollars a week as against four, and I had to have that coat.

It was a queer experience, stepping into the big, gloomy barn-like department, smelling of leather, machine oil, and bales of canvas. Queer, but not the least depressing. The whirring motors of the machines, the rows of long windows, opening out upon the water, created a far from dreary atmosphere.

Mr Clemetson, the boss, was a grave and kindly man, and the two girls at the whizzing machines were wonderfully decent.

Margot was a brusque, dapper individual, efficient to her finger-tips. Bertha, her cousin, had the sweetest nature of any girl I have ever met. She was a very plain person, and suffered from chronic bronchitis, but she had the kindest eyes, the swiftest thought for others, and not one shred of feline malice in her whole dear body.

My first day was spent getting the feel of the big power machine; feeding it miles and miles of double strips of canvas. Then came the light-flies, and, when my seams were sufficiently straight and trustworthy, eight-ounce wedge and wall tents.

Bertha, ever helpful, rescued me from a couple of crazy blunders, whereafter I was well away as an honourable tent-maker.

There was an old scallawag of a pock-marked sailor in the shop: Old Nelson, and what a card he was! Nothing but the patience of Mr Clemetson kept him there, despite his efficiency with the mallet, ropes, and riveter. Nelson was true to the ancient type of salt-water sailor, and could not, for long, eschew the tempting bottle. The dear thing drank like a fish.

Every so often the old boy disappeared for a couple of days, only to creep in with the distressed air of a beaten pup, his ugly, scarred hands all a-quiver, and his whole, ungainly hulk jittery with nerves. But, oh, how meek! How painfully industrious! And how ignored by the boss – who, when the poor old thing was not looking, winked at us wickedly.

At his best, old Nelson was, to me, at least, an entertaining study. Squatting on a stool, a mass of tent before him, he whacked away with the mallet, punctuating every tenth ring with a spurt of tobacco juice, expertly aimed at the tin pail some paces to the right. And, when the mood was on him, he chattered of the sea, and especially of the dog-gone-danged heathen island where his ship lay quarantined with the pest.

For every ailment of the flesh Nelson had the same remedy: whisky and turpentine. Whisky for your guts, and turpentine to kill the dog-gone-danged germs. Sometimes, in the stress of honest emotion, it was quite a cross, holding to these ladyfied expletives; but the boss was a terrible stickler for the nice proprieties – if it killed him, the lion must bed with the lamb.

Old Nelson was very decent to me, cheerfully coming to my rescue if a huge tent became inextricably tangled behind my machine. Sewing a twelve by fourteen wedge tent of twelve-ounce duck is not quite the same as stitching up a fancy apron, or a cambric dress. Until I became accustomed to the weight, and had the skill to guide the cumbersome bulk expertly over the machine apron with my left elbow, it was back-breaking business.

To begin with, the mere sitting still, hour upon hour, after months of racing about from dawn to dark, was extremely trying. The constant drag of unaccustomed weight upon my arms and shoulders made me feel like a rheumatic old woman, before the day was done. And, cursed with a ridiculously sensitive hide, my finger-tips were a raw and painful mess.

But these whimsies passed: my fingers sprouted a protective callous, and my arms stopped complaining. I reached a point where even oiled canvas, stiff as a board, held no terror, and the bigger the tent, the better I liked it.

One day, jumping up to straighten the folds of a huge house-tent, I got my finger under the needle. Fortunately, I had not depressed the foot pedal on sitting down again, but only spun the wheel. The needle bit through the nail, and, of course, obeying a purely reflex impulse, I foolishly yanked the finger away.

Good old Nelson rushed to the colours with his trusty turpentine tin, a most abominably filthy tin!

'Here now! Here now! In you go!' said he, thrusting the silly digit into the can, and holding it there for fully five minutes. 'Ha! That's good! Let her bleed!' said he, shifting his quid, and peering lovingly into the murky oil. 'Many's the cut that little cup o' hell's fire's fixed! By Gar!'

Margot clipped the nail as well as she could. Bertha made a bandage from a handkerchief, and the boss poured out a cup of coffee. They were all as good as gold, and the many months spent with them is a pleasant memory. There were problems enough to solve, however. In the fall papa's job played out, and he went to Winnipeg. Before leaving, he decided we must find a cow. If we had a cow, we should be in clover.

The only way to realize this marvel was to borrow forty-five dollars from a loan shark at almost 50 per cent interest. It would be my pleasant duty to discharge this obligation in weekly dribbles from my pay envelope. I can't imagine a less thrilling Saturday excursion than those trips into the musty office of that fussy benefactor, who always seemed to be worrying about, looking for some invisible mouse.

Peering at me from under a counter, from the grill of a small cage, the dark hole of a steel vault; dark and dusty, with a smile that cracked his face uncomfortably; he seemed to my exaggerated fancy a horrible little man. I hated his pleasantries; his smiling, 'So here you are, young lady – on time, as usual. And how are we to-day?'

Sometimes, when the weather had grown cold, and I shivered in my spring coat and thin, unprotected boots, I used to wonder what the old owl would say if I were to suddenly shout the truth. If I said: 'I'm cold, drat your hide! Wet as a netted fish, thanks to your robbing usury!' But such things are not said to a nice, Christian gentleman who still owns the head and horns of your cow.

As the weather sharpened we discovered that the little house was uninhabitable. It seemed to be a question of fewer hamburgers and a warm bed, or freezing to death on a smug stomach. After all, we had the cow. Rice with skim milk was filling enough for any enlightened soul.

In the course of time the blessed creature was paid for, thanks to a windfall from papa; whereupon, instead of investing in a warmer habit, I bought a giddy rocker and a high-boy. That was a proud moment, celebrated with much coffee and grand talk.

But, in the main, the season was dreary, with irascible weather, and nothing by way of entertainment. I had lost my taste for church socials, even if I could have indulged the extravagance. *Lutefisk* gave me the shudders, and the lame programmes acceptable to Pastor Bjerke left me wondering if the dead were all below ground.

Sometimes I wondered what I was doing on the top deck myself. More especially in the morning, when, at six-thirty, I went streaking for the car that meant an hour's misery before I escaped into the friendly gloom of the wholesale house. Five miles, night and morning, on the only conveyance that, for some strange reason, turns me to jelly! For weeks I really suffered acute carsickness. After that, it steadied down to a sort of groggy feeling that introduced the day with a kind of dizzy leer.

But everything has its compensations. I used to turn my back on the flesh and the devil, so to speak, and rivet my attention to the street; setting myself the entertaining task of discovering odd characters; fixing this and that curious scene in my mind; forming a habit that has served me rather well. But, at the time, it was nothing but an antidote for nausea!

It was during this year that I also reverted to the infant habit of holding imaginary conversations in my head, selecting my subjects from the crowded car, putting words into their mouths which I thought fitted their expressions, dress, and gestures. It used to give me a start, sometimes, when these people lived up to the part, breaking into the exact sort of speeches, on greeting some acquaintance, that I had imagined for them.

It used to amuse me, too, despite the wooziness amidships, to watch the chance flirtations under way; to distinguish between the expert philanderer, with his quick appraisal, and the innocent youth with his obvious crush. Poor dears, they needed a practised eye in those days! It was the age of Gibson girls; the age of pompadours, stocks, stiff collars, whalebone, pads, ruffled corset covers, stuffed brassières, long skirts, and tailored blouses. It must have been a tricky business, distinguishing how much, if any, girl there was under all this armour. And when the sweet thing finally yielded to her lover's arms, the yielding was about as responsive as steel plate!

Of course, there were cunning tricks: peek-a-boo blouses for dress wear gave naughty hints of pink flesh; and a really daring miss seldom forgot the Anna Held method of exposing a wicked ankle. There was a way of grasping the skirt, in getting on and off vehicles, and even over the curb, which definitely published the alluring line of hip and thigh – providing it was a hip and thigh, and not just cotton padding.

In the evening, these tailored Gibson dummies gave place to effigies in princess gowns, dolmans, feather boas, floating veils, and enormous picture hats tacked to mounds of rats and rolls with murderous hatpins. But it remained a stiffly corsetted company, secure in virtue and discreet lisle hose.

None of this sartorial elegance was possible to me. My select wardrobe consisted of two serge skirts and four cotton blouses, which I had made myself at the extreme cost of twenty-five cents, and with these, I wore the approved starched collar and plain black tie. I made my own hat from buckram and felt braid, and sported a sheer wool veil. Not a giddy outfit, but oh, my, *how* modest!

One thing I never would accept, however, were rats and a corset, which made me as lax in style as I was odd in lack of enthusiasm for hikes, picnics, Epworth Leagues, oratorios, and cantatas. I couldn't breathe inside a casket of whalebone, and I couldn't think inside conventional chicken-runs. Except for occasional qualms about Bannister, of whose rambling round the country Bob kept me informed for over a year, I was quite content to spend the nights alone.

I had discovered old Miss Rudd one day, selling books in a department store, and had begun reading Shakespeare. Not because it was smart, or elevating, but because I had begun to hunger for ideas expressed with power, wit, and beauty; to read for the sake of reading, which is nothing rare in an Icelander.

Once in a while I visited the Careys. I had met them years ago, but, as they lived in East Duluth at the very end of Boulevard Drive, that famous roadway that circles the brow of the hills and commands one of the finest views in the Middle West, I seldom went there in my schooldays.

They were a jolly family. Mrs Carey was a German woman with all the German virtues, married to an Irishman of good family, a little run to seed. Mr Carey was a surveyor, and I had often, in my vacations, gone with the family into the logging areas.

One memorable winter I was stranded with them, in a camp, due to a terrific blizzard. I had to get back to school, and decided to walk. Maybelle, the daughter, and another friend, volunteered to guide me to the nearest village, which was five miles away. There was no road, just a blazed trail, which we followed over windfalls and waist-deep drifts of snow.

At Nea an old Norwegian woman took us in, dried our clothes, fed us fresh bread, rosettes, and quarts of coffee, put us to bed for the night, and all next day regaled us with the private lives of the villagers. Mrs Swanson lived in my mind, undimmed, for years, and eventually, like so many other chance acquaintances, popped into a book.

The next morning I set out for Duluth with a teamster hauling logs, and quickly discovered that it was better to walk than to imitate an icicle atop the load. It was a twenty-five mile jog, and earned me a neatly frozen foot.

At the Careys, there was always a lot of laughter at my expense. They were all outdoor people, and tried their best to infest me with the holy fervour, with no better results than a good laugh at my incompetence.

I loved them very dearly, and until the day of her death Mrs Carey was Mother Carey to me. But now that I was a young lady, Mother Carey thought I should make something of my figure. Really, a few decent stays in a foundation would give me quite a fashionable turn! Then, too, I ought to mingle with young folk, not moon about the books.

Now and then I went with the Careys to a party: real German jamborees, with fiddles and harmonicas, old-fashioned dances, beer, and *Wienerwurst*. But there was always something heavy-handed about German humour, something possessive about the men, which displeased me. I was much happier with the family, under their own roof, where the local youngsters often forgathered to sing around the old piano, while Mother Carey fed us raisin cakes and lemonade. And Grandma Rabb, spryest of old ladies, was always there in her corner, smiling approval, vain of her appearance and carefully curled bangs. And there was always a remarkable cat walking about, inviting an audience for his feline gifts and graces.

It was a friendly house, but a severely regimented house, where every tick of the clock defined certain duties to a hair's breadth. I think that was what fascinated me at first. Mother Carey was a perfect Bismarck for discipline and efficiency. Everything, from the combing of her magnificent hair to the peeling of cold potatoes for the next morning's breakfast, was regulated to the exact minute. Not only were there specific days for specific duties, but every hour of every day was predestined to its little dot of labour. Such a state of affairs would have driven mamma crazy. In our house, a new book, or the weekly paper, pushed everything to the wall. You did things that had to be done, but nothing was so sacred that it could not wait for a jolly yarn or a bit of political bickering in the paper! A trip to the Careys was a like a dash of salt in the soup: it stiffened the moral digestion, but a dash was enough. Coming back to the funny little house where mamma sat with her knitting beside the glowing stove, with its heavy, happy kettle humming and the coffe-pot screaming for attention, was always a revelation most welcome. A rediscovery of other, older, mellower values that made you content to curl up like a cat and be your lazy self.

38

And so farewell

There was a nasty jolt in store for me one morning when I
arrived at the shop. Business was slack, and Mr Clemetson had
been notified to cut down the staff. Naturally, since I was the
youngest employee, I should be the victim. But Mr Clemetson
understood how desperately I needed the job. It was all we had
to live on the most of that year. He had made a tentative arrangement with the chief. In former years huge orders of 'flies' had
been sent to a small jobber, who turned them out at low cost. If I
could make these things as cheaply, turn out a sufficient number
to justify my salary, I could stay on. The job would tide me over
into the busy season.

Heavens, what a day that was! In this day of motorcars, the
honourable 'fly' is long forgotten. It was a net of coarse twine
that covered the horse from head to tail. It had to be seamed
down the middle, hemmed all round, leather clasps attached at
strategic places, eyeholes sewn and taped. To earn my seven dollars I should have to make at least twenty in the day. The
machine was second nature by now, but the material was tricky,
killing to the hands.

I went at the stuff in a sort of angry despair, timing each fly,
racing the horrid clock. At five I had finished sixteen, but was in
such a state of jitters I felt myself getting sick. Not figuratively
speaking. A few moments recess, a dash of water in my face, and,
more peaceable within, back I run to produce two more flies
before six o'clock.

By the end of the week I had struck a stride of twenty-eight flies a day; my job was safe, and I had the pleasure of knowing that no other female had covered so many horses in a single day. I even had the thrill of finding an extra dollar in my pay envelope. Such are the rewards of virtue!

Time literally whirled by after that, with nothing untoward to fix my attention. Then, without much warning, Bertha came down with a severe bronchial attack. For a day or two we thought nothing of it; she was never strong, and the weather had produced no end of colds, sinus, and other ills.

One morning Margot came to work late, visibly distressed. Bertha was very ill, and she wanted to see me. After work I hurried to the house to see my dear friend for the last time. Patient and sweet, though every breath was torture; groping for my hands, she smiled at me:

'Don't grieve for me, dear,' she said. 'I've been tired for so long – so very long. We will meet again – in some happier place ...'

A plain, soft-spoken girl, doing her colourless duty without complaint or criticism, and slipping away for ever, gently, as the seasons glide into the great years. The old machine stood silent for a few days, and none of us dared look at it openly. It was so strange not to see her there, a little bent and ungainly, her red hair tumbled over a fine, white brow; never to catch that quiet smile, so intimate and kindly. Tents must go on: the machine raced once more under another hand. Minnie Nelson joined our small ranks, and quickened the rhythm of existence with her merriment and mischief.

In the late spring papa wrote to us from Winnipeg that he had a permanent job with my uncle, and had taken a small house. In a few days the packing was done, the precious cow sold, and mother and the two children had taken their departure. I elected to stay behind, and moved in with the Careys.

Hope and a hundred dazzling plans flared high in my head. I should get myself some clothes, and then save enough money to tide me through the Normal Course. It seemed such a simple business now that I had only my board to worry about. For a time, everything went on gaily. Mother Carey selected sensible material, and made me two dresses and a very perky blouse. I bought a woollen suit, shoes, and a hat.

By this time it was midsummer. I had a fourteen-block climb up the steepest of hills every night, after an eight-hour tussle with the heavy tents, and the long race with time and the flies all winter had not done me much good. One fine night, after dragging up the hill without much enthusiasm, I suddenly keeled over. Mother Carey trotted me to the doctor, who promptly told me I was slated for the heavenly realm if I did not behave. I was anaemic, suffering nervous depletion, etc. etc. – in fact, a general mess. In plain words, I needed a complete rest, and what was more, I'd get it one way or another, no matter what I did about it!

The only thing I could do about it was to go on working until I had enough money to pay my fare to Winnipeg. Which took longer than I expected, thanks to a ruptured blood-vessel, and the patching process. However, I was accustomed to physical tantrums. The only thing that upset me to any extent was the explosion of so many fine hopes. Something else caused me deeper pain, however.

I had seen little of Laura for a long time. Now I unearthed the fact that she was ill in the hospital, about to undergo a critical operation. Nothing that had happened to me hurt so much as the hour I spent with her in the little white hospital ward. She seemed to be all eyes, as though every ounce of vital energy had centred in their wide, grey depths – eyes, and a poignant smile that wrung the heart.

Her voice was a thread of sound that had in it an earnest of will, like the notes of a little bird singing out a captive heart. What happened to her did not matter, she said. She had managed to accomplish something, after all.

Last spring, she had taken out a life insurance in behalf of her little sister. Alma would have a chance. Alma would have a thousand dollars for her education! To manage it, she had – well – taken a leaf from the blonde virgin who managed sirloins on three-fifty a week. But God would understand!

Strange, how the heart can weep and the eyes record indifferent images. Stepping out of the hospital, with its medicated chill and deceptive serenity, the loveliness of the day shocked me into a kind of nerveless subjection, as though some terrible power were forcing upon me some ritual service. A beautiful day: one of those rare, still days, that quiver with deep, integral grace; earth and air and wide blue water conjoined in peace; even the noises of the street had a muted quality that scarcely ruffled the quiet. The sun, heavy with its freight of gold, hung in a smooth canvas of misty coral, veined with violet. The lake was an inverted sky, with one dark ship in its bosom.

Strange, to see these things so clearly through a prism of tears; to see them with the occult vision of the mind, as one sees in sleep the essence of beauty framing a dear, loved face.

39

Back to the Canadian scene

It was early in September when I stepped off the train at the Canadian Pacific depot in Winnipeg. There was no one to meet me, so I was free to experience what I always experience on coming back to the golden west: a quite irrational thrill, as though something in the air itself is a missing part of me, and that now I am complete. A queer sense of coming home that has nothing to do with houses or people, or any tangible thing acceptable to reason.

I did not recognize a single thing, except the crook in Main Street, but I recognized the old heart-beat under the fine new habit. With my case in my hand, I walked up the old dog-trail, now so proudly paved and builded, and I was glad that no one had met me: that the old city that was, and the little girl that was, had this moment together. Then I boarded the River Park car, and, in a manner of speaking, put behind me one lifetime, to begin another.

A very patchy interlude followed: a queer series of conglomerate experiences that had no particular meaning, leaving behind them nothing more significant than provocative memories. To begin with, uncertain health made me more introspective than ever, more inclined to sit in the side-lines, watching the parade go by.

I had some difficulty in adjusting myself to Icelandic society, which seemed to me alien from anything I remembered. Something distinctive and treasurable had given place to Canadian commonplaces. Having suffered ostracism and condescension because of their foreignness, it seemed as though all the national energy of the people had been expanded to acquire a blameless Canadian skin, Canadian habits, and Canadian houses.

This struck me as a little ironic, considering how contemptuous the general run of Canadian was of his own country. The deprecating manner towards everything Canadian was something else that struck me very forcibly, coming, as I had, from a country that believed in its own destiny, and took pride in American endeavour.

I should have been utterly lost without the friendship of my cousin, Gudrun Johnson, who took me under her wing, as she took any stray creature, and in addition provided me with odd jobs, sewing in her shop. She introduced me to many amiable families, and finally anchored me to the Young People's Society of our old Lutheran Church. That particular attachment had not the best effect, however. I met several young intellectuals who, while they fired my own desire to amount to something, made me painfully aware of my own ignorance – an ignorance that I then stubbornly refused to believe could be mitigated except in schools.

I used to listen to these youthful orators flinging borrowed phrases at the audience, and feel myself shrivel inside with helpless shame. And if these bright beings employed a word that was strange, I seized on it like a dying soul. And the same with the subject matter. Some one mentions Sophocles, and I rush to the library and bed myself down with *Antigone*, only to find, to my horror, that the yarn affects me like any other melodrama.

Creon behaves like the typical stage heavy; Antigone, like every other doomed demoiselle, hangs herself just a second before the rescuer arrives; all of it exactly what Mr Mack would have called 'good theatre,' but, so far as I could make out, not particularly profound, in the ethical sense, at least. But, of course, I am convinced that something is wrong with my head. I desperately pursue the incestuous descendants of Laius, and come to no better conclusion than that it still smells of melodrama.

What a crazy lot of reading I did that winter, and all of it out of respect for a plain young man who worshipped Schiller and Goethe as inimitable masters, and George Eliot for her approachability. Some day, when his education was completed, he meant to translate *The Mill On the Floss* into Icelandic. Some day, he meant to write.

Well, there it was. Overflowing now with all sorts of wisdom, he still thought it impertinence to attempt any original writing. So, what of my secret – my most impertinent dream of doing that very thing myself? Obviously, it was shameful to harbour such a crazy notion. It was then I made an abortive effort to try again for that tempting Normal Course.

After an interview with the principal, I suggested to mamma that I should borrow the necessary money. Heavens above! Had I lost my mind? How would I, always sick and ailing, ever discharge such an obligation? And so on and so forth? No doubt a more enterprising mortal would have gone ahead, in spite of any such opposition, but I had lived all my life under the foolish fear mamma nursed of my supposed frailty. No matter how many ailments I threw off, or whatever drudgery I performed, she still insisted on believing that heaven was my rightful home.

But in the meanwhile I had to work. I put in some agreeable months at Eaton's, in the Mail Order Department, copying orders. During the Christmas rush I worked as a cashier.

A siege of pleurisy put an end to that, but introduced me to the country and the fine old settlers of Gimli and Icelandic River. All lame ducks were sent to my Aunt Oline to fatten and rehabilitate; and all such derelicts she welcomed with cheerful hospitality. If I have reason to be proud of anything, it is of my three remarkable aunts, for braver women never faced the world. The essence of their service became the theme and the fibre of my first novel, *The Viking Heart*.

I made other visits to these settlements, and in my own fashion, tabulated the gossip to which I idly listened. I also spent a happy summer with my sister Anna, in Saskatchewan, where, for the first time, I saw with adult eyes the grand prairie, in all its original wild beauty. Sister's little house was a humble log dwelling then, shining with cheer and shouting hospitality. It was a magnet for endless visitors, many of whom were extremely interesting, professionals in the making, working their pre-emptions, or teachers.

But whether they were interesting or dull, Anna had the priceless gift, peculiar to my father's people, and completely lacking in me, of knowing how to conduct a fluent conversation out of nothing at all. It used to waken all my former infant awe, to hear her break into spell-binding repartee with any chance traveller. She could have held concourse with a rabbit, and left the little fellow gloating with pride in his social graces.

I found in my brother-in-law, Svein, a quiet dignity and forbearance that deeply impressed me – the spiritual fortitude which I, so many years later, tried to interpret through the character of Bjorn, in *The Viking Heart*. It was Svein who drove me from Wadena through twenty miles of Virgin prairie on my first visit to the farm. In company less in keeping with the spirit of the land, perhaps I should not have had so vivid a recollection of ageless beauty to remember.

Perhaps I should not have seen, in the long, tawny grass of the sweeping plain, that gleaming skull which the rays of a westering sun illumined with unearthly light. Poor, bleaching thing! How swiftly the ghost of the noble past sprang from the dust! All the vanished host of the adventurous days now done! An age reincarnated in the twilight smile of the reticent plain; in this deeply silent land, that kept the peace of centuries; in a soft amber light, and a silence unbroken, save by the creak of a solitary buckboard and the muffled trot of ponies' hooves.

It seemed to me then, and seems so still, that anything destined to endure, whether art or other creation, must do so by virtue of elemental strength. Let it be crude, let it be faulty, yet if it have, for its foundation, the decent, fearless strength of natural things, the bare bones of the skeleton will endure to give direction to the genius of New Times.

Something else that old skull brought home to me, and the spirit of the unpeopled plain confirmed it: as the leaves of grass, so are the generations; as a dream within a dream, so is our comprehension.

The prairie has become a living book to me, every mood a page, each intimately associated with some deeply moving human experience, my own, or some other. There is a sunset never seen beyond the confines of Saskatchewan and Alberta, a conflagration of golden flames, that sets the whole heaven afire – a sort of jubilee of light, that cannot be confined to one small horizon, and flings its lambent banners across the entire sky. The whole heavens on fire, and the earth, sweet as a young bride in early summer greenery, exalted, yet humble, and so softly still: that is a page that brings me back a proud young face, a-hungered with long, long thoughts. Whenever I see this rarest sight, a dear day comes back to me, and a voice, silenced for ever at Passchendaele, speaks in my ear.

For that, I love the prairie. In that, I place my faith. Dreams never die. There is another mood of the great plains that invades the heart with tender melancholy. Grey rain, falling obliquely, refracting pale sunlight in shards of delicate hue, and all the tangled meadow touched with misty colours, aquamarine, mauve, blue. That, too, belongs to the voice: to the memory of two foolish young people walking bareheaded through the rain, over the tender spring grass, lamenting the golden age when deeds of daring were to do. Life was so barren now. So safe! Sold to prosperity and commercialism. A man should be the master of his own fate, the captain of his own soul. Grey rain, and a quiet field, and somewhere, in the misty dawn, the clear voice lingers.

40

My prairie argosy

There are gay, amusing moments I like to remember, from that first visit to Saskatchewan. A brilliant but woefully absent-minded minister used to visit the house – so absent-minded it was said he had forgotten his own wedding day, which so upset the bride she put it off for ever. He used to stride up and down the little room reciting *De Profundis* by the chapter, and, by way of real substance, passages of Greek. Needless to say, his sermons were above the heads bowed to hear him in the district church. But what a grand man he was for words! said the good folk. Blest if you could make out a thing he said, so fine was his learning.

When he did emerge from his abstractions he was very gay, and, to me, a fountain of inspiration that fired my mind with even greater curiosity. For the first time in my life I had the privilege of sharing ideas with a man whose thought was profound, groping, painfully serious, not merely erudite.

He had the humility peculiar to great minds, which made him a comfortable mentor; made it easy to ask even foolish questions. But the fearful thing I learned from him was an irrefutable confirmation of something I had suspected, but dared not believe, by my own inference: that most people did not think, and perhaps could not think, but seized upon popularized concepts as lazy women seize upon a delicatessen shop to save themselves the planning of a meal.

Naturally, such a mind as his, plagued with scientific groping, could not stay in the Church, where no suspicion of the Christian premiss is possible. He was forced to resign, and later held a chair at Cambridge University.

Thanks to this encounter, as soon as I was back in Winnipeg I fixed upon a different type of reading. History went by the board, while I wallowed in *The Soul of Man Under Socialism*; Tolstoi's *The Kingdom of God is Within You*, and, more important in its lasting effect, the ancient *Dialogues* of Plato.

In all my vexed reading nothing had so deeply moved me as the closing paragraphs of Socrates' defence:

'But, my friends, I think that it is a much harder thing to escape from wickedness than from death. And now I, who am old and slow, have been overtaken by the slower pursuer: and my accusers, who are clever and swift, have been overtaken by the swifter pursuer, which is wickedness. And now I shall go hence, sentenced by truth to receive the penalty of wickedness and evil. And I abide by this award as well as they.

'You have done this thing, thinking that you will be relieved from having to give an account of your lives. But I say that it will be very different from that. For if you think that you will restrain men from reproaching you for your evil lives, by putting them to death, you are very much mistaken.

'And now the time has come, and we must go hence; I to die, and you to live. Whether life or death is better, is known to God, and to God only.'

Reading these things over and over in the chill of my ugly little bedroom, I used to whip myself into angry despair at the stupidities of existence; at the blind, who lead the blind, and perforce, would not see. It was not until years later that I found anything written that affected me so deeply. Not until Johan Bojer sounded the same luminous courage through the character of Peer, whose life is symbolic of man's evolving consciousness.

'And it came to me that in himself man must create the divine in heaven and in earth. And I began to feel an unspeakable compassion for all men upon earth – yet, in the last resource, I was proud to be one of them. I understood how blind fate can strip us, and yet something will remain in us at the last that nothing in heaven or earth can vanquish.

'Our bodies are doomed to die, and our spirit to be extinguished, yet still we hear within us the spark, the germ of eternity, of harmony, and light for the world and for God. And I knew now what I had hungered after in my best years, neither knowledge, nor honour, nor riches, nor to be a priest, or a great creator in steel; but to build temples; not chapels for prayers, or churches for penitent sinners, but a temple for the Human Spirit, where we could lift up our souls in an anthem as a gift to heaven.'

But, although the sudden passion for the ancients undoubtedly made me a trying companion for the girls in the neighbourhood, I had my humorous adventures. Shortly after my return from Sister Anna's I saw an advertisement in the *Winnipeg Free Press*. The tailoring and alteration department of a certain fashionable establishment wanted experienced power operators.

Well, thought I, 'flies' were not quite the same as my lady's trousseau, but they required proficiency with the machine. I applied for the job, and, on the strength of experience, got it.

I was put on stitching suits, a critical operation in a tailored garment, but a straight seam is a straight seam, whether in a tent or a riding habit. However, I had one comical argument with the tailor.

Why on earth did I reverse the time-honoured process of seaming from the right? For a moment I wondered what he meant, then I saw that every one else sent the material under the machine head, an utter impossibility in the making of tents.

'Why not?' said I, bold as brass. 'The result is the same, and the material doesn't wrinkle so badly.'

'Oh, is that it?' He looked at me quizzically. 'Perhaps you're right!'

That was the beginning of an amusing tangle. Mr Frank (which is, of course, not his name) developed the habit of perching on the end of the machine at odd moments, ostensibly to watch the progress of some garment, though, to be sure, no one would have guessed it from the course of his remarks. He was a sophisticated, handsome man, just come from New York to

stylize the department. He looked like a swashbuckler masquer-
ading as a fashion plate. He had a curt way of speaking, suited to
the swashbuckler, and a mechanical smile that served the trade.

That he chose my table for a resting-place can be readily
excused. The five or six other operators were either middle-aged
or hopelessly drab – like the freckled finisher, whose tow-
coloured hair was a hard fist on her neck, and whose blouse and
skirt were never on speaking terms.

Then, too, it chanced that it was handier to use me as a
dummy for a thirty-six dress of jacket than the plaster model,
and, I dare say, after a man has stuck pins down your back,
across your breast and thighs, he just naturally developes a pro-
prietary feeling. At any rate, the poor dear began to worry about
me. It was a pity for a nice little thing like me to work for her
living, said he. A terrible shame, really. There were much more
agreeable ways of – well, being independent.

Not being an utter dunce, and wanting very much to keep the
best job I had ever had, I affected a pleasant stupidity. The
gentleman retaliated by putting the screws on me. Not in person – oh dear no! That would have been too crude. But the head
fitter, a pompous female, who loved fault-finding, began pounc-
ing upon everything I did; always discreetly hinting that Mr
Frank was disappointed in me. Sadly disappointed. Really, I
should have to do better!

So one fine night I waited until the girls were gone, and then
said my piece. I was quitting to save Mr Frank the pain of dis-
missing me.

Which fetched a nice little storm, to be sure, an argument that
seemed to get nowhere. I could not walk out: he refused to sanction it; without his sanction, I would not get my wages. I was a
dear little fool, and should go home and use my head. Yes, that
was the thing to do, go home, like a nice little girl, and get over
my temper. And come back with my wits about me – what was
there so glorious about sewing suits for a living?

To be quite truthful, I wondered about that in not the best of
spirits as I tramped home through the snow. What was there
glorious in any of the tiresome drudgery that kept one barely

living? What indeed was there glorious in living such a life at all? Millions of harassed creatures like myself were scurrying to and from stupid tasks that went on and on, irrespective of who performed them; millions of meaningless lives, trapped in a meaningless round.

And then I came to Central Park, where the poplars rimmed with hoar frost stood like the shining ghost of fairyland, and the job I had tossed away, and the flattering independence I could not accept, were alike forgotten. This thing, at least, was mine: a quick responsiveness to transient grace; a singing of the heart that made the earth my own.

Cousin Gudrun was the only one to whom I confessed this silly episode, and on her suggestion I decided to work at home hereafter, and occasionally to go out on a job she recommended. There was something to be said for such an arrangement. I could work when I pleased, and had much more time to read. It brought me in touch with all sorts of queer characters; earned me many a choice morsel of gossip, for women seemed to shed their reticence with their petticoats, to bare their souls at the first touch of a tape-line.

Standing forth in all their weaknesses, perhaps they feel called upon to confess the sins of the flesh and the sorrows of disillusionment. There was a lady who, quite unprovoked, assured me she never would have taken a lover if her husband had not been such a glum brute; and a quaint old maid who for twenty years wore the same shade of blue because that was the colour Henry had loved on her when she was a girl. Henry was dead all these years.

There was a fat woman who boasted of having once been no weight at all. 'My dear, when I was first married, my husband used to span my waist with his hands!' But children were such a complication: with each baby she took on pounds and pounds! Married women, who started off by bemoaning the cost of serge and herring-bone, and finished up at the taxes, the expense of modern plumbing, and the destructive habits of husbands who smoked in bed. And there were young shopgirls, who sang an old familiar strain, and sometimes threw in a reckless chorus.

But it was during a week's plain sewing in an old house on McDermot Street that I ran into fresh and irremediable disaster. If there were any possibility of forgetting that hot, sultry day, the shrilling cry of a newsboy precluded it.

'Sinking of the *Titanic*! Giant Steamer Sinking!' he shouted.

The very nice old lady for whom I was making batiste lingerie waddled away on her fat little feet to buy the paper. And, in the midst of her tearful hopes that the passengers might be rescued, the telephone rang for me.

Cousin Louise, a young clever musician, wanted me to fill in on some sort of programme that was part of the YMCA celebration to be held that night in old Elm Park. Some one had failed her, and she knew that I perpetrated reading now and then in the church hall. I hated all picnics, but after a stifling day devoted to the moist charms of a much too vital old lady, the thought of fresh air was too tempting to refuse.

How often and how fervently I have wished that I had been aboard the *Titanic*, and not on a street car heading for Elm Park! It was there that I met a young man who completely upset all my senses, the only man I have ever loved as every good novelist would have his heroines love, without rhyme or reason, to the exclusion of everything else under the sun. An Irishman, with all the Irish virtues and vices: irascibility, tenderness, imagination, and a love of good literature that was quite sincere. That, of course, finished the matter. But I had met many young men who were literary – very few Icelanders are not – and many who were much more intellectual; many young men, for whom I had an abiding friendship that still persists. This was something different, as I was soon to discover, to my lasting regret.

I cannot pretend that the charming creature returned this foolish affection, but he gave a fairly convincing performance to that effect. I suspect there were moments when he wanted to believe something of the sort. But he was an awful snob: he was ashamed of my nationality, ashamed of the place I called home; ashamed of my work.

Yet, with all this, and much more at fault, he kept tormenting himself with my company. He had my picture taken, to send to his parents in Belfast, along with some ridiculous essay I had written on heaven knows what.

He used to send me endearing little tokens, some bit of verse he knew I would love; a picture, or a book, and then finished up by being frightfully rude. How did we keep clean, he wondered, in a little semi-modern cottage? How on earth could I have so many superior qualities, coming from such an environment?

He was a minister's son, of which he was secretly proud, although he had left home because he hated his father for his narrow bigotry. The pious parent had spanked the children regularly every Friday night; never in anger, but to fulfil the holy injunction of the chastening rod. Huddled in their little beds, the children would wait in terror for the slow steps of the father, coming nearer and nearer to administer the justice of God.

He hated these memories, and all they represented, yet they gave him a distinction which he felt was utterly lacking in my immigrant heritage. It used to amuse me, in spite of the hurt to my feelings, and sometimes I was tempted to confess that ministers were thick as fleas in my suspect ancestry; that, under stress, I could dig up several knightly honours, one supremely great scholar, and more poets than did any family good; that, at the moment, my cousin was Governor of Iceland, and all my kin over there battling with force and intelligence to secure the full autonomy of their country.

But no child of mamma's would have dared say such things. He was the product of his own training, and I found no fault with that. It was a queer attachment, that struck its first serious snag when he took me to task for speaking to a friend on the street one summer day – a young woman for whom I had the sincerest respect; the sort of girl one hears eulogized in the pulpit. All her life was devoted to the care of her mother and an ailing sister. She was a not unhandsome girl, but inclined to be dowdy, although her clothes were good for she held a responsible secretarial position.

What in the world made me select such hopeless companions, my Irishman demanded, and out flew my Icelandic claws. To question my personal habits, whether hygienic or otherwise, was one thing; to deride my friends, quite another!

That was the beginning of many squabbles, many queer jealousies, and much heart-ache. I came to the conclusion that we had better take civilized leave of each other. I wanted to remember the happier side of this curious alliance. To which he agreed, and I, at least, should have been spared further disillusionment if he had kept to that.

But he came back, which, to my quaint old-world reasoning, was unquestionable proof of devotion. He came back long enough to inflict the sort of wound which lies at the back of the mind like a two-edged sword.

His way of final leave-taking was, to me, an added insult. We were to have gone to some theatre. I remember I had made myself a little cinnamon-coloured frock, edged with hand-painted borders of green and rose. There I sat, watching the clock. In the morning he sent a letter, which I did not read for some time. When mamma brought the wretched thing I quietly escaped and, for the one and only time in my life, lost consciousness from sheer emotion.

It was good to find myself in mamma's kind arms, to lie there, saying nothing, and having nothing said. After a bit, we went into the kitchen and drank some coffee, then I finished a blouse I was making for some one. In the evening I went to the old Province Theatre, had a good cry, and came away obsessed with only one thought: no matter what my own feelings, I wanted to think well of him, to nurse no distorted ill will – for who can command the affections, or dictate the whims of the heart?

Resolutions have their merits, but what a chilly comfort in a world that has suddenly lost all meaning. Everywhere I went, everything I looked at, reminded me of what I most wished to forget. Worst of all, I dared not read, for all my treasured preferences were bound up with intimate memories.

In the end, I conceived the notion of writing to my aunt in Duluth. I knew that she had always hoped that some one of her nieces would follow in her footsteps. Perhaps I might cultivate a taste for nursing. At any rate, I should get away from Winnipeg, and possibly come to understand my relative as she deserved.

41

The face of virtue

That much I did accomplish. I came to love and honour my aunt, to see her in reasonable light, and to appreciate the work she carried on with such admirable common sense. It would require several books to tell the tales of the women who passed in and out of the little hospital that winter. Suffice it to mention a few characteristic types.

There was a spoiled young wife, who despite an easy delivery, kept every one hopping with her tantrums. In the morning, when I came to bath her and dress her hair, she reminded me of Topsy. Her whole head was a mass of intricate curls, knots, snarls that stood up like angry snakes, impossible to describe.

Oh yes, said she, ever since childhood, emotion, anger, or pain made her do this to her hair, and no one but herself could possibly undo it. Then she demanded a mirror to keep under the pillow.

'I must watch the ravages of my suffering.' she said.

There was a girl who, on quitting the hospital, stole a sum of money away from another patient, which my aunt promptly paid, although the girl had left an unsettled bill. Two days later the culprit returned. Uncle caught sight of her, and called out in astonishment:

'Ja, here comes the thief, Haldora! She's sitting down on the step!'

'Well, why don't you let her in?' said my aunt, looking up from the medical tome she was reading. 'What are you waiting for?'

'You mean to say you'd let her in again? A thief?'

'Tut! tut! man dear! What can you expect from a girl like that? Let the child in!'

There was a young stenographer from St Paul, who looked like a scared kitten, all eyes and quivering nerves. She was so terrified of what lay before her that it was misery to come near her. The morning after her baby was born I was wondering what sort of collapse to expect, when I brought up her breakfast. What I saw was a pair of glowing eyes and a broad grin:

'Gee!' she piped. 'The kid's dead – ain't that great!'

Endless women, endless babies, all trailing threads of private history, joyous, tragic, commonplace, and sometimes frankly amusing. Like that of the jolly Irish Lady who had put off her marriage for ten years to save on a family, only to start off with twins.

'And would you be seein' the darlin's,' says she, beaming with pride. 'As like as two eggs, so they are, and not a nose between them!'

But only one out of the long procession remains to haunt me. She came on the wings of the storm, blown to the door like some wreckage cast to the elements. Because of the gale, her feeble scratching for the bell she could not see failed to rouse us.

I was writing at a little desk, immersed in the vexatious correspondence regarding little Ruby, whose tale has been told. My aunt was in her bedroom, snatching an hour's sleep, tired out from a difficult case. It was the sound of something heavy striking the door with the muffled impact, heard in a lull of the wind, that brought me out of the letter.

What a sight, the unhappy soul presented! More dead than alive, her face had a greyish pallor terrible to see, and her limbs would scarcely support her.

My aunt took one look at her, ordered a bed made ready, and half carried the girl up the stairs. To the casual glance, her condition would have passed unnoticed. She was laced within an inch of her life – a terrible lacing that had turned her limbs an enpurpled blue. As a result of this extreme congestion, although her labour was swift and comparatively easy, she suffered haemorrhage after haemorrhage.

Aunt worked over her with the energy of exasperation. She was angry and pitying in the same breath; angry with a world that elected such insanity, and pitying the life she fought to save. Something exceptional about this girl touched a deeper vein than professional duty.

In the midst of the battle, while my aunt still hesitated to leave her patient for any length of time, a most indignant lady descended upon the hospital. Was it true that Lena was here? Was it possible that the shameless girl had had a baby?

Quite true, my aunt told her bluntly, appraising with a hard eye the silly female, standing there in her sleek furs, lashing herself into righteous fury. That such a scandal should have come to her Christian household! Why, she had never failed to impress upon Lena the beauty of church attendance. The ladies of the congregation had arranged a club for working girls! Oh, it was too awful! To think that she had had such a snake in her house!

Said my aunt, in the tone of voice that always finished any argument: 'Seems to me you had two snakes in the house. Your very fine brother, madam, will have to deal with me!'

Meanwhile, Lena lay upstairs, caring nothing whether she lived or died. She had, in her tragic exhaustion, that white, ethereal beauty that grips the heart with fingers of pain. I used to look at her, lying so unearthly still, her long lashes casting quivering shadows on her alabaster cheeks, and the two heavy plaits of her lovely hair falling like ropes of spun gold on either side of her breast; and seeing her so reawakened all the bitter queries I had sought to side-track with idealistic theories.

What was the good of brave parchment and fine rhetoric, if it were perpetually reserved for parlour diversion; for snobbish pastime, to be laid aside like a Sabbath garment, in the active world? What was the point in shouting the excellence of virtue, of charity, of equality, and the universal brotherhood of man, in a society that defeated all these things by the very nature of its economic structure? What was the point in ranting against sin and degradation and decadence, in a world so lacking in social consciousness that it made no sane provision for such girls as this?

Fine words cannot feed a starving body. Prayers do not equip illiteracy with logic, or the means of a decent livelihood. A condescending smile and a dish of beans in church do not feed the hunger of human loneliness!

I thought even more heretical things the day the church women sent the minister to shrive the sinner. For, true to her type, Lena's mistress, to make everything right with her own conscience, had not hesitated to broadcast the deceitful girl's shame. God knew, she had set her a good example, with family prayers, and patient counsel about the evils of night life. But now the poor wretch was thought to be dying. Naturally, one forgot and forgave under such circumstances. A dying sinner is so much more interesting than a living slave.

The minister chosen for this mission of grace was hardly more than a stripling; a well-meaning youth, I have no doubt, but with all the earmarks of an individual whose severest hardship was a hole in the sock, and whose idea of poverty was the limitations imposed by the cheque from home during his seminary imprisonment.

The poor thing arrived, visibly braced for the effort, Bible in hand, and a definitely scared look in his eye. When he saw the pale beauty in the bed he cleared his throat, muttered something meant for greeting, dropped into the waiting chair, and hastily thumbed the book. That was all I witnessed, until, some while later, on the point of re-entering, the door flew open in my face, and out shot the young man, with the Bible in full pursuit!

All very funny, and rather typical of what passes for charity and righteousness in this complex world; an amusing burlesque, except for the consequences. For the comforter left Lena in a state of violent hysterics, that brought on an almost fatal haemorrhage, costing her weeks of invalidism and dark despair.

I like to think that I helped her sometimes in those black moments, and once, in an interval of near madness, saved her from tragedy. It was after she was up and trying to care for her infant, although the task was far beyond her indifferent strength. I happened to be pottering about upstairs, this particular morning, just as she was struggling with the baby's bath out in the back hall used for that purpose.

I could hear the infant mewling with the aggravating insistency of the new-born, and suddenly a sharp cry from Lena sent me scurrying to see what was wrong. There she was, white as a sheet, a crazy light in her eye, her hands on the baby's neck, shutting off the maddening yowls.

'Oh, my God!' cried the poor thing, when I had snatched away the baby, 'what have I done? My God! Now you'll tell —'

'Shut up,' said I. 'Shut up, and say nothing yourself.'

42

I settle in my own country

Histories no end. But I had not my aunt's passion for delivering babies. A messy business at best, for which I had no taste or talent. I decided on a much more ordinary career. I had met a breezy young man from Montana who thought he could put up with me for better and for worse, despite my confession about the faithless son of Erin. What's an Irishman, more or less, to a Norseman!

In June 1913 I married George Salverson in the old Lutheran manse in Winnipeg. A good way to end all my foolish fancies, and assume a time-honoured business of commonplace existence.

What a time we had, to be sure! George was twenty-seven years old, but, even so, it was something of a battle for him to free himself from home ties. Ever since he was a boy of twelve he had been the main support of his family. He had bought his mother a comfortable house; his sisters were married; his youngest brother was quite able to take care of their mother; yet it shocked them terribly that George should contemplate such a step.

His father, who, since quitting the sea, had served no worthy purpose, was suffering with cancer. All the money George had in the world he paid out for an operation. He arranged that the house should be sold whenever his brother deemed it advisable, and the proceeds divided between him and his mother. What we proposed to begin the matrimonial venture on was five hundred dollars that he had loaned to an old man who had taught him telegraphy. Needless to say, the loan was never paid.

We set up house in prophetic fashion, with a few sticks of furniture bought on the instalment plan, on a salary of eighty dollars, less than half of what he had been getting in the United States, where the cost of living was a great deal lower than in Canada. But I had the fixed notion that here I must live. I supposed I wanted to feel rooted somewhere, to feel that, other things failing, I had at least some sort of spiritual home.

There is nothing remarkable to remember of those first few years. I balanced the budget by renting rooms and keeping the odd boarder, usually some young man from the telegraph offices. The War put an end to the Winnipeg job, just as we had found a suitable little house, and thought we should have a breathing-space from the bills and the demands upon George from his home. In the nick of time he found a position as manager of the Grand Trunk Telegraph offices in Regina.

That winter I dawdled away in a suite, with nothing to do except cook for ourselves and a young telegrapher who worked with my husband. For amusement I undertook to sew some clothes for a couple of Russian families that the Metropolitan Church discovered in need. I had no friends, except a middle-aged lady, Mrs Tanner, who is still dear to me as a living example of true Christian conduct.

There is nothing to say of my baby, except that the prospect bored me, and to give it an enterprising turn, I decided to travel fifteen hundred miles two weeks before he was born, to test the twilight sleep, administered by a doctor who had been studying the novelty in Germany when the War broke out. In spite of all that was said against the method in those years, it was entirely successful, and my baby suffered no ill effects whatsoever.

We moved to Saskatoon, and I settled down to honourable housekeeping; pickling, cold-packing vegetables and fruit, and conducting myself with ancient propriety, getting duller by the moment, and thoroughly fed up with the good life.

As luck would have it, we were surrounded by people who, with the exception of my next-door neighbour, were alarmingly devoted to all sorts of extreme religions. They did their best to convert us, and, out of sheer boredom, I did my best to see the light.

Speaking seriously, however, I had more decent reason than mere curiosity in these various beliefs. My people, of the older generation, at least, have always been concerned with spiritual values; in the conquest of essential truths that bear upon the inner life of man. That so many extreme religions sprang to the fore at this time was undoubtedly due to the same hunger in so many human beings to whom the horrors of the War were ever-present.

I was a pacifist then, as I still am, not because I cannot perceive that, in an age of semi-barbarism, war as an instrument of policy commends itself to many earnest people; or that I believe war in itself is the greatest of human evils; but because I had come to see that organized warfare, like every other organized human institution, camouflaged ulterior motives, and was employed, not to maintain liberty for the common man, but to advance the trade monopolies of private interests.

I had come to suspect, albeit vaguely, that industry, under the present system, is an even more merciless warfare than its violent progeny that marches under resplendent banners; that the millions of workers toiling in factories and mines are nothing but conscripts in a service dedicated to wealth and privilege, and not those rights and liberties that sound so bravely on the lips of sentimentalists. Conscripts, whose slow and lingering death in the economic skirmishes brings them not a cenotaph, but the dole, degrading poverty, misery, and crime. Death for one's country – if one had any share in that country or that country's wealth – was not what repelled me.

My practical Scandinavian nature stood aghast that some less costly solution should not be found by so-called enlightened nations, for purely economic, commercial problems, and all my instincts were revolted that the dearest ideals of the human heart should be preyed upon by propagandists, to feed the sinews of war.

My husband did not altogether share in these beliefs, but, as an American, he was more or less satisfied with a neutral attitude, until the United States joined in the conflict. Many dear friends, and not a few relatives, were at the front. My cousin served as a surgeon, my brother-in-law left with the first contingent; the two young men who had lived with us a year in Regina died on the Western Front; another, equally dear friend, died from maltreatment in a military prison, because of his religious convictions. These things preyed upon my mind. What solution had the devout to offer?

Nothing practical, I must confess. Yet there was one sect that interested me somewhat, because of its stress upon mercy and divine compassion – until I discovered that these blessings were reserved for a little flock; until I discovered that all this piety was just another garden plot of fancy, prepared as an escape from the difficulties of human relationships and social obligation.

To me, it is inconceivable, and profane, that any concept of the Divine should impose a belief in any specific preference for select cults and rituals, or that Christianity is the one and only approach to spiritual discernment. An opinion not particularly welcome to those good people bent upon my salvation.

There was a very pious group, for instance, which referred to the rest of mankind as Children of the Devil. How poisonous we really were I discovered one fine day when I bought six hens from such a believer. I had no place for the chickens at the moment, and asked that they might remain where they were over the week-end. Saturday night, a timid knock called me to the door. There, bashful and barefoot, stood a small saint:

'Please, missus,' said the child, 'could you take the chickens now? Mamma says we can't keep things that belong to the Children of the Devil.'

There was another brave fiction that rested its case for salvation on Faith in the Blood; works were vanity, and no justification of man's essentially evil nature. It set me to thinking, at any rate. As I had formerly mapped out a programme of reading, I now decided to dip into theology. I waded through Thomas

Aquinas, and other early fathers, who had sought to codify the Christian doctrines into a logical system, based on premises accepted for so many centuries. I took a look at Wycliffe, and Huss, and Luther, and read some of the unpleasant sermons of Cotton Mather. In the end, I bought myself an anthology of non-classical religions, and finished the season with the primitives.

Surfeited with all these human theories that had cost so much pain and bloodshed, I fled back to the old favourites, which I had resolutely shelved since that unhappy interlude of disquiet romance. I remember well the autumn day when I dug up my copy of Ruskin's *Art and Architecture*, for I propped it up against a row of sealers while I stoned peaches for jam.

To the same accompaniment I re-read Hardy, Eliot, and Victor Hugo, who has always held first place in my affections. The result was an inner discontent that drove me nearly silly. I used to lie awake at night, with endless dialogues running through my head. I used to drive poor George to distraction with my diatribes on human justice, the evils that negative goodness fosters unknowingly, and the cruel subjection of women.

'Well, great scott, what's wrong with you?' the poor dear would exclaim. 'Who is subduing you, I'd like to know?'

'But it isn't me!' I would declaim. 'It's all women. They are the slaves, every one of them, slaves of convention, of religion, of the house – slaves in their mentality. Even the modern woman, who thinks herself free, has only exchanged the bondage to one man, to make herself the slave of many. Even in art, women reflect men, ape men, say what the smart man expects the smart woman to say.'

'Oh, good Lord, have it your way,' George would wash his hands of me.

'It isn't my way,' I would retort, feeling frightfully maligned. 'That's what's the matter with me. I can't see the sense of going on and on for ever, reflecting images and ideas like a dead mirror. I can't see the sense of doing everything in exactly the say it always has been done, thinking as you're told to think, believing as you are told to believe – and the highest blessing, to cook in somebody's kitchen!'

Poor George! That finished every argument. I was a good cook, and if he said so, I accused him of prizing me for that alone, and if he didn't say so, I felt abused. As a matter of fact, I had too much nervous energy to be satisfied with just running a house and minding a baby.

When the child was two years old I started a dress-making shop in a seven-room cottage on the edge of town, where he could be safe in the open, and I free to work off some of this spleen. I had done a lot of sewing for various neighbours, and, by way of recompense, these friends brought me trade.

In a few weeks I was so busy that I hired an English-woman to assist me. I managed the house, did all the cooking, kept a boarder, fed my son by the clock, and very shortly was earning enough money to pay my assistant more than I had ever been paid for similar services; and had something more than pocket money for myself.

However, I began to suffer continuous, excruciating head-aches, for I had not only to work through the day, but to do most of the fitting and cutting by night. Strange as it may seem, I had never suspected something might be wrong with my eyesight until now, when working with endless black materials, I found it increasingly difficult to stitch a fine seam and to thread the needle.

The specialist to whom I finally went was not very compli-mentary. Any one but a fool would have consulted a doctor long ago, etc., etc. The adjustment reduced me to bed for a couple of days, but I shall never forget my astonishment thereafter, when a whole week went by without any return of the familiar torment. The migrains remained like a faithful lover, but what was an occasional bout, compared with the daily misery formerly accept-able as an inescapable attribute of existence!

The little shop flourished, and I had the pleasure of buying some furniture, a lovely, brown Wilton rug, and clothes for us all. I even had the strange experience of buying a Liberty bond, and saving fifty dollars for a rainy day. And then George, who had never been free of an office in his life, caught the sort of fever every living creature suffers at least once in a lifetime. He wanted to go on the land, to revel in the marvels of the wide open spaces.

What really ailed him was overwork and nervous exhaustion. The office was short-handed, and subject to the tantrums of the sort of official who suffers from a superiority complex – a common ailment in men risen to petty power through political influence, irrespective of any exceptional ability.

George had been working hard and conscientiously, all his spare time that winter devoted to a course in business management and kindred subjects; but, as a long life of service was to demonstrate beyond cavil, such efforts, unless dovetailed with obnoxious subservience and political hobnobbing, are of little benefit.

43

Homestead and boarding-house

And now George had the grand vision of the independent life of a landowner! Shades of dear papa's dream! There was nothing to be done about it, except to let the disease run a swift, unhindered course. I hated to give up the little shop, just as it was well under way, but I had no desire to support throughout life, as mamma had done, a suspicion of blame for blocking a cherished dream.

George quit his job and returned to the Bonus Wires in the CPR telegraph office in Winnipeg. By his working double time, and our living in two small rooms, we managed to save enough money to make the fine gesture. He had filed a claim twenty-five miles north of Prince Albert, and during this winter the logs were cut for a house.

In the spring George set off in fine fettle to purchase a team of horses, a wagon, lumber for flooring, a pump, and such other requirements found necessary for the initial venture. I stopped off at Saskatoon to make arrangements about our furniture, some of which had been in storage, some rented to a supposedly reputable couple, who had disappeared with most of it.

I spent a couple of weeks with my former neighbour, Mrs Gibson, an Englishwoman of great common sense and diversified talents. Before her marriage she had been the matron of a London hospital, and this gave us a common interest, for, to both of us, the human element was a source of endless speculation.

While I waited for George to send for me, I had the pleasure of helping my good friend prepare for a long-desired visit to England, doing my utmost to invade her innate modesty with frivolous ideas of personal adornment. It used to amuse us no end that Flo should be setting out to dazzle society, and I heading for the sticks to hibernate with a cow and eight chickens.

The important day dawned at last. Encumbered with small George, two grips, and a box of canned supplies, I left for Prince Albert, to be met there with the most comical sight that ever greeted my eyes. Friend husband was standing beside a spick new wagon, prefaced with the oddest team-mates that ever hugged a whiffle-tree. A mournful chestnut Clydesdale, and a stiff-legged western pony, who dangled in the traces like an ill-advised participle in a pompous speech. Catching my eye, George hastened to explain that the mare, a precious purchase two weeks past, had suddenly developed a lame foot, but the pony would serve our purpose for the moment. The three of us, atop the bright green wagon, made a pretty spectacle as we rattled out of town, the chestnut clomping sedately, and the pony dog-trotting jerkily, with insult in his eye.

The first part of the curious excursion was not too bad, although sitting in a springless wagon with a heavy youngster in your lap is not particularly restful; but a few miles out from town the air began to thicken with smoke fumes. Forest fires were raging in the north, and each slow mile brought us increasing discomfort. The rancid air stung the eyes and choked the breath.

The baby began to whimper and wail with thirst, his little eyes reddened from smoke. It was not much farther now, friend husband encouraged us, a few more miles and we should be there, or almost there. It was true that we should have to camp a few days in a deserted hut some distance from our land, but how fortunate the hut was there, since our own cabin was still unroofed.

What the dear man failed to mention was, that the last mile traversed a section that still smouldered and represented nothing so much as the remains of a gigantic Indian bivouac. The horses refused to budge through a field hot underfoot; and I envied them the comparative luxury of the road, where they were tethered, after I scrambled with George in the darkness over hummocks that scorched the soles of my shoes.

The cabin was not a thrilling habitation. It had been swept, it is true, and George had set up a bed. There was a table under a hole in the wall that was meant for a window, and there was a rusty iron box stove in the middle of the floor. A lantern gave us glimmering light, by which sickly beam I managed to make tea, fry bacon on a tin plate, and heat canned milk for the baby.

A wind sprang up, and freshened the air, which was gratifying, and I thought to myself that at least we should get a fair night's sleep. But I had bargained without the mischief of the elements conspiring against a roof of shrunken poles draped with cracking clay. I had hardly settled the forty million kinks that were my body into a semblance of ease, when I realized that every gust of wind sent down a shower of fine dust and sundry creepy creatures that wriggled over my face.

That put an end to sleep, so far as I was concerned. I preferred to watch a huge silver moon racing dark dragon clouds through the night, to wrestling with sleep under a blanket of worms.

The next day George set up a tent, borrowed from a man who, with his sons, had filed on the claim next to ours. For which charity, and their help in finishing our own log cabin, I cooked endless meals for inexhaustible appetites, over open fires and the rickety heater, through the hottest weeks of the short, hot summer.

There was a cow which I had to learn to milk, and the chickens to keep from the hawks, clothes to wash, without any facilities, and the baby to mind. Finally, when the roof was up, the floor down, and a door in place, there was the familiar job of unpacking the household effects we had shipped, and creating a semblance of order and comfort within this shelter of Saskatchewan logs.

George had a grand time ploughing up a bit of land, cutting trees for firewood, finishing the well, clearing a road to the trail that meandered through the bush toward the one and only highway.

Then, suddenly, we awakened to the fact that the last of our money had magically disappeared, and the prospect of living off the bounty of the wilderness lost its fine allure.

Forthwith, he decided to go back to Winnipeg for a grubstake, and, in the meanwhile, I could keep the castle against the enemy.

The idea of being left alone in the depths of scrub timber, with my nearest English-speaking neighbour five miles away, was not a cheerful prospect. I had visions of myself in the black night, listening to the serenading of coyotes, and waiting for the brown bears that were plentiful in the bush to crash through the flimsy plank door on a friendly call, and the vision did not amuse me.

Fortunately, there was a Swedish family some miles away, whose eldest daughter, Ella, consented to spend the night with me. She could not be spared from home until late in the evening, but the thought of riding one of our ponies through the woods night and morning struck her as a glorious adventure, so that she was more than willing to hire out as my keeper. A grand girl she was, at that; cheerful and strong, and full of rough counsel that was both amusing and helpful. When work was less exacting at home she often spent the morning with me, which time we put to excellent use.

The cow took to wandering, and one rosy dawn we discovered that Bessie, the pony Ella rode, a beautiful little bay mare, had disappeared. A few hours' search, and I found her fast to a willow shrub, in which the stake she was dragging had become tightly entangled. I decided that we must make some sort of corral for safeguarding our three obstreperous animals.

Tony, the pinto who had suffered the shame of teaming with a plough horse, Bessie, our pet, and the important cow had to be protected. Sure, said Ella, that's no trick at all. Between the two of us we could saw the trees needed by dinner-time, and maybe dig the post-holes. To-morrow, we could finish the job; and so it was done, with, I must confess, some bruising of thumbs on my part, and much good-natured scorn from Ella.

During the long afternoons spent alone I finished chinking the house, using chips of poplar, and coating the seams with clay. I built a pen for chickens, roofed over with saplings to keep out the hawks. I made butter with a wooden dasher in a tin pail.

All was going merrily, until one morning, when a strange man arrived on the scene with a rifle under his arm.

'Howdy, missus,' said he, sober as judgement, 'I heard you was here by yourself, and I got to thinkin' you should have a firin' piece. There's a heap of vermin in these woods. So I brung you my rifle.'

That I had never touched a weapon in my life did not alter his good intentions. I must have it, and so he hung it on two nails over the bed, where the sight of it would be a comfort, and the reaching of it handy in emergency.

Thereafter, I naturally glanced twice at every shadow and suspected every clump of harbouring at least a lean, hungry bear, if not a desperate vagrant.

But the evening that actually produced a bear, the last thing I thought of was the rifle. I shut the door on the baby and myself, and, from the window, watched Mr Bruin nosing round the yard, and never even remembered the comforting weapon hanging on the wall.

But my most frightening exploit had to do with the old mare who limped about the yard. It outraged my sense of justice that the creature should give up the ghost before she was paid for! Something must be done.

'Well,' said Ella, 'pa says it sometimes helps to scrape the hoof, and put on a manure poultice.'

To do it, then, thought I, my heart sinking to the level of my boots. Ella fetched the mare to a sawed off tree stump, tied a rope round her leg, and heaved up the rotting hoof to the impromptu operating slab. While she held the animal captive I prodded and scraped, leaping back in terror each time the poor thing reared in the air when I struck a sensitive spot. No monster of nightmare was ever so huge and menacing as that mild old plug dancing on heavy hind legs! Every snort set me quaking like jelly, but I have yet to start a job I have not finished. The hoof was scraped clean, the foot firmly bandaged, and, I am pleased to say, the operation was entirely successful.

These crazy months had their value. It gave me an insight into the lives of pioneering people that no amount of visiting and yarning could have done. It gave me two memorable histories of brave women. The first of these was Ella's mother. She would like me to visit her, the daughter said, for so few came to see her, and she was lonely. Ella could act as our interpreter, and, besides, mamma was beginning to understand a little English; and I had a little Swedish.

I shall never forget that first visit. The house – such a small, insufferable house for so many occupants – was spotlessly clean. The table, set in the middle of the rough floor, was covered with a fine cloth, and loaded with innumerable Swedish dishes. Two beds flanked either wall; a wooden settle stood under the window; the stove and cupboards filled the far corner. A sideboard, at the foot of one bed, and some benches, completed the furniture – no, there was an amazing picture on the wall; the picture of a beautiful country estate in beautiful southern Sweden.

Ella saw me staring at it, and in an almost surly tone said: 'That was mamma's home.'

Then Mrs W. came hurrying in from some chore or other, and I knew that her daughter had spoken the truth, and, to some extent, why her voice betrayed an element of resentment. Between the tall, gentle, sad-eyed woman who greeted me in a soft, restrained voice, and the sturdy peasant who was her daughter, no affinity was remotely possible. They were so dissimilar that I could guess for myself the kind of rude, elemental, handsome creature Mrs W. had married, heaven knows why.

And I was right. Mr W. was the sort of male who stomps through life with hooves of iron; proud of his word; proud of his vitality – he was never sick, never wrong, never defeated. He had been a contractor, and had lost his money. No matter. He would make more, another, better start on the land. His wife and children could work the homestead, while he plied his trade in town. Work was good for the soul, and women were designed for the hearth and the comfort of men.

By degrees, I learned something of what this finely nurtured woman had endured, and what had come to be the most insupportable. It was not nice, she said, in her faltering, fumbling English, to be so many in one room. It – it hurt so, inside – it was not nice, having the children grow up so – so insensitive.

She seldom said anything of the endless back-breaking drudgery, except the day following a heavy rain, when I found her carrying all the bedding out of doors to dry. Then half apologetically, she said:

'If only Mr W. would fix the roof, it would help so much. I can't seem to get the sod right myself.'

Mr W. had no time for such nonsense. A little water in the house didn't hurt any one. There were kids enough to help her haul the stuff about. Time meant money, and money was more important than pampering kids and women folk.

What she did confess with restrained bitterness was the one thing she found so hard to forgive: the death of her little seven-year-old boy. Not so strong as the others, yet he had to take his turn helping papa in the woods, lopping branches of the newly felled trees. It was cold, perhaps the child was benumbed, and a little stupid with chill and weariness. He had not been quick enough when a spruce crashed down. It had crushed his skull.

'Oh, dear God! I cannot forget it, she moaned, hiding the tears with her reddened hands, 'I cannot forget – when I take him to my arms – the brains spill over my apron —'

My other friend had no such tragic memories, nor was she bound to a man of incompatible temperament or desires. But she had her troubles, none the less which she faced with that amiable cheerfulness characteristic of most English people.

Before the War this charming couple, whose courtesy and way of life amused some of their neighbours, had been upper servants in one of those places that Noel Coward has satirized as *The Stately Homes of England*. Mrs F. had been lady something or other's personal maid; Mr F., the butler. He went to war, was wounded and honourably discharged. While convalescing he began to ponder his former ways of life, only to discover that he had lost all taste for such a moribund existence. Anything would be better than a senseless round of bowing and scraping and polished dissembling. He heard of the lands opened up to returned soldiers in Canada. So here they were, and here they were glad to be.

I used to visit them regularly, once a week, and quite an adventure it was, packing a three-year-old five miles, coming and going, over a blazed trail. But it was worth any effort to reach that bright little home, where a cup of tea and intelligent conversation enriched the hours with peculiar charm. There was no place like it in the entire settlement. It was a lovely bit of England, going on bravely amid the sticks.

Flowers bloomed at the windows, and in the young garden before the house order and neatness prevailed as much as within. All the usual clutter and claptrap of Canadian homesteads was noticeably missing. Nearly all the furniture was made from boxes and crates that had crossed the sea and half a continent. Little cupboards for pretty dishes; bookshelves, and a dressing-table – which vastly amused bucolic housewives who found no merit in well-groomed hair and a good complexion. I had met that ridicule myself; been loudly laughed at by Ella for fussing with my hands after each bout with the chores. Fancy going to the trouble of making hand lotion from carefully rendered fat, boracic acid, and a dash of toilet water! Oh, she would get over all that nonsense, the practical ladies assured my little friend: curling her hair, wearing white aprons, using sheets, instead of grey blankets, and – of all things! – napkins at the table!

'But I do not want to get over these things,' said little Mrs F. 'We came to Canada to preserve our self-respect. These things mean just that to me. See, I have made my little everyday napkins from bleached flour-sacking, to save my few good ones. It may be long before we can buy anything of the sort – but I should hate to save work on the decencies of life.'

There was a moment, however, when she had been faced by a sore dilemma. It was when her husband's last trousers showed a treacherous tendency to fall apart. There was no money to buy even a cheap, ready-made pair, but she remembered a length of tweed cloth she had brought from England. So, with as much fear as I had attacked that rotted hoof, the resourceful lady took the precious trousers apart, studied their mysterious details and then fashioned a creditable copy from her tweed. The fit was not perfect, she admitted; a bit baggy perhaps, and lumpy about the pockets. But how proudly they had dressed and gone to church that Sunday! How sure that any and all miracles were possible in Canada!

My own experiment in homesteading was coming to a swifter conclusion than I had anticipated. One dark and chilly night I heard my husband's voice singing on the trail, announcing in his fashion his unexpected return. There was no more extra work, and, judging from the slump in business, no likelihood of immediate improvement.

Taking stock of our scant resources next day, it was obvious that we should not be able to remain where we were. The cabin was not proof against Saskatchewan weather; there was no shelter for the cow and the horses, no crop of any kind, and not enough money to feed ourselves for more than two or three months. So far as I could see, the only possible solution was to use what money we had to bring our furniture from Saskatoon, pay a month's rent on a house in Prince Albert, and set up a boarding-house.

In less than a week I had found a big, rambling, nine-room brick and stucco dwelling. It had good lines, and an attractive yard, well treed, and not too unkempt; but the interior was dingy from indifferent housekeeping. While we waited for the household effects we scrubbed and scraped floors and wood-work and wainscotting, varnished and painted and cleaned the wall-paper with oatmeal and brown paper.

This done, I had sixteen windows to curtain, lengthening, shortening, dipping, and refrilling what material I had. Then I organized the kitchen. Fortunately, I had nearly a hundred sealers of fruit and vegetables left from my cold-packing orgy, when, on the whiff of pickles, plums, peaches, I had eased myself through the religions of the world. This, with a thirty-five-dollar grocery order obtained on credit from our Saskatoon grocer, was my stock in trade. No, not quite all – I had the cow, and I knew how to cook!

Well, any one who has tried this easy way to fame and fortune knows what the first few weeks entail. The anxiety that no one may appear to patronize the shining rooms, enjoy the menus planned and pinned on the kitchen wall; the even greater anxiety when the first two or three angels draw out of the dark!

However, in a little over a month the rooms were rented, and I had thirteen people to cook for. Most of them were students, some of whom only came in for their meals. There were two young lawyers, a dentist, and a poor, shell-shocked soldier, whom I had not the heart to turn away, although he often frightened the girls with his bursts of violence. He did not take his meals in the house – people worried him too much – but he liked his quiet room. He liked to have me talk to him, now and then. He had a passion for *The Lady of the Lake*, which he read and re-read as he nibbled hazel-nuts.

It was a hectic period. To begin with, when a new roomer appeared I had to dash off to purchase, on the strength of his rent, what was required for his or her comfort. I had not enough beds or bedding, and every sort of goods was outrageously high in 1918. Food was scarce and the price prohibitive, especially of eggs and butter; flour was often of very poor quality. To set an attractive table on a limited budget under these circumstances required some resourcefulness. I used to buy meat by the quarter. I baked twenty-two loaves of bread weekly; eleven brown at one setting, the same number of white, the next. I had no help, a huge house to keep in order, a child to care for, and all those endless meals to prepare on a coal range. George attended to the outside chores, and helped me with the dishes and peeling vegetables when he could. But his principle occupation was to cut firewood in the bush, and haul it to the house. An occupation we find amusing in retrospect, although it was not so funny in sub-zero weather.

It was not a perfect holiday. I was so tired by the time I went to bed that sleep was usually a lottery with few fine prizes. I would toss about, going over the meals, racking my brains for new ways of serving the same old vegetables, making frantic note of the things Mr So-and-So could not eat, and Miss So-and-So must not eat, and trying to anticipate something which might please them.

It was not just a matter of getting three orderly meals prepared. Not all these people took breakfast, or lunch, at the same time; dinner was the only meal to which I might expect them all at the same hour. Breakfast repeated itself until nine, and lunch until two. That left a short afternoon to bake pies, cakes, and bread, shop for supplies, dress myself and the baby, before getting down to the business of cooking the main meal of the day.

The dinner dishes done, I had to scour milk pans, set the milk, get things in order for the morning, bath the baby, and, after he was put to bed, wash his little clothes. I had always changed his things twice a day, making little checked rompers for the morning, and something more cheerful for the afternoon.

He was an attractive child, with heavy fair hair and a clear, healthy complexion. He was very little trouble, for he had never been fussed with, was never fed between meals, nor allowed pastries or candy, and had his own little meals on a kindergarten table, and therefore was quite content to amuse himself in his own small corner. Even so, I sometimes used to wish I had four pair of hands and at least two heads.

There was a morning that stands out in my mind as something of a test of patience. One of the roomers had come in very late, and had failed to close the door properly. When I came down to get breakfast the house was like ice, all my cherished houseplants frozen, and the water pipes emitting gay fountains all over the kitchen floor. The floor was a miniature lake, but, being at a lower level than the dining-room, the water had not penetrated there.

But breakfast must go on. While George, who is a cheerful soul, though sometimes short on temper, fired the furnace with something more than wood, and flew about with a wrench, dismembering water pipes, I fed my sizable family, sloshing through the icy water in rubbers. When the meal was over, one of the young lawyers stepped into the kitchen.

'Lady!' said he, 'I take off my hat to you! Most women would have sat and wept, and sent us packing!'

A welcome pat, bless him – warming to the heart, if not to the pedal extremities.

For the most part, they were all nice young people. I used to enjoy their chatter at dinner. It gave me an opportunity to compare their reactions and opinions, to mark how differently those youngsters, with ample allowance for all their needs, accepted life, as compared with those whose background was less secure and comfortable. How certain those fortunate ones were that all was well with the world, and all their opinions correct! How utterly unconscious of the fact that nothing but the accident of birth had given them this happy philosophy. How easy it was to foresee them as the future solid citizens, suspicious of new things, and sworn to the comfortable, easy virtues!

I like them all: the little prigs and the little rebels equally. If I had any preferences, it was for the lonely soldier and the young lawyer, who had always a happy word in awkward moments – although such moments were usually of his own creating, for he was an incurable tease and an outrageous flirt. The girls were in a continual dither. The moment he entered, on went their company faces, and out cropped all their sweetest guile; and none of it made the slightest impression.

This matriarchal regime was not destined to survive. The flu epidemic struck Prince Albert with such violence that it produced near panic. Ill reports multiplied daily, and all conversation turned, sooner or later, upon some unfortunate and speedy death.

One morning, the young dentist could not rise from his bed; and no sooner had he been taken to the hospital than all my young folk fled; all but the aforementioned lawyer and the soldier. So here we were, with an empty house, the town in a panic, and no means of subsistence; back where we started, all the work and worry equally futile.

Then I came down with the flu. That did not particularly upset me. I had had a bout with it when it struck before; had it in

Saskatoon, at a time when I happened to be alone in the house, my husband away in the country.

There is no point in labouring that experience; but, since I had survived nights and days of raging fever, when, drenched with perspiration, I had to drag myself out of bed to tend to the baby, I certainly had no reason to fly into a panic now. George was home, and did what he could for me, keeping the house warm, fetching me hot lemonades, putting wet cloths on my head, and caring for the child.

To be sure, when three days passed and I was still on my back, his patience cracked a bit. If I were as ill as this, I should have a doctor. I didn't seem to be making much headway at this rate, etc., etc.; all very sensible, but not particularly soothing. I did not want a doctor, for I was suffering from the complex an empty pocket so readily creates. I was thinking of the rent to be paid, of the grocer, and the butcher, and the vacant rooms; of the fixed overhead, which neither doom nor death altered. I had not the heart to run up bills for myself.

Meanwhile, George was not idle. I question that even the ease of Paradise would reduce him to such luxury! He flew about doing a thousand things, sending wires and letters, scouting some job, going to the bush for firewood, tending the cow and the horses and the house. He had discovered he was not born to the soil, so he contracted with a returned soldier to take the homestead off his hands. And, at the darkest moment, as so often happens, he found an opening in the railway service. An operator was needed at Biggar, Saskatchewan. He had to leave at once.

So there I was, scarcely able to leave my bed, with a barn of a house in midwinter. The furnace was of the old-fashioned variety, fed four-foot logs of wood. I had to sit down on the cellar steps after each stoking orgy.

However, in a few days I had sufficient energy to form some sort of plan. I decided to auction all the household effects, except my books, the piano, some kitchen ware, and dishes; and thus square my accounts and be free to make another start.

When it came to making ready for the sale and packing what I could not keep, one of the girls came back, offering to help me – a girl of mixed blood and limited means; and my soldier insisted upon crating the books and tying boxes. He also insisted upon spending the last night in the house, after the furniture was sold, sleeping on a mattress in his empty room. It has been my experience in a not too easy life that publicans and sinners, and the humble of earth, are more dependable in an unpopular hour than their respected brethren.

44

Birth of an author

It is true that every evil has its germ of good. Life looked pretty black – which, doubtless, was just the state of my liver; it seemed to me that all my best efforts to conform to the time-honoured duties of women had brought me nothing but endless work and disillusionment. I had no life of my own, no inner satisfaction, no feeling of justifying my existence. When I watched the sale of piece after piece that represented so many dresses sewn, so many coats, so many hours of placating the whims of fussy customers; hours that other housewives spent in social pleasures, I made up my mind that I should appropriate something of the spoils. I made up my mind to use some of this money for a course in English.

Biggar was not an inspiring village, nor were the houses to let any woman's dream of bliss. We found a small cottage, minus all modern improvements and on the very edge of a windswept plain, that, after the usual painting and varnishing, was comfortable enough. It was heated by stoves and lighted with lamps, in the good old ancient manner. As soon as I had completed the household arrangements, I enrolled with the Extension Department of an American school, and put my mind upon syntax and composition.

While the March wind howled and filled the earth and air with snow, I sat there under the kerosine light, trying to recapture my one-time passion for words, tearing through dry lessons on technicalities, some quite familiar, and perceiving by degrees that none of this was what I really wanted.

I wrote to the school, asking to be permitted to submit compositions for corrections, rather than papers on parts of speech, and so forth. But, of course, that was out of their province.

So I disregarded their scholastic advice, and wrote for myself, with no better guide than my sense of rhythm and dislike of useless verbiage. I wrote verse for two reasons: first, because the simple forms were no effort; and secondly, because it focused my thoughts to a restricted, short, set medium. But I should never have dreamed of imposing these gymnastics upon any one. Not until I had written quite a batch of rhymes that showed a minimum of promise did I commit the stuff to any one else; and then to Mr Reeve, former editor of *The Writer*, for correction and comment.

One of the pleasant memories of Biggar arose from these lamplight experiments. Mr Watt, one of the train dispatchers, who at this time was initiating my husband into that phase of railroading, took it into his kind heart to furnish me with better illumination. I shall never forget the terrible, stormy day when, trudging through knee-deep snowdrifts, he arrived at the cottage with an Aladdin lamp under one arm and a bundle of neatly shaved kindling wood under the other! But then, as I was to learn from others, Mr Watt was the kind of soul who seeks out kind deeds for the doing, as others seek out pleasures for themselves.

The next year we were back in Regina, George working the third trick as train dispatcher, and I wrestling with words, as poor Jacob wrestled with the angel. I began to mail out some of this pain and agony, and, I am glad to say, most of it came back. In time, however, an occasional verse was printed in country papers.

I dug out my old Latin grammar, with some notion of perfecting my sense of derivatives. I wept over Victor Hugo, and would have liked to bathe his feet with these tears! I cared nothing whatsoever for my mental offspring. I had not listened to papa satirizing inane verse without acquiring some sense of what constituted poetry. I had not the slightest ambition to become a homespun poet. What I wanted was the language of ideas, and liberty to express ideas in a medium that should transmit something of my national flavour. I tried my hands at a few bits of prose, and found them feeble and foolish. Then I wrote two short stories, one of them destined to win the Canadian Club prize the following year.

But all of this went on under disheartening circumstances. I had no literary friends – no friends at all, in fact, except Mrs Tanner; and my health was steadily going down hill. Everything I ate seemed actually to poison me. Dr Henderson, to whom I had finally to admit this defeat, put me on various diets, which gave temporary relief. The flu had left me this gift, said he, but the serious thing was my heart. It was strained – whatever that means – which explained my shortness of breath, and sundry other unreasonable aberrations. Thankful that the old bogey of tuberculosis had not overtaken me, I returned to my scribbling, my canning, my cooking, and seemingly made no more progress than a cat chasing its tail.

Then fate took a hand. Dr and Mrs Andrews became interested in my verses. They did more: they took me to their home, and their hearts, thereby opening up a new world to my starved spirit. Not long thereafter, the University Women's Club began making preparation for Bliss Carmen's first visit to Regina. Mrs Andrews suggested that I should write a verse of welcome to the poet, which I did in fear and misgiving, never dreaming what was to come of it.

Nothing would have prevailed upon me to read the thing, or to have my name mentioned. Mrs Andrews elected to do it, and did it so well that the poor little effort acquired merit through the sympathy of her voice. In the audience was a young Scotsman, whose passion for letters made him eager to follow any glimmer of Canadian talent: the late Austin Bothwell whose faith in my ability decided my future, and to whom I owe a debt of gratitude that words cannot express.

Without the encouragement of Mr Bothwell and his dear wife, Jessie, I should never have dared to attempt a serious piece of work, or come to recapture the hope which had always lain at the back of my mind since that long-gone day in the West Duluth Library, when my heart quickened with the determination to write a book. But to dream and act are not quite the same. I had yet to conquer my self-mistrust, my fear of ridicule upon the ultimate discovery that I was just what papa would call another miscreant of letters; and I was sorely depressed.

However, enheartened by Mr Bothwell's report upon the few things I sent him, I kept scribbling away, jotting down scenes and dialogues that ran through my head as I went about the household chores. It was then that I realized how good a service nausea had done me during those dreaded street-car rides. I could carry on pages of conversation as I flew about, dusting, sweeping, ironing, and baking, and never lose a word of it! I could visualize, without any particular effort, scenes that I had thought long since forgotten. I had only to recall some quaint turn of speech heard in the drug store, on the street corner, or in the theatre, and all of it was there in my mind's eye. Without this ability I should never have been able to write as much as I did write in the next few years.

All those years of bondage to stupid duties had taught me to regiment and perfect mechanical labours to an extent that left my mind free to pursue more fascinating speculations. And I could support a terrific grind. For instance, when I was doing research for *Lord of the Silver Dragon*, I worked at that particular task from midnight until three in the morning. The first part of each day was devoted to housework. After lunch, I wrote usually from two to five. When dinner had been disposed of I became a human being, entertaining a few friends, or going out somewhere with my husband.

Except on rare occasions, I was back in my own room by ten o'clock. From then until eleven, when I made my husband's midnight snack before his going to work, I amused myself with some sort of extension work.

But all this was in the future. I was still in Regina, full of doubt and hesitations, much more certain that I should can the vegetables from the garden than write a book. That I gradually recovered a modicum of courage I have to thank the literary society which met every week in the public library. It was there that I partly learned to creep out of my mental shell. It was there I met my faithful friend, George A. Palmer, whose amiable humour and catholic interests so greatly helped to put me at ease.

The outstanding event of the winter, however, was a little party given in honour of Mrs McClung, who had just returned from England, and was lecturing in Regina. Just an intimate, friendly gathering, at the home of Mr and Mrs McLeod, but, for me, it was a memorable occasion – my first introduction to a Canadian author. I am forced to admit that I knew very little of Canadian literature, in general, and had only read Mrs McClung's *Sowing Seeds in Danny*. But I had loved her for painting, with sympathy, obscure, inconsequential folk, and more especially for the work she had done on behalf of women.

Naturally, I looked forward to the occasion with a mixture of pleasure and dread. So many idols are better left in their shrines; so many actors are disappointing out of character. To bolster up my timidity, I made myself a new dress, sitting up half the night to do it, and bought my first pair of really good shoes. Thus, shod with respectability, if not clothed in my right mind, I sallied forth to make my bow to Canadian achievement. Recalling those nervous qualms, I am tempted to laugh. For surely no famous person ever wore laurels more gracefully than Mrs McClung!

It was a pleasant evening, and I was purring with contentment that a woman both celebrated and handsome was free of all vanity and pretence. Yet I was a little disappointed that nothing was said of books, as such. I had, without being conscious of it, I suppose, a purely European attitude. I should have liked the guest of honour to hold forth in fine Bjornson style on some aspect of politics, or discourse upon points of literature after the famed Anatole France pattern. Certainly I could not imagine any group of Icelandic intellectuals behaving so mildly! Like the Jews, we have a passion for ideas; and the more provocative they are, the better we like them. It is not escape from ourselves and the problems of existence that we seek in our mental diversions, but a stimulus to curiosity and thought.

What I chiefly remember of that amicable evening is my impression of Mrs McClung; her generosity to any writer mentioned and the delightful quality of her slightly husky voice.

Before the little gathering broke up something was said apropos of beginners in fiction – something I accepted without reservation, and which I fervently wish had never been uttered. According to this opinion, if you knew your subject, and had the perseverence to master a plain, lucid style, eventual success was a foregone conclusion. I also gathered that editors were sitting on the edges of their chairs, waiting for the Canadian product, and all the intellectual world searched the heavens for signs of a forthcoming great Canadian novel.

I had no delusions of grandeur, but, if this were true it seemed to me that I had less to fear; more reason to hope that my individualized reaction to the Canadian scene might meet with some favour.

As a matter of fact, what I should have been told was to shed my Icelandic hide and every vestige of national character as quickly as possible! Saying which, I do not mean to imply that I, as an individual, have suffered any discrimination because of my nationality. That would be far from true. It is a long time since any one thought me suspect for no better reason than that. Of course, I have still to explain, with slightly diminishing enthusiasm, that Icelanders are a Norse people, with social institutions a thousand years old; that the country is not an ice cake, but a sizable cauldron of volcanoes and hot springs. And I have still to smile politely when helpful mortals rush to my rescue by saying: 'Oh, I knew an Icelander, once – such a *nice* person, too!'

What I should like to make clear has nothing to do with such harmless commonplaces. It was something quite different, and much harder to define, something instinctive, that affected my point of view and made it strange, and even offensive, to other popular beliefs. I had been conditioned in liberal thought, and came naturally by a genuine curiosity in every shade of opinion. In spite of her individual preference for the forms of the high church, my mother imposed no dogma upon her children, and she considered all attempts to censor reading and other common amusements insulting to the human intelligence.

I remember her disgust with a pious lady who expressed surprise that I should be reading a novel. A book that, most likely, dealt with disgusting examples of depravity and sin! Imagine the effects it would have upon me!

'Don't be an ass!' said mamma. 'If such things are written about, they must exist, and its high time we found out about it. There is little merit in sanctimonious blindness!'

All her life mamma read whatever came to hand, and her last request in this world was for light – plenty of light, and a good story!

As for my father, any new discovery, any theory, of whatever kind, he seized upon with eagerness and interest. We never enjoyed material blessings, but we certainly had the benefits of complete mental freedom and boundless interest in the lives of our fellow creatures; in human beings, as they were, not as we wished them to be! Such an attitude toward life was the first obstacle in the way of successful authorship.

Humanity was for me a sort of living hieroglyphics of the life principle: generations upon generations translating into acts and deeds the strange forces that impelled them; a fancy which lent fascination to the dullest life.

The second, and greater obstacle, was my conception of the purposes of fiction. Old-fashioned Icelanders did not look upon the sagas as something to kill time. They had, indeed, no predilection for such a curious desire. Even as an old woman my mother hated to go to bed – sleep seemed such a waste of life! To our way of thinking, even light fiction failed of its purpose to interest or amuse if it did not in some way extend the mental horizon. If there was nothing in the story to provoke a novel train of thought, nothing that gave you an intriguing glimpse of human foibles, nothing that touched on the springs of beauty in nature or in man, then why trouble to read the thing? A cup of coffee would do just as well, if all you wanted was mental oblivion!

With such an unfortunate conviction rooted in mind, it never even occurred to me that I should sit down to invent a sort of Punch and Judy show, mechanically timed to a prescribed tune, which changed with epidemic propulsion at cyclic intervals. Glad books, sad books, mad books, bad books – like the plagues of Egypt! For instance, when I finally resolved to write of such people and events as were thoroughly familiar, the pioneers of the west, the fiddler had called another tune. The American continent had discovered sex! It had discovered *thoughts*!

Just how the world wagged along before this flaming revelation shook the continent, was a mystery. The only mystery – everything else, from Grandma's wandering *thoughts* as she munched a lettuce salad with vital relish, to the gurgling of a baby nursing its toes, was ripped of pretence, and bravely shown in its full, erotic significance. The poor old earth writhed with complexes and repression. Even sleep afforded no escape. The demon pursued you down Elysian fields with matchless subterfuge and cunning.

Such a horrible state of affairs ought not to be endured, shouted the glandular prophets. Mankind must be free as its fiercest desire, free as the elk and the goose. Dreadful indeed were the psychopathic tragedies depicting the warped women whose horrid husbands snored in their sleep, and served no romantic purpose in their waking hours. Bold were the modern Judiths who beheaded the monster Restraint, and went a-hunting the proper mate. Gallant souls, who, it must be admitted, reminded me just a little of the less enlightened ladies at the court of the Merry Monarch.

To fly in the face of this brave new convention, with tales of antiquated mortals who stubbornly believed in the larger loyalties of social obligation, in honour and friendship and the human spirit, was not a sensible course. In fact, it was an almost fatal course, since the only other popular medium of fiction – mawkish sentimentality – was just as impossible to me.

Any single week in my aunt's hospital would have supplied me with material for six turgid novels. With no arduous invention, I could have acted upon the advice of a successful author who, after reading *Lord of the Silver Dragon*, said to me: 'When you can write like that, why waste your time? Write of love – and make it illicit!'

Honest council, but, like my deluded characters, I had my own peculiar loyalties. There were the ancestors – which is to say, there were obligations of common decency to men and women who had laboured long and hard in the service of humanistic ideals.

At this point I should like to make clear another peculiarity of Icelandic ideology. When a group of old friends gather round the coffee table, and suddenly trot out Grandfather So-and-So, and Great-grandmamma Something-Else, it is not done to create an impression. The Icelander rakes up the ancestral fires in search of some glowing ember of integrity and merit whereby to light his own spirit and quicken his heart with courage against the dark future. The ancestors were a sort of spiritual scourge. When a scholarly old gentleman once told me of an ancestress who, in ancient times of famine, retired to the church to write poetry 'in the peace of God, until He claimed her,' it was not told as an example of family distinction, but given as the reason for his own dutiful striving to surmount the obstacles of poverty and ignorance. He was not proud of his ancestors. He only hoped he had not disgraced them.

All of which will doubtless seem a strange invention, but the fact remains, that to the immigrants of Canada this need to justify their race was a powerful and ever-present incentive to courageous effort. It did not surprise me, therefore, that papa's first comment upon being told that I intended to write a book was not very flattering.

'My dear,' said he, 'are you sure it will be a good book? There are so many bad books the old bards must shudder to see!'

But I am anticipating. I was still writing verse, in the queerest moments. I was getting breakfast one morning when a sudden burst of melody drew me to the window. There, on the telephone wires, a meadow lark sang out his little heart, and, having done, soared off into the sky. I used to feed the little singers oatmeal, bits of suet, and crusts. I loved them, as the most beautiful attribute of the beautiful prairie. Now, it seemed to me I should fix this affection in some way. So, while the bacon frizzled in the pan, I sat down on the threshold and wrote: 'The Creation of the Birds.'

> When brooding o'er the earth newly created —
>   Where in her pristine splendour fair she lay,
>   A beryl beauteous, 'mid encircling waters —
> The Lord grew lonely through the dragging day.
>
> So, from the sun He took a spark of glory,
>   And from the clouds their lovely summer hue,
>   And from the winds the breath of dreaming ages,
> And from the fern the ever-sparkling dew:
>
> With all these things, in love and exultation,
>   The little birds He formed, with deep delight;
>   And cast them forth from out His holy bosom,
> To make Him glad with song from morn till night.

Hidden Fire, my first short story, was awarded the Canadian Club prize in the summer, and I had the terrifying experience of receiving it from the hands of Lady Byng, with nothing better to wear than a voile dress and a newly dyed hat, which smelled to high heaven.

My happiness in the event derived from the pleasure the Bothwells took in this small success. They were so sure it prophesied better things ahead. It was not so difficult to believe it, on the rare occasions that I spent in their invigorating company. Mrs Bothwell was like a fine flame that melted the chill in my heart. Austin Bothwell was a scholar and a Scotsman. I dared not doubt him. If he said that I could write, I had to write. It became a duty that obsessed me night and day.

A fortunate obsession, no doubt, for I was not privileged to enjoy this inspiring friendship for long. In the fall we went to Edmonton, where my husband worked as swing-dispatcher, which means that he relieved the regular trick men in Edmonton on their allotted days off, and then repeated the process in Biggar.

We found a suite on the wrong side of town, where rents were supposed to be cheaper, and when I had settled the place to the best of my ability, I began to think about the task Mr Bothwell had charged me with: to write a book about my own people. I had never heard any technical points discussed. I had no idea that such material was available. I knew nothing, in fact, except what I wanted to represent.

That was clear enough, after a fashion. I wanted to write a story which would define the price any foreign group must pay for its place in the national life of the country of its adoption. I wanted this payment to express spiritual values, which, to my way of thinking, are the true measure of national greatness, the only riches that abide, and which make a nation endure.

How to do it was still a mystery. I wrote to my father, at the time living in Gimli, and, through him, arranged for a meeting with two elderly gentlemen who had kept a record of the early Icelandic settlement. While I waited for my flying vacation, so to speak, I began jotting down episodes with which I was familiar, and almost at once the characters who were to enact these experiences took shape in my mind.

They did more: they began to haunt me in my sleep. I had one peculiar experience that was repeated two nights running. I had no more than dropped off to sleep than a woman drew out of the shadow. A sad, distraught, creature, who bore, in her extended arms, a beautiful child, whose golden curls and small, waxen figure were dripping water. It was so real, so tragically moving that I woke with a start. I must be getting a little mad, I thought – altogether too obsessed with my subject. I had no memory of any such incident, and had no intention of incorporating it into my book.

But when, some ten days later, I met the two old gentlemen in Gimli, the first tale they told me was of a poor woman whose child had been drowned, while she was charring for the daily bread; drowned in a little creek that used to traverse Market Square, where the Winnipeg City Hall now stands. So small Lillian found her place in my book. As a matter of fact, I seemed to have little to say as to how any one behaved in that book.

For instance, I had a dear old gossip in mind to act as a sort of spiritual buffer when I invented Finna, but Finna refused to be invented: she took on flesh and blood, and ran away with the story.

Back in Edmonton, I hired a second-hand typewriter, bought a kitchen table and some Manilla papers, and shut myself up in a slice of room to draw up the skeleton of the story. As I said before, I had no knowledge of the mechanics of writing. But I did have sense enough to know that it was impossible to create a story out of vague, disconnected scenes. I had to see the end before there could be any beginning. When the last paragraph finally came to me – and it came while I was doing the week's ironing – I knew that I should somehow find the right opening. When the ironing was finished, I wrote down my last paragraph:

'For in such strength alone do nations live, have their beginnings, and everlasting power. Out of the hearts of men, out of their joys and tears, their toil and tribulation, springs that illusive, and holy thing, the Soul of a Nation.

'Out of the sore travailings of men, and out of their quiet death, spring hope and faith, and that great love which, transcending the grave, revitalizes life, and makes a nation indestructible.'

I looked at these words, and there swept over me the same emotion which I had experienced so often as a child, when I saw the sun go down, leaving the world in grey widow's weeds. How often I had watched such a scene from a small, uncurtained window, opening out upon the little creek, and, with a queer ache at the heart, tried to imagine what argosies of human joys and sorrows, completed and done, were drawing beyond the rim of the world on the brave banners of the sun. Here, in these stray words, were harmonic colours that must be made to live on my canvas, to burn and radiate in varying degrees of intensity in the hearts of my characters.

I had still no plan, but now I had a definite mood within myself: an emotional disquiet, that I had long since come to recognize as the forerunner of almost photographic invention; when,
in my mind's eye, I would see and hear and feel imagined or
remembered scenes with extraordinary intensity. I began to draft
leaders in verse for my chapter headings, trying to make each
one carry forward my basic theme. That done, I mapped out the
actual experiences I wished to incorporate in the story; and then,
as I had known I must, I spent a sleepless night, struggling with
the flood of images that crowded into my mind. In the morning,
when my housework was done, I began the story.

Now all should have been simple. I had two weeks each
month when there were only myself and my son to care for; but
I was really ill. There were days on end when I sat at the machine
with a mustard plaster on my head, because it was less disturbing to suffer the burning sensation than the sickening throb in
my temples and at the base of my skull. I knew I should go to a
doctor, but I wanted to finish the book. I had hardly any sleep,
ate scarcely anything, and doped myself with aspirin. On the few
occasions I went out I had to brace myself like a dope addict.

I went on with the book. When several chapters were completed, George suggested that I should ask Mrs McClung what
she thought of them. I should never have had the courage to do
such a thing, and, I am glad to say, it is the only time I have ever
inflicted such punishment upon anybody.

Mrs McClung was kindness itself, and, when I had committed
my little crime, assured me that the story was good. I had begun
my manuscript in Victorian fashion, where the settlers arrive at
Fisher's Landing, *en route* to Winnipeg. Mrs McClung thought
that a more colourful opening would enhance the story – some
flash back into the lives of the people in their native land. I
thought she was right, and think so still.

But what lasting scorn I drew upon my innocent head by
embroidering a symbolic introduction! I did not want to disturb
the story itself, and therefore decided upon an opening scene
that would combine an intimate glimpse of an old-fashioned Ice-

landic homestead, and something of the disasters from which the country had so often suffered through the centuries.

I knew, as well as any one, the exact year of the last volcanic eruption, which had, for its aftermath, the misery and hardship which drove so many to emigrate. I certainly knew that the great volcanoes were inland – how should I not, when my father had once lived under the shadow of Mount Hecla! But I did not see that such specific detail was necessary to an introduction that was obviously nothing but symbolism.

However, the Icelandic people were so indignant that I should have played fast and loose with their landscape, shrinking it, so to speak, until the volcano came down to the sea, that the story itself had no merit. That I had tried, to the best of my ability, to represent those spiritual qualities of the people themselves, which must commend them to their Canadian brethren, was completely discounted. I had made a fool of myself by not invoking a verbal map of the country for a frontispiece!

It is never pleasant to be wounded in one's dearest affections. I loved the brave past of my little country. I thrilled to the courage of a tiny nation that neither poverty nor tyranny could reduce to spiritual bondage. This courage and integrity of purpose, under whatsoever cloud or affliction, were the qualities that I tried to represent as the payment Canada might expect from my people for their place in national life. However, although I and all my works have been tacitly repudiated by my own people, with but few exceptions, it has not changed my own affection, which is all that matters. There are no losses, except they rob the heart.

Driven by a panic of fear that I should not finish the manuscript because of illness, I wrote in a kind of frenzy. As each batch of my manuscript was finished, I dictated it to my husband, who typed the final copy, and I revised, to the best of my ability, at the reading. Not a very satisfactory method, I will admit, and one I should shudder to attempt in a serious book to-day. I had no better knowledge at the time, and little enough vitality to wrestle with the story itself.

When the manuscript was suitably prepared, I sent it to Mr Bothwell, and waited on tenterhooks for his opinion. The day that his first little note came back was undoubtedly the happiest moment of my life.

'Hurrah! You have done it!' wrote he. What that meant to me, no words can convey. That an unpopular author was about to dawn upon the horizon is not of much importance to any one. I shall come to a better reason for writing this disconnected history. But that the feat was accomplished at all is due, not alone to Mr Bothwell's inspiration, but to another man whom I must mention, for, without his very concrete support, I should have had to give up almost the beginning.

I refer to Mr J.H. Cranston, formerly editor of the *Toronto Star Weekly*. When every other periodical rejected with cryptic dismissal my human interest tales of the pioneers, Mr Cranston found them sufficiently meritorious to publish. It would be no exaggeration to say that these short stories supported my books. Those earnings paid for the preparation of the manuscripts, for my husband could not undertake such a task as a fixed pastime. He had his own work, and, like myself, was engaged in his own self-improvement, taking extension courses in traffic management, etc., efforts which he hoped might be beneficial to his advancement.

Those *Star* stories also made it possible for me to undertake the research required for historical novels. There is nothing which I can possibly say, by way of gratitude to Mr Cranston, except that I have tried my best to justify his faith and encouragement. That the Cranstons are enshrined with my dear and honoured friends is not flattery, but an abiding fact. It may not be the mission of Canadian editors to support native talent, but without some such interest I fail to see how Canadian letters are to develop.

I had the rather unique experience of having *The Viking Heart* accepted on the merit of its first eighteen hundred words, with the provision, naturally, that the rest would measure up to this promising beginning. That took a load off my mind, and so the book was finished in three months – a race which I have never been able to repeat.

That it was possible even then can be explained after a fashion. The story was in complete possession of my mind, mood, and feeling, and I wrote all day long, and far into the night, for five days out of the week. Saturday I had reserved for a thorough house-cleaning, marketing, ironing, mending, and so on. Sunday I kept for my few friends. I had the good fortune to have a neighbour, Mrs Gertrude Acheson, a Press woman, and member of the Canadian Authors' Association; and a neighbour she was, in the best sense of the word. There was also, in Edmonton, a former girlhood acquaintance, Mrs Johanneson, of whom more later, whose hospitality and kindness brightened a toilsome period.

When the book was done, I began to go to pieces. My husband thought that we should leave the suite, which was noisy, and the building itself fronting the street-car tracks, and find a quiet house with a bit of garden. We located an attractive old place, and I used up my flagging energy getting settled. I was so delighted with the garden, which was treed, and had lovely honeysuckle shrubs in the front of the porch. There was a little sun-room, with bright windows, that I instantly saw full of flowers. I bought some second-hand chairs, and a table, and after removing the old stain, enamelled them in dove grey, with touches of blue. I even painted an old congoleum rug in the same colour.

I had a grand time, sewing cheerful cretonne curtains and little table mats. My husband brought me a dear little puppy. It seemed to me that the whole earth had a brighter, more beautiful aspect. It was the first real home I had ever had. And I had it exactly thirty days! Then my husband came home one morning with the news that he was 'bumped' – that an older man had taken his job.

I had a vision of what it meant – of the endless hours wasted in fixing and refurbishing the old house; taking down the bright curtains that had hung so gaily for only two weeks; of the packing, and crating and general turmoil and eternal expense. For the first time in our wanderings, I sat down and cried – the foolish tears of sheer physical exhaustion. I just could not see how I should manage another bout of moving.

When the fit was over I went downstairs to get the breakfast. Then I took down the curtains, fetched a barrel from the basement, and began to pack the dishes.

I was not destined to follow our goods to Melville, however. I had to undergo medical treatment that made it impossible to leave. How we should have managed without the Johannesons, I cannot imagine. Mrs Johanneson herself insisted upon taking my son and myself into her own home.

She had a young baby, and not too much room. But what of it, said she. I could have the porch, and could cook my own special food, and young George would be safe while I underwent my treatments. The sort of sacrifice plain people make for each other without thought of reward, and which gets little enough publicity in smart writings.

Those many weeks, despite the daily jogs to the doctor, are a pleasant memory. We drained so many pots of excellent Icelandic coffee out on the little porch in the summer evenings; reviewed so many memories of old Winnipeg; and I began to mend. For the first time in many years I could eat without discomfort, walk up a flight of stairs without the weight of Atlas on my chest. When my blood tests were satisfactory, the infection from which I suffered eliminated, the doctor consented to my departure, cautioning me, however, not to work round the clock.

By this time George had gone to Calgary, so that I was spared one hop, at any rate, and our few sticks of furniture escaped a second crating. Calgary was not the happiest place in which to test a new-found strength – the extreme altitude is no respecter of persons. But at last we were settled in another house, the old floors dressed with linseed oil to permit a descent camouflage with varnish, the windows decked out in altered curtains, the furniture, which had stood in a railway warehouse, cleaned of grime. These gentle employments over, I sat down to plot another story.

45

So dreams come true

So we came at last to a strange morning, when my husband said: 'Your book is out. I think we should go down to Osborne's and have a look at it.'

Strange as it may seem, I did not want to look at it. I was suddenly afraid to meet this thing face to face. For this was not just a book to me; it was the epitome of a terrible desire that had given me no rest; that had hounded me relentlessly for twenty years.

In a way, it was the ghost of the shabby little girl who had dared to dream this thing so long ago. I wanted nothing so much as to rush away into some dim, dark hill, where wisdom breathes in the silence, and the mind grows still as the stars.

But a sensible housewife, busily stoning plums, does not say such things. I would go, of course, said I, but I first must finish the jam.

'Good heavens!' cried George, who was perfectly willing to forego his sleep after a night's work. 'Can't the jam wait? I should think, after all this fury of housework you'd want to get away from it.'

True. Yet, how can I explain that the physical act of leaving the house did not necessarily take me away from it? That what I really wanted was an hour to myself – an hour spent on the little balcony that overlooked a sweep of dun-coloured hills, and the silver crescent of the Bow River – an hour to cut myself off in spirit from pots and pans and the four enclosing walls of a jealous house.

It was late afternoon before we started down the hill on this intimate errand. I cannot say that I experienced any of that marvellous elation that embryo authors are supposed to feel on such an occasion. My mind was too full of jumbled memories.

I was seeing a girl reading Victor Hugo in an attic bedroom, of a house where she was nothing but a drudge; and that other young thing, going home from the tent and awning factory, through sleet and snow, to struggle with an assignment in English literature; I was hearing kind old Miss Rudd: 'Laura, whatever happens, never lose your sense of the beautiful. Never let yourself dream little dreams!' God bless her!

I was remembering all the hundred things that had stood in the road of this simple ambition. All the young heartache, all the humiliations, real or imagined – all real enough, since they had cut so deeply. All the ugliness which I had set myself to dispel by the force of a curiosity strong enough to penetrate to bed-rock of some underlying good – all that was lovely, the winsome way of a furry pet, the smile of old faces that had looked on life with courage, the beauty of the embroidered sky; and the miracle of the ever fruitful earth. These were the enduring realities that had kept my soul alive and my heart responsive to the lives of others.

And here we are at last! Here, before a commonplace plate-glass window, where a little stack of books in sunset jackets make a colourful mound. But I cannot see what this fine wrapper represents. I have to pull my hat down, and hide my eyes.

I will not enter – no, not for any gay persuasion! I have seen what I came to see. I have seen the fulfilment of a dream.

That is something, in a world that prides itself on materiality. A small triumph, for so many years; but a small thing can demonstrate a great truth. That I accomplished so little is beside the point.

That truth may serve a bolder spirit to better purpose: what you want, you can do, no matter what the odds against you! And to say just that, with something more than mere words, is the whole purpose of this rambling narrative. That I formed the resolution I must blame an unknown voice, speaking over the radio. A man's voice, pleading on behalf of Canadian literature.

Somewhere, said he, on some bleak little homestead, there may be another Frederick Grove, another Salverson, dreaming of a book to be written. Something to that effect – the words have escaped me. They escaped me because of the shock they produced. That there is another Grove somewhere, I earnestly hope; but if ill luck has fastened such an ambition upon some little foreign girl circumstanced as I was, I could weep for her. Yet it may be so. It may be that, like myself, some child of immigrants longs to justify her race as something more than a hewer of wood; dreams in the starlight of the lonely prairie of some fair burnt offering to lay upon the altar of her New Country, out of the love of a small, passionate heart.

How to do it, in a strange, new language? How to do it, in the face of poverty and isolation, and the cold indifference of an alien people? How to hold fast to a purpose that no one counts as precious as a new-turned furrow, a pelt of furs, or a load of grain.

It can be done, as simply as the seasons follow the sun. It can be done by the simple, undistinguished feat of snatching at straws; a word, a phrase, a tantalizing speech, to be stored in the mind, analysed, thumbed over, as a miser thumbs his gold; sights and sounds; the way a bird wheels in the wind; the moonlight dappling deep water; the sound of withered grasses telling their rosaries of frost and seeds; a thousand images to feed the mind in the sterile days of drudgery. It can be done by robbing sleep to hobnob with the thinkers of times present and past. It can be done by accepting pain, which, like a sharp sword, cuts through the stupidities that shut us off from our neighbours.

It can be done by keeping true to the thing within you, that no man sees, and only the great gods cherish! For each living creature has its own, inalienable covenant with the universe; its own small service to perform; every creative thought is a part of that universe, and has, within itself, the essence of its fulfilment. This I believe, and this I hope I shall always believe. Life to all men is not the same thing, but it is the same in this: that it becomes for them what they earnestly believe and relentlessly strive to make it.

All things are in the eye of the beholder. A fall of leaves from a scarlet maple-tree trembles for an infinitesimal point of time on the air, vibrates rhythmically, giving off ruby tints of light, and, in its drifting flight, arrests the eye of a chance observer.

Something in him responds. Beautiful! Beautiful! His senses leap, as to the sound of bugles. His imagination soars as on wings; and a thousand frets of life are instantly forgotten.

To another, the lovely miracle does not exist. Dead leaves have blown across his path. The shining incarnation has passed unseen, unheard. The little rustling of the ruby leaves taking their joyous departure, has passed the way of all spirit. No god was crucified on the flaming tree for the redemption of his earthbound senses. There was nothing in the wood; nothing in the winding road; nothing in the pale, evening air.

It is so with everything in the world: *out of the heart are the issues of life!*